SCOTLAND

NATIONAL GEOGRAPHIC
TRAVELER

SCOTLAND

by Robin & Jenny McKelvie

National Geographic
Washington, D.C.

CONTENTS

■ **Pages 2–3: Glenfinnan Viaduct—aka Harry Potter's "Bridge to Hogwarts"—
arcs over the Finnan Valley at the head of Loch Shiel, as The Jacobite steams
along the West Highland line. Left: Isle of Skye pipe band leader**

TRAVELING WITH EYES OPEN

Alert travelers go with a purpose and leave with a benefit. If you travel responsibly, you can help support wildlife conservation, historic preservation, and cultural enrichment in the places you visit. You can enrich your own travel experience as well.

To be a geo-savvy traveler:

- Recognize that your presence has an impact on the places you visit.

- Spend your time and money in ways that sustain local character. (Besides, it's more interesting that way.)

- Value the destination's natural and cultural heritage.

- Respect the local customs and traditions.

- Express appreciation to local people about things you find interesting and unique to the place: its nature and scenery, music and food, historic villages and buildings.

- Vote with your wallet: Support the people who support the place, patronizing businesses that make an effort to celebrate and protect what's special there. Seek out local shops, restaurants, and inns. Use tour operators who love their home place—who love taking care of it and showing it off. Avoid businesses that detract from the character of the place.

- Enrich yourself, taking home memories and stories to tell, knowing that you have contributed to the preservation and enhancement of the destination.

That is the type of travel now called geotourism, defined as "tourism that sustains or enhances the geographical character of a place—its environment, culture, aesthetics, heritage, and the well-being of its residents."

SCOTLAND

ABOUT THE AUTHORS

■ **Robin McKelvie** *(robinmckelvie.com)* is a native Scot with a master's degree in English literature and a passion for traveling that has taken him to more than 80 countries. In over a decade as a professional travel writer, Robin has written more than 30 travel books, had articles and photographs published in more than 50 magazines and newspapers across five continents, and also worked in radio and TV. His travel adventures have included taking the train from Edinburgh to Hong Kong, swimming with sharks in Belize, and canoeing with crocodiles in Australia. An active member of the British Guild of Travel Writers, Robin makes more than 30 trips a year, at least half of them around his favorite country in the world, which, with his hand on his proud heart, he can honestly say is Scotland.

■ **Jenny McKelvie** is an adopted Scot who has been a travel writer and photographer for over a decade, visiting more than 50 countries on the way and living in three of them—Scotland, England, and Australia. Jenny has co-authored more than 20 travel guidebooks with her husband, Robin, and written travel articles for more than 20 magazines and newspapers in the United Kingdom. She also writes travel intelligence reports on global trends and weaves being a full-time mother into her busy travel schedule. Jenny's number one country remains, of course, the country she married into: Scotland.

ABOUT THE UPDATER

■ **Christopher P. Baker**—the Lowell Thomas Award 2008 "Travel Journalist of the Year"—researched, updated, and wrote new features and other text for this edition. Born and raised in Northern England, he first explored Scotland by motorcycle on assignment for *Robb Report*, and currently leads annual photography tours to the Scottish Highlands, Isle of Skye, and Outer Hebrides. He is the author of the *National Geographic Traveler* guidebooks to Cuba, Dominican Republic, and Panama, as well as Colombia and Costa Rica, both of which he also photographed. He has written and photographed widely about destinations worldwide for publications as diverse as CNN Travel, *National Geographic Traveler, Travel + Leisure,* and the *Los Angeles Times.*

CHARTING YOUR TRIP

One of the world's most spectacular countries is blessed with thousands of rugged hills and mountains, hundreds of Atlantic islands, and myriad lochs and rivers, all brimming with bountiful wildlife. Dramatically interwoven into the natural drama are rich layers of history and culture in a country that overflows with world-class cities, ancient castles, and historic towns and villages.

How to Get Around

Getting around Scotland is all part of the fun, but journey times should not be underestimated. This is a nation, after all, with a heavily indented coastline

Admission Costs

The £–£££££ scale used in this guidebook delineates entry fees into attractions in British pounds:

£ = Under £10
££ = £10–£15
£££ =£15–£20
££££ = £20–£25
£££££ = Over £25

NOT TO BE MISSED:

The panoramic views of Edinburgh from Arthur's Seat 73

Rekindling the passions of William Wallace and Robert the Bruce at Stirling 144-145

A feast of world-class Scottish seafood at Oban 155

A cruise on Loch Ness in search of Nessie 221

Hiking up Ben Nevis to the highest point in the United Kingdom 222-223

Sampling your favorite wee dram in the distillery where it is conjured up 261

Sifting through the ghosts of Neolithic man on Orkney 316

twice as long as that of either France or Spain. The trip between Glasgow and Campbeltown, for example, takes just over 20 minutes by air but well over three hours by car!

Driving, though, is by far the best way to get around, as it offers the chance to really see the scenery unfold and stop off wherever you like. Visiting Scotland is as much about discovering little back lanes and hidden spots as it is seeing its famous cities. But you will still need a hand from the ferries (tel 0800/066 5000, calmac.co.uk) to get your car to the islands. Scotland's rail routes (tel 0344/811 0141, scotrail .co.uk), meanwhile, are among the most spectacular on the planet, though they are seldom quicker than traveling by road, so are best enjoyed as an experience in themselves. The Orkney Islands and Shetland Islands can also be reached by ferry *(tel 800/111 4422, northlinkferries.co.uk)*, but the more remote islands are most easily reached by air *(tel 0344/800 2855, loganair.co.uk)*. Flying can also be an efficient way of reaching more distant parts of the mainland if you're short on time.

In 2021, the new Highland Explorer between Glasgow and Oban made life easier for cyclists with dedicated carriages for bicycles, while the number of budget airlines serving both Edinburgh and Glasgow airports continues to grow.

Visitor Information

The place to go for information is **VisitScotland** *(tel 0131/472 2222, visitscotland .com)*, the country's national tourist office. Here you'll find all kinds of information about accommodations, sightseeing, and activities throughout Scotland. In addition to the terrific website, most cities and towns also have walk-in VisitScotland iCentres, where you can pick up brochures and maps, learn about local tours, and book accommodations. See Travelwise pp. 328–339 for more information on planning your trip.

A Week-Long Visit

If this is your first visit to Scotland, you will want to start in its picturesque, historic capital, Edinburgh, and then make a foray into the scenic Highlands, before returning to the central region and its largest city, Glasgow, another historic and deeply cultural hub. Most direct flights from North America land into one or other of these two cities, which also have great air links to London and Europe.

Starting out in Edinburgh on **Day 1,** make sure to visit Edinburgh Castle and enjoy a long lazy stroll down the Royal Mile, through the centuries, to the Palace of Holyroodhouse. Don't miss the city's string of national galleries and, in the evening, its lively pubs.

Using Edinburgh as the base for **Day 2,** drive half an hour south to Roslin and its fascinating Rosslyn Chapel, thought by some to be the home of the Holy Grail. Enjoy lunch by the water's edge in the relaxed and picturesque suburb of South Queensferry before visiting its grand Hopetoun House. An afternoon drive 7 miles (11 km) west brings you to Linlithgow Palace to swirl in the ghosts of Scotland's most romanticized monarch, Mary Queen of

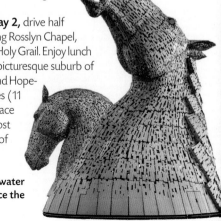

Statues of two Kelpies, mythical water horses, standing at 98 feet (30 m), grace the Falkirk landscape.

■ The Scottish mountains offer everything from gentle excursions to great skill-testing challenges, such as reaching the summit of Aonach Mor, a stone's throw from Ben Nevis.

Scots. Return to the UNESCO World Heritage charms of Edinburgh for either an eerie ghost tour on the Royal Mile or a dip into its rich performing arts scene.

Day 3 starts with a two-hour drive north to Perthshire, passing over the River Forth via a dramatic bridge before entering the rolling landscape. After lunch in the town of Perth make the short drive north to Scone Palace, where Scotland once crowned its kings. Rejoin the A9 north and you are soon engulfed in the majesty of the Highlands, with mountains crowding all around on the approach to the busy resort town of Aviemore two hours farther north. If it is still light when you arrive, head up the Cairngorm Mountain Railway, which takes you high into the rugged wildscape for the sunset.

On **Day 4,** ease farther north just over an hour by car to the only city in the Highlands, Inverness. Detour to Culloden en route; a catastrophic defeat for the Jacobite Highlanders here in 1746 led to the destruction of the Highland clan way of life. Inverness itself offers cultural attractions and riverside strolls, plus a kiltmaking center.

Day 5 begins with a scenic drive along the famous shores of Loch Ness keeping an eye out for Nessie, its famous monster. Head out on to the water with a boat tour from the trim little town of Fort Augustus, which will also allow you time to ramble around the romantic ruins of Urquhart Castle. A 1.5-hour drive will take you across to the

When to Visit

You can visit Scotland at any time of year, but be aware that many visitor attractions close or operate restricted opening times from late October to Easter. The snows of winter give the Scottish landscape even more appeal, and Christmas and Hogmanay (New Year) are great times to be in Scotland's cities. The favorite month among Scots is May, which is often the sunniest and the driest. July and August can be afflicted by the harmless, but annoying, biting midge insects, especially in the Highlands and islands. Photographers swear that October offers the best light.

Atlantic coast and the former garrison town of Fort William, with great views and plenty of facilities.

The fit, brave, and well equipped can kick off **Day 6** by embarking on a full-day hike up the United Kingdom's highest mountain, Ben Nevis. More sedentary souls can still enjoy the high altitude by taking the Nevis Range Gondola and then mountain biking, embarking on a short walk, or just taking in the views from the café/restaurant.

On **Day 7** take the narrow, twisting A82 road south from Fort William. This road, while not the fastest route, provides spectacular views of some of Scotland's finest scenery, passing though Glen Coe and along the western shore of beautiful Loch Lomond. Once you have descended from the Highlands, Glasgow awaits with an easy-to-navigate city center replete with grand Georgian and Victorian buildings and world-class cultural attractions. Leave time to also head west from Fort William to Glenfinnan to photograph the Jacobite steam train crossing the iconic Glenfinnan Viaduct.

Tipping

Tipping is not so straightforward in Scotland. In cases where paying for service is optional, locals simply add a little extra onto the bill, while others add an additional 10 percent. As a general guide, add 10 to 15 percent for good service in a café or restaurant. Tipping is not expected in a bar. You may, however, hear the bar person being told to buy one for themselves; when this happens, they will usually add the price of a drink to the bill and take this as a tip. For taxi fares, round up the fare to the nearest pound or add on a couple of pounds.

If You Have More Time

You could spend months in Scotland and still not see all of it. If you do have more time, we recommend taking two or three days to explore south of Edinburgh and Glasgow. Southern Scotland boasts rolling hills, a rugged coastline, a string of ruined abbeys (including the majestic Border abbeys of Melrose, Dryburgh, and Jedburgh), and quintessential towns such as Portpatrick, Melrose, and Kirkcudbright. Here you can revel in the writings of Sir Walter Scott and Robert Burns, the two men who have most romantically captured Scotland in prose and poetry, respectively, better than anyone. Or consider exploring the kingdom of Fife, just north of Edinburgh, a region that boasts the "home of golf," St. Andrews, as well as picturesque fishing villages and historic sights. Head up the coast, past stunning Dunnotar Castle and other scenic ruins to Aberdeen, on the east coast about 120 miles (193 km) north of Edinburgh. This city is known for its grand granite buildings and easy access to Royal Deeside, once a favorite mountainous playground of Queen Victoria.

Also worth exploring to the north and west of Glasgow is the indented and island-strewn coast of Argyll. Often ignored by tourists, this region is home to numerous sea lochs, hills, and historic attractions, as well as trim towns such as Inveraray (about a 1.5-hour drive northwest of Glasgow) and Oban (on the west coast, 2 hours north of Glasgow), the latter having reinvented itself as the "seafood capital of Scotland."

The ancient city of Stirling, located about an hour's drive north of Glasgow, is a must for history buffs, as the key battle between the Scots and the English took place here. It is also a gateway to the famous Highlands, which, beyond Inverness and Avemore, stretch from the North Sea to the Atlantic Ocean. The scenic North Coast 500 route marks a spectacular way to explore this sparsely populated but tremendously beautiful region. With more than 800 islands, almost 100 of them populated, Scotland offers plenty beyond its mainland. The best plan is to focus on one island or a group of neighboring islands. The biggest, Skye, is ideal for those short on time, as it can be reached by road from Glasgow in about 4 hours. Arran is even easier to get to, and can be reached within 2 hours by car and ferry. The little-visited Outer Hebrides, located 50 miles (80 km) off the northwest coast of Scotland, offers an end-of-the-world feel and stunning scenery. The Orkney and Shetland Islands, north of the mainland, are whole archipelagos with as much Norse as Scottish history. All of these islands can be reached by ferry or short flights from Edinburgh or Glasgow.

More Outdoor Possibilities

Wherever you go in Scotland, the scenery is universally remarkable. Lovers of the great outdoors will be in heaven, and even if you are not normally an active type there will be something for you. Choose from myriad walking opportunities, from skill-testing dangerous ridges, to coast-to-coast trails, to gentle lochside strolls. Then there is mountain biking, with Scotland widely acclaimed as one of the world's best destinations for this pastime. The country has both well-organized mountain-bike centers and wild rural trails where you see more deer than people. Throw in river rafting, kayaking, canyoneering, surfing, windsurfing, sailing, and skiing, and Scotland offers a diversity of things to do as varied as the histories of its clans. Wherever you go and whatever you do, it will all come wrapped in that famously infectious Scottish hospitality and friendliness. Enjoy Scotland, *sláinte*–"health." ■

Inveraray Castle, one of Scotland's many tourist destinations

HISTORY & CULTURE

SCOTLAND TODAY

Scotland is a land of stunning natural beauty—a cultural oasis with a complex history steeped in tradition. The Scots are justifiably proud of their land, which has branded itself onto the global map through its whiskies, bagpipes, tartan, and so much more. The country's vitality is seen in many ways, from an influx of top chefs to soul-searching talk of independence.

Scotland's story is long and complex, to say the least. This is perhaps not surprising given that within its genetic makeup runs the blood of fierce Pictish warriors, Celtic kings, Roman legionnaires, marauding Vikings, and the Germanic Angles. Scotland was first an independent nation more than a millennium ago. The country is today part of the United Kingdom—a political and economic union (with a shared monarchy) with England, Wales, and Northern Ireland. But don't make the mistake of confusing Scotland with England (more about that later). The soul-searching following the 2014 Independence Referendum and 2016 "Brexit" vote has really stirred up the political and cultural landscape.

> **The Scots wear their history firmly on their sleeves, and often you almost forget which century you are in.**

Old & New

Modern Scotland is a fascinating place to visit and continues to offer a complex web of old and new. The Scots wear their history firmly on their sleeves, and often you almost forget which century you are in. Here, tales of old battles and ancient rivalries simmer in the fissures of the rocks. If you want to revel in this Scotland of heart-stirring clichés, the world of Mel Gibson's *Braveheart* (1995) is still out there and is thoroughly enjoyable.

Your visit will be far richer if you make the effort to also delve beyond the tartan-draped clichés. Modern Scotland embraces new technologies, has an economy based firmly on the service sectors, and is home to a people with a passion for succeeding in the high-tech world of the 21st century. Scotland's cities still have those gorgeous castles, cobbled old towns, and all the traditional tourist trimmings, but look farther than the view from an open-top bus tour and you will see that they also have funky modern art galleries, dynamic glass-and-steel architecture, and a plethora of more stimulating and cerebral tourist attractions.

A *cèilidh* (a traditional Scottish gathering) is where the modern and historic

▪ Scotland's vibrant culture is an exciting mix of the traditional and the new.

■ Life in the Highlands retains its traditional pace and simplicity.

Scotland most happily join hands. This thoroughly fun Celtic celebration has its roots in the mists of clan history, when the tribespeople would party with music and dancing. The tradition continues, and you will find a real mix of creeds and clashing personalities at a modern ceilidh, dancing as a group to traditional fiddle music.

The Scotland that you will discover with your eyes, as well as your heart and mind, is as multifaceted as it has ever been. After a day or two, you will realize that you have been lucky enough to discover a truly unique place. Scotland is a land that may lie on England's doorstep but will never be content to be anything less than an equal partner, and it lies in a corner of Europe where geopolitical fault lines are as shifting as any of the tectonic plates that have so spectacularly formed this beautiful nation.

The Scots & the English

Scotland's relationship with England is a defining one. Millions of years ago the two regions lay an ocean apart and in some ways they still feel that way. Its larger neighbor has been a constant source of torment through the centuries with a series of wars and periods when the "Auld Enemy" (the English) tried to occupy Scotland. Even when they were not engaged in open warfare, the Borders were alive with skirmishes and power struggles, and the next bout of saber rattling was never far away. Today, a large part of the Scottish national identity is formed by "not being English," something the Scots feel they have to actively proclaim, as they are often grouped with their southern neighbors by international visitors unsure of the relationship between the two countries and, worse still, ignorant inhabitants of England. Referring to the country as England will instantly lose you Scottish friends. It is, regardless, rare to find Scots who express genuine hostility toward the English—for many the centuries-old conflict has become little more than a good-natured rivalry.

The issue of Scottish independence has occupied a great deal of Scottish political discussion since the Act of Union joined Scotland with England in 1707, but it is not a straightforward one. Many observers outside Scotland were surprised that Scotland did not take the opportunity to regain its autonomy in the 2014 Independence Referendum, with 55 percent of those who voted answering

EXPERIENCE: Celebrate Hogmanay

It will probably be when you have been hugged by a stranger for the 100th time, with your body warmed by the whisky, that you decide that no matter how many times you have celebrated New Year's Eve, you have never before savored anything quite like "Hogmanay."

Hogmanay flaunts in bizarre traditions. On the isle of Skye, a bull's hide was once burned, with every guest having to sniff the smoke to ward off evil spirits. If the hide went out as you sniffed it, this meant bad luck. An equally wacky tradition, "first footing" considered it good luck for the "first footer" to step into your house to be a dark-haired male stranger carrying a lump of coal, symbolizing warmth and fuel. This "first foot" spirit of friendliness is still alive in all of Scotland's cities at the end of December, with visitors welcome to join the party. There are Hogmanay festivities throughout Scotland, with the scale and type of events varying considerably between communities **Edinburgh** (edinburghfestivalcity .com) offers the biggest of all the nation's Hogmanay parties. Its fierce rival, **Glasgow** (glasgowlife .org.uk), Scotland's largest city, throws its own Hogmanay Ceilidh in the city center. Just along the road in **Stirling** (whatsonstirling .co.uk), it is mostly the locals who turn out for the seriously fun festivities in the dramatic setting of Stirling Castle. Here the ramparts come alive with the sound of the massed bagpipes and drums, as well as homegrown pop stars. It's an experience you will never forget.

"no" when asked "Should Scotland be an independent country?" The picture is complex and while many Scots firmly wanted to remain within the U.K., others were nervous about the political and economic ramifications of leaving, so opted for the status quo. The 45 percent who voted for independence remain a very vocal lobby, one whose voice has grown louder since the 2016 U.K. "Brexit" vote to leave the European Union—a move very much against the wishes of the Scottish people. Having an interest, or at least a basic knowledge of these issues will inform your trip, enhance your experiences, and win you new friends in this proud nation.

Highlands & Lowlands

Every country has its internal rivalries; the biggest in Scotland is the seismic rift between the Highlands, in the north of the country, and the Lowlands, in the south. The country is actually split into three different geographic zones determined by two fault lines (the Southern Uplands, the Lowlands, and the Highlands), administered by 32 local councils since 1975, when the 33 former counties were abolished (nonetheless, Scots still commonly refer to the counties).

> **While many Scots firmly wanted to remain within the U.K., others were nervous about the political and economic ramifications of leaving, so opted for the status quo.**

The divisions in Scotland are not only physical. Highlanders tend to see themselves as more rugged—people of the earth—and this is where the remnants of traditional Gaelic culture survive and where the Celtic language is still spoken. The Highlands was the region that was decimated after the tragic defeat at Culloden in 1746 (see p. 48). In many ways, the people and the economy here have never fully recovered. Romantic tales of the old clans are still immortalized in poignant songs and poetry. Inhabitants of the Lowlands (or *Lallans* in Scots, Scotland's own rival language to English) take on many hues, but their world is generally a more urban, connected place with cities, highways, and all the trimmings of modern living. The two worlds coexist and inevitably intertwine continuously, but it is a useful division to note, one that will help your understanding of the country's rich history and culture.

Becoming a Tourist Destination

Scotland as a tourist destination was once an unlikely prospect, even after the grand tour of Europe's cities toward the end of the 17th century really kicked off sightseeing in foreign lands. Who would want to spend an arduous, uncomfortable trip battling the elements on bumpy tracks and negotiating threatening mountains in a country notorious for its rebellious people? Indeed the whole idea of mountains being somewhere you would actually want to spend time did not really exist until relatively recently. In 1773, English writer Samuel Johnson concluded after his rugged three-month tour that "Seeing Scotland … is only seeing a worse England. It is seeing the flower gradually fade away to the naked stalk." While the wildly popular works of author Sir Walter Scott (1771–1832) conveyed a romanticized view of the country to a broad readership, the love of British monarch Queen Victoria (1819–1901) for the Highlands makes a convenient starting point for the emergence of tourism within Scotland. She first visited in 1842 and was so deeply moved and impressed by the wild beauty of the brooding hills and tumbling glens that she bought an estate, Balmoral. She spent many a happy holiday wrapped in the charms of her expanded castle and exploring her beloved Deeside (today known as Royal Deeside in her honor) and beyond. She swathed the Highlands in platitudes and virtually single-handedly made them a fashionable escape, with some of England's wealthier families even establishing substantial residences (their Highland estates) in the north.

Tourism developed throughout the 19th century, but getting around the extremities was still a problem—although perhaps not as difficult as it was in 1773, when Johnson reported that there were no roads on the isle of Skye and so had to travel everywhere on horseback. With the improvement of the railroads, making it possible to travel deep into the Highlands in a modicum of comfort, more people south of the border discovered the country's natural beauty. Scots concentrated in the central belt also started to escape to the wilderness—many in the west heading "doon the watter" to the isles and resorts of the Firth of Clyde, seeking refuge from the nation's increasingly industrialized cities.

Through the 20th century, Scottish tourism continued to grow. However, the advent of cheap jet travel in the 1960s sounded the death knell for the great boom of the Clydeside resorts, as Scots of all social classes headed for the Spanish Costas instead. In recent decades the growth in demand for short city breaks has helped Scottish

(continued on p. 22)

Soccer: A National Obsession

If you want to take route one into the Scottish psyche, go to a football match (as a soccer game is called in Scotland) or just talk "footie" or "fitba" in any pub. The sport is used as a way of demonstrating traditional rivalries along regional and even religious grounds, but it is also a crucial way of venting tensions that might otherwise be expressed in more dangerous places than a football stadium. The greatest rivalry is the "Old Firm" rivalry between Glasgow Celtic (Catholic and Irish nationalist) and Glasgow Rangers (Protestant and Unionist), with even many less avid fans having a preference between the two, as well as supporting their own "lesser" teams.

HIGHLAND GAMES

The Highland Games, or the Highland Gathering, is integral to Scottish culture, celebrating and also harking back to layers of history and tradition. These events have their origins in the days of King Malcolm III, when the Scottish monarch used the games as a way of finding the bravest, strongest, and most skilled warriors.

The Highland Games took on another practical role when the occupying English banned Scottish men from military training for fear of rebellion. The Scots simply traded their swords and daggers for cabers and weighty stones as a way of developing their stamina, physical strength, and, of course, preparing for conflict.

Today, Highland Games take place annually at various venues throughout Scotland. The earliest events take place in May and carry on through September, which makes them accessible to many people visiting Scotland. The games are massively popular events that, despite their name, are not limited to the Highlands. In fact, they stretch from the Borders right up to the top of Scotland, with the isles of Arran, Bute, Lewis, Mull, and Skye among those hosting their own games.

Perhaps equally surprising is the fact that the largest Highland Games in Scotland is the Cowal Gathering in Dunoon. This extravaganza ripples through Dunoon during the last weekend in August and attracts more than 3,000 competitors and 20,000 spectators. Other major gatherings take place at Braemar (see pp. 189–190)—an event traditionally attended by members of the British royal family—Grantown-on-Spey, and Crieff, but there

EXPERIENCE: Try Your Hand at Highland Dancing

Highland dancing is an expertly choreographed and thoroughly athletic performance, which is always performed solo and usually undertaken in traditional Highland dress to the accompaniment of bagpipes. It is a far cry from the rough-and-tumble of the games' sports, having more in common with ballet than warfare. On your visit you have the best chance of catching a performance at a Highland Games, but regular competitions are also held across the country during the summer. Key dances to watch for include the Highland Fling, Sword Dance, Shean Truibhais, Reel and Sailor's Hornpipe, and the Highland Laddie. If you are staying longer in Scotland you can sign up for lessons with one of the dance groups. For more information contact the **Scottish Official Highland Dancing Association** (sohda.org.uk)—the governing body for this national tradition, mostly performed by women.

■ **The hammer throw tests the warrior's strength and balance at Inveraray Argyll Highland Games.**

are countless other events, and each has charms of its own.

Traditional Events

Perhaps the most famous Highland Games event is the caber toss. This sees a variety of pine logs being lifted by burly men, who then run with them before hurling them through the air. Other events include the hammer throw, a variety of weight throwing events, and hurling a weight over a bar.

The traditional sports are often accompanied by athletics events, such as running various lengths on a track or up (and back down) the nearest steep hill. There are also traditional music performances, with the highlight usually a Highland band that consists of talented pipers and drummers.

Each Highland Games has its own traditions and events. Some include cattle shows, while others have sheepdog trials. There is also the spectacular sight of dancers performing traditional Highland dancing, mimicking the movements of the stag on the Highland hillsides.

At many games there are also plenty of modern distractions to entertain children, which vary from venue to venue but may include carnival rides and games, police dog demonstrations, children's entertainers, spectacular shows featuring birds of prey, children's races, gig tents with live music, and even pet dog shows. For the adults, the food stalls and beer tents often prove an added attraction.

Whichever Highland Games you choose to attend you will get a glimpse of the traditional Scottish way of life and the events that once kept these traditions alive. For more information about any of the Highland Games in Scotland visit the Royal Scottish Highland Games Association *(rshga.org)* or stop at the local tourist information center to ask about the nearest events.

tourism—now a multimillion-dollar industry employing 210,000 people—with Edinburgh and Glasgow particularly popular destinations for both domestic and international visitors. Today's $4 billion tourism industry is multifaceted. Some people come for the traditional castle-and-shortbread bus tour, while others prefer to get away from it all on a romantic Hebridean isle. Still others come to the highlands to test their mountain-bike skills or tackle the mountains while the North Coast 500 is considered a must-do for motorcyclists. Scotland remains a place of magic for many, including fans of the popular *Outlander* series (see pp. 55–57), as well as a refuge from the real or perceived threat of terrorism. The COVID-19 pandemic refocused travelers' priorities, as visitors opted for staycations and domestic breaks closer to home. Post-lockdown, Scotland has witnessed a shift toward wilderness-focused travel and less crowded rural and coastal areas, boosted by the Highlands being named one of National Geographic's top five "Best of the World" nature destinations for 2023.

Scottish Sporting Profile

Perhaps it is because Scotland is not an independent nation that its people constantly strive to raise their country's global profile across myriad fields of endeavor. This is keenly displayed within the sporting arena, where supporters usually wave Scottish and not British flags. This even happens during the Olympics, where their countrymen can only compete under the Great Britain and Northern Ireland banner. The two main team sports of soccer and rugby are passionately followed in Scotland. Fittingly for a nation that historically has often seemed to snatch defeat from the jaws of victory, its teams tend to do the same. Scotland's national soccer team spectacularly qualified for five World Cup finals in a row from 1974 through 1990 but then failed to progress beyond the first round in any. Since then Scotland has only qualified for one soccer World Cup and that was back in 1998; although the team once again failed to get past the first round, the famous Scottish fans, known as the "Tartan Army," won the hearts of many

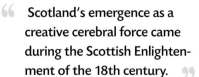

Scotland's emergence as a creative cerebral force came during the Scottish Enlightenment of the 18th century.

French hosts with their sporting and lighthearted behavior. Individual sports stars have been more successful. Scotland invented golf, and in recent years the country's golfers have made their mark with the likes of Sam Torrance, Colin Montgomerie, Russel Knox, and Sandy Lyle. Then there is seven-time world snooker champion Stephen Hendry. He has been followed by another successful Scottish talent, John Higgins. The current Scottish sporting success story is tennis player Sir Andy Murray. He has made three Grand Slam finals and won a flurry of tournaments, including Wimbledon twice. He was also crowned the

■ **Off the tourist trail at Elgol, with the Cuillin Mountains looming beyond**

world's number one tennis player in 2016. Multi-Olympic gold medalist Sir Chris Hoy is another Scottish sporting hero in the field of track cycling. He suffered a horrendous crash in 2009 that could have ended his career. He bravely battled back and after, incredibly, suffering another chilling crash in the qualifying rounds, went on to win his tenth world title and fifth Olympic gold medal.

Scotland's Gifts to the World

Within the United Kingdom, Scotland has a reputation for being a nation of inventors and creative thinkers. The achievements are less well known farther afield, strange as this nation of more than five million people has given the world perhaps more inventions per capita than any other country. If that sounds like a bold statement, and you think you could do without Scottish inventions, you had better switch off your TV, not make any calls, not drive on a road (you couldn't anyway without tires), and not use your bike. All of these were Scottish inventions, and the list goes on and on.

Scotland's emergence as a creative cerebral force came during the Scottish Enlightenment of the 18th century. Two of its main luminaries were Adam Smith (1723–1790), whose *Wealth of Nations* remains a seminal economic tome today, and empiricist philosopher David Hume (1711–1776). Then there was John Logie Baird (1888–1946), the man who gave the world the TV, while his contemporary Alexander Graham Bell (1847–1922) first set tongues wagging on the telephone. It was John Boyd Dunlop (1840–1921) who gave us pneumatic rubber tires to drive on. Many of us owe our dry clothes at work to Charles Macintosh (1766–1843) and his handy waterproof coats. And next time you take a stroll in the park, spare a thought for John Muir (1838–1914), whose love of nature stirred him to advocate the preservation of wilderness areas and the creation of U.S. national parks, including Yosemite and Sequoia.

Where would medicine be without James Young Simpson (1811–1870), who invented chloroform, and Alexander Fleming (1881–1955), who has saved millions of lives through his discovery of the antibiotic penicillin? And that is not even mentioning Scottish physician Alexander Wood (1817–1884), who invented the hypodermic needle, or Alexander Cumming (1733–1814), who invented the S-bend flush toilet. Lesser known inventors, unfamiliar even to many Scots, include William Murdoch (1754–1839), who invented gas lighting, and Robert Watson-Watt (1892–1973), who invented radar, without which the Allied success in World War II (1939–1945) would have been far more tricky and protracted—and by no means guaranteed. Then, of course, there was the creation of one of Scotland's most famous inhabitants, the hugely innovative and controversial "Dolly the sheep"—the first cloned mammal, with the Midlothian-based Roslin Institute the pioneering force behind this particular science. Dolly at least is still drawing attention, now at the National Museum of Scotland in Edinburgh (see pp. 71–73).

Scotland's Political & Economic Profile

Scotland rushed into the new millennium flush with the success of gaining devolution (with increased political powers being transferred to Scotland from Westminster in London) and establishing its first parliament in 300 years in its capital city. However, crucial political decisions, such as defense, foreign affairs, and the economy, stayed in London.

But there is no underestimating the boost to Scottish confidence that devolution engendered. A burst of new legislation driven by a more Scottish viewpoint soon emerged, including the establishment of the nation's first two national parks and the landmark Land Reform Act in 2003. This act laid to rest the lingering embers of the Highland Clearances (one of the darkest periods in the nation's story; see p. 252) and solidified in law the people's right to walk or cycle on the vast estates that emerged during feudalism and still occupy large swaths of Scotland today. In 2007, the Scottish National Party (SNP) won a landmark victory in national elections, and it has remained in power ever since, most recently being reelected in 2021. The SNP has repeatedly stood up for Scotland's interests in the U.K. Parliament, too, where it won 44 of Scotland's 58 seats in 2021. One of the most seismic political events of recent years, the aforementioned Independence Referendum of September 2014, was preceded by two years of passionate debate that at its best invigorated the country and its rich cultural scene, but at its worst split friends and even families. As the vote approached and one poll showed a majority favored independence, the U.K. government panicked into making "The Vow," a promise of more devolution if Scotland voted to remain within the U.K. There is little doubt that this helped sway some voters; however, some voters on both sides still feel they were cheated by this last minute offer, as neither the substance nor the spirit of The Vow have yet been delivered. Matters became further complicated by the "Brexit" referendum held in the U.K. in June 2016. Most of England voted to leave the European Union, while Scotland voted to stay. This has fueled calls both to find a way to keep Scotland in the EU or to gain full Independence within the U.K. The picture remains confused and fast moving.

Other economic and social problems remain in 21st-century Scotland. The decline of traditional heavy industries has left some communities bereft of jobs and, in some cases, devoid of hope. There is serious deprivation, especially in and around parts of Glasgow, the hub of Scotland's once booming heavy industries, and in areas of Fife, where the mining industry has suffered a collapse. But Scotland's overall unemployment rate remains low, the resurgence of oil prices since 2020 has reversed a slump in the Aberdeen and Shetland economies, Edinburgh has rebounded as one of Europe's leading financial centers, and the 3.2 million overseas visitors to Scotland in 2022 almost equaled 2019's pre-pandemic visits. ∎

■ **A march for Scottish independence under the banner of the national flag** (January 2020)

FOOD & DRINK

Despite boasting some of the world's finest seafood and red meat—in the form of Aberdeen Angus beef—Scottish cuisine has not always enjoyed the best of reputations. All that has changed over the last two decades, with a slew of Michelin-starred restaurants being backed up by much better use of the local ingredients throughout the country at all levels.

Traditional Food

For centuries, Scottish food was based around the needs of its largely poor population. Easy to grow and filling staples such as the potato emerged as popular favorites, and there was also the widespread use of oatmeal. This is, after all, the home of porridge, which remains the most popular way to start the

> **The most famous (or perhaps infamous) food is the national dish, haggis. Much maligned and misunderstood, its ingredients are really no worse than most sausages.**

day in 21st-century Scotland. To really fit in, have it made with water and seasoned with a little salt.

The most famous (or perhaps infamous) food is the national dish, haggis. Much maligned and misunderstood, its ingredients are really no worse than most sausages. It consists of sheep's offal mash bulked up by oatmeal and then seasoned with various spices and onion, giving it an extremely pleasant flavor. These days, it is increasingly rare to find haggis served as it used to be—inside the lining of the sheep's stomach. Instead it is used in imaginative ways and featured on menus from take-out shops to high-end restaurants. Haggis is traditionally eaten with neeps (turnips to the Scots, swedes to the English, and rutabaga to Americans) and tatties (potatoes); the most renowned producer, Macsween (macsween .co.uk), also makes excellent vegetarian and gluten-free versions.

Another staple is, of course, shortbread. This sweet buttery treat originated in Scotland, and it is as popular today as it has always been with both locals and tourists, making for an ideal souvenir or gift.

Scottish Soups

Another Scottish staple is soup. Scotchbroth is a filling soup made up of barley; root vegetables such as carrots, turnips, and rutabaga; and cheap cuts of meat—traditionally mutton but sometimes lamb and (rarely) beef. This popular winter warmer has been around for hundreds of years. Traditionally, the

A selection of Scotland's internationally renowned seafood

OYSTER BARS

meat was removed after cooking and served as a main course, but today it is retained and eaten as one delicious meal.

Cullen skink might be the soup of choice for more adventurous foodies. This thick, creamy soup is made up of smoked haddock, potatoes, and onions and is thought to originate from the fishing village of Cullen on the northeast coast. Another traditional soup, cock-a-leekie, dates back to the 16th century and is a popular starter to a Burns Night supper (see sidebar below). This nutritious soup is made by boiling fowl such as chicken in a stock with vegetables such as leeks. In the past, chefs added prunes to improve the flavor of the soup. Prunes are rarely added today since they are not to everyone's taste, and even traditional chefs who cook the soup with prunes will remove them before serving.

World-Class Seafood

Scotland's rich seafood larder is often underrated, even within the country, perhaps because most of the freshest produce is spirited off to the fine-dining tables of London, Paris, and Madrid, where it fetches a far higher price.

The west coast is the real star, especially when it comes to shellfish. Here the cold, nutrient-rich, and unpolluted waters are ideal for plump wild lobsters and langoustines, the latter known confusingly as prawns in some parts of Wester Ross. Scallops are also excellent—both king scallops and the smaller queenies—with some of the biggest king scallops the size of tennis balls. The most prized are hand-dived king scallops, which are best served simply seared to really let the full flavor speak for itself. Regionally, Orkney crab is excellent and Shetland is generally considered the best source of large, plump, and flavorsome mussels. The best places to try cheap seafood are around the ports themselves, with Oban (see sidebar p. 155), establishing itself as the "seafood capital of Scotland," a good bet. Many of the best Scottish restaurants now have plenty of west coast seafood on their menus, as demand has increased and the prices the fishermen can get locally have risen.

Over on the east coast the specialty is whitefish, caught farther afield in the North Sea, although Eyemouth in the Borders is an excellent shellfish port,

Burns Night

Burns Night, on January 25, is one of the biggest nights of the year, when the birth date of national bard Robert Burns is celebrated. He was a legend with an eye for both booze and the ladies and certainly knew how to party; after all, he was the seminal poet and songwriter who penned the world's number one end of party anthem "Auld Lang Syne." Scots traditionally mark Burns Night by eating the national dish of haggis, served with neeps and tatties—a surprisingly tasty treat, especially when accompanied by a liberal serving of culture and traditional dancing.

■ **A traditional haggis ceremony—piping in the bearer**

too. The main whitefish ports are Peterhead and Fraserburgh in Aberdeenshire (see p. 197), Arbroath in Angus (see p. 181), and the litter of smaller ports on the southern flank of Fife. Species to look for are haddock (the most common staple in the fish and chips sold up and down the east coast) and the increasingly rare cod.

Scottish salmon is world famous. The majority of it is farmed in sea lochs. Much has been made of the poor conditions in some fish farms, and the situation has certainly improved in recent years. One highly regarded fish farm operator is on Loch Duart (lochduart.com), where environmentally friendly methods reap rewards on the flavor and texture front. Wild salmon, mainly caught in salmon-rich rivers such as the Tweed and the Spey, are greatly prized, but you will usually have to catch one for yourself.

Scottish Red Meat & Game

Scottish beef is universally excellent and highly acclaimed. The most famous breed is the Aberdeen Angus, which produces a consistently good flavor no matter what the cut. In recent years, the Highland breed (the furry beasts with the big horns) has been appearing on more menus, though the slightly richer flavor does not suit all palates. Many Scots hail Buccleuch beef, and Buccleuch fillets and rib eye are indeed hard to beat.

Scottish lamb is also usually very good, with lamb from the Borders particularly highly prized. Venison—the lean and healthier red meat from deer—is growing in popularity, although its gamey richness can be too much for some and is best offset with a tangy berry-based sauce. Many Scottish butchers also produce excellent homemade sausages, and the famous "Square," or "Lorne," sausage is

Visitors taste whisky at the Isle of Harris Distillery.

a favorite hangover cure.

Game is more of a niche market, but during the shooting season it appears on menus in more expensive hotels and restaurants. You will usually find grouse and pheasant on offer, with the wild, rich, and often overpowering taste too much for some. When fresh and cooked properly, however, game meat can be excellent.

Regional Specialties

Scotland boasts many regional specialties. One of the most famous is the Arbroath smokie, which is a brand of locally caught and smoked haddock. In Aberdeenshire, look for butteries—a highly calorific pastry treat.

In recent years, Scotland has also been producing some award-winning cheese. The highlights among blues are the Lanark, Dunsyre, and Strathdon blue varieties, while the finest cheddar is the isle of Mull cheddar, which is usually unpasteurized. Traditional cheeses have become immensely popular in recent years, including Caboc (which dates back to the 15th century) from the Highlands and Grimbister from the Orkney Islands.

Today's Dining

You can still "savor" the various deep-fried abominations served up in Scottish fish-and-chips restaurants, or "chippies." Examples include deep-fried pizza and even deep-fried chocolate bars. Standards have improved across the board, however, helped in part by the rise of the celebrity TV chef and a determination of the government to promote a healthy lifestyle. With this has come greater sophistication. Edinburgh leads the way, with no fewer than 31 Michelin-starred restaurants in 2023. Glasgow's eateries are more egalitarian, but there are still many great places to eat. All major towns and cities now boast good, and often great, restaurants. Smaller operators have also opened in the likes of Kinlochleven and Kishorn to offer boat-fresh seafood in informal surroundings. So you can savor the same seafood you would pay a fortune for at the finest dining tables of London or Paris.

Drinks

For Scots, whisky is known as *uisge beatha* (see sidebar opposite), and little excuse is needed to persuade one of the locals to enjoy a wee dram. Beer is also popular, with the deliciously creamy and full flavor "heavy" similar, but often better, than warmer English beer. Independent microbreweries have also blossomed lately. Brews to look for include those from the excel-

Whisky—the Quintessential Highland Tipple

Scottish whisky has never been more popular around the world than it is today. However, how many people enjoying a wee dram in Singapore or New York, for example, are really aware of the story behind whisky's early illicit days, or that there are three types of "Scotch"?

The production of whisky—whose recipe of malted barley, yeast, and water is wonderfully simple—had been going on in Scotland centuries before it became fashionable elsewhere in the world. *Uisge beatha,* the Gaelic name for whisky, which translates as "water of life," was a lifeblood of the Highland clans who used to roam the wild mist-shrouded glens.

After the 1707 Act of Union, the British government heavily taxed whisky, which was produced in small stills across the country. This drove production underground, and the Scots started to play a whisky-drenched cat-and-mouse game with the tax collectors.

These days whisky is big business. There are many hundreds of distilleries dotted throughout Scotland, with each region offering different flavors and incarnations. Many of the distilleries are open to the public, offering free or cheap tours with, of course, the chance to sample the hallowed amber spirit.

There are three types of Scotch whisky: grain, malt, and blended. Single malts are the purest of whiskies and are the product of a single distillery, with the fresh water going in one end and whisky coming out the other. Grain malts are similar but usually rougher in taste and these are rarely available for purchase. Blended whisky is made up of at least two different whiskies, usually a single malt that is mixed with a grain whisky. Some blended whiskies have more than two blends mixed into them, including whisky that comes from other distilleries located in totally different parts of the country. A blend that has only single malt whiskies and no grain whisky is called a vatted malt. Most whiskies are blends.

lent Black Isle Brewery *(blackislebrewery.com),* the award-winning BrewDog *(brewdog.com),* and the Orkney Brewery *(orkneybrewery.co.uk),* whose Dark Island is a world-class tipple.

In recent years, following the global trend back to craft cocktails, gins infused with a variety of locally sourced botanicals have taken hold. Such elements as marsh marigold from the Shetland Islands, heather from Islay, and bramble from the Highlands lend distinctly Scottish tones to diverse batches of the spirit produced by some 20 distilleries, from small start-ups as well as long-established whisky brands. Try an impromptu tasting or attend a juniper festival leading up to World Gin Day, in June *(worldginday.com).*

Of the soft drinks, the ultrasweet Irn Bru is an indigenous fizzy drink that rivals Coca-Cola and Pepsi in national sales and is rated much higher in the country's affections. ∎

LAND & ENVIRONMENT

The geography of Scotland is one of the most remarkable in the world. Slightly smaller than South Carolina, the country boasts an unparalleled natural diversity for its size. Scotland has a coastline twice as long as that of either France or Spain and is adorned with mighty mountains, voluminous sea cliffs, and silvery lochs that handily fall into three main geographical areas.

Scotland is split between the Southern Uplands, the Lowlands, and the Highlands, with each region having its own unique natural attractions and features—although all three exhibit the classic effects of glaciation. The country stretches for 274 miles (441 km) from north to south and is between 154 miles (248 km) and 24 miles (39 km) wide, with a total land mass of more than 31,000 square miles (80,290 sq km). The natural stories of the trio of geographical regions and their landscapes dovetail with the human history; in Scotland the imprint of man has always been firmly dictated by the environment. Indeed, some Scots joke that it was the Highlands, and not the Highlanders, that kept the ancient Romans at bay. The country is one of Europe's top wildlife-viewing destinations. Any trip is enhanced by both the flora and fauna of this dramatically scenic corner of Europe.

> **In Scotland, the imprint of man has always been firmly dictated by the environment. Some joke the Highlands, not the Highlanders, kept the ancient Romans at bay.**

Southern Uplands

Scotland's most southerly geographic zone borders England and then runs southwest-northeast, parallel to the English border, along the line of the Southern Uplands Fault, which angles from Girvan on the west coast across to Dunbar on the North Sea coast. It is a highly attractive area replete with mile upon mile of rolling hills, with a large spine of barren peaks (the actual Southern Uplands) that stretch around 120 miles (190 km) from west to east, although there are no Munros (mountains more than 3,000 feet/914 m). The highest peak is Merrick (2,766 feet/843 m). The region's western and eastern fringes are more fertile, with sweeping glens (valleys) dropping down toward the coastal plains. On the coast are sea cliffs and sandy beaches awash with birdlife. The Southern Uplands region is also home to large forest areas, including Mabie Forest and Galloway Forest.

▪ The wild cliffs of Orkney are home to many species of seabirds.

The Lowlands

The Lowlands describes the rift valley that separates the Uplands and Highlands. Geologically, the area extends north to the Highland Boundary Fault—roughly from Dunoon in the west and angling northeast to Stonehaven in the east. It is rich in sedimentary rocks and hence rich in minerals, which has brought it wealth through the mining of coal and iron deposits. It is also the flattest geographic region of Scotland and the most fertile, which means that it has also become the most agriculturally significant and the most populated, with around 80 percent of the country's population and five out of its six biggest cities (Inverness is in the Highlands).

The main hill ranges in the Lowlands are the Pentlands and Lammermuirs in the east and the Campsie Fells in the west. The region is also home to a number of extinct volcanoes—most significantly Arthur's Seat and Castle Hill in Edinburgh. Of the smaller groups of hills of note, the Bathgate Hills are particularly lovely; they run between the country's two main cities of Edinburgh and Glasgow and offer views across the Forth and Clyde Valleys.

The central Lowlands are indented with a series of river estuaries, known locally as firths. In the west, the Firth of Clyde opens up after the River Clyde passes through Glasgow to end in a wide sweep replete with isles such as Arran and Bute. The River Forth runs east through Stirling before widening out into a firth of its own, and meets the sea east of Edinburgh. Meanwhile, the Firth of Tay merges with the North Sea just east of Dundee.

The bleak beauty of the Isle of Lewis highlights the ancient ruin of Dun Carloway Broch.

The Highlands

The north and west of Scotland is the most awe-inspiringly scenic part of the country. The Highlands is one big dramatic geography lesson on uplift and glaciation, as you can see and feel the effects of the mighty glaciers that, during the last ice age, rumbled seaward from the high mountains, carving out the glens and scything deep cuts into the ground, which today are the country's myriad lochs (lakes).

Mountains formed from ancient rock abound in the Highlands. Both Torridonian sandstone and Lewisian gneiss are thought to be among the oldest rocks in the world, with the latter dated to more than three billion years ago. The region abounds with towering peaks and is home to the massive Munro mountains, which attract climbers and walkers from all over the world. The Munros come in all shapes and sizes. Some stand alone—real monarchs of the glen like 3,169-foot (966 m) Ben More, the most northerly—while others are more unassuming, forming part of a chunky range of mountains, such as the Cairngorms.

> 66 **The scenery in the Highlands is unremittingly majestic. At every turn another mountain looms into view or a gushing burn (stream) rushes past.** 99

The scenery in the Highlands is unremittingly majestic. At every turn another mountain looms into view or a gushing burn (stream) rushes past. At its heart is the Great Glen. This fault line northeast from the Atlantic town of Fort William in the southwest to the Moray Firth and the city of Inverness in a series of slender glens and lochs, all dwarfed by the massive mountains that rear up spectacularly on both sides.

Inland Waterways

Scotland is richly veined with burns and rivers across all its regions, all either running into the North Sea or the Atlantic Ocean. The longest three rivers are the Tay (120 miles / 193 km), which meets the sea at Dundee; the Spey (107 miles / 172 km), which runs into the North Sea at the Moray Firth; and the Clyde—Scotland's most industrial river, which runs through Glasgow (106 miles / 171 km). These three are also the largest rivers in terms of catchment. Other major rivers include the salmon-rich Tweed in the Southern Uplands and the Forth, which runs through the central Lowlands and widens its firth into the North Sea, east of Edinburgh.

Climate

Much is made of Scotland's supposedly terrible weather, but for its northerly locale (Aberdeen is on the same line of latitude as Juneau, Alaska) the country's climate is actually surprisingly temperate and, of course, maritime. The chilly northerly winds and the influence of the Arctic are tempered by the warming influence of the Gulf Stream, which flows across the Atlantic from the Gulf of Mexico. The Gulf Stream helps to make the west coast particularly mild, with visitors often being surprised by palm trees growing happily in villages such as Plockton in the Highlands. Even when the weather is extreme, it just adds to the natural drama.

Of course, there are many regional variations. To generalize, the east tends to be cooler and drier, while the west is the first place the tempestuous Atlantic weather systems hit, meaning that the west coast is considerably wetter. Fickle best sums up Scotland's weather. The Scottish summer—June, July, and August—can be especially unpredictable. Both spring and fall are good times to visit, as temperatures are still mild, with May usually the driest month. In contrast, winters can be harsh, with frequent snowfall affecting transportation, particularly in the Highlands. The islands can be a law unto themselves, with westerly isles such as Tiree and Coll reporting comparatively tiny amounts of rainfall, while Skye often earns its Gaelic moniker of the "isle of mist."

Flora & Fauna

Scotland is not only the most richly diverse part of the United Kingdom for wildlife, but it is also one of Europe's most valuable wild havens. There is a wide range of wildlife to spot, from a species of field mouse that lives only on two of the islands in St. Kilda to soaring ospreys (sea hawks) and giant killer whales (orcas).

Scotland is free of large predatory wild animals; the native wolves died out in the 18th century at the hands of game hunters and farmers who wanted to protect their livestock. The largest wild land animal is the deer, with the red deer being the

The John Muir Way

Scotland, a country awash with long distance walks, has a trail of particular interest to conservationists. Opened in 2014, the John Muir Way (johnmuirway.org) pays tribute to the Scottish luminary who played a pivotal role in establishing the United States' National Park System. Although Muir famously had a great love for the mountains, this 134-mile (216 km) trail—which snakes from his birthplace at Dunbar on the North Sea to Helensburgh, where he left for America at age 12—is largely flat or at least low level. It does, though, offer a green pathway through Central Scotland and has become a favorite with both walkers and cyclists. It is best hiked west to east with the prevailing winds.

■ Iconic Highland cattle, known as "hairy coos," graze above Loch Lomond.

most ubiquitous species. Deer are found all over Scotland, but prosper most in the Highlands and islands. The unspoiled isle of Jura is named for the Gaelic word for deer and is one of the finest places in the land to spot them, with deer vastly outnumbering the tiny human population (see pp. 267–268).

The famous Highland cow is unmistakable and is now a common sight, even outside the Highlands. Its shaggy red coat and impressive horns combine with its laid-back nature to make it a favorite with camera-toting tourists. These cattle roam semiwild on large Highland estates. It can be quite an experience having to dive into a ditch to avoid an oncoming herd of Highland cows heading down a narrow track.

Other fauna to spot include the elusive otter, which is found in lochs around Scotland's coast, and the pine marten—another predator that lives in forested areas. The critically endangered Scottish wildcat is now restricted to mixed woodlands of northern and eastern Scotland. Birdlife generally thrives in Scotland. Large birds of prey include the common buzzard (now even found in and around Scotland's urban areas) and the less seen, but deeply impressive, golden eagle—a majestic sight soaring above a Highland glen. Lucky hillwalkers will come across a symbol of the nation: grouse. These chiefly ground-dwelling birds, including the rare capercaillie and the ptarmigan, shed their brown camouflage in winter to adopt a white snow-colored sheen.

Out at sea, the elusive sea eagle is a rare but enthralling attraction in the isles, while the cute puffin is a more ubiquitous and fun vision with its awkward flying technique, splash landings, and brightly colored beak. St. Kilda and the Shetland

Islands are fantastic places to spot storm petrels (see sidebar p. 322) and puffins (see p. 323), although they can also be found within sight of Edinburgh Castle on the islands of the Firth of Forth.

In the water, you can watch for everything from small porpoises to large bottle-nose dolphins, as well as a range of whales and sharks, including basking sharks, minke whales, and the predatory killer whale (orca). In recent years, the Isle of Mull has emerged as something of a hub for marine wildlife-watching trips, although any boat trip off the Scottish coastline can reap rich rewards.

Conservation

Scotland is very serious about conservation. Devolution in 1999 gave the newly formed Scottish Parliament increased political powers, and it wasted no time in swinging them into action when it came to the conservation effort. Unusually, Scotland had no national parks when the SNP came to power, so the new government quickly declared Loch Lomond and The Trossachs National Park and Cairngorms National Park the first two in the country. Various nature reserves and protected areas exist around Scotland, and real attempts are also being made to atone for the natural cost of land mismanagement and the Clearances by replanting swaths of the Caledonian forest that once used to cover the nation in a rich, green cloak.

Direct interventions are also being made to control particular species. The native red squirrel (more than 75 percent of the U.K.'s dwindling population reside north of the border) has been under serious threat from the gray squirrel. A concentrated effort has been made to control the latter's numbers. In 2009, the beaver was reintroduced to great success; by 2021 its numbers surpassed 1,000 animals across 254 beaver territories. More success has already been secured with the nation's birdlife, with the rare osprey (or fish hawk) now thriving. ∎

Stag by a "passing place" on the Isle of Harris

HISTORY

Scotland's history is a complex, romantic, and controversial tale of heroes, battling peoples, and deadly power struggles. The story begins around 7,000 years ago, when Neolithic settlers eked out a rudimentary existence, and continues through to 2023, when the U.K. Supreme Court ruled that the Scottish government couldn't hold an independence referendum without Westminster's consent.

The Earliest Peoples

The earliest remaining imprints of humans in Scotland are to be found on the Orkney Islands. Indeed, the well-preserved sites at Skara Brae, Knap of Howar, and Maeshowe are actually the oldest preserved Neolithic dwellings in Europe. Archaeological evidence from the sites suggests that people from mainland Europe drifted into the region around 7,000 years ago and then settled. These people eked out a simple life, but as their settlements became more secure, and their grip on the land became stronger, they cemented their world with the building of large burial cairns and the stone circles that today still stand shrouded in mystery on the Orkney Islands and the Outer Hebrides. The finest is at Callanish on the isle of Lewis, whose stones date back as far as 2900 B.C.

> **Archaeological evidence from the sites suggests that people from mainland Europe drifted into the region around 7,000 years ago.**

The coming of the Bronze Age brought new tools that made farming far more productive but also gave people the ease to kill others. Struggles for land and food spilled into violence and necessitated the building of defensive crannogs (dwellings built out on lochs with access through one retractable wooden walkway) and more extensive hill forts. Added to the immigration from the Continent came a new wave of arrivals from the south—the Celtic Britons. As competition between the warring tribes escalated, and new threats developed from the sea, a string of brochs (hollow fortified stone towers), where richer families could hunker down and withstand a siege, mushroomed along the coast. The best preserved of these are Dun Carloway on the Isle of Lewis and the remarkable Mousa Broch on the eponymous island in the Shetland Islands, which is part of a network of more than 500 brochs that once stood guard around Scotland's coastline.

■ **Next page: Skara Brae on Mainland, the largest of the Orkney Islands**

Romans & Picts

It was the Romans who first coined the term *Picts* (from the Latin *pictus,* which means "painted") to describe the tribes of face-painted warriors that they encountered on their forays into the northern reaches of the British landmass—a region that the Romans named Caledonia. The Romans had dabbled with incursions into southern Britain before, and their fully fledged occupation kicked off in A.D. 43 under the leadership of Emperor Claudius. They soon pacified what is now England and Wales and began their efforts to homogenize the local culture and transform the territory by building infrastructure and their own cities. They did not have such an easy time with the northern tribes in what is now Scotland.

The Romans made repeated attempts to quell and then subjugate the Picts but lost legions of men and valuable resources as they were beaten back by both stiff resistance and the wild Highland weather and landscape. So troublesome did the mighty Romans find the battling northern tribes that they built not one but two defensive walls to keep them at bay. They started building the stone Hadrian's Wall in northern England in A.D. 122 and then the turf Antonine Wall in A.D. 142 farther to the north across Scotland's central belt, from the large fort at Cramond on the outskirts of Edinburgh in the east across to Old Kilpatrick in the west. The Romans eventually left Britain around A.D. 500 after half a millennium of occupation. They left without having pacified Scotland, a rare blot on an otherwise unblemished record of military victories across Europe in those centuries. The resistance is something that many Scots are still proud of today.

The Coming of Christianity

The geographical area of Scotland that the Romans left was made up of three main tribes. The Celtic Britons held what is now southern Scotland, while the Picts held vast swaths of the north and east. Added to the mix were the Scotti (Celts from Ireland), who began to arrive on the isles and Scotland's western coast in the latter stages of the Roman occupation and were unwittingly to give the country their name. They spoke Q-Celtic, similar to Gaelic and Irish, while the Celtic Britons and (less conclusively) the Picts are thought to have spoken varying versions of P-Celtic (akin to Welsh and Cornish). Some historians think the Scotti may have been given their name by the Romans.

While the Scotti and the Celts followed the Christian faith, the Picts were a pagan people. As a result, missionary work began to convert the Picts to Christianity. The most famous of these missionaries were St. Ninian in the fourth century and then the Irish Abbot Columba, who was more successful in his quest. Columba fled

■ **Statue of Robert the Bruce at Stirling Castle**

Ireland in the sixth century and set up a monastery on Iona—a rebuilt version of the same monastery still stands today. Canonized as Saint Columba, he dedicated his life to converting the northern Picts of Caledonia. According to legend, he is also credited with getting rid of the original "Loch Ness Monster.

Forming a Scottish Nation

In a land riddled with rival tribes, the formation of a nation was never going to be an easy task, although by sharing a common enemy of the Romans and facing the emerging threat from the Norse Vikings helped to bring all the groups together. Thanks to the efforts of the missionaries, the tribes also increasingly shared a religion. Until recently, the accepted historical wisdom was that the first Scottish king was the Scotti Kenneth MacAlpine (800–858), leader of the Scotti kingdom of Dalriada, who moved to unite his lands with the Picts in 843 to create the nation of Alba, latterly Scotland.

Alba did not include Strathclyde, the Lothians, and southern Scotland, and some historians argue that you cannot even speak of a "Scotland" until as late as 1468, when Shetland and Orkney came under control. Yet MacAlpine did form a nation that encompassed much of what Scotland is today, paving the way for further consolidation by setting his capital at Scone, as well as giving Scotland what is still its most sacred artifact—the Stone of Destiny—where the fledgling nation's kings were to be crowned.

MacAlpine and the line of succession

Scottish Time Line

5000 B.C. Neolithic man builds structures on the Orkney Islands.

A.D. 43–500 Romans fail to conquer Caledonia.

843 Kenneth MacAlpine, first king of Alba, unifies the Picts and the Scotti.

1314 Robert the Bruce defeats the English at Bannockburn.

1371–1714 Stuart monarchy.

1707 Act of Union passes with England.

1715–1745 Jacobite rebellions attempt to restore the Stuarts and independence.

1746 Battle of Culloden ends traditional clan system.

1746–1886 Highland Clearances.

1887–1945 Scotland's cities prosper as part of the British Empire.

1945–1970s Heavy industries decline; postwar economic strife.

1970s Oil and gas boom in the North Sea rekindles calls for independence.

1999 First Scottish Parliament in three centuries.

2014 Scotland holds Independence Referendum; 55 percent of electorate votes to remain in the U.K.

2016 With "Brexit," the U.K. electorate votes to leave the EU. The Scots overwhelmingly vote to remain.

he established brought some stability to Scotland. One of his family's royal line, Malcolm II (954–1034), went on to defeat the Northumberland Angles at the Battle of Carham in 1018, which secured the land south of the Firth of Forth, including Edinburgh. As the kingdom expanded, so the country became more sophisticated. David I (1083–1153) oversaw the establishment of royal burghs and the foundation of the Borders abbeys, and the cultural and religious dimensions that came with them. Feudalism, at least in the southern and central regions, started to replace the traditional clan system, although the Highlands remained as wild as ever. To the north and northwest, the Norse kings held sway over Shetland and Orkney and also harried many other isles, as well as coastal areas.

The Wars of Independence

The Battle of Largs in 1263 saw a scrambled victory over the Vikings, and the Norse invaders never posed the same threat again. Instead, an even more ruthless threat was brewing south of the border. England watched her neighbor with envious eyes. Skirmishes in the Borders badlands were common, but these broke out into outright invasion in 1296 when King Edward I (1239–1307), the "hammer of the Scots," butchered his way north with a 30,000-strong professional army.

The Scots were never keen on being subsumed into England, and unrest simmered throughout the land. This unrest bubbled to the surface in the unlikely form of man-of-the-people William Wallace (1272–1305), a character portrayed famously by Mel Gibson in the film *Braveheart* (1995). Wallace was not a royal, or even of noble blood, but he showed what could be done by a determined "inferior" force using his knowledge of the landscape to the full with a stunning victory over the English at the Battle of Stirling Bridge in 1297. The feudal nobles, more keen to make deals and garner additional land, were never truly behind Wallace, and he was infamously betrayed after the Scots' defeat at the Battle of Falkirk the following year. Wallace met a horrific death—"hung, drawn, and quartered" by the English in 1305. Another man, who was both popular with the people and more palatable to the nobles, had learned the lessons of

Two Flags

Scotland has two flags—the Saltire (or St. Andrews Cross) and the Royal Standard (or Lion Rampant). The St. Andrews Cross flag, with its distinctive white diagonal cross on a blue background, is the one you will see most often. The "Saltire" is actually only the white cross associated with St. Andrew that apparently once appeared in the sky before a Scottish victory on the battlefield. Today, the name is given to the whole flag. Meanwhile, the Lion Rampant, a fiery red lion on a bright yellow background bordered by lilies, was originally used by the Scottish monarchs. These days it is only flown by representatives of the monarchy, and at royal residences when the king is not in residence.

■ **Mary Queen of Scots, painted by Sir James I around 1580**

Wallace's victories. Initially, Robert the Bruce (1274–1329) suffered many defeats, but he persevered in his quest to protect the country and won the Scots their most famous triumph over the English in 1314. On the field of Bannockburn, in the shadow of Stirling Castle, Robert the Bruce led the massively outnumbered Scots to an incredible victory. This not only secured his crown but brought Scotland another four centuries of liberty, and the English were "sent hame tae think again," as the words of the unofficial national anthem, *Flower of Scotland*, famously proclaim. The acceptance of the Declaration of Arbroath by the pope in 1320 put the seal on the independent Scottish nation with a defiant and rousing certainty that many Scots still proudly feel today: "For as long as but a hundred of us remain alive, never will we on any conditions be brought under English rule. It is in truth not for glory, nor riches, nor honors that we are fighting, but for freedom—for that alone, which no honest man gives up but with life itself."

Scotland's independence was officially recognized by the English king Edward III (1312–1377) in 1328, ending the 30-year War of Independence. Robert the Bruce and then his son, David II (1324–1371), ruled Scotland until 1371, when the House of Stuart came to power with Robert II (1316–1390), David II's nephew on his mother's side. But the fight for freedom was by no means over—the next 200 years were smattered with bloody skirmishes between the two countries.

Religious Strife & Mary Queen of Scots

More storm clouds emerged in the 1500s with the immense passions, intrigue, and upheaval generated by the Protestant Reformation. The effects of the Reformation, a backlash against what was seen as the extravagance of the Catholic Church (deemed to have lost its way in its worship and its relationship to God), were felt throughout Europe, but they lashed into Scotland like a tornado.

At the helm of the Scottish Reformation was the firebrand cleric John Knox (1514–1572). In 1561, Knox was granted an audience with the Stuart monarch Mary Queen of Scots (1542–1587). She could not have mistaken the passion for

The Scots' devastating defeat at the Battle of Culloden marked the end of the Jacobite rebellions.

Protestant reform that spat from this impassioned soul. Mary, perhaps the most fondly remembered and romanticized of all the Scottish monarchs, had to play a delicate and increasingly desperate game of cat and mouse to placate her Catholic supporters, the reformers, and the fledgling Protestant Church.

Mary was a monarch draped in controversy. Born at Linlithgow Palace in 1542, she was proclaimed Queen of Scotland when her father James V died less than a week earlier. Her colorful childhood saw her spirited off to France and at one point she was crowned Queen of France, with aspirations for the English and Spanish thrones, too. Perennially embroiled in scandal, her first husband, Lord Darnley, had her supposed lover David Rizzio murdered in front of a pregnant Mary. Many historians attribute Darnley's subsequent murder to Mary herself. Mary eventually fled Scotland in 1567, seeking refuge with her cousin Elizabeth I in England, who was so distrustful of her scheming relative that she had her imprisoned. After being accused of numerous plots, and never tasting freedom again, Mary was executed on Elizabeth's orders in 1587.

As Scotland lurched between a Catholic monarchy and—thanks to John Knox's tireless work—demands for Protestantism, the nation was in turmoil. In 1610, Protestant James VI (1566–1625), also by now James I of England and Wales, restored the bishops, which added fuel to the fire. His son, Charles I (1600–1649), tipped the situation over the edge in 1637, imposing a new prayer book on the Scottish Church. In response, Presbyterian reformers organized a National Covenant to outline their opposition to Charles' reforms. Charles I could not stop the movement exploding across the country, with Covenanters raising an army and taking control of the country. Their stint lasted until 1650, when Charles II (1630–1685) was persuaded to sign the Covenant. His rule was a short one. Oliver Cromwell's parliamentarian army pushed north and took Scotland, ruling until the 1660 Restoration under Charles II.

EXPERIENCE: Visit Scotland's Battlefields

Bannockburn

Bannockburn (see p. 146) is the most celebrated of Scotland's victories over England. Mention this victory to any red-blooded Scot and expect his or her patriotic fires to instantly burn. It can be hard to get as passionate about it as a visitor, but a trip to the excellent visitor center will help you understand the history.

Once you have the background, head for the enormous statue of Robert the Bruce and imagine him standing in 1314, wondering just how his heavily outnumbered and previously defeated forces were going to beat King Edward II's well-drilled army.

But win they did. Robert the Bruce's skillful tactics, and innovative use of the local terrain, turned the unwieldy English army's strengths into weaknesses in what became a bloodbath that famously turned the Bannock Burn red. The English fled in chaos, with only one sizable force making it back across the border. Edward scrambled to escape by sea from Dunbar.

You can visit Bannockburn most weekends in the summer, when actors play some of the roles of the warriors, further enhancing the experience and giving you a clearer insight into the famous victory that paved the way for the next 400 years of independence.

Culloden

While the visitor center gives real insight into events leading up to the battle, you need to stand on the bleak moor itself to really appreciate the horror of the battle (see pp. 208–209). Look for the fluttering red flags that line up near the parking lot and mark government lines. Cast your eyes west to the blue flags, which note where the Jacobites massed in 1746 and took shattering rounds of cannon fire while their leader, Bonnie Prince Charlie, dithered. Try hauling yourself across this unforgiving ground, and you will see how difficult it must have been for the men who were weighed down with weapons and being blasted with grapeshot as they struggled on. Those who did make it to the government lines were quickly dispatched, as "Butcher" Cumberland had drilled his men in new techniques for fighting at close quarters with the Highlanders. After your trip to the battlefield, enjoy a well-earned pit stop in the visitor center café.

In 1689, James VII of Scotland (1633–1701, also James II of England), was forced into exile, partly as his Catholic views clashed with the English Church. His Protestant daughter, Mary II, took up the reins with her Dutch husband (and cousin), William of Orange. The couple failed to produce an heir, however, as did her sister Queen Anne, so as agreed in the 1701 Act of Settlement, the throne passed to George I (James I's grandson), prince-elector of Hanover, in 1714, and a new dynasty—the Hanoverians—started a lineage that stretches all the way to the modern British royal family.

The Clan System

Under the clan system that existed up until the Highland Clearances, the local men pledged to take up arms for their chief in return for land and their place in society. Under the new feudal system, the British government banned many traditional Scottish activities, including wearing tartan and playing bagpipes, and it prohibited the clan chiefs from having their own armies. The clan chiefs who supported the Jacobite uprising lost their lands.

Union With England

Controversy still surrounds Scotland's union with England. The Act of Union was passed by Scotland's parliament in 1707, uniting the countries as Great Britain. It remains a dark day for many Scots—the day that independence was officially surrendered. The signatories insisted that the decision was good for the economy, because it would open up new trade routes for Scotland through England and make the country's future safer and more secure. Others felt that England's economic bullying should not be rewarded with Scotland being subjugated into an unequal union with England. National bard Robert Burns later proclaimed, "We're bought and sold for English gold, Such a parcel of rogues in a nation!" He was referring to the nobles and schemers who had accepted bribes to smooth the passage of the Act of Union—an act that was greeted with rioting and unrest in many parts of Scotland when it was made public.

Jacobite Rebellions

The supposed economic benefits that were promised when the Act of Union was signed did not materialize quickly, which fueled popular unrest and the desire for independence. Bound up within these calls were demands to bring back the pre-1714 Stuart monarchy. In particular, the Highlands were struggling economically, and there was a real sense that bringing back the Old Pretender, James VII, was the way forward—an act, it was felt, that would give Scotland her independence back. The Jacobites (named after the Latin for *James*) kicked off their first major rebellion at Braemar Castle on September 1, 1715, and were soon on their way. The British government was surprised by the speed of the uprising. Initially, the Jacobites made some progress, and James himself returned triumphant, with hopes high in many Jacobite hearts both in Scotland and England. However, the pivotal Battle of Sheriffmuir in November of the same year had no clear victor and left the Jacobites weakened and unfocused, with the rebellion petering out as quickly as it had begun. James was soon on his way back across the North Sea to remain the "king over the water," a moniker that survives today in romantic Jacobite songs and dreams.

Desires for independence and for a Stuart monarch to be put back on the throne did not dissipate, however, and the cause was taken up by James VII's son, Charles Edward Stuart (1720–1788), who became popularly known as the Young Pretender, or Bonnie Prince Charlie. The latter moniker hints at his good looks and the manners he had learned in his upbringing in French royal circles. He was an unlikely leader for the 10,000 or so rugged clansmen who joined the "45," as the rebellion of 1745 became known.

This time the success of the Jacobites was quick and impressive. After taking Edinburgh and defeating the British Army at Prestonpans, the Jacobite army battled confidently south, with Bonnie Prince Charlie's claims that the English Jacobites were waiting to rise up in support and that the French military invasion was imminent, echoing in their ears. After crossing the border the army reached Derby, and even London was panicked as its population feared an impending and decisive attack. However, the English Jacobites did not rise in significant numbers, nor did the promised French attack materialize, leaving the Jacobites divided over what to do next. Reluctantly, Bonnie Prince Charlie led his troops on a thoroughly morale-sapping retreat north, with the eager Duke of Cumberland, son of the Hanoverian George II, and his professional army (now free from battling the French on the Continent) in hot pursuit.

In 1746, after a draining winter, the undefeated Bonnie Prince Charlie resolved to take on Cumberland and his British Hanoverian army. An ambitious attempt to surprise the British government forces by marching overnight to catch the duke on his birthday failed. Instead, the shattered Jacobites were dragged into battle the next morning, immediately after their exhausting night march. To date their infamous "Highland Charge" had seen them outmaneuver the organized British army, but this time the prince chose his battlefield poorly—the boggy moor at Culloden—which made their bloodcurdling charge almost impossible. Badly led and demoralized, the Jacobite army was decimated in a horrendous carnage that saw more than 1,500 men slain for the loss of a couple hundred British troops.

The Highland Clearances

The defeat at Culloden was cataclysmic for the Highland way of life. The Highlands were hammered by "Butcher" Cumberland and his men. Months of systematic murders, beatings, and rapes ensued as Cumberland's army sought revenge.

The new regime that took over the Highlands following the defeat at Culloden destroyed the clan system forever. The clans' medieval *runrig* system was based on communal farming and grazing rights, but with the industrial revolution land began to be seen as a source of profit. Even before the Jacobite rebellion the feudal clan system of joint-tenancy was being replaced by large-scale pastoral farms stocked with sheep—the same social model that already operated in the Scottish Lowlands to some extent. After Culloden, the new breed of landowner, or laird, backed by the British government, set about pacifying the Highlands and making the land more economically viable. Highlanders were forced from their homes to make way for sheep, in a human tragedy that has become known as the Highland Clearances (the Duke of Sutherland brutally evicted 15,000 crofters from his estates, 1811–1820). Displaced tenants were moved to coastal "crofting" communities where they were expected to be employed in small-scale industry such as fishing; others were forced on to infertile plots over which they had no security of tenure, resulting in overcrowding and famine. Soon, thousands of Scots were leaving the Highlands on "assisted passages" for new lives in far-flung corners of the world. The Clearances continued until the Crofters' Holdings Act of 1886, which finally granted security of tenure as well as other essential guarantees and reforms.

Industrial Revolution & Scotland in the Empire

The Act of Union had been slow to boost the Scottish economy. But the start of the industrial revolution and Scotland's role both in it and in the establishment of the British Empire soon brought the nation and its people the possibility of fame and fortune. As a western port crucially offering easier access to the Americas, Glasgow was the spearhead of this surge in trade.

With rich natural resources, particularly coal and iron, Scotland was well placed to grow during the industrial revolution. The River Clyde soon became the birthplace of many of the world's ships. This economic transformation brought with it social change, too, as the country's population increasingly flocked to the central belt, and particularly Glasgow, looking for work. The Scots were in a unique position, being both keen colonists in the British Empire and a colonized nation within the United Kingdom, but the bureaucrats in London still called the shots.

Scotland in the 20th & 21st Centuries

World War I (1914–1918) brought massive suffering to Scotland. It is estimated that 20 percent of British deaths during the Great War were Scots soldiers, despite Scots making up only 10 percent of the British population. Scotland had still not fully recovered when the economic depressions of the 1930s hit. Systemic problems in Scotland's heavy industries and cheaper competitors started to bite—a trend that World War II (1939–1945) merely delayed. The war helped prop up Scotland's failing heavy industries, such as shipbuilding, and other factories were turned to munitions supply, keeping workers not off to the battlefields employed. But in the postwar years, a slump hit as domestic demand died away and foreign markets offered cheaper alternatives.

The discovery of North Sea Oil in the 1970s proved a huge boon for the Scottish economy, as Scotland received a proportional percent of oil tax revenues. Aberdeen evolved as a major industrial center and "capital" of the oil industry. The period also saw tensions with the government of the "Iron Lady," Margaret Thatcher, who was seen as dismissing the Scots and any desire they had for devolution or independence.

In 1997 a resounding 75 percent of Scots voted for devolution, and in 1999 the first Scottish Parliament in three centuries sat in Edinburgh. The Scottish National Party has gone on to win control of the Scottish Parliament and also the lion's share of the Scottish seats at Westminster in London. This support did not translate into a vote for independence in 2014, when 55 percent of Scots voted to remain in the U.K. in the Independence Referendum. More than 16,000 Scots died in the COVID-19 pandemic, which briefly devastated the tourism industry, which had rebounded by 2023. ∎

> **In 1997 a resounding 75 percent of Scots voted for devolution, and in 1999 the first Scottish Parliament in three centuries sat in Edinburgh.**

Oil rigs in the North Sea off the coast of Scotland

THE ARTS

Scotland's rich cultural heritage harks back to the days of oral clan culture, when the storytelling ballad was key. Over the centuries, this gift has evolved, leading Scots to create some world-famous works in the fields of art, architecture, literature, film, music, and the performing arts. A vibrant arts scene is integral to the psyche of the modern nation.

Painting & Sculpture

Scotland's earliest art was created by its prehistoric people, but little remains. The same can be said of the art of its clans, who for centuries relied on oral storytelling more than fixed art mediums. In the 18th century, however, some famous Scottish painters emerged, including Sir Henry Raeburn (1756–1823) and Allan Ramsay (1713–1840), the latter most famous for his portraits. In the 1870s, the Glasgow Boys emerged with a Scottish take on impressionism, using its styles to reinvent the city and the surrounding countryside. Chief among them were Joseph Crawhall (1861–1913), Sir James Guthrie (1859–1930), and George Henry (1858–1943). From here, the artistic movement of the Scottish Colourists emerged in the early 20th century, as exemplified by John Duncan Fergusson (1874–1961), who spent time with Picasso and became influenced by the Fauvists. On the east coast, the Edinburgh School emerged in the 1930s. William Gillies (1898–1973) and Anne Redpath (1895–1965) stand out, as does Sir Eduardo Paolozzi (1924–2005), whose sculptures may be seen at the Scottish Gallery of Modern Art in Edinburgh, along with a re-creation of his former studio at Modern Two.

Scotland's most famous living painter of the 21st century is undoubtedly the controversial Jack Vettriano (1951–). This self-taught artist has been embroiled in accusations of being too commercial, but his fetishistic paintings are as appealing in art galleries as they are on the walls of homes around the country. In May 2015 another famous Scottish artist, Edinburgh-born Peter Doig (1959–), set a new record when "Swamped" became the most expensive painting ever sold by a living European artist (it sold for US$26 million). Until recent decades, women artists struggled to gain recognition. Multimedia artist Alberta Whittle (1980–) addresses such current themes as racism and the climate crisis to evoke empathy and collective care.

Literature

Scotland's rich canon of work came to global attention in the age of Romantic literature. The most famous Romantic Scottish writer was Sir Walter Scott (1771–1832), who penned perhaps the first ever historical novel with

Waverley (1814) and went on to weave a succession of romanticized historical novels, eulogizing folk heroes such as Scotland's own Robin Hood, in *Rob Roy* (1817). Scott also collated some of the traditional Borders ballads, as did Scotland's national bard, Robert Burns (1759–1796), who is most renowned for his colorful poems in the Scots language and, of course, for writing "Auld Lang Syne." Every bit the tragic romantic poet, his all too short life was peppered with love affairs, illegitimate children, and all sorts of scandal. The 19th century brought the great Robert Louis Stevenson (1850–1894), a novelist whose renowned *Strange Case of Dr. Jekyll and Mr. Hyde* (1886), while set in London, satirizes the duality of Edinburgh and the Scottish psyche. His works *Kidnapped* (1886) and *Treasure Island* (1883) perfectly bridge the divide between thriller and children's literature. Stevenson's contemporary, Arthur Conan Doyle (1859–1930), studied medicine at the University of Edinburgh before going on to create the famous detective Sherlock Holmes—a character based on the Edinburgh physician and forensic scientist Joseph Bell.

> 66 **Scotland's rich canon of work came to global attention in the age of Romantic literature.** 99

The *Scots Quair* trilogy by Lewis Grassic Gibbon (1901–1935) is a lucid insight into life in Aberdeenshire in the years swirling around World War I; *The Silver Darlings* by Neil M. Gunn (1891–1973) does the same with the aftermath of the Highland Clearances. Then there is Muriel Spark (1918–2006), whose seminal *Prime of Miss Jean Brodie* perfectly captures 1930s Edinburgh; she wrote 20 other novels as well. In the

Scotland's Book Capital

Wigtown *(wigtown-booktown .co.uk)* **has held the title of Scotland's designated National Book Town since 1998. This southern charmer is a real haven not only for writers, but also for visual and performance artists. They say you can browse more than a quarter of a million books around town, with numerous opportunities to buy and sell them. There are a flurry of events and festivals throughout the year, with the highlight being the Wigtown Book Festival** *(wigtownbookfestival .com).* **Its 10-day run each autumn caters to all ages, not only through literature, but also through the mediums of music, film, theater, and arts and crafts. One of the most appealing things about the town is that most of the little bookshops and galleries are owner run. Their real passion shines through.**

▪ **A piano designed by Charles Rennie Mackintosh at House for an Art Lover, Glasgow**

■ **Choose a second life! Jonny Lee Miller and Ewan McGregor in *T2 Trainspotting*.**

field of poetry, Hugh MacDiarmid (1892–1978) emerged as a true giant of language and thought, celebrating the use of Scots and vehemently defending its increasing usage and written form. By contrast, Edwin Muir (1887–1959) showed what could still be done writing about Scottish themes in English, while Sorley MacLean (1911–1996) did the same for the threatened Gaelic language. Other Scottish writers of note include Alasdair Gray (1934–2019), whose groundbreaking novel, *Lanark* (1981), has been dubbed "Scotland's *Ulysses*." Irvine Welsh (1958–) violently committed Scots, and even more extreme dialects, to the novel format with a series of shocking novels, including *Trainspotting* (1993). Ian Rankin (1960–) is known for his gritty Rebus detective novels, painting a vivid Edinburgh, while Iain Banks (1954–2013) penned beautifully perceptive novels such as the disturbing and powerful *The Wasp Factory* (1984) and the unorthodox Scottish family saga *The Crow Road* (1992). The most famous living Scottish-based author is, of course, J. K. Rowling (1965–), whose seven Harry Potter books, and subsequent adult novels, have achieved global fame.

Film

Hollywood has always had a love affair with Scotland, with blockbusters such as *Local Hero* (1983), starring Peter Riegert as a cynical oilman being won over by the local community; *Rob Roy* (1995), a depiction of one of Scotland's most romanticized outlaws; *Braveheart* (1995), telling the story of William Wallace (with a few historical shortcuts on the way), and *Outlaw King* (2018) that of Robert the Bruce. The Disney–Pixar animated epic *Brave* (2012) was

(continued on p. 58)

THE *OUTLANDER* EFFECT

Not since the seismic success of the Hollywood blockbuster *Braveheart* has a television show or movie had such a dramatic effect on Scottish tourism. *Outlander,* a remarkably successful TV series particularly in North America, has not only boosted Scotland's global image, but it has also ramped up the popularity and appeal of a flurry of Scotland's historic attractions, which viewers can now visit for themselves.

■ **The picturesque town of Falkland substitutes for long-ago Inverness in** *Outlander.*

For the uninitiated, *Outlander* is based on a series of romantic historical novels written by American author Diana Gabaldon. The story of the first seven seasons (2014–2023) revolves around the two protagonists, English nurse Clare Beauchamp Randall and kilted Highlander Jamie Fraser. Clare is catapulted away from 1943 through a mysterious set of standing stones and finds herself amidst the tumultuous 1740s, when Bonnie Prince Charlie's Jacobite rebellion is brewing across Scotland.

While it is the romance of indomitable Clare and dashing Jamie that is the key character focus, the real star of the show, of course, is Scotland, with its sturdy fortresses, ancient standing stones, and spectacular Highland scenery. Whatever you think of the far-fetched story line or the flowery prose, Gabaldon's love for Scotland is passionately translated onto the television screen. Viewers savor lingering shots of rugged mountains, silvery lochs, and plunging glens. The Highlands are the main attraction here, though the action sweeps all around the country. Season two even sees Scotland stand in for France, while by season three, much of the action moves to America in the build up to the Revolutionary War.

Numerous sights star in *Outlander* (see *visitscotland.com,* type "Outlander" in the search field). The list below focuses on those that have seen the biggest upsurge in visitors.

Blackness Castle

This sturdy ship-like bulwark is spectacularly located on the banks of the Firth of Forth, just 17 miles (27 km) west of Edinburgh. In *Outlander* it stands in for Black Jack Randall's headquarters and a fort that no longer exists in the town of Fort William. Fittingly its role in the series echoes its former use as a prison (see p. 95; *Blackness, West Lothian, tel 01506/834 807, historicenviron ment.scot, £*).

Bo'ness and Kinneil Railway

This charming volunteer-run railway stands in for Milford Station in London, where Clare says an emotional goodbye to her husband during World War II. Today you can enjoy a wee trip along the line and even travel on a steam train—although these trips are less regular—to really evoke the action in *Outlander* (see p. 95; *Union Street, Bo'ness, West Lothian, tel 01506/825 855, bkrailway.co.uk, ££*).

Doune Castle

A number of castles feature in *Outlander,* but the pivotal one is Castle Leoch, or rather Doune Castle in Stirlingshire. You might also recognize it as a Monty Python location.

In the show it is the home of clan chief Colum MacKenzie, and its grand 100-foot-tall (30 m) gatehouse is suitable for his status (see p. 145; *Castle Hill, Doune, Perthshire, tel 01786/841 742, historicenviron ment.scot, ££*).

The Rebellion's Long Reach

There have been rumors that the British government tried to ensure *Outlander* did not hit U.K. screens before Scotland's Independence referendum in 2014.

Whether these rumors have any truth or not, the show certainly paints the English redcoats as vicious, callous baddies, most of all "Black Jack" Randall, who is superbly played by actor Tobias Menzies.

The *Outlander* story hurtles through clan rivalries and skirmishes between the British troops and the Highland clansmen, taking in the mounting historical backdrop of the Jacobite rebellions as it goes. Events build toward the inevitability of the Battle of Culloden and the tragic aftermath that saw the traditional Highland clan way of life torn apart forever. By season four the setting had shifted to the American colonies, with its slavery, tensions with Cherokees and Mohawks, and surging swell for American independence.

Highland Folk Museum

The romance of a traditional Highland village oozes from *Outlander,* with its thatched traditional houses and smoking peat fires. Many viewers imagine these are a set built just for the series, but you can walk among them at the Highland Folk Museum in Newtonmore (see p. 216; *Newtonmore, Inverness-shire, tel 01349/781 650, highlifehighland. com/highlandfolkmuseum/, £*).

Hopetoun House

This grand country house 13 miles (20 km) west of Edinburgh commands dramatic views of the Firth of Forth. Fittingly it is the palatial setting for the Duke of Sandringham's home in *Outlander.* Avid watchers will recognize the lavish Red Drawing Room and the West Lawn at the rear, the location of the dual between Sandringham and the head of the MacDonald clan. Eagle-eyed fans will also notice that the area around the current Stables Tearoom doubled as France in season two. (see p. 84; *South Queensferry,* *Edinburgh, tel 0131/331 2451, hopetoun .co.uk, ££*).

Linlithgow Palace

The birthplace of Mary Queen of Scots also has a key role in *Outlander,* where it stars as Wentworth Prison. It is in the dungeons here that some of the most harrowing scenes of the whole show are set during Black Jack Randall's excruciating degradation of Jamie Fraser (see pp. 93–94; *Kirkgate, Linlithgow, West Lothian, tel 01506/842 896, historicenvironment .scot, ££*).

Royal Burgh of Culross

This stunning heritage village situated in Fife on the banks of the Firth of Forth is the ideal setting for the fictional village of Cranesmuir, thanks to its rich treasure trove of 16th- and 17th-century buildings. Walk around this immaculately preserved hamlet and you are literally on the *Outlander* set. At Culross Palace (see p. 171; *tel 01383/880 359, nts.org .uk, ££*), look out for the herb garden where Clare works.

Linlithgow Palace and loch

clearly inspired by the brooding Highland landscapes and brought in a wave of family film tourists, while Hollywood's most recent Shakespeare adaptation, *Macbeth* (2015), brilliantly brought Skye to the big screen. At the other end of the spectrum, director Danny Boyle (1956–) did not so much burst onto the world's cinema screens as explode in a pile of gritty realism that shocked global cinema audiences with *Trainspotting* (1996). Boyle's other global successes include *Slumdog Millionaire* (2008) and *T2 Trainspotting* (2017). Also of note is director Kevin Macdonald (1967–), whose *Last King of Scotland* (2006), about the notorious Idi Amin, was a global hit. Scotland's most famous actress was Deborah Kerr (1921–2007), star of *From Here to Eternity* (1953) and *The King & I* (1956). The most famous actor was undoubtedly Sean Connery (1930–2020). In recent years, a new generation of male leads has emerged with Ewan McGregor (1971–) and Robert Carlyle (1961–), who used *Trainspotting* to launch their careers.

Architecture

Scotland's treasure trove of prehistoric architecture stands among the finest in Europe—particularly the well-preserved sights at Skara Brae and the Knap of Howar in the Orkney Islands. The Romans also left their mark with a higher density of marching camps than anywhere else in Europe, with most places yet to be excavated. Sturdier remnants are the rugged stone brochs built around the coastline to fend off seaborne intruders, especially from the north.

For buildings created in the days of a united nation, David I goes down in architectural history for commissioning the remarkable Borders abbeys, whose romantic ruins are graced with a variety of styles. Following the 1707 Act of Union and the increasing concentration of Scottish society into her cities came the refined era of Georgian architecture. This period saw Edinburgh's graceful New Town emerge in a sophisticated revolt against the medieval Old Town. Seminal Scottish architects at this time included William Henry Playfair (1790–1857), William Adam (1689–1748), and his son Robert Adam (1728–1792). Neoclassical styles ruled the day and were adopted in Glasgow as well as in grand country houses found in far-flung corners. As part of the British Empire, Scotland's cities prospered during the reign of Queen Victoria (r. 1837–1901), an affluence expressed in graceful stone town houses. Sir Walter Scott created one of the country's most impressive Victorian temples, with his Abbotsford retreat.

Charles Rennie Mackintosh (1868–1928) brought a unique brand of art nouveau to his seminal Glasgow School of Art and a whole host of other remarkable buildings that feature his characteristic use of geometric shapes and decorative roses. Probably Scotland's most dramatic—and certainly the most contentious—building of the 21st century has been the new Scottish Parliament building in Edinburgh, which again weaves in old and new styles and very much reflects the zeitgeist of modern Scottish architecture. The distinctive jagged roof of the Riverside Museum in Glasgow also demonstrates Scotland's continuing willingness to erect bold modern architecture, a tradition continued by Dundee's new V&A Museum of Design.

Music

Music was integral to life under the old clan system. Mournful ballads drifted through the glens centuries ago as an oral culture that both celebrated and recorded the history of the day. This tradition has carried on into modern times, with much Scottish music atmospherically harking back to the themes of lost kinship and struggles for independence. The key proponents of traditional folk music once included the Battlefield Band, the Corries, and Alba. But Scotland's music, like the country around it, has constantly evolved. Exciting talents on the current folk music scene include Meursault, RM Hubbert, and King Creosote.

The bagpipe, the accordion, and the fiddle are key instruments in Scottish folk music, but the more recent addition of the acoustic guitar, and then the more powerful electric guitar, opened doors for global rock success stories such as Big Country (with guitars sounding like bagpipes) and Simple Minds. Singer Annie

■ **Students rehearse at the Royal Scottish Academy of Music and Drama.**

Lennox, who grew up in Aberdeenshire, continues to record, as does superstar Rod Stewart, born to an English mother and Scottish father. Increasingly, Scottish music in the 21st century is entwining traditional forms into modern media. Kilsyth's dark alternative rockers the Twilight Sad and Selkirk's mournful but jaunty alternative posters Frightened Rabbit have both incorporated enigmatic storytelling in their work with dramatic results. In recent years, well-known acts on the pop front have included KT Tunstall, Glasvegas, and Calvin Harris. These Scottish pop acts are not afraid to use their own accents, which isn't the issue it once was and is a sign of a nation brimming with musical confidence. In Scotland, dancing along to a powerful alternative rock band is as much part of the musical landscape as taking in an informal folk session in a traditional pub.

Other Performing Arts

The performing arts are crucial to Scottish culture, with the huge Edinburgh International Festival in August (*eif.co.uk*; see p. 74) now the world's biggest arts extravaganza. This is a sure sign of how Scotland views the performing arts. Indeed, there are five national performing arts bodies. On the classical music front, the Royal Scottish National Orchestra (*19 Killermont St., Glasgow, tel 0141/226 3868, rsno.org.uk*), formed way back in 1891, is one of Europe's leading symphony orchestras. The highly regarded Scottish Chamber Orchestra (*4 Royal Terrace, Edinburgh, tel 0131/557 6800, sco.org.uk*) performs in venues throughout the country. The largest performing arts organization in the country is Scottish Opera (see Travelwise p. 366), with a base at the Theatre Royal in Glasgow—the oldest theater in the country. Meanwhile, the Scottish Ballet (see Travelwise p. 364) continually tours from its dramatic new base at the Tramway, Glasgow. The mission of the National Theatre of Scotland (*125 Craighall Rd., Glasgow, tel 0141/221 0970, national theatrescotland.com*) is to take the arts to the people, which it does by performing around the country and nurturing budding local talent.

> **The performing arts are crucial to Scottish culture, with the huge Edinburgh International Festival in August now the world's biggest arts extravaganza.**

While these official organizations are the most renowned, they are backed by a plethora of groups, companies, and performers of all shapes and sizes. They appear at a multitude of venues—from world-class performance spaces in Scotland's cities to more modest village halls and schools. Take in any manner of performance and your visit will be the richer for it, and even better if you can make it to Edinburgh in August. ∎

Steeped in culture and history, a vibrant and cosmopolitan capital standing proudly on rocky crags overlooking the Lothians

EDINBURGH & THE LOTHIANS

EDINBURGH & THE LOTHIANS

Scotland's capital city does not so much wear its history on its sleeve as overflow with intoxicating tales of feuding upper classes, medieval villains, and royal and religious intrigue. This sense of history spills into the surrounding region of the Lothians, which offers premier golf courses, picturesque villages, and areas of stellar natural beauty.

Edinburgh has always been at the heart of Scotland's turbulent history—whether it was when the city's castle held out against Bonnie Prince Charlie during his ill-fated quest to reclaim the British throne or as the epicenter of the seminal Scottish Enlightenment.

Today's Edinburgh is a modern and vibrant city with a personality that stretches deep into the past, while continually looking to the future. Now full of boutique-style shopping and stylish

hotels, Edinburgh maintains its unique neighborhoods—each with its own character. Scotland's capital has a renewed identity, since 1999, as home to the country's parliament after a gap of 300 years.

Edinburgh has earned plaudits such as "the Athens of the North" with its combination of stunning natural setting and well-preserved classical architecture. More importantly, the city won recognition from UNESCO with both the medieval Old Town and Georgian

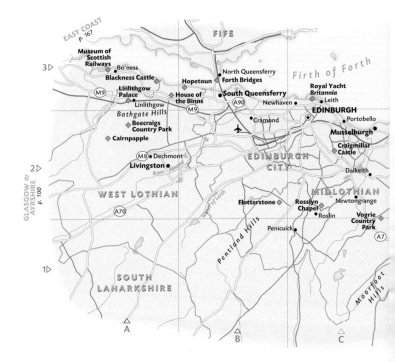

New Town as well as the Forth Bridge commended on the World Heritage List. And its grand location, graced with peaks of volcanic rock, rugged hills, and the mighty River Forth estuary has always given the city a certain air.

Further charms await outside the city center in the old port of Leith, now reinvented as a gastronomic hub, and the suburb of South Queensferry, home to three great bridges. With so much to offer, it is easy to see why Edinburgh is Scotland's most visited city.

The three regions surrounding Edinburgh—East Lothian, Midlothian, and West Lothian, collectively known as the Lothians—have their own treats to offer, from the resort towns and top golf courses of East Lothian, the rolling hills and historic churches of Midlothian, and the royal castles and palaces of West Lothian. ■

NOT TO BE MISSED:

Edinburgh Castle, dominating the Scottish capital 67–70

Exploring the sights along the Royal Mile, from castle to palace and everything in between 68–69

The National Museum of Scotland, a cultural mecca at the heart of historic Scotland 71–72

Hiking up Arthur's Seat, remnant of an extinct volcano 73

Strolling through the beautiful Royal Botanic Garden 80

South Queensferry's world-famous bridges, cozy restaurants, and grand country houses 83–86

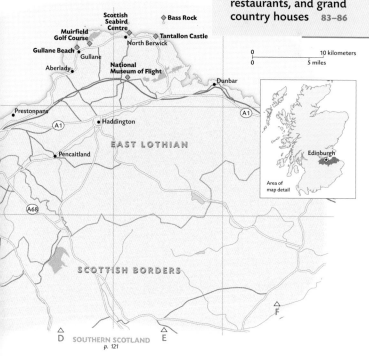

D SOUTHERN SCOTLAND
p. 121

EDINBURGH

With a stunning castle perched atop the remains of an extinct volcano and a distinctly medieval Old Town set against the well-heeled New Town to the north, which is itself more than 200 years old, Edinburgh does not just impress on first sight, but blows away your senses and steals your heart.

Edinburgh's History

The story starts at Castle Rock, the imposing volcanic plug that lies at the very heart of modern Edinburgh. The city's original Gaelic name, Dunedin, comes from "Eidyn's Fort," which is a name given by the Celtic tribes who once held sway in these wild lands. Historians think that Northumbrian invaders first anglicized the name to its current Edinburgh.

Further English incursions followed as various Scottish kings tried to establish their authority over what had become a deeply strategic fortress. A small settlement grew up around the ridge that climbed to the castle (today's Royal Mile), and by the 12th century Edinburgh had its own mint and was emerging as a serious national player. By the 14th century, Scottish king Robert the Bruce had bestowed a new charter on Edinburgh and brought the port of Leith within its bounds.

In 1707, Edinburgh's status as the capital of an independent nation was snatched away as the Act of Union joined Scotland and England. London would always be Britain's capital. Yet the loss of political power was mitigated by the advent of the British Empire. Ed-

inburgh benefited from the increased prosperity and emerged as a center for finance, invention, learning, and philosophy as luminaries such as David Hume and Adam Smith came to the fore.

Edinburgh Tram Network

Edinburgh's tram system (edinburghtrams.com) opened in 2014 after a controversial series of delays and cost hikes. The project took eight years to complete, and the price rose from £375 million (US$497 million) to a whopping £776 million (US$1 billion) for an 8.7-mile (14 km) line running from Edinburgh Airport to York Place in the city center. Today, the line extends to Leith and Newhaven. For visitors the most useful of the 23 stops are at the airport, Murrayfield rugby stadium, and those that run by the shops along Princes Street. While smooth and enjoyable, the journey in from the airport can take longer than the bus and is about a pound more expensive.

Edinburgh 62 C2, 65 **Visitor Information** 249 High St. (0131) 473 3820 **edinburgh.org**

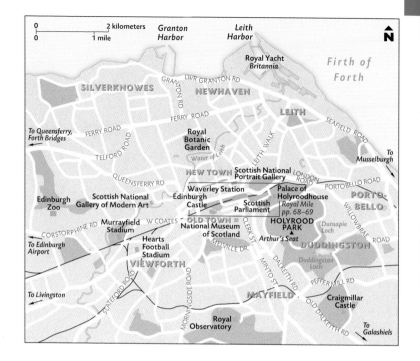

Granton Harbor
Leith Harbor
Royal Yacht Britannia
Firth of Forth
SILVERKNOWES
GRANTON RD
LWR GRANTON RD
NEWHAVEN
LEITH
FERRY ROAD
SEAFIELD ROAD
To Queensferry, Forth Bridges
FERRY ROAD
TELFORD ROAD
Royal Botanic Garden
Water of Leith
LEITH WALK
To Musselburgh
QUEENSFERRY RD
NEW TOWN
Scottish National Portrait Gallery
LONDON ROAD
PORTOBELLO ROAD
Waverley Station
Palace of Holyroodhouse
PORTO-BELLO
Edinburgh Zoo
Scottish National Gallery of Modern Art
Edinburgh Castle
Scottish Parliament
Royal Mile pp. 68–69
CORSTORPHINE RD
W COATES
OLD TOWN
National Museum of Scotland
CLERK ST
HOLYROOD PARK
Dunsapie Loch
WILLOWBRAE
ROAD
Murrayfield Stadium
Arthur's Seat
DUDDINGSTON
To Edinburgh Airport
Hearts Football Stadium
MELVILLE DR.
Duddingston Loch
VIEWFORTH
MINTO ST
DALKEITH RD
PEFFERMILL RD
To Livingston
STATEFORD ROAD
MORNINGSIDE ROAD
MAYFIELD
OLD DALKEITH RD
Craigmillar Castle
Royal Observatory
To Galashiels

INSIDER TIP:

Holyrood Park, just a few minutes' walk from town, presents a glimpse of the raw Scotland that forged the rhapsodic character of the great conservationist and Sierra Club founder John Muir.

—BOB SIPCHEN
National Geographic writer

As Edinburgh expanded, the new wealthy citizens turned their back on the medieval squalor of the Old Town, building a perfectly planned city to the north, just across the drained Nor Loch. Wide boulevards, a neat grid-like street plan, leafy squares, and elegant sandstone town houses graced the New Town—the brainchild of architects James Craig (1739–1795), Robert Adam (1728–1792), and William Henry Playfair (1790–1857). The Georgian order and style of the New Town was the complete antithesis of the nefarious and ramshackle Old Town. This helped to add to the sense of duality that has pervaded Edinburgh's heart and soul through the centuries.

Holyrood Park 🏔 65 ✉ Queen's Drive ☎ (0131) 557 4685
historicenvironment.scot

Two world wars depleted Edinburgh's population, but its lack of industrial development compared to other Scottish cities spared it the worst of the World War II air raids. In the years following, the city found an outlet to promote its charms on the global stage with the founding of the Edinburgh International Festival in 1947.

As Scottish oil generated billions of pounds for the British economy in the 20th century, this new source of wealth helped fuel a desire for independence that had lain dormant, like Arthur's Seat (the extinct volcano in the heart of Edinburgh), but by no means expired. This desire culminated in a 1997 referendum that solidly backed the establishment of a devolved parliament. The new parliament first sat in 1999 and moved to a striking modern home in Holyrood in 2004.

By the Millennium, Edinburgh was struggling economically, but ongoing revitalization efforts anchored in the St. James Quarter have helped lend a fashionably hip new touristic appeal to this unique city.

Edinburgh's Old Town

Edinburgh's Old Town is a deeply evocative warren of medieval streets, where ghosts of the past swirl around the cobbles and seep into every pore of the narrow wynds (lanes) and closes (alleyways). The streets are awash with cafés, pubs, and restaurants, and the Old Town is very much the tourist epicenter.

Edinburgh Castle is the capital's iconic landmark and offers sweeping views over the city center.

Edinburgh Castle: The castle hangs omnipresent over the city on its volcanic perch and must be visited for its rich history and dramatic views. Once home to Mary Queen of Scots, the castle is remarkably well preserved. Its unique structure encompasses the military innovations of various eras, while the many exhibits shed further light on the nation's history. Over the centuries, the castle held off at least 23 sieges; today it is only besieged by visitors, as the country's most visited tourist attraction. The best way to get a real feel for the fortress is on a short guided tour, followed by an in-depth, self-guided audio tour where you can wander at your own pace.

Key features to look for include the expanse of the **Esplanade** as you enter, home to the Military Tattoo (see sidebar right). Inside the castle, the **National War Museum** covers Scottish soldiers after the Act of Union with a cornucopia of arms, medals, and well-preserved uniforms. A poignant addition includes portraits of Scottish troops serving in Afghanistan and other recent conflicts.

In the **Crown Room** you can view Scotland's Crown Jewels—the Honours of Scotland—and the deeply symbolic Stone of Destiny, over which Scottish kings were once crowned. This important relic was repatriated from Westminster Abbey in London in 1996.

Military Matters

The Edinburgh Military Tattoo at Edinburgh Castle, held every August, is one of the wonders of the modern military world. The sight of the massed pipes and drums of the Scottish regiments parading proudly beneath the floodlit castle ramparts is unforgettable. The tattoo is sold out well in advance (for tickets: *tel 0131/225 1188* or *edintattoo.co.uk/tickets, £££££*) as 200,000 people flock to watch the bands perform. In past years, camels and elephants have joined the show, along with eclectic performers who light up the pageantry with dancing and flag-waving. At the castle, expect the unexpected.

The Great Hall was once the venue for lavish banquets and all sorts of regal revelry. It was built during the reign of James IV and once served as the seat of the Scottish Parliament; it has been more prosaically a hospital and barracks. Its most recent, and somewhat ostentatious, makeover came in the 19th century.

Tiny **St. Margaret's Chapel** is the oldest surviving part of both the castle and the city, dating back to the 12th century and the reign of King David I.

If you have a taste for the darker side

(continued on p. 70)

Edinburgh Castle ⛰ 59 ✉ Castlehill ☎ (0131) 225 9846 💲 £££
edinburghcastle.scot • **National War Museum** ⛰ 68 ✉ Edinburgh Castle, Castlehill ☎ (0300) 123 6789 💲 £££ **nms.ac.uk/national-war-museum**

A WALK DOWN THE ROYAL MILE

English writer Daniel Defoe once described the Royal Mile as the "finest street in the world." Despite the blight of a number of tacky souvenir shops, the majestic regal thoroughfare remains breathtaking. The Royal Mile originates in the craggy heights of Edinburgh Castle and descends in a tumble of cobbles—and three name changes—to the green expanse of Holyrood Park and the Palace of Holyroodhouse.

Descending from **Edinburgh Castle ❶** (see pp. 67 & 70), the Royal Mile starts at Castlehill, with sweeping views of the city at its western extremity, before stopping at the **Camera Obscura ❷** *(549 Castlehill, tel 0131/226 3709, camera-obscura .co.uk)*, home to more breathtaking views. These views are projected onto a disk in its distinctive tower using an archaic system of mirrors to the delight of young and old alike.

Across the road, **The Scotch Whisky Experience** *(354 Castlehill, tel 0131/220 0441, scotchwhiskyexperience.co.uk)* is essential for lovers of a wee dram, and tours *(£££)* start with a cute whisky barrel ride and end with a tasting, the more extensive the more expensive. The Royal Mile then rushes through two name changes, the Lawnmarket and then High Street. As you cross at the junction that marks the end of Lawnmarket you will see the old headquarters of the once mighty **Bank of Scotland ❸** *(The Mound)*, which nearly collapsed and lost its independence following the global recession of 2008. **St. Giles'**

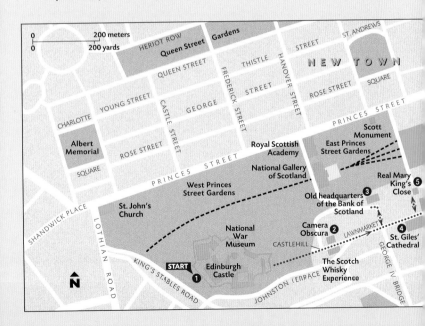

Cathedral ④ *(High Street, stgilescathedral .org.uk)* proudly welcomes you to High Street. A religious edifice has stood on this site since 854. The oldest sections date from 1120, and Charles I designated it a cathedral back in 1633. If you are brave, you can meet the city's famous ghosts close up at the **Real Mary King's Close ⑤** *(2 Warriston's Close, tel 0131/ 225 0672, realmarykingsclose.com)*. As the grand Georgian Edinburgh evolved, many poorer plague-ridden inhabitants were quarantined to die here, and the foundations of the City Chambers (which still stands) were built over them. Sections of their former quarters can be explored on distinctly eerie tours *(££)*.

As you leave High Street, glance to the south to see the **Tron Kirk ⑥** *(122 High St.)*. Today the former church functions as an information center, a market, and a venue during festival time. If in need of a break, the **Inn on the Mile**

(1–3 South Bridge, tel 0131/556 9940, theinnonthemile.co.uk) is on hand with its friendly bar, which demonstrates how the city has constantly reinvented its buildings while retaining their grandeur. You won't enjoy such frivolous revelry at the **John Knox House ⑦** *(43 High St., tel 0131/558 8137, tracscotland.org)*, farther down High Street. Now part of the Scottish Storytelling Centre *(£)*, it provides insight into the strict firebrand religious campaigner who led the Protestant Reformation of Scotland in the 16th century.

The penultimate stop is the ultramodern **Scottish Parliament ⑧** *(Holyrood, tel 0131/348 52000)*. Fittingly, you have now traveled from the old seat of power—the castle—to the new Scottish one. At the end of the Royal Mile, the British royal family keeps an eye on proceedings from the **Palace of Holyroodhouse ⑨** *(Holyrood, tel 123 7306; see p. 70)*.

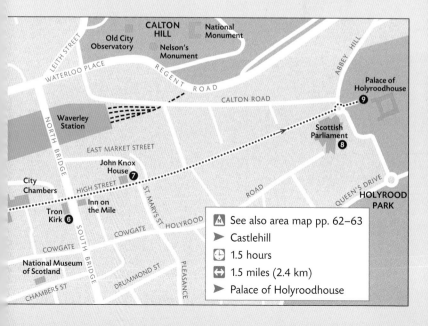

🅰 See also area map pp. 62–63
➤ Castlehill
🕐 1.5 hours
↔ 1.5 miles (2.4 km)
➤ Palace of Holyroodhouse

of life, you can delve into the bowels of the castle and explore its vaults, which served as a military prison. Watch for the graffiti etched into the walls by the poor souls once condemned to eke out their days here.

Palace of Holyroodhouse: This palace, at the foot of the Royal Mile, is the British royal family's pad in town. Next door is **Holyrood Abbey,** today a rambling but dramatic ruin. In the 12th century, during the reign of David I, the abbey was a mighty religious icon but was sacked by rampaging English armies.

The palace dates back to the days of

INSIDER TIP:

Take a tour of the Real Mary King's Close [see p. 69]. This step back into 16th-century city life allows you to experience firsthand the difficult living conditions of these crowded alleyways.

—NICOLE ENGDAHL
*National Geographic
Development Office*

James I, and despite its role as a regal residence, you can visit when the royals are not around. The interior is awash with fine fabrics, delicate oil paintings, and period furniture, but the highlight for many is the bed of Mary Queen of Scots. On this spot, Mary almost miscarried her baby (the future King James VI), later born in Edinburgh Castle, after she witnessed her alleged lover being murdered at the hands of henchmen under the instructions of her husband, Lord Darnley.

South of the Royal Mile: This is a wonderful place to come to grips with the Old Town and evoke its medieval character. Delving down **Victoria Street** is like leafing through the pages of a dusty old history book. The cobbled crescent descends in a curl of antique shops, bookshops, custom-made clothes stores, and some characterful pubs and

Greyfriars Bobby

Although perhaps not as famous as Snoopy, Lassie, or Scooby Doo, the tragically romantic tale of "Greyfriars Bobby" is more alluring for being true. Bobby, the faithful little Skye terrier, became a resident of **Greyfriars Kirkyard** when his master died in 1858. Bobby spent the rest of his 14 years in a vigil by the grave. The dog became a local celebrity, and when he died, a statue was erected just outside the graveyard. Disney made a film out of the story *(The True Story of a Dog)*, and Bobby lives on in the hearts of generations of tourists.

Palace of Holyroodhouse 🗺 65 ✉ End of Royal Mile ☎ (0303) 123 7306 💲 £££ rct.uk/visit/palace-of-holyroodhouse • **Greyfriars Kirkyard** ✉ Greyfriars Pl. ☎ (0131) 225 1900 greyfriarskirk.com

Old pubs offer outdoor dining along Grassmarket in the Old Town area.

restaurants. Look above to see a second tier leading up to the castle.

Victoria Street spills onto the **Grassmarket,** a scenic cobbled square that was once home to a popular market and, more gruesomely, where the city dwellers used to gather to witness public hangings. **The Last Drop** (74–78 Grassmarket, tel 0131/225 4851) is a pub based around the macabre theme as is its neighbor, **Maggie Dickson's Pub** (92 Grassmarket, tel 0131/225 6601), named for a woman said to have been hanged as a witch who was bumped back to life as the undertaker's cart thundered over the cobbled streets. Maggie won a reprieve that had more people believing she was a witch than ever before. Scotland's Shakespeare—the poet Robert Burns—wrote some of his most memorable verse a few

doors along at the **White Hart Inn** (34 Grassmarket, tel 0131/226 2806).

At the end of Grassmarket, across the dramatic sweep of George IV Bridge on Chambers Street, is the building formerly known as the Museum of Scotland—a grand swish of modern architecture that somehow manages to blend seamlessly with the older Royal Museum building. Following a massive renovation project, the two museums have now merged into one, known as the **National Museum of Scotland,** with exhibits on six levels spanning a complete spectrum of learning. Exhibitions on all six floors plus the basement brilliantly tell Scotland's story from the arrival of primitive man to the wild years when the people fought to forge their nation in the face of English dominion, through

National Museum of Scotland  65 ✉ Chambers St. ☎ (0300) 123 6789 **nms.ac.uk/national-museum-of-scotland**

■ **Princes Street in New Town Edinburgh**

Art, Design, and Fashion galleries, six Science and Technology galleries, and ten Natural World and World Cultures galleries feature thousands of objects plus more than 200 interactive displays, films, and touchscreens, where you can delve into everything from 18th-century court dresses to generating your own power in a giant hamster wheel.

This is the city center's most popular attraction with families. Among the perennial favorites are the homemade bicycle of "Flying Scot" Graeme Obree, a very Scottish hero who famously set the world record in a velodrome. Obree's record is all the more amazing given that he saw off his competitors on a contraption fashioned with parts from an old washing machine. There are also a *Tyrannosaurus rex* and stuffed Dolly the sheep, plus intricate scale models of once glorious steamships and rail engines.

The voluminous **Grand Gallery** is an airy marvel and a work of art in itself. Also check out the collage of ancient Greek and Roman pieces, the ghoulish Egyptian mummies, and the Maori war canoe. After you have exhausted the exhibits at the museum you can linger in the Balcony Café, take in views from the roof garden, or enjoy lunch in the ground-floor bistro-style Museum Kitchen.

to Scotland's pivotal role in the rise and fall of the British Empire, ending with "Scotland: A Changing Nation (early 1900s-present)." The museum's four

Farther east back toward Holyrood Park, **Our Dynamic Earth** takes a more scientific, geological look at the story of Scotland in a striking sail-like avant-garde building that nestles in the shadow of Arthur's Seat (see

Our Dynamic Earth ✉ 112–116 Holyrood Gait ☎ (0131) 550 7800
💲 ££ dynamicearth.co.uk

INSIDER TIP:

Don't let the name "New Town" deter you from leaving the Royal Mile. This side of the gardens has beautiful buildings filled with less-touristy restaurants and interesting boutiques.

—MARY NORRIS
National Geographic contributor

sidebar right). This is one of the city center's premier family attractions. Its amazing array of interactive exhibits thrills the senses in an exciting and energetic experience that allows you to face the dangers of a volcanic eruption, dive beneath the waves and explore a coral reef, take flight over the glaciers of Norway and Sweden, and wander through a tropical rain forest. Those without children in tow may want to give it a miss, but a call to all parents—don't even think about skipping this attraction if you are visiting Edinburgh for any great length of time.

New Town

Edinburgh's New Town is not so new anymore. The area dates back more than two centuries to the days when the city's rich and prosperous citizens employed visionary architects and town planners to create an idyllic new abode away from the maelstrom of the Old Town. The New Town retains its dignified neoclassical air, with green spaces, arrow-straight streets laid out largely on a neat grid, grand town houses, and some of the finest art galleries in Britain.

The most dramatic way into the New Town is descending from the Royal Mile down **The Mound,** a sinuous descent that offers fine views over the newer quarter below as it winds from the Old Town. Today, the castle lies proudly to the west while the grand facades of the New Town greet to the north. In between lie Princes Street Gardens.

(continued on p. 76)

EXPERIENCE:
Climbing Arthur's Seat

Join the locals who like to hike up this 823-foot (251 m) dormant volcano in the heart of the city center. The best place to start is the steep trail that leads off **St. Margaret's Loch,** but there are many ways to the summit. Just take care and avoid the west face, which has been the site of a few fatal accidents. The rocky summit offers the best possible views of Edinburgh, with the entire city and its suburbs unfurling below as you chat with the equally breathless locals. Now descend to the south and the village-like suburb of **Duddingston,** where the famous **Sheep Heid Inn** (*43–45 The Causeway, tel 0131/661 7974, thesheepheidedinburgh.co.uk*) and its traditional skittles alley await.

EDINBURGH SUMMER FESTIVALS

Every summer, Scotland's capital explodes with myriad festivals, collectively known as "The Festival" to locals and visitors alike. There is an amazing vibe in the city as celebrities, performers, and festivalgoers flock to its concert halls, theaters, and pubs to soak up the many various forms of entertainment on offer.

Fireworks light up a distinctive Scottish skyline during the annual Edinburgh Military Tattoo.

Since its inception in 1947 this global megaevent has morphed into a cocktail of overlapping and constantly evolving festivals that keep the city buzzing from late July through early September. Repeat visitors say this is the best time to visit, if you can secure a place to stay.

The **Edinburgh International Festival** *(mid-August–early September, eif .co.uk)* is the traditional linchpin of the Edinburgh summer festivals, with classical music, theater, and dance gracing grand venues like Festival Theatre and Usher Hall. Past highlights include innovative performances by the Scottish Ballet and the Budapest Festival Orchestra. For many, its spectacular fireworks finale and concert, held in Princes Street Gardens, is the crowning glory.

The **Edinburgh Festival Fringe** *(August, edfringe.com)* has also been going strong for more than 70 years. This massive event—ticket sales are well in excess of two million and the number of shows, in myriad venues, is mind-boggling—delivers everything from famous stand-up comedy acts to risqué amateur productions. Randomly picking a show, rooting out an obscure venue, and learning that you are a lone spectator is all part of the fun and captures the true essence of the Fringe.

The **Edinburgh Military Tattoo** *(August, edintattoo.co.uk)* is the hugely popular signature event of the festival, staged in the large esplanade at Edinburgh Castle. Thousands flock to watch military bands from around the globe parade and perform in this deeply atmospheric arena; the sight of bekilted Scottish regiments marching and playing their pipes and drums beneath the floodlit ramparts is unforgettable. Offshoots of the Tattoo can now be found around the world, but the original is very much still the best and the most spectacular.

The **Edinburgh International Book Festival** *(August, edbookfest .co.uk)*, one of the most prestigious in the world, first graced Charlotte Square Gardens in 1983. Today, more than 230,000 visitors pour through its gates for an audience with authors, poets, journalists, and thinkers from around the globe. Previous Book Festival favorites include the likes of Ian Rankin and J. K. Rowling, as well as best-selling authors Julia Donaldson and Jonathan Safran Foer.

Established in 1978, the **Edinburgh Jazz & Blues Festival** *(July, ejbf .co.uk)* has morphed from a low-key pub-based event to one of the biggest festivals of its kind in the U.K. A colorful Mardi Gras—the Edinburgh Festival Carnival—and a three-hour jam in Grassmarket set the pace for this musical jamboree.

World-class visual art, meanwhile, arrives in the city's galleries and museums each summer via the **Edinburgh Art Festival** *(late July–late August, edin burghartfestival.com)*. The U.K.'s largest annual celebration of visual art spreads throughout the city's many galleries, museums, and artist-run spaces, which each stage exhibitions, talks, and insider guided tours.

The **Mela** *(August)*, a colorful extravaganza of dance, theater, food, and music, celebrates Scotland's ethnic and cultural diversity. However, it wasn't offered in 2022 or 2023, and its future is uncertain.

The **Edinburgh International Film Festival** *(mid-August, edfilmfest .org)*, long a staple of Edinburgh's summer festivals, briefly made the brave decision to move slightly outside the main event in an attempt to create a separate identity, before returning to the core mid-summer dates. A relative newcomer that shows the ever evolving nature of "The Festival, " **Foodies Festival Edinburgh** *(August, foodiesfes tival.com)* brings an epicurean extravaganza to the city's Inverleith Park. This three-day event showcases the talents of the country's celebrity cooks. Ticket holders can also participate in cooking classes, sample and buy the finest Scottish produce, and take advantage of an array of free live entertainment.

Much of "The Festival" action is out on the city's streets. Grab a prized seat in a Royal Mile café and watch the hectic street life bustle by during the world's biggest and best festival.

Princes Street Gardens: Both parts of the gardens are replete with benches and grassy areas ideal for a picnic. **West Princes Street Gardens** is also home to the Ross Bandstand (venue for the city's famous Hogmanay concerts; see sidebar p. 17), the striking gold Ross Fountain, and **St. John's Church,** a religious edifice as renowned for the views from its terrace as its splendid interior. Look, too, for the **Scottish-American War Memorial,** which was commissioned by the Scottish-American War Memorial Committee to commemorate those Scots who fought in World War I. Sculpted by Scottish-Canadian R. Tait McKenzie (1867–1938), the memorial was unveiled in 1927 by then U.S. ambassador to Britain, Alanson B. Houghton.

East Princes Street Gardens is less grand, but things brighten up during the Christmas period, when an ice rink and Ferris wheel are assembled, and a German Christmas market helps locals and visitors alike get in the festive mood. This is a great time for families to visit.

Crowning The Mound itself are the **National Gallery of Scotland** and the **Royal Scottish Academy.** William Henry Playfair (1790–1857) designed these two Georgian temples—the academy in classical Doric style and the gallery in Ionic style. The two buildings are connected by an underground walkway

St. John's Church 🖾 68 ✉ West Princes Street Gardens, Princes St.
☎ (0131) 229 7565 **stjohns-edinburgh.org.uk** • **National Gallery of Scotland** 🖾 68 ✉ The Mound ☎ (0131) 624 6200 **nationalgalleries .org** • **Royal Scottish Academy** 🖾 68 ✉ The Mound ☎ (0131) 624 6110 **royalscottishacademy.org** • **Arthur's Seat** 🖾 65 **visitscotland.com**

A walk up Calton Hill offers a spectacular view across the city center.

INSIDER TIP:

The Beltane FireFestival is an incredible spectacle, with hundreds of drummers and torchbearers on Calton Hill at midnight on April 30, escorting the May Queen on her ancient pagan pilgrimage of rebirth.

—JIM RICHARDSON
National Geographic photographer

extension, the **Weston Link** (opened in 2004), which is an architectural marvel in itself. Make sure you relax with a drink or enjoy a meal in the Weston Link to appreciate the views out across East Princes Street Gardens to the landmark Balmoral Hotel and Princes Street.

The more time you can afford in the galleries the better. They are a real treasure trove of domestic and international art displayed in an environment that brings out the best in the paintings. Must-see works include "The Reverend Robert Walker Skating on Duddingston Loch" by Scottish artist Sir Henry Raeburn (1756–1823; see p. 51), "The Feast of Herod" by Peter Paul Rubens (1577–1640), "The Virgin and Child" by Raphael (1483–1520), and "The Three Tahitians" by Paul Gauguin (1848–1903).

East of the galleries, East Princes Street Gardens leads on to the nubby spires of the **Scott Monument.** This tribute to Scotland's greatest historical novelist, Sir Walter Scott (1771–1832), was funded by his avid fans and was completed in 1840 by George Meikle Kemp (1795–1844). Some see it as a fittingly towering tribute to the great man, others as a prime example of Victorian pomposity. Whatever you think, don't miss the chance to climb the hefty steps to the top of the rocket-like 200-foot-tall (61 m) tower offering great views over the city center.

More sweeping views await at the east end of Princes Street on the other side of the **Balmoral Hotel** (see Travelwise p. 341), the city's finest hotel and an impressive piece of Victorian architecture. The hotel was originally built to serve the needs of **Waverley Station,** a 19th-century station with an elaborately decorated dome, during the golden age of the railroads. A few hundred yards beyond the hotel lies the access to Calton Hill. Take the steps on the north side of Waterloo Place.

Calton Hill: Scottish writer Robert Louis Stevenson (1850–1894) thought this modest hill offered the finest views of the city, and he had a point. You can see both the castle and Arthur's Seat, as well as right down the Firth of Forth, out to the open sea, with the Ochil Hills in the distance to the northwest. Calton Hill is also home to the **National Monument,** which was to be Scotland's very own Parthenon.

Scott Monument 68 ⊠ East Princes Street Gardens ☎ (0131) 529 4068 £ *edinburghmuseums.org.uk* • **Waverley Station** 68–69 ☎ (03457) 114 141 *networkrail.co.uk*

However, the project ran out of steam, and all that was ever built were the slightly bereft looking Doric columns of the facade. Also up here is **Nelson's Monument** and the **Old City Observatory,** built in 1818 but redeveloped in 2018 as the Collective, displaying the City of Edinburgh's contemporary art collection.

George Street: Back down from Calton Hill, two blocks north of Princes Street and separated by the narrow and largely pedestrianized **Rose Street**—itself a great place to stop off in one of the many pubs and restaurants—is **George Street.** Once the seat of many wealthy banks and financial institutions, its grand Georgian buildings have been reinvented as trendy bars, chic restaurants, and designer stores.

Two charming squares lie at either end of George Street. On the eastern end is **St. Andrew Square.** Its seating and coffee stall are popular with locals and visitors alike, who are watched over by the **statue of Lord Melville** (1742–1811), the corrupt right hand to the British Prime Minister William Pitt the Younger (1759–1806), surveying the scene from his lofty perch.

Some of the homogeneity of this Georgian square was lost to 1960s and 1970s functionalism, but in 2018 the £1 billion (US$ 1.2 billion St. James Quarter *(stjamesquarter.com)* redevelopment project began. To bring the city firmly into the 21st century, the retail-based, multiuse project will include an Everyman Cinema, plus a futuristic, metal-

Nelson's Monument 🅰 69 ✉ 32 Calton Hill ☎ (0131) 556 2716 💲 £ edinburghmuseums.org.uk • **Old City Observatory** 🅰 69 ✉ Calton Hill ☎ (0131) 556 1264 **collective-edinburgh.art** • **Scottish National Portrait Gallery** 🅰 65 ✉ 1 Queen St. ☎ (0131) 624 6200 **nationalgalleries.org**

Edinburgh's Scrap Metal Sculptor

Sir Eduardo Paolozzi (1924–2015) was born into Edinburgh's large Italian community. His parents ran an ice-cream shop in Leith until World War II broke out, and he and his family were interned as enemy aliens. He was released after three months, but his father, grandfather, and uncle drowned when a ship transporting prisoners to Canada was sunk by a German U-boat. In 1943, after maintaining the family business for several years, Paolozzi left the city to study sculpture in London.

Paolozzi went on to become a successful sculptor, creating many high-profile works of public art, and his art and ideas were major influences on the pop art movement of the 1960s. He is most famous for his sculptures made from machine parts, scrap metal, and other discarded items.

■ **Revelers enjoy themselves in an Edinburgh bar.**

sheathed W Hotel as centerpiece of the development.

One block north of St. Andrew Square is the **Scottish National Portrait Gallery.** In contrast to the austere Georgian architecture elsewhere in the New Town, this gallery is an ostentatious riot of Gothic architecture made all the more dramatic by its striking red sandstone hue. The portrait gallery is as much a historical gem as an artistic one, since it is made up of portraits of celebrated Scots through the ages. Highlights include seminal figures such as Mary Queen of Scots and Bonnie Prince Char-

lie, right through to more contemporary notables such as Sir Sean Connery.

At George Street's western end awaits exclusive **Charlotte Square.** Designed by Robert Adam (1728–1792; see sidebar p. 117) a year before his death, it's now a focus of the city—Scotland's First Minister resides at number six, **Bute House.** The house sits on the northern flank, while neighboring **Georgian House** is open to the public. Owned by the National Trust for Scotland, this grand building retains the dignified air of Edinburgh life in the first half of the 19th century. Keep an

• **Georgian House** ✉ 7 Charlotte Sq. ☎ (0131) 225 2160 $ ££ **nts.org .uk/visit/places/georgian-house**

eye out for paintings by Sir Henry Rae-burn and Allan Ramsay (1713–1784).

Across the Dean Bridge: West of Charlotte Square and Princes Street, the land slopes down to Edinburgh's modest river, the Water of Leith. The photogenic views from Bell's Brae Bridge and the Water of Leith Walkway are among the city's most iconic. Farther west, this area is home to a world-class art gallery in a plush and spacious wooded setting, the **Scottish National Gallery of Modern Art One.** Before you even enter, take in the sculptures dotting the grounds—the highlights are works by Henry Moore (1898–1986) and Barbara Hepworth (1903–1975). Inside, avant-garde legends such as American Andy Warhol (1928–1987) and native Brit Damien Hirst (1965–) are celebrated alongside less well-known local talent.

Next door, the **Scottish National Gallery of Modern Art Two** is most renowned for its collection of sculptures by Sir Eduardo Paolozzi (see sidebar p. 78). He left the gallery thousands of pieces when he died, including some of his finest work, and a re-creation of his studio sheds light on the work of this homegrown genius. On the ground floor, the Roland Penrose Gallery and Gabrielle Keiller Library have a collection of Dada and surrealist art featuring Pablo Picasso (1881–1973), Joan Miró (1893–1983), and Salvador Dalí (1904–1989).

Royal Botanic Garden: North of New Town is the world-class Royal Botanic Garden. In addition to beautiful plantings, the stunning views back toward the New Town and Old Town skyline, with the castle clearly visible overlooking the scene and seemingly within touching distance, are not to be missed. The grounds have an eclectic mix of trees and shrubs from all over, with themed gardens throughout. Late spring is the best time to visit, when the flowers are in bloom.

It is well worth the modest admission fee to visit the 10 huge greenhouses (called "glasshouses"), which are heated to different temperatures to house flora from around the world. Pools laden with carp and little bridges ideal for strolling also emerge from the lush greenery. Don't miss the serene **Chinese Garden** or **Inverleith House,** home to ever changing art exhibitions.

A glorious addition to the botanic garden is the multimillion-pound **John Hope Gateway** at the West Gate. It has information on the gardens, interactive displays, a plant sales section, a gift store, and the airy **Gateway Restaurant** (*Arboretum Pl., tel 0131/552 2674, atthebotanics.co.uk*), offering garden views and a large terrace for summer dining. ∎

Scottish National Gallery of Modern Art One 🅰 65 ✉ 75 Belford Rd. ☎ (0131) 624 6200 **nationalgalleries.org** • **Scottish National Gallery of Modern Art Two** ✉ 73 Belford Rd. ☎ (0131) 624 6200 **nationalgalleries.org Royal Botanic Garden** 🅰 65 ✉ Inverleith Row ☎ (0131) 248 2909 💲 Grounds: free; greenhouses: £ **rbge.org.uk**

LEITH & THE DOCKS

Leith was once a separate town from Edinburgh, and some of the residents of this waterfront district continue to proclaim their independence. Visitors often ignore this charismatic quarter, but Leith and its docks boast a rich history. In recent years, the area has reinvented itself as a culinary and nightlife oasis.

■ Barges and trendy bars and restaurants line The Shore, where the Water of Leith widens into the port.

Although it lies beyond the city center, the lively medieval port of Leith has played a major role in the history of the capital. In the 15th century, Mary of Guise (1515–1560) presided from here on behalf of her young daughter, Mary Queen of Scots (1542–1587). When Oliver Cromwell's (1599–1658) men were in town, they chose Leith as their base. Right up until World War II, Leith was a major port, with a bustling hinterland.

After World War II, Leith's port slumped into major decline. By the 1980s, it was a rundown area with serious drug problems and an active red-light district, as described by Irvine Welsh in his first novel *Trainspotting* (1993), later made into a hit film.

Since 2000, investment by both public and private sectors has rejuvenated the area with large-scale developments, including tourist attractions, shopping malls, and upmarket waterfront housing. Since June 2023, Leith has been connected by tram to Edinburgh airport and west to Newhaven.

Visiting Leith

The best way to get to Leith is to wander down the lengthy **Water of Leith Walkway**—a wide thoroughfare that runs 13 miles (21 km) through the heart of Edinburgh, from Balerno to Leith. On the southwest side of Edinburgh, the **Water of Leith Visitor Centre** *(24 Lanark Rd., 0131 455 7367, waterofleith.org.uk)* provides fun exhibits on the life of the river.

Just as Leith Walk reaches its northern

Leith 🗻 62 C3, 65 **Visitor Information** ✉ Leith Mills, 70–74 Bangor Rd., Edinburgh ☎ (0131) 555 5225 **edinburgh.org**

INSIDER TIP:

Book ahead to dine at Leith's top foodie destinations: Restaurant Martin Wishart and The Kitchin.

—MARY NORRIS
National Geographic contributor

---

terminus, the **Leith Links** appears to the east. This modest parkland does not look like much, but the locals insist that it has a stronger claim than St. Andrews to being the "home of golf." Documents suggest that King James IV of Scotland (1473–1513) banned his men from playing golf on the links and that the rules were codified here a full decade before they were committed to paper in St. Andrews.

The cobbled harbor area of **The Shore** is a charming send-off as the Water of Leith widens into the port area. The once grand merchant and seafarer houses are being revitalized with quirky shops, new pubs, welcoming restaurants, and the Michelin-starred Restaurant Martin Wishart (see p. 97) turning this area into a hip evening haunt.

Running west from The Shore is **Commercial Quay.** Once a bustling network of warehouses, alive with boats and cranes, it is now home to more restaurants, including The Kitchin (see p. 96)—another Michelin-starred establishment. One block north, on Victoria Quay, the massive utilitarian building you see is the administrative home of the Scottish government.

Victoria Quay opens west to **Ocean Terminal** *(Ocean Drive, tel 0131/475 9400, oceanterminal.com).* This giant shopping mall and multistory leisure oasis boasts more than 70 stores, a cinema, spa, and panoramic views out over the Firth of Forth. If that isn't enough, Leith's most famous tourist attraction, the **Royal Yacht** *Britannia* (see sidebar below), is moored below.

A massive transformation of the run-down waterfront area includes completion in 2023 of the **Port of Leith Distillery** *(tel 0131/600 0144, leithdistillery.com, guided tours £££££),* a vertical whisky distillery a stone's throw north of the Royal Yacht *Britannia.* ∎

Britannia Rules the Waves

The Royal Yacht *Britannia* is a permanent fixture on the Leith waterfront. Edinburgh demonstrated its drive and ambition by fighting off Glasgow, where the ship was launched from John Brown's Shipyard in Clydebank back in 1953, to become the resting place of this slice of floating history. You can explore the rooms where the British royal family entertained foreign royalty and dignitaries, as well as sneak little insights into the royal way of life on board the ship. Make sure to enjoy the quintessentially British tradition of tea in the café, where you can even splurge on a glass of champagne.

Royal Yacht *Britannia* 🅰 62 C3 ✉ Ocean Terminal, Leith ☎ (0131) 555 5566 💲 ££ **royalyachtbritannia.co.uk**

OUTSIDE THE CENTER

Edinburgh is not a very big city by global standards, but in its outskirts you'll find a brace of charming waterfront communities—including Cramond, South Queensferry, and Portobello—as well as a sweep of hills that offer great views over the city.

Cramond

Cramond lies on the western fringe of Edinburgh and has a charmingly forgotten feel. This seaside suburb was once a Roman stronghold, and the sparse ruins of the fortress can still be made out. The village itself is a pretty affair, with a row of white-washed houses lining the banks of the River Almond, a small sailing club making the most of the widening Forth estuary, and both a pub and a cozy little restaurant.

It is also possible to walk over to **Cramond Island,** but check the tides in advance, which are usually posted on a sign at the start of the mile-long (1.6 km) tidal causeway to the island. The island is a bird-watcher's dream, but the tides are frighteningly quick here, so don't take any risks. Every year, visitors and locals alike get stranded as the causeway disappears.

South Queensferry

South Queensferry is quite simply one of the prettiest coastal settlements in Scotland. Although it lies within the official city boundaries, it feels a world away from Edinburgh, surrounded by protected countryside on three flanks and the Firth of Forth on the other.

■ Hardy souls brave the icy waters of the Firth of Forth, South Queensferry, during the "Loony Dook."

These days, South Queensferry is most famous for its mighty bridges—the Forth Bridge (which carries trains) and two others (see pp. 85–86).

South Queensferry takes its name from Queen Margaret (1045–1093), the monarch who first commissioned the ferries across the river. Some pedantic locals may insist that you are in the Royal Burgh of Queensferry, but most still call it South Queensferry to distinguish it from North Queensferry across the Forth.

South Queensferry's charming cobbled High Street is lined with well-preserved stone buildings, some painted in pastel hues. The oldest, the **Black Castle** (38–40 High St.) dates back as

Cramond 🗺 62 B2 • **South Queensferry** 🗺 62 B3

far as 1626. Pop into the **Queensferry Museum** to learn about the suburb's rich history, from its pagan Burry Man Festival to the "Loony Dook," when the locals, and any visitors daft enough to join them, welcome in the New Year with a chilly dip in the Forth.

South Queensferry is surrounded on three sides by private estates, each home to a grand country house. Dundas Castle is not open to the public, but **Dalmeny House** offers guided tours, including of its impressive art gallery, but was closed for renovation at press time. The star attraction is **Hopetoun,** which has been dubbed "Scotland's Versailles" and is one of the finest houses in the land. The grounds are also impressive, with views of the Forth and a selection of flora to enjoy as well as the chance to spy deer. The on-site café serves teas and cakes and even offers a suitably grand champagne afternoon tea.

Portobello

The name hints at the romance of the Mediterranean, and Portobello, 3 miles (5 km) east of the city center, does have a dash of seaside romance. Before the days of cheap jet travel, the city's residents flocked to the beach on sunny days. Today, the suburb is a little down-at-heel, but the views across the Firth of Forth are superb, the sands are still wide and welcoming, and the walks are always refreshingly bracing—the sense of better times having slipped through its sands giving it an extra layer of romance. ■

EXPERIENCE:
A Walk on the Wild Side

This lovely 7.5-mile (12 km) walk is something of a local secret. The best plan is to take a train from Edinburgh northwest to Dalmeny, South Queensferry's nearest train station, and walk north down to the Forth Bridge. Follow the track that leads into the Dalmeny Estate to the east. Highlights include grand Dalmeny House (see main text), superb views of the Forth Bridge and Edinburgh, the **Eagle Rock** where a Roman legionnaire once carved graffiti, and the sea life scattered along the sandy coastline. The ferry across to Cramond no longer operates, but this allows a scenic detour up to **Cramond Brig** and a walk back down a marked walkway along the **River Almond** into the village. For further information visit *roseberyestates.co.uk/dalmeny-house/the-shore-walk.*

Queensferry Museum ✉ 53 High St., South Queensferry ☎ (0131) 331 5545 **edinburghmuseums.org.uk** • **Dalmeny House** ✉ 2 miles (3.2 km) from Dalmeny train station; follow signs off the A90 Forth Bridge Rd. ☎ (0131) 331 1888 🕐 Open Sun.–Wed. June–July for scheduled tours 💲 ££ **roseberyestates.co.uk** • **Hopetoun** ✉ 12 miles (16 km) W of Edinburgh via the A904 ☎ (0131) 331 2451 🕐 Closed Oct.–March 💲 ££ **hopetoun.co.uk**

FORTH BRIDGES

The world-famous twin Forth bridges, which span the Firth of Forth 9 miles (14 km) northwest of Edinburgh and link the capital to the kingdom of Fife, were joined by a new arrival in 2017. Each is a testament to the finest engineering of its time—the grand iron Victorian Forth Bridge, the sleek 20th-century Forth Road Bridge, and the gleaming new 21st-century Queensferry Crossing.

You can walk, cycle, drive, boat, or take a train across the water to appreciate the bridges; a visit to the picturesque Edinburgh suburb of South Queensferry offers good vantage to admire the mighty trio.

The River Forth estuary has long been a natural obstacle for people. Back in the 11th century, Queen Margaret of Scotland commissioned the first ferry service to transport pilgrims from the capital to the emerging religious centers of Dunfermline and St. Andrews, and today the estuary traffic is busier than ever.

Forth Bridge

The Forth Bridge (the railroad bridge), first opened in 1890, is almost everyone's favorite. UNESCO is a fan, too, placing the bridge on its protected World Heritage List in 2016. One of the finest examples of Victorian engineering in the world, this rich iron-red monster proudly vaults 1.5 miles (2.5 km) across the river in an unusual triple cantilever design. The Forth Bridge was the work of engineers Sir John Fowler (1817–1898) and Sir Benjamin Baker (1840–1907), who had learned from the mistakes of the 1879 collapse of the Tay Bridge farther north.

The amount of materials involved in the bridge's construction is staggering: 58,000 tons (53,000 tonnes) of steel, 637,000 cubic feet (18,000 cubic m)

The Forth bridges provide a visual time line of the advances in bridge-building down the decades.

of granite, and more than eight million rivets. The human effort was equally immense, with a whole community of workers billeted in the suburb of South Queensferry; almost 100 of them paid for their work with their lives. The bridge also crossed over into popular culture, appearing in Alfred Hitchcock's 1935 film *The 39 Steps.*

UNESCO shouldn't fear for its durability, as surveys have shown that the steel and iron used is of a high and consistent quality. The days when a never-ending task in Scotland was said to be "like painting the Forth Bridge" are gone, too, with the current paint job said to be good for another couple of decades.

Forth Road Bridge

Somewhat forgotten in the shadow of its famous sibling, the Forth Road Bridge is a grand suspension bridge that bears a strong resemblance to its relative in San Francisco. It was the largest of its kind in Europe when it opened in 1964. It has also been immortalized as the focus of Iain Banks's highly regarded novel *The Bridge* (1986).

Eventually, the Forth Road Bridge carried much more traffic than it was designed for, and remedial work is ongoing to ensure that it continues to operate. Note that it is the only bridge open to walkers and cyclists and now plays a secondary role to the new Queensferry Crossing, with limited access for cars.

Queensferry Crossing

The latest Forth bridge, opened in 2017, is a fittingly grand addition to the family. It spans more than 1.7 miles (2.7 km) and soars 25 percent higher than the Forth Road Bridge, making it the highest bridge in the British Isles and the longest three-tower cable-stayed bridge in the world. The steel required for the north and south viaducts weighs 7,716 tons (7,000 tonnes). As the bridge is part of Scotland's motorway network, both pedestrians and cyclists are banned from using it and should take the Forth Road Bridge instead, from which they can admire the new bridge's soaring lines.

Travel Information

The Forth Bridges website *(the forthbridges.org)* offers an excellent comparative profile of the three bridges, including up-to-date information about ways to experience each. ScotRail *(scotrail.co.uk)* runs trains across the Forth Bridge from Dalmeny Station in South Queensferry to North Queensferry. The family-run *Maid of the Forth (maidoftheforth.co.uk)* and the *Forth Belle (forthtours.com)* cruise under all the bridges on sightseeing tours. Anyone can walk or cycle across the Forth Road Bridge, which affords visitors easy access from both sides of the river. The circular, 5-mile-long (8 km) Forth Bridges Trail was opened in 2022, with interpretive signs regaling fascinating tidbits on history, literary references, and natural history. In South Queensferry both Orocco Pier *(oroccopier.co.uk)* and the Boat House *(theboathouse.online)* restaurant/bar offer stunning bridge views. Or try the Railbridge Bistro *(railbridge.co.uk)*, dedicated to the Forth Bridge, with intriguing displays of memorabilia, information boards, and even a scale model.

THE LOTHIANS

Many visitors to Edinburgh never bother to venture beyond the city limits to sample the Lothians that surround the city. Those who do can look forward to a scenic region graced by hills, the Firth of Forth, and the North Sea. The area is studded with ancient palaces and mysterious churches, as well as the little-known town that claims to be the site of the world's first oil production.

Bass Rock, near North Berwick, East Lothian, is home to a colony of around 80,000 gannet nests.

East Lothian

East of Edinburgh, **Musselburgh,** with its famous racecourse, is worth a visit for horse-racing fans. Fans of ice cream should stop at legendary **Luca's** *(32–38 High St., tel 0131/665 2237, lucasicecream.co.uk)*, scooping up delight for more than 100 years.

A must for golfers is **Musselburgh Links** *(Balcarres Road, tel 0131/653 5122, musselburgholdlinks.co.uk; see p. 193)*, the world's oldest golf course. It's been documented that golf was first played here in

1672, and some say that Mary Queen of Scots played here in 1567.

After passing the now defunct Cockenzie power station, East Lothian becomes less urban with a string of sandy beaches lining the littoral. The finest is perhaps **Gullane Beach,** a generous oasis of clean sands that rise up to meet unspoiled dunes. In the summer, people flock here from the city, but off season, you will have it largely to yourself. Keen golfers will take more interest in the superb **Muirfield Golf Course**

East Lothian 63 D2–D3, E2–E3, F2–F3

(Duncur Road, Muirfield, tel 01620/842 123, muirfield.org.uk; see p. 193), which has previously hosted the British Open.

The most charming of the coastal settlements is undoubtedly **North Berwick.** This grand resort town experienced a golden age in the Victorian era, when trains ran direct from London to service stressed city types looking for fresh air and a healthy dip in the waters. To get an idea of the layout of the town head just south of town and take a one-hour hike up to the top of **North Berwick Law.** The distinctive craggy hill offers tremendous views over the town and East Lothian in general.

North Berwick's main attractions are its beautiful sandy beach, a trio of fabulous golf courses, and the excellent **Scottish Seabird Centre**—a modern attraction constructed to open up the remarkable Bass Rock just offshore. **Bass Rock** is a volcanic rock stack that looms out of the Firth of Forth's icy waters like a giant submarine beginning to surface. This towering 350-foot (107 m) monster looks impregnable, and largely is, except to its huge population of seabirds. Greedy gannets and cute puffins are among its colorful and noisy residents. Members of the public are not allowed to land on the protected island, but the mainland center reveals the rock's daily life story through a system of well-placed cameras. In summer, boat tours take you much closer. The sheer variety of birds that flock here make Bass Rock a key scientific research station.

East Lothian's Hinterland

Farther east, the coastline becomes wilder and rockier. A dramatic imprint of man is at the rugged ruin of **Tantallon Castle** *(2 miles/3.2 km E of North Berwick, tel 01620/892 727, historicenvironment.scot, £)*, with its spectacular views overlooking the sea. This stalwart 14th-century castle was once the refuge of one of Scotland's most famous historical families, the Douglas Earls of Angus.

Dunbar is a last flourish as East Lothian turns south toward the Borders. This honest and attractive fishing town is replete with some sturdy sandstone architecture and a busy little port.

Farther inland, a world-class attraction is the **National Museum of Flight** at the

Flying on the Concorde

Although the supersonic airliner Concorde retired in 2003, the National Museum of Flight (see above) lets you enjoy a touch of the high life on the excellent "Concorde Experience." Once you have your "boarding pass," the journey begins with an audio tour around main parts of the aircraft, with flight attendants and pilots offering their insights into life aboard this amazing passenger airliner. You even get a glimpse into the surprisingly cozy cockpit.

North Berwick 🗺 63 E3 • **Scottish Seabird Centre** 🗺 63 E3
✉ The Harbour, North Berwick ☎ (01620) 890 202 💲 £ **seabird.org**
• **Dunbar** 🗺 63 E3 **ourdunbar.com**

■ Hiking in the Pentland Hills, near Edinburgh in Midlothian

old military airfield at East Fortune. On show are scores of well-preserved aircraft from over the ages, either displayed in newly-restored hangars or even more atmospherically out on the aprons. The trusty old Spitfire, which played a crucial role in World War II during the Battle of Britain, as well as the Vulcan bomber that caused a political storm when it made an emergency landing in Brazil during Britain's Falklands War with Argentina, are the highlights. Other impressive exhibits include a rocket-powered Messerschmitt Komet, the fastest plane of World War II. The Scottish National Air Show is hosted here each July.

A few miles from the museum is the neat inland market town of **Haddington,** which was first recognized by King David I back in the 12th century. Haddington is a relaxed place for a stroll and café stop. The most visually appealing part of town is **Church Street,** with its well-preserved 18th- and 19th-century architecture. The most alluring building is **Lennoxlove House,** 0.5 mile (1 km) south of the town, which dates back to the 14th century and boasts a sprinkling of remnants from one of its most famous guests, Mary Queen of Scots, including a death mask. The only way to explore Lennoxlove House is on one of the excellent guided tours on select days only.

This may not strike you as whisky country, but East Lothian boasts its very own **Glenkinchie Distillery,** one of the "Four Corners of Scotland" distilleries that produce the regional malts—in this case the distinctive Edinburgh Malt—that are blended to make Johnnie Walker whisky. The distillery runs excellent tours that explain how they mercurially turn the local water into this hallowed dram.

National Museum of Flight 🄰 63 E3 ✉ East Fortune Airfield, East Lothian ☎ (0300) 123 6789 🕐 Closed Mon.–Fri. Nov.–March 💲 *£££* **nms.ac.uk/national-museum-of-flight** • **Lennoxlove House** ✉ Lennoxlove Estate, Haddington ☎ (01620) 823 720 🕐 💲 *££* **lennoxlove .com** • **Glenkinchie Distillery** ✉ Pencaitland, Tranent, East Lothian ☎ (01875) 342 012 💲 *£–£££* **malts.com**

Midlothian

The **Pentland Hills** are a chunky necklace of rolling hills that form a natural border along the western side of the old county of Midlothian, or "Edinburghshire." Most of the Pentland area is protected but open to the public. Just off the Edinburgh Bypass road lies Hillend at the east of the range, which is home to the **Midlothian Snow Sports Centre—**, offering daytime and floodlit nighttime skiing on one of the longest dry ski slopes in Europe. Farther into the Pentlands, the land turns more rugged, and the hustle and bustle of modern life quickly eases away. **Flotterstone** is the best access point for a hike, with a free parking lot, information center, walking trails marked on maps, and an inn for sustenance after the walk. The highest point is only 1,900 feet (579 m), which makes the Pentlands an appealing and safer winter alternative to Scotland's more serious mountains. Further hiking awaits in the **Moorfoot Hills,** south of Midlothian on its boundary with the Borders.

Midlothian's star attraction is undoubtedly **Rosslyn Chapel** at **Roslin,** which has recently been made world famous by Dan Brown's best-selling 2003 novel *The Da Vinci Code* (see sidebar below) and the subsequent Hollywood blockbuster. Sir William St. Clair (1404–1482) was the man who realized his dream in seeing the chapel completed in 1446. Its newfound fame has helped finance essential ongoing renovation work. However, the increase in visitors has caused problems of its own.

The exterior of this atmospheric building is a collage of flying buttresses and scary-looking gargoyles, but the intricacies inside the church are what really excite. The genius of the master stonemason, with all manner of symbols and allegorical images, speaks through the centuries. The walls of the 69-by-42-foot (21-by-13 m) church are covered almost entirely with hundreds of carvings, depicting everything from knights on horseback and the pagan Green Man to a nativity scene and Lucifer bound, gagged, and hanging upside down.

The Da Vinci Code

Rosslyn Chapel plays a central role in Dan Brown's best-selling novel *The Da Vinci Code,* in which the author suggests that it was once the resting place of the Holy Grail. The book's central characters, Robert Langdon and Sophie Neveu, visit the chapel to seek out the Holy Grail but find that it has been moved to France by the shadowy Priory of Sion. While in Scotland, Neveu speaks to her grandmother and learns more about her own ancestry, which links her directly back to the supposed lineage of Jesus and Mary Magdalene.

Midlothian Snow Sports Centre ✉ Biggar Rd., Hillend ☎ (0131) 445 4433 💲 ££ ski.midlothian.gov.uk • **Rosslyn Chapel** 🅰 62 C2 ✉ Chapel Loan, Roslin ☎ (0131) 440 2159 💲 ƒ rosslynchapel.com

Rosslyn Chapel is a special place, and it is no surprise that its Freemasonry and Knights Templar connections add further fuel to fire the imaginations of its many visitors. Adding to the intrigue are the carvings of North American plants that date back to before the apparent discovery of the Americas by Christopher Columbus (1451–1506) in 1492. Recent research found an underground chamber, adding to the speculation in some quarters that the Holy Grail lies buried beneath the chapel. Conspiracy theorists and those with vivid imaginations might like the fact that "Dolly the Sheep" was genetically engineered nearby at the Roslin Institute. Visits to this private chapel, run by the Rosslyn Chapel Trust, are by reservation.

Midlothian was once a major coal producer and provided the fuel to power Scotland's thriving capital during the industrial age. The demise of industrialization has cast an economic shadow over the area; however, the excellent **National Mining Museum Scotland** commemorates the once booming industry. Located in one of the best-preserved Victorian-era collieries in Europe, the museum features two exhibitions—"The Story of Coal" and "A Race Apart"—plus a Pithead Tour usually led by a former miner. Re-create the mining experience with the aid of helmets fitted with audio gear, which go down well with young visitors, as does the play area.

Roslin itself is not all about world-famous churches. **Roslin Glen Country Park** is a bucolic escape, with walking trails and a ruined castle—both attractions come without the crowds that can hamper a visit to the chapel itself. Another green oasis is **Vogrie Coun-**

National Mining Museum Scotland ✉ Lady Victoria Colliery, Newtongrange ☎ (0131) 663 7519 💲 £–££ **nationalminingmuseum.com** • **Roslin Glen Country Park** ✉ Bet. Roslin & Rosewell via the B7003 **midlothian.gov.uk/info/200283/parks** • **Vogrie Country Park** 🗺 62 C1–C2 ✉ 12 miles (19 km) from Edinburgh; S on the A68, right on the B6372 for 1.2 miles (2 km) to park entrance ☎ (01875) 821 716 **midlothian.gov.uk/info/200283/parks**

The Tragic Life of Mary Queen of Scots

The real life of Mary Queen of Scots reads more tragically and unbelievably than *Outlander*, although the 2018 movie *Mary Queen of Scots* does the tale justice. Born in Linlithgow Palace in December 1542, Mary became Queen of Scotland as a six-day-old baby. After spending much of her childhood in France, Mary returned to Scotland to rule in 1561. As a staunch Catholic, Mary's attempts to undermine the Protestant faith failed, and she was forced to abdicate. She fled to England to seek refuge with her cousin, Elizabeth I, but was jailed and spent the rest of her days under house arrest, implicated in various plots–and executed in 1587.

■ The austere sandstone facade of Linlithgow Burgh Hall

try Park, which is a short drive away. At the center of the park is the eponymous house, which includes a café with play area, a golf course, some interesting public sculpture, and some walking trails.

West Lothian

West Lothian, perhaps the most underrated corner of central Scotland, is largely off the beaten tourist track. Its claim to fame is that it is the "home of oil," and it lays a decent claim—it was here that the Scottish chemist James "Paraffin" Young (1811–1883) first produced oil from shale.

At one point, more than 13,000 people worked in the local oil industry that Young established here. His legacy is a landscape underpinned by mine workings and the very visible slag heaps, known locally as "bings," that resemble miniature versions of Uluru (Ayers Rock) at sunset.

Visitors can explore the days of shale mining at the **Almond Valley Heritage Trust** in the planned New Town of **Livingston.** One section re-creates a mine shaft with pitch-black tunnels and mine trucks. Large maps show the extent to which the mining spread its tentacles out over West Lothian. There is also a children's farm at the trust, which is guaranteed to keep younger visitors happy for at least half a day. The farm area slopes down the hillside toward the **River Almond,** with a series of enclosures and buildings housing a cornucopia of animals. As well as learning about the animals, you can take a ride on the narrow-gauge rail track or on a trailer pulled by a tractor.

On the fringe of the Livingston greenbelt is the village of **Dechmont—** the unlikely setting of one of the world's most famous UFO fantasies. In 1982, a local man and his dog were knocked

Almond Valley Heritage Trust ✉ Millfield, Livingston ☎ (01506) 414 957 ⑤ ££ almondvalley.co.uk

unconscious and suffered burns at the hands of what he described as a floating spherical-type object. Scientists and the media descended on the area from all over the world, but the only legacy today is a small plaque at the landing site near Dechmont Hill, between Dechmont and Livingston.

Many of West Lothian's towns are rather scruffy affairs, but one shining star, north across the **Bathgate Hills** from Dechmont, is **Linlithgow.** The birthplace of Mary Queen of Scots is a richly historic town, and it is handily located on the main Edinburgh–Glasgow railroad line. The cobbled High Street is awash with cafés and stores, making it the perfect location for a relaxed stroll and lunch stop. A good day to visit is on the fourth Saturday of every month,

when a lively farmers market descends on the town. Before heading to the palace, stop by the imposing stone. **Linlithgow Burgh Halls,** former headquarters of Linlithgow Burgh Council. Recently transformed into an art gallery following an extensive renovation, it hosts touring exhibitions of contemporary works by Scottish and international artists. Now follow the cobbled path to the rear, noting the wall plaques listing the kings and queens of Scotland, then pass beneath the arch that opens to **Lunlithgow Palace.**

The palace is a breathtaking 15th-century building that rises robustly from a grassy knoll overlooking the waters of **Linlithgow Loch.** Mary Queen of Scots was born in Linlithgow Palace in 1542. The building is now a ruin, but there is

Linlithgow 🅰 62 A3 • **Linlithgow Burgh Halls** ✉ The Cross, Linlithgow ☎ (01506) 282 720 **linlithgowburghhalls.co.uk** • **Linlithgow Palace** 🅰 62 A3 ✉ Boghall, Linlithgow ☎ (01506) 842 896 💲 £ **historicenvironment. scot**

■ **A jousting tournament captivates crowds at Linlithgow Palace, birthplace of Mary Queen of Scots.**

Visiting Beecraigs Country Park

The Bathgate Hills offer a bucolic escape, but you'll need a car or bike to get to its highlight—Beecraigs Country Park *(The Park Centre, near Linlithgow, tel 01505/284 516, westlothian.gov .uk/beecraigs),* with its new visitor center and café. Head south from Linlithgow into the heavily forested park, home to a deer farm and a fishing reservoir where you can rent boats and tackle. You can camp overnight in a forest clearing or limber up on the fitness course. People from all over the region flock here in summer, so you will meet a cross section of West Lothian society.

still plenty worth exploring, not least the views from six stories up over the town and loch. Unlike many castles in Scotland, Linlithgow is not bedecked with hordes of memorabilia. Indeed, much of the charm of the place is imagining what it might have looked like in its day. Legend has it that the fountain in the courtyard, built during the reign of James I (1566–1625), flowed with wine when Charles I (1600–1649) visited in 1633. In more current fame, the palace was featured in the hit television show *Outlander* as the prison corridors and entrances in episode 15, "Wentworth Prison."

The centerpiece of the palace is the magnificent and voluminous **Great Hall,** where you can let your imagination wander back to the past, when the palace walls echoed to the cries of a baby girl who was to have a monumental effect on the nation into which she had just been born.

If you visit the castle, make sure you also have a look at **St. Michael's Church** next door. The church itself dates back to the 13th century, but the structure is topped by a spiky aluminum crown that has divided the critics since it was added just after World War II. Back across the High Street and up the hill past the railroad station is another more modern addition, the **Union Canal,** which was built as a transportation link between Edinburgh and Glasgow. The canal basin is home to the **Linlithgow Canal Centre,** which has a modest museum and runs short canal cruises to the Avon Aqueduct in spring and summer.

If you prefer to explore the area by foot, the walk around **Linlithgow Loch** is an enjoyable experience. This circular adventure is best taken heading west, away from the palace. The first stretch is awash with eager ducks and swans touting for tidbits from passersby. Soon the town center disappears as you ease past some exclusive houses with views back across the waters to the

St. Michael's Church ✉ Cross House, The Cross, Linlithgow ☎ (01506) 842 188 **stmichaelsparish.org.uk** • **Linlithgow Canal Centre** ✉ Canal Basin, Manse Rd., Linlithgow ☎ (01506) 840 574 🕐 Closed Oct.–early-April & weekdays April–June & Sept. 💲 Boat trips: £ **lucs.org.uk**

palace. Information boards illuminate the route and both the loch's human and natural history. Look for the site of an old crannog—an island hideout used centuries ago by the local people to live their lives in a modicum of safety. The path rejoins the main road back into the center, but stay on the marked trail to the loch, which provides a thrilling denouement in the approach up to the palace from the lochside.

There are two more historic buildings within easy reach of Linlithgow, both back toward the city center. They can be savored with a first-rate lunch as part of the experience at the **Champany Inn** *(tel 01506/834 532, champany .com)* or just a burger in the chophouse.

The grand, crenellated **House of the Binns** has been in the Dalyell family for more than four centuries. Its most famous recent resident is the controversial politician Tam Dalyell, former Labour Member of Parliament, who always furrowed his own path and raised tricky questions about the political makeup of Britain. Children are challenged to "spot the peacock" in each room of the house, as well as in the large parkland of the estate.

Often ignored, **Blackness Castle** can be found sturdily guarding the shores of the Firth of Forth. This fortress and its drama were brought to the screen in Mel Gibson's film *Hamlet* (1990), when it was used as a location, as well as in the television show *Outlander,* where it stands in as Fort William. There is a superb riverside and forest walk east from the castle back to South Queensferry, where you can also take in Hopetoun (see p. 84), dubbed Scotland's Versailles. Allow at least three hours for the strenuous hike, after which you can pick up a taxi back to your car or a bus into the city center or back to Linlithgow.

A marvel of transportation is the restored stretch of railroad and station at **Bo'ness.** After being mothballed, the project was brought back to life by a team of volunteers. The station houses the **Museum of Scottish Railways,** which is the country's largest dedicated railroad exhibition, with sheds full of locomotives, wagons, and other exhibits. Summer brings regular train trips on the **Bo'ness and Kinneil Railway** *(bkrailway.co.uk)*—many hauled by steam engines. There is the option to visit an old mine to break up the return journey, with a café and tourist information center at the station, too.

The best view in West Lothian is the one from **Cairnpapple** in the rolling hills, taking the road just south of Linlithgow past **Beecraigs Country Park** (see sidebar opposite). Cairnpapple offers wide views of central Scotland, and there is also a burial cairn to explore. ∎

House of the Binns 🅰 62 A3 ✉ Linlithgow, West Lothian ☎ (01506) 834 255 🕐 House closed Nov.–March 💲 ££ **nts.org.uk/visit/places/house-of-binns** • **Blackness Castle** 🅰 62 A3 ✉ Blackness ☎ (01506) 834 807 💲 £ **www.historicenvironment.scot** • **Bo'ness** 🅰 62 A3 • **Museum of Scottish Railways** 🅰 62 A3 ✉ Bo'ness Station, Union St., Bo'ness ☎ (01506) 825 855 🕐 Closed Nov.–March 💲 £ **bkrailway.co.uk**

Where to Eat & Drink in Edinburgh & the Lothians

THE BOAT HOUSE

22 HIGH ST., SOUTH QUEENSFERRY

(0131) 331 5429 | theboathouse.online

Panoramic views over the Firth of Forth and its bridges would be reason enough to eat here, but first-rate seafood and service make it a special pleasure. Its menu also features venison and lamb, plus ramen and curry dishes. Note: Access involves stairs but it has disabled-access.

££ AE, MC, V

EDINBURGH LARDER

15 BLACKFRIARS ST.

(01506) 844 445| edinburghlarder.co.uk

This cozy café just off the Royal Mile is an absolutely delightful stop for a lighter lunch or brunch, with a welcome variety of healthy and hearty options, all locally sourced. Choose from amazing sandwiches and soups, plus artisanal coffee and teas.

£ MC, V

L'ESCARGOT BLEU

56 BROUGHTON ST.

(0131) 557 1600 | lescargotbleu.co.uk

A piece of Paris transplanted, this bistro-style French-inspired restaurant fuses fresh Scottish ingredients into a Gallic menu under chef-patron Fred Berkmiller. Bean stew with confit duck, braised pork, and sausage is a typical delight.

£££–££££ Closed Sun.–Tues. except August MC, V

HERON

87-91A HENDERSON ST.

(0131) 554 1242| heron.scot

Opened in 2021, this relaxed and old-world styled newcomer immediately earned a Michelin star for its inventive contemporary Scottish dishes using the freshest farm-to-table seasonal products. Perhaps partridge with cherry and pink peppercorn, or mackerel with fig leaf and hazelnut, followed by a divine Gubbean cheese with heather honey?

££££–£££££ Closed Mon.–Tues. All major cards

THE KITCHIN

78 COMMERCIAL QUAY, LEITH

(0131) 555 1755 | thekitchin.com

Celebrity Michelin-starred chef Tom Kitchin lures locals and visitors alike to his clubby and uber-hip Leith eatery with fresh and expertly cooked British produce. Highlights on a creative menu and seasonal cooking include sautéed Devon snails and Dornoch lamb.

££££–£££££ Closed Sun.–Mon. AE, MC, V

MUMS

4A FORREST RD.

(0131) 260 9806 | monstermashcafe.co.uk

Cheap and cheery, Mums offers tasty and affordable British comfort food at its best. Here diners happily tuck into such classics as sausage and mash, shepherd's pie, fish and chips, and haggis (a vegetarian haggis is also available), all served with a smile. This is the place to try the classic treacle and date pudding. Menus include nods to such pop-culture icons as Monty Python, the Beatles, and the classic spy show *Get Smart*. The selection of draft beer and cider is also on point.

£ MC, V

P Parking   Opening Hours   Credit Cards

PRICES

An indication of the cost of a three-course meal without drinks is given by £ signs.

£££££	Over £50
££££	£40–£50
£££	£25–£40
££	£15–£25
£	Under £15

THE MUSSEL INN

61–65 ROSE ST.

(0843) 225 5979 | mussel-inn.com

Delicately spiced mussels served by the kilo are the highlight at this aptly named restaurant just off Princes Street in Edinburgh's New Town. Fresh oysters and scallops also tempt from the menu. The Aberdeen Angus beef burger and the vegetarian pasta are a nod to non-fish-eaters. The relaxed atmosphere makes this a family-friendly destination.

££ 🖼 AE, MC, V

NUMBER ONE

THE BALMORAL, 1 PRINCES ST.

(0131) 557 6727 | roccofortehotels.com/hotels-and-resorts/the-balmoral-hotel/dining/number-one

Utilizing fresh Scottish produce to magnificent effect, Jeff Bland's Michelin-starred restaurant within the landmark Balmoral Hotel blows away all the old anachronisms about the quality of Scots cuisine. Fine food is complemented by fine wine and first-class service in a hotel restaurant that is anything but run of the mill.

£££££ 🕐 Closed Tues.–Wed. 🖼 All major cards

LA POTINIERE

34 MAIN ST., GULLANE

(01620) 843 214 | lapotiniere.co.uk

If you are looking for East Lothian's best restaurant then you don't need to look much farther than this relaxed local eatery. Here the focus is firmly on food, where the short but decadent menu features the likes of braised halibut, fillet of Scotch beef, and poached nectarines.

£££ 🕐 Closed Sun. dinner, Mon.–Wed. 🖼 All major cards

RED SQUIRREL

21 LOTHIAN RD., OLD TOWN

(0131) 229 9933 | redsquirreledinburgh.co.uk

This pub, located near the tourist area but not full of tourists, has a very fun and young atmosphere. While it specializes in burgers, it's fine simply to stop in for a drink, or you can go straight to the sticky toffee pudding.

£ 🖼 MC, V

RESTAURANT MARTIN WISHART

54 THE SHORE, LEITH

(0131) 553 3557 | restaurantmartinwishart.co.uk

For many visitors to Edinburgh this is the place to dine. Leith's most established Michelin-starred restaurant doesn't disappoint with the likes of roasted Scottish lobster and Ross-shire beef gracing the French-influenced menu. Indulge in the six-course tasting menu, available in vegetarian and fish-only versions. A set lunch is served Wednesday through Friday. Tables are at a premium, so reserve well in advance.

£££££ 🕐 Closed Sun.–Tues. 🖼 All major cards

WHITE HART INN

435 LAWNMARKET

(0131) 226 2806 | belhaven.co.uk/pubs/midlothian/white-hart

Self-described as "probably Edinburgh's oldest pub," this popular stop in the Grassmarket area of the Old Town may be touristy, but that doesn't mean it's not welcoming. It offers basic pub fare, plus Scottish folk music on some nights.

£ 🖼 D, MC, V

A sprawling cosmopolitan city that occupies the valley of the River Clyde, below the rolling hills of agricultural Ayrshire

GLASGOW & AYRSHIRE

Glasgow's bustling city center

GLASGOW & AYRSHIRE

Over the past decades, Scotland's largest urban center has been transformed from run-down industrial sprawl into one of Europe's most dynamic, culturally savvy, and enticing cities. A string of awards—not least as a UNESCO City of Music—has cemented its status. But further attractions await beyond the city center, around the River Clyde and out along the stunning Ayrshire coast.

Glasgow—or the "dear green place" as it poetically translates from its Gaelic moniker—is a bustling city that swirls in layers of history and

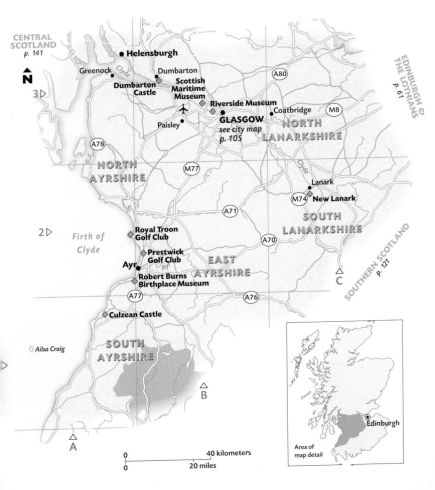

a vibrant sense of culture. In the decades following World War II, the days when Glasgow was the booming "second city of the empire" and Clyde-built ships ruled the waves, post-industrial decline set in. But Glaswegians have always been a passionate, spirited people, and they set about turning around perceptions of their city in the 1980s. Since then, Glasgow has been awarded the honor of European City of Culture and City of Architecture and Design. This meteoric renaissance was crowned by the vastly successful 2014 Commonwealth Games held in the city of Glasgow. This international sporting event brought not only glory to Scotland's athletes, but also an extreme financial boost to the city, providing new and polished tourist facilities and a rise in their global popularity.

A City Transformed

In recent years, massive development has transformed the city center. The area including once raffish Buchanan Street is now known as "Style Mile," laced with designer stores. The city has plenty of great places to eat and drink, frequented by a mix of working class, local pop stars, and hallowed soccer players.

While Glasgow may not have the immediate visual appeal of Scotland's celebrated capital, the more effort you put in, the deeper the rewards. Who cannot be charmed by a city that was once home to the seminal architect and designer Charles Rennie Mackintosh (1868–1928), who created some of Glasgow's finest buildings and who made such an impression on the world stage with his creative—yet practical—designs, which are unmistakably Glaswegian?

Beyond the city center and well off the beaten path, the Clyde Valley boasts the immaculately preserved New Lanark Heritage Centre, a world-class attraction. To the south, the rolling hills of Ayrshire were once the haunt of Scotland's most romantic poet, Robert Burns. ∎

GLASGOW CENTER

Glasgow's city center is easy to navigate—the uniform grid layout makes sightseeing simple, and all the main attractions are within walking distance. Much of the city center has been redeveloped, so the area is also alive with lively bars, cafés, restaurants, and smart stores.

City Center

In such a sprawling city, it can be hard to pinpoint Glasgow's exact center, but **George Square** is a good starting point. The square is handily sandwiched between the two main railway stations—**Central Station** and **Queen Street Station**—and lies in the middle of the urban grid of Georgian and Victorian architecture, a legacy of the city's industrial heyday. Take a seat on a bench and admire the grandiose **City Chambers** (*George Sq., tel 0141/287 2000, guided tours twice daily*), which appeared in a lavish swirl of Victorian pomposity in 1888 (and were inaugurated by Queen Victoria herself). Take a guided tour and walk through time to the days when the British Empire dominated the globe. Friezes of all the countries within the empire at that time cement the sense of Union swagger.

Nearby, the **Gallery of Modern Art** (*Royal Exchange Sq., tel 0141/287 3050, glasgowlife.org.uk*), also known as GoMA, focuses on contemporary artists.

Merchant City spreads its refined tentacles across a neat grid of stately streets immediately southeast of George Square. The elegant sandstone

■ Spiral staircase at the Mackintosh Interpretation Centre.

buildings were erected in the 19th century by ostentatious cotton and tobacco traders, as well as businessmen who grew rich from the blossoming shipyards. They now house residences, shops, bars, and restaurants. One of

Glasgow 🗺 100 B3 **Visitor Information** ✉ 158 Buchanan St.
📠 (0141) 566 4083 **visitscotland.com, peoplemakeglasgow.com**

INSIDER TIP:

A fun way to tour Glasgow is by bike. These can be easily rented on a pay-as-you-go basis from well-marked locations across the city, and returned to the same or another station when you're done.

—ANDREA WOLLITZ
National Geographic subsidiary rights manager

the most impressive redevelopments here is the **City Halls** *(Candleriggs, tel 0141/353 8000, glasgowlife.org.uk/whats-on/glasgow-life-tickets).* Luminaries as diverse as writer Charles Dickens (1812–1870) and comedian Billy Connolly (1942–) have performed here. Special events are held at the **Trades Hall,** Robert Adam's finest contribution to the city, which was built as a meeting place.

One block to the west of George Square lies **Buchanan Street—** Glasgow's "Style Mile." Much of Buchanan Street has been pedestrianized, making Glasgow one of the finest British shopping cities outside London. At the southern end of Buchanan Street is the sparkling redevelopment of the **St. Enoch**

• **Trades Hall** ✉ 85 Glassford St. ☎ (0141) 552 2418 **tradeshallglasgow.co.uk**
Buchanan Galleries ✉ 220 Buchanan St. ☎ (0141) 333 9898
buchanangalleries.co.uk

Centre *(st-enoch.com)*—a shopping and entertainment complex that's a telling symbol of new Glasgow. One block northwest on Buchanan Street is **Princes Square** *(princessquare.co.uk),* a stylish shopping mall that is home to a flurry of designer stores, niche shops, and multiple restaurants. The retail frenzy continues as you head

(continued on p. 106)

EXPERIENCE:
Under the Skin of Mackintosh

The unique architecture and design of Charles Rennie Mackintosh (1868–1928) is inexorably woven into the fabric of Glasgow. You can start along his trail at the **Mackintosh Interpretation Centre** *(The Lighthouse, 11 Mitchell Ln., tel 0141/276 5365, thelighthouse.co.uk).* City center sights include the **Glasgow School of Art** *(visitor center, 164 Renfrew St.),* **Willow Tea Rooms** *(217 Sauchiehall St.),* and the **Daily Record Building** *(20–26 Renfield Ln.).* In the West End, the highlight is the **Hunterian Art Gallery** *(University Ave.).* On the city fringes watch for the **Scotland Street School Museum** *(225 Scotland St., currently closed for refurbishment),* **Ruchill Church Hall** *(15–17 Shakespeare St.),* and the **Mackintosh Church** *(870 Garscube Rd.).*

WALK AROUND GLASGOW

With so many modern shopping malls and new building works, Glasgow city center may appear rather uninspiring on first impression. Take a closer look and you will see many interesting sights and sounds. Georgian- and Victorian-era buildings are all around—the legacy of the city as a major player in the expanding British Empire.

Rainswept George Square in the center of Glasgow

Leaving **George Square** on North Hanover Street, cut east along Cathedral Street to the landmark **Glasgow Cathedral ①** (*Cathedral Sq., glasgowcathedral .org.uk*). A church has stood here since the 12th century, but today's incarnation dates back to the 15th century. Some find the haunting cathedral a touch oppressive, but that perhaps misses the point—the building was meant to instill rectitude in its worshippers.

Just beside the cathedral, the **St. Mungo Museum ②** (*2 Castle St., tel 0141/276 1625, glasgowlife.org.uk*) is an ambitious attempt to portray the world's six major religions in a reconstruction of the medieval Bishops' Castle. For sheer uniqueness of vision,

it is worth visiting. The museum also organizes guided tours of the sprawling **Necropolis ③** (*glasgownecropolis .org*), which lies just across Wishart Street to the east. Here some 50,000 Glaswegians are buried in one giant ornate city of the dead.

Cutting south down High Street takes you to the unmistakable hulk of the **Tolbooth ④**. This used to be Glasgow's center, home to both the town hall and a prison. Now that the center has moved farther west, all that remains is this mighty 126-foot (38.5 m) tower topped with a clock that watches over the traffic below.

NOT TO BE MISSED:

Glasgow Cathedral • Necropolis • People's Palace • Gallery of Modern Art

Proceed south down the Saltmarket, and the city's favorite green lung, **Glasgow Green,** opens up to your left. The highlight is the **People's Palace ⑤** (*Glasgow Green, tel 0141/276 0788, glasgowlife.org.uk*), which tells an informal story of the city and its lively citizens.

Head back up the Saltmarket, and this time turn left at the Tolbooth to follow Trongate west to the **Tron Theatre ⑥** (*63 Trongate, tel 0141/552 4267,* *tron.co.uk*). Originally an old church, topped with a 16th-century steeple, the Tron was revamped in the late 1990s as a contemporary arts venue. Pop into the bar/restaurant and take the artistic pulse of this booming cultural city. More culture can be gleaned a stone's throw west at **Trongate 103** (*tel 0141/276 8380*), galleries and studios spanning the arts spectrum.

Pushing west, Trongate turns into Argyle Street, and you will pass under the massive Victorian expanse of **Central Station ⑦**. To find the station's grand main entrance, turn right up Hope Street and right again on Gordon Street. Step inside and look up at the colossal roof, which once filled with steam billowing out from the old

engines. Some of that glamour can still be felt as today's trains romantically set off in search of the old Clyde piers.

From the station, cut two blocks east to Buchanan Street and continue into **Merchant City** (see p. 102) through Royal Exchange Square to the imposing **Gallery of Modern Art ⑧** (see p. 102). Opened in 1996, GoMA is the most visited art gallery in Scotland, with a range of exhibitions, plus a children's creative area and a café.

See also area map p. 100
George Square
A half day
4 miles/6.4 km
George Square

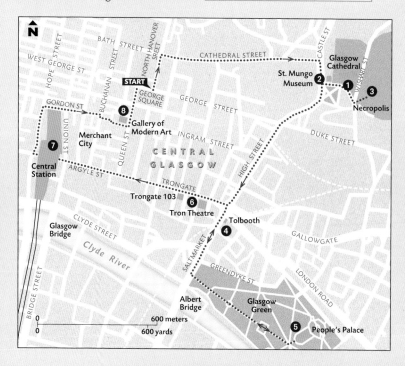

EXPERIENCE: Soccer in the City

Glasgow's two main soccer teams—Rangers and Celtic—together known as the "Old Firm," possibly garner as much support around the world as the national team does from their fun-loving and friendly "Tartan Army." Snaring a ticket for an Old Firm derby is tricky given the fierce rivalry between the two teams, but you can often find tickets for games with less demand online or by visiting their box offices in person. The same applies for friendly internationals. It's well worth the price of a ticket, since hearing the Tartan Army in full voice is a moving experience, not least for the weight of history that echoes around through their patriotic songs. **Rangers** *(rangers.co.uk)* offer guided tours of Ibrox Stadium as do **Celtic** *(celticfc.co.uk)* at Celtic Park and the **Scottish Football Museum** *(scottishfootballmuseum.org.uk)*, housed at Hampden Park.

north to the grand **Buchanan Galleries** shopping mall, just north of Georges Square. While here, pop into the iCentre information office within the mall; here you can buy tickets for the excellent open-top bus tours of the city *(citysightseeing.com/en/92/glasgow)*, as well as pick up a range of maps and leaflets. Immediately south of the mall, the junction with George Street is punctuated by the spire of **St. George's Tron** *(sgt.church)*, an imposing church built in 1808. To the north one block, at the upper end of Buchanan Street stands a patinated statue of a rather unimpressive-looking bespectacled man. Donald Dewar (1937–2000) was the inaugural First Minister of the first Scottish Parliament, which sat in Edinburgh in 1999—the first time in more than 300 years. Dewar sported a deep sense of intellect and patriotism, and he was a popular political leader.

Immediately beyond the statue, Buchanan Street ends with the **Royal Concert Hall** *(2 Sauchiehall St., tel 0141/353 8000, glasgowconcerthalls.com)*, home of the lively **Celtic Connections** music festival *(celticconnections.com)* in January, as well as a string of cultural events throughout the year. West of the concert hall is **Sauchiehall Street**—a much less salubrious shopping street and very much "old Glasgow." In 2008, Glasgow was named that year's UNESCO City of Music. The award was given in recognition of the litany of classical, folk, and pop musicians who have emerged from Glasgow over the years. The award also recognizes the fact that the city actively promotes music in all its forms. Famous Glaswegian musicians include Lulu and the late Lonnie Donnegan, as well as modern stars Franz Ferdinand and Glasvegas. The highlight of Glasgow's musical calendar is the Celtic Connections, but there are also regular concerts at a variety of other venues, from massive events at the SSE Hydro (see p. 111) as well as such eclectic spaces as **King Tut's Wah Wah Hut** *(kingtuts.co.uk)*, **Barrowland** *(barrowland-ballroom .co.uk)*, and the O_2 Academy *(academy musicgroup.com)*.

West End

Glasgow's West End is far less hurried and much greener than the city center, which is more in keeping with the city's "dear green place" origins. The West End was built later in the 19th century, however, when the city's wealthy looked for space and clean air. The West End is also a place of learning and culture—the home of Glasgow University and a collection of first-rate galleries and museums.

Kelvingrove Park: The large green lung of Kelvingrove Park is the star of the West End, and at its heart is the **Kelvingrove Art Gallery & Museum.** To call this fantastic museum/gallery just a museum or an art gallery is selling it way short. Within its palatial Victorian walls, you can see a Spitfire fighter plane soaring above, get up close and personal with an elephant, take in one of the most famous works of Salvador Dalí (1904–1989), "The Christ of St. John of the Cross," and then explore some of the mysteries of Egyptian mummies.

In all, more than 8,000 objects are on display in 22 state-of-the-art galleries, which make use of the excellent natural light and drama afforded by this massive building. For those

(continued on p. 110)

Kelvingrove Art Gallery & Museum ✉ Argyle St. ☎ (0141) 276 9599 **glasgowlife.org.uk/museums • Kelvin Hall** ✉ Argyle St. ☎ (0141) 276 1450 **kelvinhall.org.uk**

▫ "Old Firm" clashes between Glasgow Celtic and Glasgow Rangers echo with history; go with a local to best appreciate the songs and chants that celebrate past glories and air long-held animosities.

GLASGOW'S SHIPBUILDING MIGHT

Today, many of the remnants of Glasgow's once mighty shipyards and shipbuilding industry look rusty and forlorn. Delve deeper into their history and you can uncover an era when the city's bustling shipyards were alive with men and machines and half of the world's ships were "Clydebuilt"—a term that both reflected the origin of the ships and attested to their quality.

■ **The Riverside Museum spikes along the waterfront behind the** *Glenlee*

During the halcyon days of the British Empire (at its pinnacle from the late 19th to the early 20th century) Britannia really did rule the waves, and there was a huge demand for ships to sustain this maritime power and to meet the needs of Britain's burgeoning trade with the colonies. Some of the most famous ships in the world were Clydebuilt.

For shipyard owners Glasgow was on the "right" coast, with the River Clyde's easy access to Scotland's west coast, the Atlantic Ocean, and the Americas. The city also supplied an abundance of cheap labor, as well as plentiful coal and iron. Scotland's legendary prowess for great engi-

neering and a pioneering spirit aided Glasgow's shipbuilding boom.

In the glory days of the 19th century, shipyards stretched along the banks of the Clyde and thousands of workers poured into Glasgow from all over Scotland as well as Ireland. Production levels continued to grow to quite staggering levels, with 830,000 tons (760,000 tonnes) of shipping launched in 1913 alone!

A series of events that included the end of World War I, the Great Depression of the 1930s, the opening of cheaper shipyards abroad, and the advent of jet travel, combined to result in a dramatic decline in demand for Clydebuilt ships. During the 1960s and 1970s the Clyde shipyards plunged into a nigh terminal decline; something that was exacerbated by Margaret Thatcher's Conservative government, which put little value in protecting an industry it regarded as archaic and unprofitable. In Glasgow unemployment and social deprivation became serious problems.

In recent years Glasgow's surviving shipyards have made themselves more efficient and there are some bright signs. In 2014, BAE Systems was contracted to build three new ships for the Royal Navy, the first of 32 frigates since commissioned through 2023. And Ferguson Marine is a leader in wind turbine fabrication, a growth area for the Clyde waterfront.

The Riverside Museum

The best place to learn more about Glasgow's shipbuilding heritage is at the great **Riverside Museum** *(100 Pointhouse Pl., tel 0141/287 2720, glasgowlife.org.uk)*. Housed in a spiky modern structure by the late architect Zaha Hadid, it is situated fittingly on the site of the old Inglis Shipyard, where the Clyde meets Glasgow's other river, the Kelvin. This expansive space shows how transport in Scotland developed through the centuries and has a host of interactive exhibits that make a visit here really enjoyable. It has justifiably won a number of international awards, including the European Museum of the Year Award (EMYA).

The Riverside Museum cost £74 million (US$120 million). It was money well spent, as it is one of Glasgow and Scotland's most visited attractions, with in excess of 3,000 objects on show. They range from model shipyards, which rotate in a large glass display cabinet and entertain younger visitors, to exhibits more aimed at adults, such as one on the Lockerbie disaster and a phalanx of old trams and trains.

The museum focuses on getting people involved rather than just looking at "hands-off" exhibits. Three mock historic streets invite you to walk through the years, popping into shops and cafés that date from 1895 through the 1980s. Another highlight is the chance to board an old Glasgow subway train, dating back to 1896, when the carriages were first constructed. Kids love to try the 90 large touchscreens peppered throughout this interactive museum, and can even help put out a fire with an interactive fire engine. Allow at least an hour or two for your visit, and don't be surprised when you end up staying much longer.

The Riverside's cafés include one on the ground floor with views out across the Clyde, that great shipbuilding river that brought Glasgow its golden age, the story of which the Riverside Museum tells in detail.

The *Glenlee*

The *Glenlee,* a tall ship moored right outside the Riverside Museum, is a three-masted barque whose air draft (the distance from the water to the tip of the tallest mast) is 137 feet and 6 inches (almost 42 m). It's a real throwback, a traditional sailing ship that was built in 1896 during the heyday of the Glasgow shipyards. Be sure you go aboard this piece of floating heritage. The artifacts on her four decks tell her story and also shed light on the city's shipbuilding and maritime heritage. For younger visitors there is a mini cinema and an under-fives play area in the cargo hold, with a café on hand for all the family *(150 Pointhouse Pl., tel 0141/357 3699, thetallship.com, admission free for groups of 8 or fewer).*

with an interest in history, an exhibition that explores how the nation's view of itself has evolved through its art is particularly compelling. So, too, is the exhibit about the remote Scottish islands of St. Kilda—handy for those unable to get out there. Of course, the city's most famous artistic son, Charles Rennie Mackintosh (1868–1928; see sidebar p. 103), has a room to himself, displaying some fine examples of his trademark furniture.

INSIDER TIP:

For a 360-degree view of Glasgow, climb the tower at The Lighthouse, Scotland's center for design and architecture, then explore its floors of interwoven exhibits.

—ANDREA WOLLITZ
*National Geographic
subsidiary rights manager*

Younger visitors are catered to as well, with plenty of interactive displays to keep them busy.

Immediately southwest of the Kelvingrove, on Argyle Street, looms **Kelvin Hall.** Serving as an exhibition hall since it was built in 1927, this mixed-use art and exhibition space includes storage (guided tours only) for Glasgow Museums' more than 400,000 items not otherwise displayed.

Glasgow University: North though Kelvingrove Park along Kelvin Way, the greenery spreads out in all directions as you approach Glasgow University. Grand sandstone buildings make this quarter feel more like a historic castle than a university, but you will still see students strolling around as they have done since 1870. The university has a visitor center if you want to learn more about the various buildings and statues. It can also organize tours up the university's voluminous tower, which offers sweeping views out across the city.

At the university's heart is the **Hunterian Museum and Art Gallery** *(University Ave., tel 0141/330 4221, gla.ac.uk/hunterian),* known for possessing the largest collection of paintings outside of Washington, D.C., by James Abbott McNeill Whistler (1834–1903). The collection consists of 80 oil paintings, a range of drawings and watercolors, and more than 2,000 prints. The gallery also houses works by the renowned group of painters known as the Glasgow Boys, represented by Sir James Guthrie (1859–1930) and Edward Hornel (1864–1933), as well as a small collection of work by the Scottish Colourists, including the movement's leading figure, John Duncan Fergusson (1874–1961). The museum also celebrates the work of Glasgow's celebrated creative genius, Charles Rennie Mackintosh (see sidebar p. 103), including an interior of his home—the pieces of his

Glasgow University ☎ (0141) 330 2000 gla.ac.uk/explore/visit/ •
The Lighthouse ✉ 11 Mitchell Ln. ☎ (0141) 276 5365 thelighthouse.co.uk

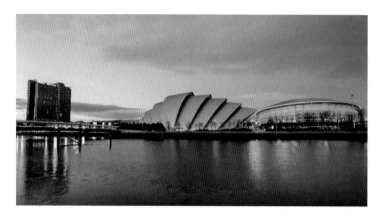

■ **The SEC Armadillo and its neighbor, the SSE Hydro Arena, on the River Clyde**

work that he deemed good enough to live with every day. Admission to the Mackintosh House is limited to a dozen visitors for self-guided tours *(£)*.

Just a five-minute walk from the gallery, off University Avenue, is one of the loveliest little lanes in the city and something of a local secret. **Aston Lane** is a cobbled gem lined with graceful stone buildings that house a sprinkling of bars, cafés, and restaurants. At the end of this exquisite lane is the city's most bohemian thoroughfare—**Byres Road**—which is also replete with eating and drinking venues, as well as stylish boutiques.

Around the Clyde

The River Clyde suffered post-industrial neglect for decades before its recent reinvention. In place of hulking shipyards (see pp. 108–109), the Clyde now sports a string of welcoming visitor attractions, as well as modern architecture. Today, tour boats and seaplanes fly its deeply historic waters.

The North Bank: The most impressively revamped stretch of the river lies west of the striking **Clyde Arc,** known affectionately as the "Squinty Bridge" due to the unusual angle at which it straddles the Clyde. Visible on the north bank is the sprawling **Scottish Event Campus** (SEC)—two dramatic, futuristic, and purely functional spaces that house music concerts and other events. The westernmost building is the distinctive **Armadillo** performance venue (seemingly inspired by the animal), designed by Lord Norman Foster (1935–), who also designed the adjoining **SSE Hydro Arena,** a concert and sports venue resembling a flying

Armadillo & SSE Hydro Arena ⊠ Scottish Exhibition and Conference Center, Exhibition Way ☎ (0141) 248 3000 **sec.co.uk**

saucer. Outside on the riverside rises the **Finnieston Crane,** preserved for shipbuilding heritage reasons. To the west, the old pumphouse that controlled Queens Dock houses the new **Clydeside Distillery,** offering tours and tastings. Beyond spikes the distinctive **Riverside Museum** (see p. 108), showcasing Glasgow's rich transport heritage.

The South Bank: Across a pedestrian bridge, facing the SEC on the opposite bank of the river, lies a brace of glass and steel structures that house the British Broadcasting Corporation (BBC) and Scottish Television (STV) companies, as well as the popular **Glasgow Science Centre** *(50 Pacific Quay, tel 0141/420 5000, glasgowsciencecentre.org, £££).* The main building—the giant titanium and glass **Science Mall**—holds an innovative visitor attraction spread across three stories. The museum emphasizes interactive displays and gadgets, which appeal to younger visi-tors. Here you can meet Madagascan hissing cockroaches, make your own hot-air balloon, conjure up a rocket to launch, and visit the planetarium.

Part of the Science Centre complex is the **Glasgow Tower** *(££),* which is Scotland's tallest freestanding structure at 417 feet (127 m). It's also the world's tallest fully-rotating tower, as the entire structure revolves 360 degrees. In good weather, you can take an elevator up to a viewing platform for unparalleled views of the city. This riverside complex also contains an **IMAX Cinema** *(tel 0141/420 5000),* showing educational movies on Scotland's biggest screen.

Farther to the south, within Pollock Country Park, is one of the greatest art collections ever gathered by a single person, with more than 9,000 objects. The renowned **Burrell Collection** *(2060 Pollockshaw Rd., tel 0141/287 2550, burrellcollection.com)* spans ancient Chinese art through medieval armor to French Impressionist paintings. ∎

Clydeside Distillery ✉ 100 Strobcross Rd. ☎ (0141) 212 1401 $ £££
theclydeside.com

▪ The Glasgow Science Centre on the South Bank of the River Clyde

BEYOND THE CITY CENTER

Glasgow is Scotland's largest city, and its suburbs radiate into the surrounding countryside. The suburbs eventually trail off into satellite towns that lie on the banks of the Clyde and south into Lanarkshire, which is home to one of Scotland's top attractions, New Lanark.

■ An 18th-century cotton mill on the banks of the River Clyde in New Lanark

One of the most interesting Glasgow overspill towns is **Dumbarton.** While depressing postwar housing characterizes most of the town, shining through the gloom is the mighty **Dumbarton Castle,** which sits atop a volcanic crag and stares out across the Clyde, guarding Glasgow from the threat of marine invasion. Indeed, Dumbarton was the staging post for its own invasion

in 1548—that of Mary Queen of Scots, when she set sail for France in her quest to become queen of the country.

If you caught the shipbuilding bug during your travels in Glasgow, you may want to check out the **Denny Ship Model Experiment Tank** (*Castle St., Dumbarton, tel 01389/763 444, scottishmaritimemuseum.org/dumbarton, £*), part of the Scottish Maritime

Dumbarton Castle 🗺 100 B3 ✉ Castle Rd., Dumbarton ☎ (01389) 732 167 💲 £ **historicenvironment.scot**

INSIDER TIP:

If you're planning to visit a lot of sights, an Explorer Pass (*historicenvironment .scot*) is a good investment. The 7-day pass grants free access to many historic sites nationwide.

—LARRY PORGES
National Geographic author

Museum. Denny Tank is the site of the world's oldest testing tank, which has launched a thousand ships.

A little farther north, on the train line from Glasgow, is elegant **Helensburgh.** Once a popular seaside resort for holidaying Glaswegians, Helensburgh has an air of nostalgia about it. It is now best known as the birthplace of John Logie Baird (1888–1946), the engineer who invented the first working television. You can sample some of the history

Helensburgh 🗺 100 A3 **The Hill House** ✉ Upper Colquhoun St., Helensburgh ☎ (01936) 673 900 💲 ££ **nts.org.uk/visit/hill-house**

EXPERIENCE: Cruise Aboard the *Waverley*

One of the most memorable and unique ways to visit the islands of the Firth of Clyde is onboard the PS *Waverley* (*Waverley Terminal, 36 Lancefield Quay, Glasgow, tel 0041/243 2224, waverleyexcur sions.co.uk*). The last seagoing paddle steamer in the world regularly plies the islands and ports of the River Clyde May through August, with a few sailings in September and October. One of the most spectacular routes takes passengers from Glasgow to Rothesay on the isle of Bute.

The original *Waverley* was sunk during the evacuation of Dunkirk in 1940. Her successor, one of the last paddle steamers built after World War II, was launched on June 16, 1947. She spent much of her time cruising from Craigendoran "doon the watter" to the

Firth of Clyde resorts, whose beaches in those days were as busy as the beaches of Hawaii are today.

Taking a trip on the *Waverley* is like delving through a history book. Feel the years peel back as you listen to an accordion performance, take in the scenery from the sundeck, nip down to the gleaming engine room, or hear the horn toot "hello" to those on shore watching for this distinctive ship bedecked in her signature colors, with a white and black hull topped with eye-catching red, black, and white funnels.

The future of the *Waverley* is perennially in doubt given the massive costs of maintaining this historic vessel. By taking a trip on her you are very much helping preserve one of the world's most precious ships.

of Helensburgh at **The Hill House,** immaculately and inspirationally crafted inside and out by another of Helensburgh's most famous sons, Charles Rennie Mackintosh (see sidebar p. 103).

New Lanark

Heading in a southeasterly direction, the Clyde narrows and starts to meander across the bottom of a large valley gripped by new developments. Beyond the town of Lanark itself is the World Heritage site of **New Lanark.** This 18th-century cotton mill is so valuable, both historically and socially, that UNESCO has given it a place on its protected World Heritage List. Your first port of call should be the visitor center, where you can learn of the enlight-

ened industrialists who founded the village in 1785 to make cotton on a grand scale, using the River Clyde as a source of power. Mill manager Robert Owen (1771–1858) made history by providing his workers with the world's first day nursery, as well as schooling for children to the age of 12. Owen realized that workers' well-being, culture, and education were vital to improve production and quality.

Highlights include the Annie McLeod Experience Ride, during which the "ghost" of a mill girl leads an unorthodox tour of life in the 1820s. Children can dress in period garb for a seat in Robert Owen's school. Leave time to follow the riverside walkway to the impressive **Falls of Clyde,** a trio of waterfalls. ∎

New Lanark 100 C2 New Lanark Rd., Lanark (01555) 661 345 ££ **newlanark.org**

The Hill House by Scottish architect Charles Rennie Mackintosh

AYRSHIRE

Ayrshire extends south from the last of the Clydeside shipyards on the Firth of Clyde down to the Irish Sea, which impresses with sweeping, sandy beaches and world-famous golf courses. County town Ayr is most famous as the birthplace of Robert Burns, Scotland's Shakespeare.

■ **Attractive gardens surround the imposing Culzean Castle.**

Golf

Ayrshire is prime farming country, but the area is best known as the home of several of Scotland's top links golf courses, including the two biggest hitters: Prestwick Golf Club and Royal Troon. Billing itself as the "Birthplace of the Open," **Prestwick,** founded in 1851, hosted the first British Open in 1860 (and for years thereafter) and is packed with desert-sized bunkers, rollercoaster greens, and magnificent

ocean vistas of Arran.

Just to the north, **Royal Troon**—the "Royal" addition awarded in 1978—boasts a trio of courses, in the form of the Old Course, Portland, and the nine-hole Craigend. The back nine on the signature Old Course may justly lay claim to be the most challenging in the world. Ayrshire is home to countless other courses, both public and private, which share gorgeous views out over sandy beaches toward the isle of Arran and Ailsa Craig.

Robert Burns

First and foremost, Ayrshire is Burns Country. Scotland's Shakespeare is venerated as a king in Alloway, the sleepy village to the south of Prestwick and Royal Troon, where he was born in 1759. It is fitting that the **Robert Burns Birthplace Museum** is located here. Make the **Burns Cottage** your first stop: It was here, as the bitter winter winds swirled all around, that one of the world's great romantics and lyricists burst into the world—the man who gave the world "Auld Lang Syne," among myriad other classics. Travel the "poet's path" over to the

Prestwick Golf Club 2-4 Links Rd., Prestwick ☎ (01292) 477 404 **prestwickgc.co.uk • Royal Troon Golf Club** 🗺 100 A2 ✉ Craigend Road, Troon ☎ (01292) 311 555 **royaltroon.co.uk**

museum, then spout some poetry over fresh-baked scones at the on-site café. A short stroll leads to the large Grecian-style **Burns Memorial** and the ruins of **Alloway Auld Kirk.** Look for the resting place of Burns's father, William Burnes, and his sister Isabella Burns Begg among the gravestones.

Castle Country

By far the most dramatic building in all of Ayrshire, and one of Scotland's most impressive castles, is **Culzean Castle,** located 12 miles (19 km) south of Ayr on the south Ayrshire coast. Once the residence of the Marquess of Ailsa, parts of this mighty structure date back to the 15th century. Constant additions and embellishments, however, made it more grand country house than serious fortified castle. The first port of call is the visitor center, where an excellent audio-visual presentation sheds light on the castle's eclectic history. Then explore the huge collection of armaments shipped up from the Tower of London back in 1812. Look too for the Oval Staircase—the work of seminal Scottish architect Robert Adam (see sidebar right)—who revamped much of the original medieval interior in his unique style between 1772 and 1790. You can see his table and chair designs as well. Then take a stroll in the vast castle grounds.

Also in Ayrshire are the ruins of **Dunure Castle,** perched dramatically on a cliff edge overlooking Ayr

Bay about 5 miles (8 km) south of Ayr. The fortified **Dundonald Castle** *(Dundonald, tel 01563/851 489, £ dundonaldcastle.org.uk),* once home to the grandson of King Robert the Bruce, has high vaulted rooms plus a visitor center, museum, and café. If time allows, more grand houses in the area include **Dean Castle** *(tel 01563/554 743, deancastlecountrypark.com),* with its collection of weapons, armor, and musical instruments; **Kelburn Castle** *(tel 01475/568 685, kelburnestate.com, £),* which offers a variety of family-friendly activities; and **Portencross Castle** *(tel 01294/823 799, portencrosscastle.org.uk),* tended to by dedicated local volunteers. ∎

Adam's Style

Robert Adam (1728–1792) was born in Fife, Scotland, the son of an architect. He traveled to Italy, where he studied the classical style, and returned to Britain with new ideas. Adam rebelled against the then dominant Palladian style. While still drawing on classical influences, his innovative light, elegant lines refused to follow slavishly classical proportion and decoration. His final project was Culzean Castle, which he remodeled in stages between 1772 and 1790 to make the most of its outlook over the sea.

Robert Burns Birthplace Museum 🗺 100 A2 ✉ Murdoch's Ln., Alloway ☎ (01292) 443 700 💲 *££* **nts.org.uk/visit/places/robert-burns-birthplace-museum** • **Culzean Castle** 🗺 100 A1 ✉ Near Maybole, Ayrshire ☎ (01655) 884 455 💲 *£££* **nts.org.uk/visit/places/culzean**

Where to Eat & Drink in Glasgow & Ayrshire

THE 13TH NOTE
50–60 KING ST.
(0141) 533 1638 | 13thnote.co.uk
Functioning as an independent music venue (which also hosts theater and art) while simultaneously maintaining a high rating for its vegetarian and vegan selections, the bar is the perfect place for vegetarians, vegans, and meat-eaters alike. Favorites include dahl, falafel wraps, spicy bean burgers, chili burritos, Indonesian rainbow salad, and sticky toffee pudding.
£ MC, V

AYRSHIRE FOOD HUB
CROSSROADS, HURLFORD
(01560) 324 335 | crossroadshub.org.uk
Deep in Ayrshire's agricultural heartland, close to Prestwick and Troon, this welcoming, community-run farm shop and café with a conscience celebrates all things local with satisfying sandwiches, salads, and snacks, and such hearty dishes as classic fish 'n' chips and Scottish breakfasts.
£–££ MC, V

THE BEN NEVIS
1147 ARGYLE ST.
(0141) 576 5204 | thebennevisbar.com
This great atmospheric pub has a particularly large selection of whiskies and a knowledgeable and friendly staff. Live traditional Celtic music is featured several days a week, usually with at least one fiddler and a dog or two joining in. Stop in for a dram or one of the many craft beers.
£ MC, V

CAFE GANDOLFI
64 ALBION ST.
(0141) 552 6813 | cafegandolfi.com
Lovely wooden furniture, ambient mood lighting, and a creative menu have ensconced Cafe Gandolfi at the top of Glasgow's informal dining scene for more than 40 years. The seasonal menu might include haggis, courgette orzo risotto, Finnian smoked haddie (haddock), and smoked venison.
££–£££ AE, MC, V

HIDDEN LANE TEAROOM
1103 ARGYLE ST.
(0141) 237 4391 | hiddenlanetearoom.com
As the name suggests, this wonderfully quirky spot is hidden down an alley, nestled in a corner behind two buildings in the Finnieston section of Glasgow's west end. The selection of delectable afternoon teas will turn anyone into a tea fiend. Vintage crockery, homemade cakes, and tasty sandwiches will warm your heart and stomach. Breakfast, lunch, and afternoon tea only.
£ MC, V

MOTHER INDIA'S CAFÉ
1355 ARGYLE ST.
(0141) 339 9145 | motherindia.co.uk
Contemporary décor and spicy Indian cooking that shies away from an endless list of sauce-laden curries distinguish Mother India from the competition. More unusual dishes on the small menu include spiced haddock; lamb, leek and mint; and chili garlic chicken.
££ AE, MC, V

RALPH & FINNS
23–25 ST. VINCENT PL.
(0141) 248 5636 | ralphandfinns.co.uk
Housed in the former headquarters

P Parking   🕐 Opening Hours   Credit Cards

PRICES

An indication of the cost of a three-course meal without drinks is given by £ signs.

£££££	Over £50
££££	£40–£50
£££	£25–£40
££	£15–£25
£	Under £15

of the Bank of England's Scottish base, this elegant brasserie—formerly Urban Bar & Brasserie—was recently rebranded, the old dark woods giving way to more contemporary décor, from relaxed and airy in the Garden Room to clubby in the Boardroom. The kitchen conjures up excellent Scottish fusion dishes under the baton of Chef John-Paul Lappin. *££–£££* MC, V

SCOTIA BAR

112 STOCKWELL ST.

(0141) 552 8681 | belhaven.co.uk/pubs/lanarkshire/scotia-bar

The Scotia Bar is renowned among Glaswegians for its live music. Visit this traditional boozer—apparently the oldest pub in the city, established in 1792—Thursday through Sunday and you've got a good chance of hearing anything from country and folk to blues or jazz (especially later in the evening). A good selection of beer, ales, and spirits is also complemented by a small menu that offers good home-cooked pub food (note, no food served on Sunday or evenings).

£ AE, MC, V

SORN INN

35 MAIN ST., SORN, MAUCHLINE

(01290) 551 305 |

At the heart of a picturesque village, this gastropub belies an unassuming exterior with its Michelin-starred fine-food brasserie, where an unpretentious

seasonal menu features superb Scotch beef and fresh seafood dishes supported by a fine wine list. Ever changing gourmet grazing and tasting menus are also offered.

££££–£££££ MC, V

UBIQUITOUS CHIP

12 ASHTON LN.

(0141) 334 5007 | ubiquitouschip.co.uk

With a Scottish menu dictated by the season and delivering delights like venison haggis, organic Orkney salmon, Aberdeen Angus steaks, and Caledonian oatmeal ice cream, the Ubiquitous Chip is a strong contender for the title of Glasgow's best fine-dining restaurant, all with an artistic flair. Lighter fare can also be enjoyed in the Upstairs Brasserie and Rooftop Terrace (the city's only rooftop bar), and the Whisky Bar awaits for post-prandial tipples.

£££ MC, V

■ **Tea and scones at Hidden Lane Tearoom**

The rolling hills of Dumfries, Galloway's dramatic coastline, and the green fields and heather-clad hills of the Borders region

SOUTHERN SCOTLAND

Galloway Forest Park is famous for its stunning natural beauty.

SOUTHERN SCOTLAND

Although southern Scotland is often overlooked by visitors heading north to Edinburgh and Glasgow, or farther afield to the Highlands, the area has much to offer. The district of Dumfries and Galloway boasts lush forests and a rugged coastline, while the Borders' crumbling abbeys speak of the region's turbulent history.

Dumfries & Galloway

Created when the historic counties of Dumfriesshire and Galloway were merged in 1975, the district of Dumfries and Galloway has a range of attractions, from the beautiful coastal towns of Kirkcudbright and Portpatrick to the trail of Rabbie Burns in bustling Dumfries. The many picturesque villages and castles scattered across the Dumfries and Galloway countryside reward curious explorers. Castles to keep an eye out for include Kennedy and Caerlaverock, while the abbeys of Dumfries and Galloway are less well known than those of the Borders but equally charming.

Natural attractions include the spectacular coastline dubbed "Scotland's riviera," which unfolds along the Solway Firth in the south; the beautifully windswept Rhinns of Galloway on the edge of the Irish Sea to the west; and Galloway Forest Park, which includes part of the Southern Upland Way. This popular walking route cuts through the heart of Dumfries and Galloway and on across the Borders.

The Borders

Scotland and England battled for control

of the region known as the Borders for centuries. Spreading across 1,800 square miles (4,600 sq km), the Borders stretch from the rolling hills and moorland in the west, through gentler valleys and high agricultural plains, to the rocky east coastline. Add pretty market towns, dramatic ruined abbeys, and some of the most attractive country houses in Britain, and it is easy to understand why people fall deeply in love with the region.

The star attractions are undoubtedly the Border abbeys, home to Cistercian and Augustinian monks in the 12th to 16th centuries, but now in ruins. The rolling hills and snaking River Tweed also have plenty to offer. Melrose is the epitome of what is so appealing about the Borders, with its impressive abbey, independent shops, affordable hotels and restaurants, and rich literary history—this is Sir Walter Scott country, after all. The Borders are great for active types, too, with some of the best hiking and biking Scotland has to offer. The Borders are awash with country houses and castles given the region's rich history and strategic importance. The pick of the bunch are Floors Castle near Kelso, Traquair House near Peebles, and the astonishing Abbotsford—Sir Walter Scott's own home. ■

NOT TO BE MISSED:

Sampling fresh seafood in the charming coastal resort of Portpatrick   128

Hiking or biking in Galloway Forest Park's forested hills   129

The charming town of Melrose, set between the River Tweed and rolling hills   132, 136

Glimpsing the legacy of the monastic orders that once lived at the Border abbeys   133–135

Enjoying some of the freshest fish with your chips in the working seaport of Eyemouth   138

DUMFRIES & GALLOWAY

From the warm beaches of "Scotland's riviera" to the rolling hills of Dumfriesshire, Scotland's most southwesterly region is a far cry from the rugged mountains of the Highlands. Its historic towns, once home to the poet Robert Burns, have much to offer lovers of art and literature.

■ Dumfries town center fountain, built of iron in 1882

Dumfries

Ayrshire may have been the birthplace of Robert Burns (1759–1796; see pp. 116–117), but the market town of Dumfries also claims a strong link to Scotland's national poet—he spent the last five years of his life here and is immortalized in a magnificent marble statue on the High Street. Burns was very much a man of the people, however, and much preferred the busy company of a pub to being put on a pedestal. The **Globe Inn** *(56 High St., tel 01387/323 010, globeinndumfries.co.uk)* was his favorite local drinking den; on its Burns-themed tour you'll hear of his notorious affairs with a barmaid, who bore his child. The **Robert Burns House,** where the poet died at the age of 37,

Dumfries 🗺 122 C2 **Visitor Information** ✉ 64 Whitesands, Dumfries ☎ (01387) 253 862 **visitscotland.com/places-to-go/dumfries-galloway** • **Robert Burns House** ✉ Burns St., Dumfries ☎ (01387) 255 297 **dgculture.co.uk/venue/robert-burns-house**

INSIDER TIP:

Threave Castle sits on a wee island in the middle of a river. Ring the bell and a boatman will come to take you over for a tour.

—JIM RICHARDSON
National Geographic photographer

is a more conventional memorial. His widow, Jean Armour, lived here until her death more than 30 years later. The most interesting exhibits are his personal letters and handwritten notes. On the same bank of the River Nith lies the neoclassical **Mausoleum,** where his body lies.

Across the River Nith, the **Robert Burns Centre** (*Mill Rd., tel 01387/264 808, dgculture.co.uk/venue/robert-burns-centre-2*) illuminates Burns's connections with Dumfries in the charming setting of an old watermill. The highlight is the excellent audiovisual presentation (*£*) in the center's cinema, which screens contemporary films outside museum hours.

Galloway

Kirkcudbright, 27 miles (43 km) southwest of Dumfries, is the star of the "Scottish riviera"; this relaxed waterfront oasis comes complete with a working fishing harbor. Today, Kirkcudbright has become more popular with artists than fisherfolk, with an active local community attracted by the quality of the light. Other sights include the remains of sturdy **Mac Lellan's Castle** as well as **Broughton**

(continued on p. 128)

Kirkcudbright 🏔 122 C1 • **MacLellan's Castle** ✉ Castle St., Kirkcudbright ☎ (01557) 331 856 🕐 Closed Nov.–March 💲 £ **historicenvironment.scot** • **Broughton House & Garden** ✉ 12 High St., Kirkcudbright ☎ (01557) 330 437 🕐 Closed Nov.–Feb. 💲 £ **nts.org.uk/visit/places/broughton-house**

Gretna Green Weddings

The town of Gretna Green in southern Dumfriesshire is a place long associated with secret marriages and romance. This tradition dates back to 1753, when a law was passed in England that prevented those under 21 from marrying without their parents' consent. As this law did not apply to Scotland, Gretna Green, just across the border on the main road to Glasgow, became a favorite spot for young English couples who wanted to marry. Scottish law allowed pretty much anyone to carry out marriages, and Gretna Green's blacksmiths performed so many ceremonies that impulsive marriages became known as "anvil weddings." Although the legal loophole was closed in 1853, the town's romantic history still draws thousands of couples every year to marry or renew their vows.

WALK: THE GALLOWAY COAST

Walking along the high cliffs north of Portpatrick, with the wind whipping up from the Mull of Galloway, it's hard not to feel that you have traveled far into the wild, empty country of the Highlands. This walk on a portion of the Southern Upland Way quickly whisks you into spectacular Rhinns of Galloway, only a few miles from civilization.

Looking north to Killantringan Lighthouse near Portpatrick

NOT TO BE MISSED:
Portpatrick • Sandeel Bay•
Killantringan Lighthouse

With its clutch of excellent hotels, pubs, and restaurants, the charming seaside town of **Portpatrick** is a popular base for those who wish to explore the dramatic coastline of the Rhinns of Galloway. The town is the western terminus of the Southern Upland Way, a 212-mile (340 km) hiking route that goes all the way to the North Sea coast. You don't have to travel great distances, however, for an invigorating and rewarding hike, nor do you have to forsake the comforts of a Portpatrick hotel in the evening.

Start this walk in the parking lot at **Portpatrick harbor ❶**, where an information board provides a primer on the Southern Upland Way (you can also consult *dgtrails.org/southern-upland-way* for route maps and details). The path rises steeply north from the harbor on a staircase cut through the layered rock of the cliffs. Look back toward the town as the steps kink their way up the steep slope and you will see the desolate ruin of **Dunskey Castle,** a 14th-century tower-house that stands high on the cliffs south of Portpatrick. This walk only takes you on the first few miles of the Southern Upland Way, so don't be daunted by the waymarkers that say there's more than 200 miles to go!

From the top of the stairs, the path runs along the cliff top beside Portpatrick golf course. After about a mile (1.5 km), you will reach the picturesque **Sandeel Bay ❷**. This beach was once popular with bathers, but there are few around today who would be willing to dive into its cold waters. Instead, visitors admire the caves and waterfalls at the edges of the beach. Continue north from the beach, up another staircase cut into the cliff. This one is a little narrower and rougher, so be careful where you step. The same advice applies to the path beyond, which hugs the cliff edge for a few minutes as it makes its way around to the next bay, **Port Kale ❸**. Here two peculiar hexagonal huts are the only remains of the first tele-graph connection between Scotland and Ireland. The steps up from this bay are steeper than the previous ones, but there is a railing for support as you climb.

For the next 1.5 miles (2.4 km) the route takes you across the open head-land above the cliffs to Killantringan Lighthouse. From the high points of this path you will get your first glimpses of the lighthouse, and on a clear day this is a good vantage point to watch the fer-ries making trips between Cairnryan and Belfast. At low tide, it's also possible to see what remains of the *Craigantlet* con-tainer ship that ran aground in 1982. The attractive white and yellow **Killantrin-gan Lighthouse** ❹ is privately owned and no longer in operation, but the out-crop of Black Head on which it stands provides great views along the coast,

including the broad sandy beaches of Knock Bay to the north.

From here you can either retrace your steps along the coast, or, if you prefer to take a circular walk, follow the single-track road inland. After 1.3 miles (2 km) this road will meet with the B738 road to Portpatrick. Turn right at the junction and follow the road south. The B738 sees slightly more traffic than the track from the lighthouse, but has broad verges for pedestrians to walk on. Follow this road for about 2 miles (3.2 km) before turning right when it joins the A77 on the out-skirts of Portpatrick. From here follow the road around 0.5 mile (1 km) into town, passing the village's war memorial and church before turning right again onto Dinvin Street, which takes you the short distance back to the harbor and your starting point in the parking lot.

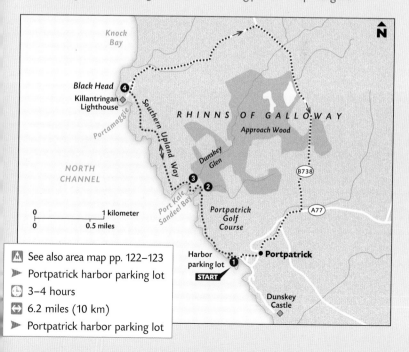

🗺 See also area map pp. 122–123

➤ Portpatrick harbor parking lot

🕐 3–4 hours

↔ 6.2 miles (10 km)

➤ Portpatrick harbor parking lot

■ Drumlanrig Castle, once home to the Dukes of Buccleuch.

House & Garden, a gorgeous 18th-century town house now open as a museum that offers insight into the town's artistic connections. Also worth visiting is the dramatic ruin of **Threave Castle,** stronghold of the Black Douglasses. Accessible only by boat, it stands on an island in the River Dee around 10 miles (16 km) north of Kirkcudbright. Both MacLellan's Castle and Threave Castle were closed for restoration at press time.

On clear days, **Portpatrick**, on Galloway's west coast, offers views of Northern Ireland hovering on the horizon of the Irish Sea. This charming vil-lage of whitewashed and pastel-painted houses curls around a sweeping bay and boasts several cozy hotels and ex-cellent seafood restaurants. No longer a major port for ships heading for Northern Ireland, Portpatrick is now basking in a tranquil retirement. It is the western terminus of the **Southern Upland Way,** a 212-mile (340 km) coast-to-coast hiking trail (see pp. 126–127), as well as a good base for exploring the western flank of the region on local walks.

Castles & Abbeys

A number of abbeys, castles, and country houses tempt many visitors

Threave Castle ✉ Threave Castle, Castle Douglas ☎ (07711) 223 101 🕐 Closed Nov.–March 💲 £ **historicenvironment.scot** • **Portpatrick** 🗺 122 A1

heading out of Dumfries. North lies a chunky Renaissance gem, **Drumlanrig Castle,** built in 1691 by the first Duke of Queensberry, himself an architect, using pink sandstone. The 80,000-acre (32,000 ha) estate also boasts a country park and a Victorian garden and is a popular mountain bike venue. Guided tours of the castle offer access to one of the finest private art collections in Scotland—the Buccleuch Collection—which includes works by Thomas Gainsborough (1727–1788) and Rembrandt van Rijn (1606–1669). The lavish reception rooms are the highlight of the interior and offer a glimpse into the lifestyles of the dukes and duchesses who have called Drumlanrig home through the centuries.

The deeply romantic ruin of **Caerlaverock Castle** (tel 01387/770 244, historicenvironment.scot, £) lies 7 miles (11 km) south of Dumfries in Glencaple. Dating from the 15th century, the castle sports a unique triangular design and a double moat. Walk around the outside and you can see right inside the very skeleton of the castle, thanks to a battering by invading armies. Cross into the castle itself, and you will have to use your imagination as the castle now lies in ruins. A modest visitor center looks at its history and the bitter sieges its inhabitants once endured.

Drumlanrig Castle 🏛 122 C2
☎ (01848) 331 555 🕐 Castle tours certain days April–May, Fri.–Mon. July–Aug.; Garden closed Oct.–March 💲 Castle £££; Gardens £ **drumlanrigcastle.com**

Take time to explore the grounds on the network of walking trails, including one that reveals the foundations of an earlier fortification.

Farther west from Caerlaverock you'll find a trio of ruined Cistercian abbeys. The well-preserved **Sweetheart Abbey** (tel 01387/850 397, historicenvironment.scot, £) lies just 5 miles (8 km) south of Dumfries. It was commissioned and later named by Lady Devorgilla in the 13th

EXPERIENCE:
Cycling in Galloway Forest Park

A number of excellent trails open up the unspoiled scenery in and around Galloway Forest Park (0330/067 6900, forestryandland.gov.scot). The **Round the Loch** trail takes in an easy 14-mile (22.5 km) route around Clatteringshaws Loch. Perhaps the most popular trail, the **Palgowan** leaves from Glentrool Visitor Centre and makes an 8-mile (12.9 km) circuit along forest roads, quiet back roads, and small hills. Bikes are for rent at **The Break Pad** (Kirroughtree Visitor Centre, tel 01671/401 303, thebreakpad.com) in Newton Stewart, which is within easy biking distance of the park. There are three park visitor centers: **Kirroughtree** and **Glentrool** both near Newton Stewart, and **Clatteringshaws** near New Galloway.

century as an enduring tribute to her late husband. Further west, some 6 miles (10 km) east of Kirkcudbright, **Dundrennan Abbey** *(tel 01557/ 500 262, historicenvironment.scot, £)* took English monks about 50 years to build in the 12th century. Here Mary Queen of Scots spent her last night before being boated off to England, never to see her beloved Scotland again.

Built in the 12th century, **Glenluce Abbey** lies much farther west, just as the land narrows into the Rhinns of Galloway peninsula, 55 miles (88 km) west of Dumfries Most of the abbey is now a ruin, but the chapter house survives intact and is well worth a visit to gaze over the grotesque characters that adorn the corbels and ceiling bosses. You can look at artifacts, including decorated floor tiles and pottery items, in the museum.

Some 7.5 miles (12 km) west of Glenluce Abbey, you'll find ruins of the last grand castle, **Castle Kennedy,** set within extensive gardens. In fact, you get two castles for the price of one. The original castle was destroyed by fire in 1716, but its ruins can still be seen around the more recent **Lochinch Castle,** which overlooks the White Loch.

Natural Attractions

The wide sweep of the Solway Firth is the main attraction in the south of Dumfries and Galloway. It is dotted with coves and sandy bays, perfect for cycling or driving around. There are plenty of places to stay and camp on "**Scotland's riviera,**" a mild holiday oasis popular with Scots but little known farther afield.

The **Southern Upland Way** (see pp. 126–127) runs through the heart of Dumfries and Galloway, and the best place to appreciate its beauty is **Galloway Forest Park**—Britain's largest forest park (see sidebar p. 129). This bucolic oasis stretches its tentacles over 300 square miles (776 sq km) of brooding hills and silvery lochs and is considered to be one of the world's best star-gazing spots. The land is rich in myths and legends, most poignantly that the Scottish king Robert the Bruce hid away here before uniting his country in victory against the "Auld Enemy," England. If you are short on time, focus on **Glentrool**—home to the impossibly pretty Loch Trool. There are plenty of trails for cyclists and walkers.

The scenic **Rhinns of Galloway** peninsula, at the southwesternmost point of the region, is surrounded on three sides by the Irish Sea. To appreciate the views, head to its southern extremity—and Scotland's most southerly point—the **Mull of Galloway.** Here it will often just be you, the wildlife, and the lonely lighthouse blinking out a warning to ships to avoid this treacherous stretch of coast. ∎

Dundrennan Abbey 🄰 122 C1 ☎ (01557) 500 262 🕒 Closed Oct.–March 💲 £ **historicenvironment.scot** • **Glenluce Abbey** 🄰 122 A1 ✉ Glenluce ☎ (01581) 331 856, Wed.–Sat.; (01581) 300 541, Sun.–Tues. 🕒 Closed Oct.–March 💲 £ **historicenvironment.scot** • **Castle Kennedy** 🄰 122 A1 ✉ Stair Estate, Rephad ☎ (01776) 702 024 🕒 Closed Nov.–Feb. 💲 £ **castlekennedygardens.com**

THE BORDERS

The Scottish Borders are no longer the disputed "Badlands" between warring Scotland and England, but there is a rich legacy of those troubled days, with ruined abbeys, castles, and grand country houses complementing attractive market towns and excellent hotels and restaurants.

■ **Picturesque Kelso on the banks of the River Tweed**

Peebles

Less than an hour's drive south of Edinburgh is Peebles, one of the most attractive towns in the region. Flanked on three sides by rolling hills, and on the other by the wide sweep of the mighty River Tweed, this prosperous little oasis is an excellent base. The busy **High Street** speaks of a Victorian golden age, with a sprinkling of little delis and specialist shops.

Just a few minutes' walk upstream from the town center the landscape becomes much more wild. Here the River Tweed is lined by parks and open land, and a footpath takes you along the pebble-fringed banks of the river toward the imposing bulk of **Neidpath Castle** (today a deluxe boutique hotel). Looking at this 14th-century tower-house from the river, you can still see the damage inflicted when it was attacked by Oliver Cromwell's army during the English Civil War (1642–1651).

Another walk, following a disused railway line from Peebles all the way to Innerleithen, passes through the village of Cardona (also reached via the

Peebles 🗺 123 D3 **Visitor Information** ✉ 23 High St., Peebles
☎ (01721) 728 095 **visitscotland.com • Neidpath Castle** ✉ Peebles
☎ (01721) 720 333 💲 **neidpathcastle.com • Kailzie Gardens**
✉ Kailzie, Peebles ☎ (01721) 720 682 💲 £ **kailziegardens.com**

B7062). Here you will find the beautiful walled **Kailzie Gardens,** the result of many decades of work finding plants that can tolerate the brutally harsh winters this exposed site experiences.

Farther along the road from Kailzie, 5 miles (8 km) south of Kelso, is the ancient **Traquair House.** According to some, this is Scotland's oldest inhabited house. The current occupants trace their family line back to the 15th century. Built in the style of a fortified manor, its facade is exquisite in its whitewashed simplicity. You can explore the stately rooms and vaulted cellars as well as the grounds, with a maze and wandering peacocks.

Off the B712, 8 miles (13 km) south of Peebles, awaits the oasis of **Dawyck Botanic Garden***(tel 1721/760 254, rbge.org.uk/visit/dawyck-botanic-garden, £)*, known for its trees. Wander among the flowering shrubs and through the Beech Walk, then enjoy the gardens over tea and cake at the cozy café.

Tweed Valley

The River Tweed is one of the defining features of the Borders landscape, marking the eastern half of the border between England and Scotland. It flows from the hills around Peebles to the English border town of Berwick-upon-Tweed.

A neat and charmingly attractive old market town, **Melrose** sits in a scenic fold of hills on the riverbanks. The cobbled town center, awash with cobbles and sturdy stone buildings, attest to its deep sense of continuity and tradition. Its history is dramatic, as for centuries this was serious "Border Country," with tensions between England and Scotland often boiling over into skirmishes

(continued on p. 136)

Traquair House 123 D3 Innerleithen (01896) 830 323 Closed Nov.–March £ traquair.co.uk • **Melrose** 123 E3 **visitscotland.com**

The Borders Railway

The reopening of the Borders Railway *(scotrail.co.uk/inspiration-hub/great-scenic-rail-journeys)* in 2015 marked the completion of a landmark rail project. Spanning 30 miles (48 km), it was the longest stretch of line to be reopened in U.K. history (the original line closed in 1969). It was also a massive moment for Borders tourism, providing direct connection to and from Edinburgh. Seven new stations were built as part of this project, including the terminus at Tweedbank, a 5-minute taxi ride from both Melrose Abbey and Sir Walter Scott's grand old mansion at Abbotsford. The pleasant train journey takes passengers out of Edinburgh's urban sprawl in search of the rolling hills of the Borders. Look out for special steam train services that run in August and September, and experience how people traveled in days gone by.

BORDER ABBEYS

The Scottish Borders have always been home to passions, struggles, and strife. The region has always been a spiritual place, too, as its great abbeys attest. Today the Border Abbeys are a necklace of ruins, which have lain in various states of disrepair since they were sacked by English invaders centuries ago. But while only hinting at their former glory, the abbeys have lost nothing of their charm and romance, although most were closed at press time for safety assessment and repairs.

The majestic Abbey Church dominates the pink- and red-tinted stone ruins of Melrose Abbey.

The Border Abbeys were founded during the reign of King David I of Scotland, who invited a quartet of monastic orders to build their abbeys in the Borders in the 12th century. King David wanted to demonstrate that his power extended even to the southern fringes of his kingdom. Over the years, the orders grew wealthy in their own right and started to wield their own power.

Once the grandest of 12th-century structures, the magnificent **Kelso Abbey** (*Abbey Row, Kelso, no tel, historicenvironment.scot*) was devastated as the land disputes between Scotland and England raged on. However, the striking Romanesque design still reveals itself in the ruins, and you can conjure up some of what life would have been like for the Benedictine

At Kelso Abbey, arched cloisters invite the visitor to walk in the footsteps of medieval monks.

monks who lived here. Take note of the towers and transepts that were part of the unusual double-cross design.

Jedburgh Abbey *(Abbey Bridge End, Jedburgh, tel 01835/863 925, historicenvironment.scot, £)* also endured centuries of attack, yet even today its majesty is a reminder of King David I of Scotland's message to England. In commissioning such a grand design, he wanted to prove that his country held sway over the Borders. The abbey was built on the site of a much earlier church, dating back to the 700s. At one stage, the abbey was heavily fortified, but it was eventually destroyed by the Scots to keep it from falling into English hands.

The remains of the abbey still cast an unmistakable presence on the local skyline and dominate the approach to the town. Jedburgh Abbey is the best one to visit on a rainy day since it has a good visitor center, where you can take in a short audiovisual show. The center is also home to the abbey's greatest treasure, the priceless Jedburgh Comb. This beautiful artifact, carved from wal-

INSIDER TIP:

Visit Melrose Abbey on an afternoon in fall, when the pink stonework of its walls positively glows as the sun sinks in the west.

—TIM HARRIS
National Geographic contributor

rus ivory, dates back over a millennium.

Hidden among the trees on a horseshoe bend in the River Tweed 10 miles (16 km) west of Kelso are the striking ruins of the medieval **Dryburgh Abbey** *(tel 01835/822 381, historicenvironment .scot, £)*. Although not as well preserved as the other abbeys, it still provides insight into the cloistered lives of the resident monks. The church has long since fallen, but large parts of the monastic quarters survive. Dryburgh Abbey is a place of pilgrimage for visitors who admire the work of the great Sir Walter Scott, whose grave lies in the chapel of the abbey—an understated granite monument unlike the overblown "rocket" that bears his name in Edinburgh. Long after its destruction in 1544, the abbey was acquired by the Earl of Buchan. At the end of the 18th century he worked to preserve the ruins and had formal gardens planted in the grounds.

Perhaps the most romantic of all the abbey ruins are those of **Melrose Abbey** *(Abbey St., Melrose, tel 01896/822 562, historicenvironment.scot, £)*. According to some, the ghost of Scotland's greatest warrior king lives on at Melrose Abbey—Robert the Bruce's heart is believed to have been laid to rest here. The Scottish monarch is said to have wanted his heart to be taken on a crusade to the Holy Land—to atone for his brutal murder of a political rival years earlier—but this request was not carried out. Extra weight was given to the idea that it lies at Melrose Abbey when a casket containing a heart was discovered in 1997.

Take the stairs up the abbey's tower for sweeping views across Melrose and the surrounding hills. Melrose Abbey's elaborate design incorporates dramatic Gothic touches to spice up the original Cistercian designs. The intricacy and creativity of the stone carvings is remarkable—gargoyles of pigs playing bagpipes being particularly memorable. Delve into the museum if you want to learn more about the expert stonemasonry.

A view of Jedburgh Abbey built by King David I of Scotland

EXPERIENCE:
Fishing in the Tweed

The Tweed offers excellent fishing with well-organized sport for visitors. The easiest way is to organize a trip through your hotel or a local tour operator. You can also seek out a permit to fish from a tackle store such as **Orvis** (*11 The Square, Kelso, tel 01573/225 810, orvis.co.uk*) or **Peeblesshire Trout Fishing Association** (*peeblesshiretrout-fishing.co.uk*).

The Tweed is one of the top salmon fishing rivers in the world, so the highlight is the chance to catch wild salmon as they make their journey upstream in the autumn. The Tweed boasts a bounty of trout, too. Some hotels, including **Ednam House Hotel** (*ednamhouse.com*) arrange fishing, while the **Tweed Foundation** (*rivertweed.org.uk/fishing*) is a good starting point for planning your trip.

a fishmonger, a wine merchant, and a well-stocked deli. A sprinkling of cafés, tearooms, and restaurants serve up the local produce.

Melrose Abbey (see p. 135) in the center of town is the starting point for **St. Cuthbert's Way** (*stcuthbertsway.info*), which is one of many excellent walking trails that run in and around Melrose. This 62-mile (100 km) trail continues across the border to Lindisfarne monastery in England. Follow the trail south out of town, and you will find yourself among the **Eildon Hills,** where it is relatively easy to climb up and enjoy a panorama that encompasses the Tweed Valley and a huge swath of the Borders, with England visible in the distance.

Seminal Scottish writer Sir Walter Scott built his mansion, **Abbotsford,** about 2 miles (3 km) to the west of Melrose. Born in Edinburgh's Old Town in 1771, Scott grew to become Scotland's most celebrated and prolific novelist (see p. 53). In his final years, the building of the grand Abbotsford retreat came back to haunt Scott as the writer struggled financially, working himself into an early grave in 1832. The great writer lived here for two decades, from 1812 onward, although building work continued for almost half that time. The exterior of this grand stately mansion borrows from a variety of architectural styles—Scottish baronial is perhaps the most striking. The rooms open to the public offer unique insight into the life and times of the novelist,

and battles. The windswept landscape around Melrose has long been associated with the quasi-mythical "Border Reivers"—bands of medieval raiders who stole livestock and took part in inter-tribal warfare. Melrose is proud of its traditional stores—first-rate butchers,

Abbotsford 🅰 123 E3 ✉ 2 miles (3 km) W of Melrose ☎ (01896) 752 043 🕐 Closed Dec.–Feb. 💲 £ **scottsabbotsford.com** • **Kelso** 🅰 123 E3 Visitor Information ✉ **visitkelso.com**

with the eclectic displays including a lock of Rob Roy's hair and the cross Mary Queen of Scots took to her execution. Also of note is the visitor center, modern café, and the opportunity to stay in what were the private living quarters of Scott's descendants.

If you are blazing the Scott trail, you should visit **Scott's View,** 3 miles (4.5 km) east of town. This was the writer's favorite overlook—the Eildon Hills rising up above a broad bend in the River Tweed, with thick forests and lush greenery filling in the rest of the picture-postcard view. So enamored was Scott by the view that it is said that his horses stopped here unprompted. His funeral cortège passed by here, too, as his last farewell to the landscape he loved.

The main attraction of the historic town of **Kelso,** 15 miles (24 km) east of Melrose, is **Floors Castle.** Despite the name, this is a grand country house, one set in a vast estate on the banks of the River Tweed. For centuries it has been the lavish country seat of the powerful dukes of Roxburghe. Completed in 1721, Floors Castle is steeped in history and romance. In the early 20th century, Henry John Innes-Ker (1876–1932), the eighth Duke of Roxburghe, married a beautiful young American, Mary Goelet, who was not only an heiress, but arrived complete with her own superb collection of fine art and tapestries. Many are still on display and make a pleasant distraction from the family portraits. Between the two world wars, the ballroom underwent a revamp, and it now evocatively conjures up the spirit of the 1930s.

Acres of scenic grounds and gardens surround the castle. Here, too, you'll find a children's adventure playground, cafés, gift shops, and even a hotel and championship golf course. There are also stores in which you can buy produce that comes from the grounds of the estate. Kelso itself unfurls in Georgian grandeur around the confluence of the Tweed and Teviot Rivers, which are spanned by a trio of bridges. It has always been a strategic town, sacked and rebuilt on numerous occasions. The grand main square is the place to start a walk. The **Town Hall** is a large building with a clock that towers over the cobbled plaza below. You can also follow a riverside walk from the main square, which starts down Roxburghe Street and leads off to Floors Castle.

Mellerstain House is another outstanding stately home, located 5 miles (8 km) northeast of Kelso. It is particularly noteworthy as it involved the work of the architect William Adam (1689–1748) and his gifted son Robert Adam (1728–1792; see sidebar p. 117).

A few miles to the southeast stands **Paxton House.** One of Britain's finest Palladian stately homes, it is replete with fine antique furniture plus paintings from the National Gallery of

Floors Castle ✉ Roxburghe Estates, Kelso ☎ (01573) 223 333 🕐 Closed Oct.–Mar. 💲 ££ **floorscastle.com • Mellerstain House** ✉ Gordon, Berwickshire ☎ (01573) 410 225 🕐 House closed Tues.–Thurs. 💲 ££ house; £ garden **mellerstain.com • Paxton House** ✉ Paxton ☎ (01289) 386 901 🕐 Closed Nov.–March 💲 ££ **paxtonhouse.co.uk**

■ Wild waters on the rocky coast of St. Abbs Head National Nature Reserve

Scotland, and the estate boasts Scotland's only functioning waterwheel. The turbulent history of the Borders is commemorated each summer when hundreds of riders take part in the annual **Common Ridings,** or Marches, that take place across the region *(returntotheridings.co.uk).* There are 11 festivals in all, which hark back to the 13th and 14th centuries, when townsfolk were forced to patrol their town's boundaries on horseback to ensure their rivals were not encroaching on the common land.

The Borders Coastline

The Borders region boasts some fine beaches along its small stretch of coastline. **Eyemouth** is a busy fishing village and a great place to sit with a steaming "poke" of fish and chips as gulls call overhead and trawlers ease out of the harbor. The **Eyemouth Museum,** housed in an old church, is worth a visit if only to see the Eyemouth Tapestry, created by 20

local women in the 1980s. It depicts the disaster in 1881 when a wild storm wiped out the fleet, killing more than 100 fishermen and crippling the town. The pretty old fishing village of **St. Abbs** *(Coldingham St., Abbs, tel 01890/771 672, stabbsvisitorcentre.co.uk)* lies about 4 miles (6.4 km) north of Eyemouth, and you can take a scenic cliff-top walk between the two towns.

Nearby, the rocky headlands of **St. Abbs Head National Nature Reserve** harbor a large seabird colony—thousands of guillemots, razorbills, and kittiwakes nest on the cliffs in spring and early summer, while shearwaters and skuas arrive in late summer. Check in at the visitor center for the best walk for the time of year, and consider one of the excellent takeout lunches from the coffee shop to fuel your trek. The St. Abbs Lighthouse, atop St. Abbs Headland and located at the end of a waymarked trail, is a fabulous place to take in a broad sweep of coastal scenery. ■

Eyemouth Museum ✉ Auld Kirk, Manse Rd., Eyemouth ☎ (01890) 751 701 🕐 Closed Sun. & Nov.–March 💲 £ **eyemouthmuseum.co.uk**
• **St. Abbs Head National Nature Reserve** ☎ (01890) 771 443
🕐 Visitor Center closed Nov.–March **nts.org.uk/visit/places/st-abbs-head**

Where to Eat & Drink in Southern Scotland

PRICES

An indication of the cost of a three-course meal without drinks is given by **£** signs.

£££££	Over £50
££££	£40–£50
£££	£25–£40
££	£15–£25
£	Under £15

BURT'S HOTEL

MARKET SQ., MELROSE

(01896) 822 285 | burtshotel.co.uk

It's easy to see why this busy restaurant in the Burt's Hotel (see Travelwise p. 346) has become something of a Melrose institution. Service is polite but not too formal, and the food is consistently good. Venison, duck, halibut, fillet steak, and Stornoway black pudding are just some of the delights you might find. The Old World feel of the dining room adds to the charm.

£££ P MC, V

THE HOEBRIDGE

HOEBRIDGE RD E., GATTONSIDE

(01896) 823 082 | thehoebridge.com

This airy, simple, stylish bistro-style restaurant is run by self-taught chef Hamish Carruthers who prepares monthly menus that showcase mouthwatering internationally influenced local dishes. Typical treats include roast cod and braised squid with chorizo, potato, and aioli, and lamb with rosemary mashed potatoes and red-currant sauce.

££–££££ Closed Sun.–Tues.
AE, MC, V

KNOCKINAAM LODGE

PORTPATRICK

(01776) 810 471 | knockinaamlodge.com

The lovely restaurant at this beautiful country house hotel (see Travelwise pp. 344–345) is open to nonguests. The food on the four-course prix-fixe menu is divine but often gives only one choice of dessert, so advise staff about any special dietary requirements in advance. The superb wine list caters to all wallets, with moderately priced fine wines sitting alongside budget-busting vintages.

£££££ P AE, MC, V

OSSO

1 INNERLEITHEN RD., PEEBLES

(01721) 724 477 | ossorestaurant.com

This chic café-restaurant with its mirrored walls, polished wood, olive green upholstery, and designer lampshades doesn't just deliver style. Chef Ally McGrath has an excellent cooking pedigree and he brings his expertise to every aspect of the menu, from lighter lunches to the superb dinner dishes like braised hare and hand-dived scallops. In the evenings a tasting menu that makes the most of local seasonal produce is also available.

££ Closed Sun.-Tues.
AE, MC, V

THE SHIP INN

1 FLEET ST., GATEHOUSE OF FLEET

(01557) 814 217 | theshipinngatehouse.com

The award-winning restaurant The Ship Inn has kept the standards high with food that is a cut above your average pub grub. The menu makes the most of Scottish produce and includes the likes of beef, lamb, pork, and venison. This inn also offers overnight accommodations, with breakfast and an option for a packed lunch. **££** P MC, V

The very heart of rural Scotland, the gateway between
the southern lowlands and the mountainous Highlands

CENTRAL
SCOTLAND

◼ Sailing ships moored on the banks of the Crinan Canal in Argyll

CENTRAL SCOTLAND

An easily accessible wonderland of attractive lochs and rugged mountain backdrops, central Scotland has an equally epic history to match. With heather-clad mountains, brooding lochs, and romantic castles, it is Scotland in microcosm.

Central Scotland is swathed in history—the heartland of William Wallace, the real life "Braveheart," and heroes such as Robert the Bruce and Rob Roy, who stamped a permanent mark on the nation. It is also blessed with wonderfully scenic landscapes: silvery sea lochs, an attractive coastline, and a backdrop of rugged mountains.

The city of Stirling is home to Scotland's most strategic castle, which proudly stands on guard at the gateway north to the Highlands. The castle is steeped in history—and it's home to the ghosts of William Wallace and Robert the Bruce. Nearby at Bannockburn, Scotland scored its most famous victory over the "Auld Enemy" in 1314. A memorial and a visitor center tell the story, while the Wallace Monument stands as a proud and defiant testament to the Scots' enduring love of the country's greatest patriot and martyr.

Central Scotland is also home to what became Scotland's first national park in 2002. Loch Lomond and The Trossachs National Park spreads across a vast swath of Scotland. The loch is the largest body of freshwater in Britain and a real leisure oasis. The Trossachs, meanwhile, are a smaller-scale version of the Highlands' peaks, whose slopes are much more accessible to walkers and cyclists. This, combined with the first-rate tourist facilities, makes the Trossachs ideal for visitors short on time.

Oban & the West

To the west, Argyll and the Cowal Peninsula shimmer around the Irish Sea. Despite its many attractions, and the fact that it is easily accessible from Glasgow, the area remains off the main tourist routes. Scotland's busiest ferry port, Oban, lies on the west coast and tempts visitors with graceful stone buildings, a distillery, and world-class seafood. Just inland, Loch Awe remains a local secret and a much less touristy escape than Loch Lomond and Loch Ness.

NOT TO BE MISSED:

The romantic Kintyre Peninsula juts out into the sea toward Ireland in a forgotten stretch of quiet roads, half-abandoned towns, and sweeping sandy beaches. Part of the same finger of land—but not actually part of the Kintyre Peninsula—is the trim town of Inveraray. Sitting on the shore of Loch Fyne, Inveraray is as historic and welcoming a town as any in Scotland and a great base for exploring this remarkable region.

Perthshire

Moving back east toward a slew of sinewy lochs, you will enter Perth-shire. The capital, Perth, is an unsung urban star with lively restaurants and cultural scenes. The rest of this affluent county is alive with Munro mountains (peaks more than 3,000 feet/914 m high), sweeping lochs, and historic castles. It is also home to Scone Palace—once the crowning place of the Scottish kings and home of the Stone of Destiny. With so much history, drama, and beautiful scenery, central Scotland is a must-see for any visitor to the country—a visit that is made much easier by the excellent transportation links. ■

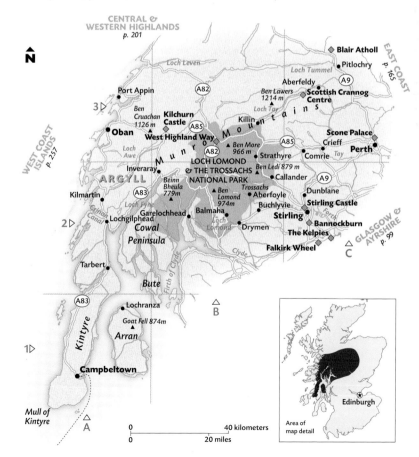

STIRLINGSHIRE

Stirling may be something of a newcomer as a city, but it is one of the most deeply historic places in Scotland. Tucked between the waterways of the Clyde and Forth—and guarded by the surrounding hills—Stirling and its historic county overflow with attractions.

Surrounded by cliffs on three sides, Stirling's castle has long been an important fortification.

Everyone from the Scots and the English, right back to the Romans, have fought for control of Stirling, such is the city's strategic importance. And they have all left their indelible marks.

Stirling Castle

The historic legacy is most obvious at Stirling Castle, used by James IV (r. 1488–1513), James V (r. 1513–1542), and Mary Queen of Scots (r. 1542–1567). In the palace you'll find some impressive Renaissance sculptures and the renovated Great

Hall, where Scottish monarchs of old once wined and dined their guests. The Castle Exhibition gives you the necessary historical background, and informative guided tours are included in the ticket price (audio tours in many languages carry an added fee).

The views from the cliff-top castle are sublime, with one flank staring back down the throat of the River Forth to the east, while the Trossachs, Ochils, and the Pentland Hills vie for attention to the west. Look too for the **Stirling Bridge,** where William Wallace's heavily

Stirling 142 C2 **Visitor Information** ✉ Old Town Jail, St. John St. ☎ (01786) 475 019 **visitscotland.com** • **Stirling Castle** 142 C2 ✉ Castle Wynd, Stirling ☎ (01786) 450 000 ⑤ £££ **historicenvironment.scot**

outnumbered men crushed the previously untouchable English in 1297.

Stirling Old Town

The castle is without doubt Stirling's main attraction, but spare a couple of hours for the fascinating **Old Town Jail,** which you see as you descend toward the town. After stopping in at the helpful Visit Scotland iCentre, you can meet "Stirling's nastiest prison warden" and learn about the experience of being locked up under the harsh regime of a Victorian jail through a highly entertaining performance tour (offered every 30 minutes) great for families.

The attractions don't end there, though, and on the same route into town there is also the well-preserved **Argyll's Lodging—**a graceful 17th-century town house *(entry fee included in ticket to Stirling Castle; closed for restoration at press time)*—as well as the **Church of the Holy Rude** *(St. John St., tel 01786/475 275, holyrude .org),* with one of the last surviving medieval timber roofs in the country. Here, in 1567, infant James VI was crowned King of Scotland. Call ahead if you wish to book a guided tour.

A little farther east you come to the attractive and historic Old Town, where the ambience is reminiscent of Edinburgh's Royal Mile. Many buildings date back to the 16th and 17th centuries

Old Town Jail ✉ St. John St., Stirling ☎ (01786) 595 024 🕑 Closed Nov.-Jun. 💲 £ **oldtownjail .co.uk • Doune Castle** ✉ Castle Rd., Doune ☎ (01786) 841 742 💲 ££ **historicenvironment.scot**

and Stirling's golden age as a royal burgh. This area is magical at night. Go for a moonlit walk and you may get it all to yourself.

About 15 minutes north of Stirling Castle, tucked strategically between steep slopes and two waterways, is medieval **Doune Castle.** With an imposing keep and vast great hall, this small outpost of the powerful Regent Albany comes alive via an excellent audio tour narrated by actor Terry Jones, aiding your imagination to conjure up the great banquets and parties of the past. It may look familiar, as it has been used as a film location for *Monty Python and the Holy Grail* as well as television's *Outlander* and *Game of Thrones* series; these are referenced for avid fans as special "stops" on the audio tour. You

Wallace Monument

One sight you cannot miss from Stirling Castle is the imposing stone skyscraper of the Wallace Monument *(Hillfoots Rd., just outside Stirling, tel 01786/472 140, nationalwallace monument.com, ££).* It is worth the short trip east of Stirling to see this grand Victorian statement and enjoy the sense of history. Be warned: The narrow 246 steps spiral up some 220 feet (67 m) to the top (there are good views from the base as well). After three levels of exhibits, you end up surveying a scene that overflows with history. Pick up an audio tour before you start. A 15-minute hike leads from the visitor center to the tower, or hop on the complimentary bus.

■ **The mighty Kelpies are the largest equine sculptures in the world.**

can clamber all over this relatively small fortress, taking in views of Ben Lomond, the Menteith Hills, and the River Teith from the ramparts.

Bannockburn

The famous battlefield of Bannockburn lies 2 miles (3 km) south of Stirling. This is the site of the famous Scottish victory over the English in 1314—where King Robert the Bruce led his brave but seriously outnumbered warriors into a fight to the death with the professional English army that had marched north to crush Scotland's desire for independence. Not only did Bruce's men win, but they annihilated "proud Edward's army" and "sent them back tae think again," as Scotland's unofficial national anthem, "Flower of Scotland," famously celebrates.

The mighty equestrian statue of a somber but defiant-looking Bruce shows the esteem in which he is still held, and the excellent **Battle of Bannockburn Visitor Centre** *(Glasgow Rd., Whins of Milton, tel 0 1786 812 664, nts.org.uk/visit/places/bannockburn, ££)* provides Robert the Bruce's full story and that of the nation he so spectacularly led. Book your tickets ahead for a timed entrance to "take part" in the battle via an interactive experience (or view your participating friends or family from the gallery above), and meet characters from the past through other innovative displays. Then explore the battleground itself. Two great days to be in Bannockburn are June 23 and 24, when volunteers dress in period costume and reenact Scotland's most famous battle against the "Auld Enemy." Other reenactments occur on occasion; check the website for more information.

Continuing south on the M9 into the historic county of Stirlingshire, follow the brown signs for the country's most popular public art project of the

past century, **The Kelpies.** You will see
the two glinting horse heads from the
road well before you wind your way to
the parking lot, but that won't prepare
you for their size. They are situated
within a family-friendly park, **The Helix,** so named for its distinctive shape
as seen from the air. The park also
hosts food kiosks, an adventure zone,
splash area, and miles of pathways to
walk or cycle. The Kelpies, named
for mythical shape-shifting creatures
of Scottish legend, are the work of
Scottish sculptor Andy Scott. Constructed of 928 skin-plates of pierced
stainless steel—an acknowledgement
to Falkirk's once-prominent place in
the iron industry—and modeled after
two Clydesdale horses from Glasgow,
they do seem to shift in mood with
the changing light (they are also lit
from within after dark). A helpful
visitor center, café, and a 30-minute

tour that brings you inside one of the
horse sculptures add to the experience.

Follow the Forth & Clyde Canal
about 4 miles (6 km) west to another
modern marvel, the **Falkirk Wheel.**
The world's only rotating boat lift,
it continues the heritage of Scottish
engineering expertise. This innovative design solved the problem of a
demolished staircase of 19th-century
locks. The wheel became the show-
piece of the successful Millennium
Link project *(millenniumlink.org.uk),* re-
establishing sea-to-sea navigation of
Scotland's canals. You can watch the
wheel in action from the visitor center,
or experience the lift yourself on an
hour-long boat trip. ∎

 **The Falkirk Wheel's rotating boat
lift may have been inspired by a
Celtic double-headed spear.**

The Kelpies 🄽 142 C2 ✉ Helix Park, Falkirk ☎ (01324) 590 600
🅂 Tour: £ **thehelix.co.uk** • **Falkirk Wheel** ✉ Lime Rd., Tamfourhill,
Falkirk ☎ (0300) 373 0868 🅂 Boat trip: ££ 🕓 Closed Mon.–Tues. Nov.–
March **scottishcanals.co.uk**

THE TROSSACHS & LOCH LOMOND

For those short on time, or who are confining their trip to Scotland's central belt, the Trossachs is the perfect "Highlands in Miniature" experience, with rugged hills, pristine lochs, and attractive towns.

The ever changing sky over Loch Lomond and The Trossachs National Park

Loosely speaking, the Trossachs is the area of wooded glens and braes that unfurls west of the twin towns of Callander and **Aberfoyle** and sweeps off in search of the famously "bonny bonny banks" of Loch Lomond (see pp. 150–151). In fact, Loch Lomond forms the western boundary of the area and is usually grouped with it as Loch Lomond and The Trossachs National Park. An enjoyable way into the Trossachs is along the scenic route west from Stirling to Aberfoyle, which takes you over the flat Carse of Stirling and past the serene **Lake of Menteith.** One of the few bodies of water known as a "lake" in Scotland, this is a lovely spot on a sunny day, where you can enjoy a boat ride out to the 13th-century ruins of **Inchmahome Priory** *(closed for restoration at press time)* before having lunch at the gracious **Karma Lake of Menteith Hotel** *(Port of Menteith, tel 01877/385 258, lake-hotel.com),* which reclines right on the water's edge.

Exploring the Area

To delve deeper into the Trossachs, drive, cycle, or take a bus up the vertiginous road that heads north from Aberfoyle and traverses the Duke's Pass to Callander. This winding trail takes you into a hilly wonderland blessed with mighty forests that occasionally give way to reveal stunning

Aberfoyle 🏔 142 B2 **Visitor Information** ✉ Trossachs Discovery Centre, Main St. ☎ (01877) 381 221 **visitscotland.com** • **Inchmahome Priory** ✉ Island in Lake of Menteith, reached by boat from pier at Port of Menteith ☎ (01877) 385 294 🕐 Closed Nov.–March 💲 £ **historicenvironment.scot**

views of glacial lochs. Check that the road is open before planning a trip during the winter months, when the snow and ice often close it.

Of all the hills in this area there are two that deserve special attention. **Ben A'an** (1,488 feet/454 m) is less than an hour's walk from the parking lot on the A821 at the west end of Loch Achray and offers one of the best effort-to-view ratios of all the hills in Scotland. A more challenging hike takes you up nearby **Ben Ledi** (2,884 feet/879 m), a brooding monster that lies above the attractive Loch Lubnaig. The walk takes you through thick forest and

INSIDER TIP:

The Trossachs offers some of the best walking of any small area in Scotland. Its appeal is greater because— unlike other ranges—it isn't bursting with hikers.

—SALLY McFALL
National Geographic contributor

out onto a bare ridge that makes its way across to the summit and a panorama that you won't forget.

Sedentary souls may want to take a trip on Loch Katrine on the historic steamer **S.S. *Sir Walter Scott.*** A minor road heads west from the Ben A'an parking lot to the small Trossachs Pier, where this charming old steamship awaits to transport her passengers back

---

EXPERIENCE:
Bike the Trossachs

One of the best ways to experience the Trossachs is on two wheels, because one of the most stunning stretches of the National Cycle Network (NCN7) runs through the region, from Loch Lomond to Killin. **Wheels Cycling Centre** (*Invertrossachs Rd., Callander, tel 01877/331 100, wheelscycling centre.com*) is your best option, with a range of mountain bikes, plus downloadable cycling routes. Or you can try **Katrine-wheelz** (*Loch Katrine, tel 01877/376 366, katrinewheelz .co.uk*).

---

in time as they slowly make their way down Loch Katrine and back.

Head back east to **Callander**, the other popular gateway to the Trossachs. This small town enjoys a busy main street, a few hotels, and some great walks. North of town is the exceptional hotel **Monachyle Mhor** (*Balquhidder, Lochearnhead, tel 01877/384 622, mhor.net*) and its excellent restaurant. The owners also run a number of businesses in town, including a superb bakery, **Mhor Bread** (*8 Main St., tel 01877/339 518*), and a first-class restaurant, **Mohr84** (see p. 163). Fans of Rob Roy should head here anyway as it is the site of the grave of the infamous outlaw.

S.S. *Sir Walter Scott* ✉ Trossachs Pier, Loch Katrine, near Callander ☎ (01877) 376 315 🕐 Closed winter, check website for timetable 💲 ££–£££££ **lochkatrine .com • Callander** 🅰 142 B2 **incallander.co.uk**

Scaling Ben Lomond is a real test of stamina.

Loch Lomond

At about 24 miles (38 km) long and up to 5 miles (8 km) across, Loch Lomond is by far the largest body of freshwater in Britain. Dotted with some 22 named islands (and many others unnamed), this tranquil oasis is one of the most stunning lochs in Scotland and remains a very popular natural attraction.

Since 2002, the loch has been protected within **Loch Lomond and The Trossachs National Park**—a wilderness area packed with hills, many more lochs, and a dizzying array of things to see and do. Loch Lomond itself is within easy striking distance of Glasgow, and many Glaswegians know it as "Glasgow's loch," which it certainly feels like on busy summer weekends when half the city's population seems to be there.

A good starting point is at the **Bal-** loch iCentre *(tel 01389/753 533, visitscotland.com)* in the red sandstone old rail depot opposite the town's current central rail station, where you can find out about the loch, its heritage, and its role today. Nearby is the **Loch Lomond Shores** *(Ben Lomond Way, tel 01389/751 031, lochlomondshores.com)* complex, where you can go for a paddle in a canoe, hang out in an aerial adventure course, have a bite to eat, or even indulge in some shopping. Here you'll also find the **SEA LIFE Loch Lomond Aquarium,** the **Loch Lomond Bird of Prey Centre,** and a selection of lake cruises. The more energetic can rent mountain bikes to explore farther afield Also here is the venerable *Maid of the Loch (maidoftheloch.org)* paddle-steamer, currently undergoing restoration with the intent of once again offering loch cruises.

The western shore is Loch Lomond's most developed side. The most charming village here is **Luss**—an idyllic escape that once starred in the popular Scottish TV show *Take the High Road.* This refers to the favorite ballad "Loch Lomond," which touches on the ill-fated Jacobite cause with the well-known refrain: "You take the high road and I'll take the low road and I'll be in Scotland before you." The loch's eastern side is less developed than the western shores. As you travel north from the pleasant town of **Drymen,** the

Loch Lomond 142 B2 • **Loch Lomond & The Trossachs National Park** 142 B2–B3 ☎ (01389) 722 600 **lochlomond-trossachs.org** • **SEA LIFE Loch Lomond Aquarium** ✉ Ben Lomond Way, Balloch ☎ (01389) 721 500 💲 *££* **visitsealife.com/loch-lomond** • **Loch Lomond Bird of Prey Centre** ✉ Ben Lomond Way, Balloch ☎ (01389) 729 239 💲 *£* **llbopc.co.uk**

EXPERIENCE: Tackling Ben Lomond

Mountains in Australia, New Zealand, and the United States have all been named for Ben Lomond. At 3,200 feet (974 m) in altitude, this majestic Munro (the name for a Scottish peak above 3,000 feet/914 m) casts an unmistakable shadow across Loch Lomond and beyond. It is the most southerly of the Munros and one of the most famous. Given its easy accessibility from the central belt, it offers an ideal introduction to Scottish mountaineering for visitors with the right equipment and an up-to-date weather forecast in hand.

To start the ascent, you will need to travel to **Rowardennan,** on the shore of Loch Lomond. Here, the main (or "tourist") trail is signed from the parking lot. Make sure you pick up a map of the area (Ordnance Survey West Highland Way Map nos. OL38 and OL39), as the route is a bit of a slog. After escaping the attractive wooded foothills, much of the time spent is on a long, featureless ridge. The trail is easy to follow since it is rough-paved.

The view from the top is staggering. Loch Lomond stretches below like a rippling blue carpet dotted with her necklace of islands. All around, hills and mountains vie for attention. If you catch "the Ben" on a good day, this is a truly wonderful climb and it may whet your appetite for another. The walk is about 7 miles (11 km) and should take 3 to 4 hours.

For more information see *nts.org. uk/visit/places/ben-lomond.* Guided walks are the specialty of **Loch Lomond Guides** (*64B Colquhoun Street, Helensburgh, tel 07870/654 658, lomondguides.co.uk*).

large caravan parks soon give way to a narrow lochside road, which is dotted with little bays and quiet stretches of beach.

Most of Loch Lomond's forested islands are privately owned, but a few are still open to the public. The best bet is to head to the island of **Inchcailloch** from the relaxed village of **Balmaha** on the eastern shore. Scottish Natural Heritage owns the island, but anyone can cross without a permit in groups of less than 12 by using the on-demand ferry *(The Boatyard, tel 01360/870 214, balmahaboatyard.co.uk, £).*

Once on the picturesque island you'll find two walking trails—the Low Path and the Summit Path. As its name suggests, the latter is the more strenuous option, but it really opens up the surrounding scenery. There is also a small picnic area and a modest campsite for anyone who has fallen instantly in love with Inchcailloch and wants to spend the night.

Balmaha is an attractive place in its own right, with an excellent visitor center *(tel 1389/722100)* on the banks of Loch Lomond. Within easy walking distance along the loch lies Milarochy Bay, a great place to relax and take in the beauty. The road eventually peters out at Rowardennan, and the only way farther north is on the spectacular long distance **West Highland Way** walking route *(west-highland-way.co.uk).* ∎

ARGYLL

If you walked the whole of the Argyll coastline—which extends from the tip of the Mull of Kintyre in the south to Oban in the north—you would have trekked an astounding 2,313 miles (3,723 km). Visitors will discover a region steeped in history and a landscape blessed with a dramatic Atlantic coastline, scenic lochs, and plenty of tempting towns.

■ The rugged Kintyre coastline is home to an abundance of wildlife.

Loch Fyne & Kintyre

The most spectacular approach to Argyll is west from Loch Lomond, up and over the legendary "Rest and Be Thankful" on a vertiginous route that follows an old military road. What opens up is an impressively rugged landscape of steep-sided mountains, tumbling waterfalls, and dense forests. The route pushes on through **Argyll Forest Park,** past the fjord-like Loch Goil, and underneath the Cobbler which, at 2,891 feet (880 m), is not Argyll's highest peak but is certainly one of its most distinctive, making for an excellent and relatively easy climb for a reasonably fit hiker.

Loch Fyne is a massive sea loch, with the world-famous **Loch Fyne Restaurant & Oyster Bar** (see pp. 163) in Cairndow at its northern tip. This seafood eatery has spawned a U.K.-wide chain and is one of the best places in Britain to savor fresh and perfectly cooked seafood.

Inveraray: Just a short drive south is the trim lochside town of Inveraray— an unmistakable sight with its church spires and whitewashed buildings glinting off the silvery expanse of Loch Fyne. Most of the action is on Main Street, which tumbles down to the loch and is home to a range of stores unashamedly geared to tourists. However, there is quality among

Argyll 🅰 142 A1–A3, B2–B3 **Inveraray** 🅰 142 B2 **visitscotland.com**

Mull of Kintyre

No fan of ex-Beatle Paul McCartney needs an introduction to the Mull of Kintyre, the most southwesterly section of the Kintyre Peninsula that was eulogized by him in his eponymous ballad. You have to hike out to the Mull on foot, with views opening up all around. Push on to the very edge of Scotland—a symbolic point so far west that it feels like you can touch the emerald isle of Ireland, only 12 miles (20 km) distant. Standing at this lonely spot, it is easy to understand why McCartney felt so compelled to immortalize its beauty. The lighthouse at its tip was remodeled by Robert Stevenson (see sidebar p. 243).

the souvenirs, with a choice of decent cafés, an old-fashioned candy store, and at the top of Main Street the highlight for whisky connoisseurs, **Loch Fyne Whiskies** *(tel 01499/302 219, lochfynewhiskies.com).* This delightful liquor store offers expert generous tastings and some very rare malts, the most expensive of which comes in at more than US$75,000 a bottle. The store also offers its own liqueur—a sweet orange and chocolate concoction that might just manage to make whisky palatable to the unconverted.

On wet weather days, Main Street has plenty to keep visitors occupied, but it's worth heading to Church Square and the **Inveraray Jail.** Exhibits, waxworks, and actors in period costume help bring to life the experience of prisoners in years gone by, including the poor children who were once holed up here.

The town's number one attraction is **Inveraray Castle.** Enjoying a prime position overlooking the town and Loch Fyne, the castle as it stands dates back to 1789. It is the ancestral home of the Duke of Argyll—a progressive figure who is very popular among the local population as someone intent on working with the local community to push Inveraray forward, rather than shutting himself away on his sprawling estate. You can take a tour of the castle and explore the lavish function rooms, and there is a café in the basement that serves light lunches and great cakes. The gardens are worth a wander too.

Kintyre Peninsula: If you head south down Loch Fyne, the Kintyre Peninsula awaits. The most appealing settlement is **Tarbert** in the north of the peninsula. This pretty little fishing village boasts some colorful houses, and it is a characterful place to spend a few hours. Check out an art gallery or antiques shop, and stop at a café for tea or coffee and homemade cake as you enjoy views of the picturesque harbor.

Kintyre sports some lovely sandy

Inveraray Jail ✉ Church Sq., Inveraray ☎ (01499)302 381 💲 ££ inverarayjail.co.uk • **Inveraray Castle** ✉ Cherrypark, Inveraray ☎ (01499)302 203 🕐 Closed Tues.–Wed.; Nov.–March 💲 Garden £; Castle £££ inveraray-castle.com • **Tarbert** 🗺 142 A2

beaches, and one of the most stunning is **Machrihanish.** Stroll along the sands and enjoy the sea views and flocks of wild seabirds that live along the rugged coast. All around Kintyre birds abound, and one of the most impressive sights is to watch the gannets dive-bomb into the water.

As you approach the famous **Mull of Kintyre** (see sidebar p. 153), the last outpost is **Campbeltown,** today known as home of the annual **Mull of Kintyre Music Festival** (mokfest.com). A few grand houses and swaying palms harken back to when this was "whisky capital of the world," with 34 distilleries; today only three remain active. Campbeltown is set in an attractive bay, with the island of **Davaar** just off the coast. Davaar is easily accessible at low tide and by using one of the regular boat trips. An on/off ferry service to Ireland (kintyreexpress.com, £££££) runs from late spring through September.

North Toward Oban

The western coastal road that pushes north from Kintyre is a scenic route. Near the village of Crinan it meets the **Crinan Canal,** a shortcut that allows boats to avoid the hours-long passage around the peninsula. Take a seat by the canal's mouth and watch the modern yachts pass by, as well as the jumble of historic sailing ships that evocatively speak of past times.

Just to the north is **Kilmartin.** Within a 6-mile (9 km) radius of the village are 350 ancient monuments, the largest collection of monuments in Scotland, many of which date back to prehistoric times. Learn more at the small but interesting **Kilmartin Museum** (A816, tel 01546/510 278, kilmartin.org), which also has a café serving tasty soups and cakes. Ask about their volunteer-led weekly walks.

Pushing north of Kilmartin you have two choices—stick to the largely coastal road or head inland in search of **Loch Awe.** Scotland's longest inland loch may not be as famous as Loch Ness and Loch Lomond, but there is plenty to see and do for visitors of all ages. It's renowned for trout fishing.

The most famous historic sight in these parts is the oft-photographed ruins of **Kilchurn Castle** (closed for renovation at press time). Climb the tower to enjoy sweeping views of Loch Awe.

A good wet weather option is **Ben Cruachan,** the "hollow mountain," at the northern end of the loch. A huge hydroelectric project is housed inside. In addition to the visitor center, it's worth it to book a guided tour (Dalmally, tel 0141/614 9105, visitcruachan.co.uk, closed Sat.–Sun., £) to learn about one of Scotland's emerging green technologies.

Oban

Oban is Scotland's busiest ferry port. Hills sweep around and enclose the

Campbeltown ⚊ 142 A1 **Visitor Information** ✉ 15-17 Main St. ☎ (07939)149 706 **explorecampbeltown.com** • **Kilchurn Castle** ⚊ 142 B3 ✉ Lochawe ☎ (0131) 668 8600 ⊕ Closed Oct.–March **historicenvironment.scot** • **Oban** ⚊ 142 A3 **Visitor Information** ✉ 3 North Pier ☎ (01631)563 122 **visitscotland.com**

town's broad bay, and the town it-self boasts some gorgeous grand Victorian guesthouses and hotels. The historic **Oban Distillery** is the town's main attraction, offering a variety of tours and tastings. Oban is a bustling town with a variety of non-touristy shops and excellent seafood (see sidebar below). The **Oban Chocolate Company** is an especially sweet treat. Visit the little factory to see artisanal chocolates being hand-made.

Heading north, look left for the pic-turesque ruin of **Castle Stalker,** then for a small signpost to the quiet village of **Port Appin**—a local secret where Scots come for cozy weekends away. Drive to the very end of the signposted road and have a drink, splurge on an excellent meal, or even spend the night at **The Pierhouse Hotel.** From here you can also zip across to pastoral Lismore on the small passenger ferry (*seasonal, £*). ■

Oban Distillery ✉ Stafford St., Oban ☎ (01631)572 004 $ *££££–£££££* **obanwhisky.com** • **Oban Chocolate Company** ✉ 34 Corran Esplanade, Oban ☎ (01631)566 099 🕒 Factory closed Sat.–Sun. **obanchocolate.co.uk**

EXPERIENCE: Oban Seafood

In recent years Oban has devel-oped a reputation as a town whose restaurants serve delicious sea-food. Today a banner welcomes visitors to the "Seafood Capital of Scotland"—and although it may be a bit tongue in cheek it is also justi-fied. The highlight for many are the informal stalls along the busy pier; here you can sit at a picnic bench and feast on scallops and squat lobster tails for a fraction of what you would pay in a posh res-taurant. This boat-fresh shellfish is accompanied by a great view over the bay.

The first stall to start serving here (and many think it is still the best) was the green-and-white **Oban Seafood Hut** (*Calmac Pier, tel 7881/418 565*), close to the ferry terminal and offering real value-for-money. It's sure to be one of the most memorable experiences of any visit to Oban as you slurp down the fresh oys-ters from the shell, and watch huge mussels and scallops the size of saucers being given the marinière treatment on an out-side burner.

Oban also boasts up-market restaurants where reservations are recommended. **Ee-Usk** (Gaelic for "fish"; *North Pier, tel 01631/565 666, eeusk.com*), situated right on the waterfront, cooks local sea-food with a creative flair. In the center of town, chic **Coast** (see p. 162) is similarly imaginative—serving the likes of seared scallops laced with pork belly, alongside classic fish and chips.

Boat-fresh seafood is also a point of pride at the **Water-front Fishouse** (*1 Railway Pier, tel 01631/567 415, waterfront fishouse.co.uk*). They use ultra local suppliers—their langoustines for example are listed on the menu as coming from "Gordon the Prawn." Book ahead for a coveted window table and gaze out over Oban Bay toward the Isle of Mull.

DRIVE AROUND THE COWAL PENINSULA

The Cowal Peninsula is a hidden gem definitely off the tourist trail. Relax and enjoy the stunning surroundings—quiet, winding roads and ferry trips are all part of the fun. The drive can be done in a day, but allow three to fully reap the benefits.

Tarbert on the shores of Loch Fyne, near Kintyre

The best way to reach the Cowal Peninsula is by taking a car ferry from the Clyde port of Gourock to Dunoon. Two operators ply the route—Caledonian MacBrayne *(calmac.co.uk)* and Western Ferries *(western-ferries.co.uk)*. The short crossing still allows time to leave the busy city behind.

Dunoon ❶, Argyll's largest town, has seen better days and is no longer a favorite of vacationing Glaswegians. The best time to visit is in August during the **Cowal Highland Gathering** *(cowalgathering.com)*—a captivating celebration of traditional Scottish music and dancing. You can visit the modest **Castle House Museum** *(Castle Gardens, Dunoon, tel 01369/701 422, castlehousemuseum.org.uk, closed Sun.–Mon. & Nov.–March, £),* where an interesting exhibit highlights the old "steamers" that once carried Glaswegians "doon the watter" for a holiday.

Head northwest on the A815; the wide loch to your right is **Holy Loch ❷**. Until the early 1990s, this loch was a nuclear submarine base for the U.S. Navy—as famous for its protestors as for its submarines. Cut west along the B836 and you leave modern life behind as the scenery grows wilder in Glen Lean.

Keep pushing west on the B836, head up the A886, then turn south on the A8003 to **Tighnabruaich viewpoint ❸**, where you get a supreme view of the **Kyles of Bute.** In Gaelic, the word *kyles* means "narrows," which refers to the narrow waters that separate Cowal from the Isle of Bute. This is prime sailing country, but the views are equally stunning from the land, too. Farther south awaits the charming village of **Tighnabruaich ❹**. Tighnabruaich is a Gaelic name meaning "house on the hill," which aptly describes the many houses on the steep hills that rise above the Kyles. A good place to stay overnight, or just stop for some delicious fresh seafood, the town offers a number of excellent

---

NOT TO BE MISSED:

Tighnabruaich • Ardkinglas • Argyll Forest Park • Benmore Botanic Garden

guesthouses, hotels, and restaurants.

Rounding the peninsula on an unclassified road you come to **Portavadie ❺**, home to a sheltered marina complex, complete with luxury spa for serious relaxation. If time allows, you can take a boat tour of Loch Fyne from here, or catch a ferry over to Tarbert across on Kintyre. Or proceed north up the B8000, rejoin the A886, and in about an hour arrive in tiny **Strachur ❻**, home to **Creggans Inn** *(tel 01369/860 279, creggans-inn.co.uk)*, great for a fresh seafood meal with stunning views of the loch.

Cowal's most unlikely attraction is the **Ardkinglas Woodland Garden ❼** *(Cairndow, tel 01499/600 261, ardkinglas.com, £)*, less than 30 minutes north on the A815. A network of paths snake through this verdant 25-acre (10 ha) oasis, with an eclectic range of trees planted as far back as the 18th century. The high local rainfall

and the moderating influence of the Gulf Stream combine to make this an ideal environment for trees. Indeed, some of the most impressive in the country stand here, including one of the tallest firs in Britain, vaulting skyward more than 210 feet (64 m) with a girth of nearly 33 feet (10 m). Head back to Strachur, but this time continue inland on the A815 and travel south deeper into Cowal and **Argyll Forest Park ❽** *(tel 0300/067 6650, forestryandland.gov.scot)*, an oasis for bikers and hikers alike.

Your last stop is **Benmore Botanic Garden ❾** *(Benmore, Dunoon, tel 01369/706 261, rbge.org.uk/visit/benmore-botanic-garden, closed Nov.–Feb., £)*, where 300 globe-spanning species carpet 120 acres (49 ha), including a spectacular avenue of giant redwoods. From here follow the A815 south into Dunoon, where the ferry back across the Clyde awaits.

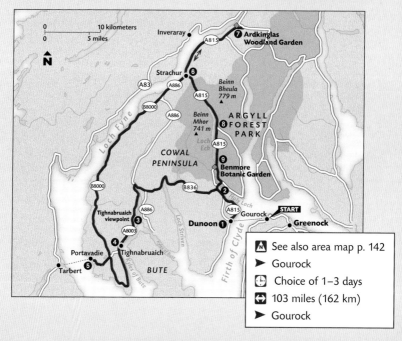

PERTHSHIRE

Perthshire is self-styled "tall tree country" and packs a powerful natural punch with its stunning landscape of thick forests, scenic lochs, and majestic mountain ranges. Then you can explore Perth, the trim capital and a bounty of historic attractions.

■ Blair Castle, ancient seat of the dukes and earls of Atholl, sits in the heart of Highland Perthshire.

Loch Tay to Pitlochry

The reflections of Perthshire's mighty Munros bounce off Loch Tay on calm days, making the loch look like a glacial grand canyon. The highest peak is **Ben Lawers,** which towers a whopping 3,984 feet (1,214 m) over the land. Experienced walkers can make a whole day of it and tackle a flurry of Munros on one arduous ridge walk. At the eastern end of Loch Tay lies the **Scottish Crannog Centre** *(Kenmore, tel 01887/830 583, crannog .co.uk, closed Nov.–March, £),* where you can learn about the old crannogs that people used for shelter and protection more than 2,000 years ago. These simple stilted dwellings were laid out in the water along a retractable walkway, which made them hard to attack. A reconstructed roundhouse contains the museum with exhibits that illuminate the lives of the people in those days. Use a guide to get the most out of your visit.

Aberfeldy is a short drive farther east. This graceful little town sports stately streets laden with grand stone

Loch Tay 🅐 142 B3–C3● **Aberfeldy** 🅐 142 C3

buildings. Scotland boasts hundreds of distilleries, but the excellent visitor center at **Dewar's World of Whisky** (*Aberfeldy Distillery, Aberfeldy, tel 01887/822 010, dewars.com/gl/en/aberfeldydistillery, tours ££–£££££*) offers one of the most enjoyable experiences, with the highlight, of course, sampling a wee dram.

On roads heading north, the conical bulk of **Schiehallion** is never far away—this mountain helped give maps contour lines as the concept was pioneered on its slopes. You will eventually end up at **Loch Tummel,** hemmed in by hills on all sides. This loch was a favorite of Queen Victoria, and a visitor center and café now stand at a scenic overlook within the Tay Forest named **Queen's View** (*forestryandland.gov.scot*). Rejoining the A9, you can head north to the sleepy village of **Blair Atholl,** where the highlight is the dramatic **Blair Castle** (*tel 01796/481 207, atholl-estates.co.uk/blair-castle, closed Nov.–March, £££*). This remarkable building lies at the very heart of a massive 145,000-acre (58,679 ha) estate, which overflows with charming scenery and fine walks.

Nearby **Killiecrankie** is a tiny place made famous by one man's great leap. In 1689, when the Jacobites smashed an English force at the Battle of Killiecrankie, one plucky and extremely lucky English soldier escaped by leaping across the gorge—an impressive feat that some skeptics file under the urban-myth category. A visitor center fills you in on the history.

INSIDER TIP:

Perthshire is legendary for its soft fruits. In summer keep an eye out for roadside signs marking the fruit farms where you can pick your own ultra-fresh strawberries and raspberries.

—SALLY McFALL
National Geographic contributor

Continue south down the A9 and you come to **Pitlochry,** the Victorian-era resort and popular tourist stop, replete with tacky souvenir shops on the busy High Street. Off the A924 is the **Edradour Distillery** (*tel 01796/472 095, edradour.com, £*). Although the smallest traditional distillery in Scotland, it still manages to conjure up a fine dram and offers fun tours, but was temporarily closed to visitors at press time

Nearby, the **Pitlochry Dam Visitor Centre** (*Pitlochry Power Station, Armoury Rd., tel 01796/484 111, pitlochrydam.com*) appears to hover above the River Tummel below. Exhibits on hydroelectricity explain the process underway at this massive station, which generates power for northern Scotland. A café is also on hand, for those who wish to make a day of their visit. Don't miss the famous fish ladder here, visible through glass windows so you can view the action—wild

---

Killiecrankie ✉ 3 miles (5 km) N of Pitlochry **Visitor Information** ☎ (01796) 473 233 **nts.org.uk • Pitlochry** 🅰 142 C3 **Visitor Information** ✉ 22 Atholl Rd. ☎ (01796) 472 215 **visitscotland.com**

salmon progressing through a series of 34 tiered pools to reach the top of the dam while avoiding the turbines. The large fish then continue their long journey back to their spawning grounds.

Perth

A trim city by the River Tay, Perth is often ignored by Scots. Its center is hemmed in by two parks to the north and south—the North and South Inch—and then on its eastern flank by the silvery Tay. The broad landscaped walkway is ideal for bracing riverside strolls.

Cultural pursuits are on offer at the funky **Perth Concert Hall** (Mill St., tel 01738/621 031, perththeatre-andconcerthall.com), which hosts an impressive roster of events. Close by is the family-friendly **Perth Museum and Art Gallery** (78 George St., tel 01738/477 022, culturepk.org .uk). Although it closed in 2022, the Fergusson Gallery's superb art collection moved to the refreshed Perth Art Gallery. It features the work of painter and sculptor John Duncan Fergusson (1874–1961), a member of what became known as the Scottish Colourist group, as well as his partner, Margaret Morris (1891–1980), a pioneer of modern dance.

Comrie & Beyond

Comrie, to the west of Perth, is the epitome of urban, or rather urbane, Perthshire. Its grand Victorian buildings hark back to the days when it was a major player and even had its own railway station. Indeed, a lot of its charm comes from this sense of faded grandeur and the passion for Comrie that lives on in today's proud inhabitants.

Comrie is also famous as the earthquake capital of Scotland, with more recorded seismic activity than anywhere else on the British mainland. Little wonder, since the town lies in the middle of the Highland Boundary Fault. You can visit the unique **Earthquake House** (The Ross, Comrie), where

Scone Palace

With its period furnishings and antiques, Scone Palace (Perth, tel 01738/552 300, scone-palace.co.uk, closed Nov.– March, ££–£££££) is today every bit the graceful country house with pleasant grounds for strolling. Centuries ago, however, this bucolic retreat was bathed in drama as the site where the independent Scottish kings were crowned. Coronation took place on an oblong block of red sandstone dubbed the Stone of Destiny. Although the famous stone now resides with the crown jewels of Scotland at Edinburgh Castle, a tangible sense of history remains. It was here that the first Scottish king, Kenneth McAlpine, was crowned in A.D. 843, on the Stone of Scone. It was last used for the coronation of Elizabeth II, as Queen of the United Kingdom of Britain and Ireland

Perth ⚘ 142 C3 **Visitor Information** ✉ 45 High St, Perth ☎ (01738) 450 600 **visitscotland .com** • **Comrie** ⚘ 142 C3

South Inch Park, a lovely green space within Perth town center.

the world's first seismometer was set up in 1874. Today you can see a model of it, as well as some more modern equipment.

There are two good times to visit Comrie. The first is for the summer festival, called the **Comrie Fortnight,** *(comrie.org.uk)* with a string of cultural events—including dances and a parade—during the last week of July and the first week of August. The highlight of the local calendar, however, is **Hogmanay** (see sidebar p. 17),when the local "Flambeaux" reaches its dramatic climax. Villagers make their way through the town center and circle its old perimeter with flaming torches in an effort to ward off evil spirits for the year ahead, then the local pipe band kicks off a shindig.

A quick hop by motorway south of Perth is **Loch Leven**—one of Scotland's most historic lochs, set in a fold of hills with a castle-topped island in the middle. The castle is, of course, linked to Mary Queen of Scots, who was imprisoned here for almost a year. You can retrace her steps by taking a small boat out to visit. Entry is by timed reservation, and you are advised to book ahead online.

The loch and its surroundings are part of **Loch Leven National Nature Reserve,** teeming with myriad birdlife. The U.K.'s largest concentration of breeding ducks congregate here, as well as thousands of migratory geese, ducks, and swans. The visitor center on the south side of the loch offers a good café and friendly advice on viewing hides. ∎

Lochleven Castle ☎ (07836) 313 769 🕐 Closed Nov.–March 💲 £ £
historicenvironment.scot • Loch Leven National Nature Reserve
✉ The Pier, Kinross ☎ (01577) 862 355 **nature.scot**

Where to Eat & Drink in Central Scotland

63 TAY STREET

63 TAY ST., PERTH

(01738) 441 451 | 63taystreet.com

Everything about this fine-dining eatery located down by the river is smooth, from the service to elegant décor complete with muted hues and subtle tartan. This culinary oasis makes the most of Scottish produce, with Perthshire-born chef Stuart Black now heading up the kitchen. Succulent venison is perfectly cooked and the well-selected wines a perfect accompaniment to an epicurean feast that will last all evening.

£££ 🕐 Closed Sun.–Tues. 💳 MC, V

BLAIR ATHOLL WATERMILL & TEA ROOM

FORD RD., BLAIR ATHOLL

(01796) 481 321 | blairathollwatermill.com

One of Scotland's few remaining watermills (flour and oatmeal are still milled here) is also the setting for one of Scotland's better cafés. Delicious sandwiches, bagels, soups, and cakes (the carrot cake is legendary in these parts) feature on the simple menu. Enjoy a light lunch and then pick up some of the mill's own oatmeal and flour, as well as jams, chutneys, eggs, and other Scottish produce. Bread-baking classes are also available.

£–££ 🕐 Closed Nov.–March 💳 MC, V

COAST

104 GEORGE ST., OBAN

(01631) 569 900 | coastoban.co.uk

Housed in a former bank, this contemporary eatery welcomes guests with crisp white table linens, soft hues of brown, and light polished woods. An eclectic menu caters to all tastes, with local seafood being the star (although there are tasty vegetarian options). Attentive service makes for an even more pleasant experience. Note that, because of licensing restrictions, children under 10 years of age must leave the premises by 8 p.m.

£££ 🕐 Closed Sun.–Mon. lunch 💳 MC, V

KILBERRY INN

KILBERRY, ARGYLL

(01880) 770 223 | kilberryinn.com

It may be off the beaten path, but diners who make the effort to find the Kilberry Inn are rewarded with mouth-watering local produce. The likes of plump Loch Fyne scallops seared to perfection and tender Ormsary rib eye steak are hallmarks of cooking that is always delicious and has earned the chef a Bib Gourmand mention. The whitewashed inn with five cozy guest rooms is a fittingly atmospheric place to enjoy an epicurean treat.

£££ 🅿 🕐 Closed Mon., Mon.–Tues. in Nov., & Dec.–March 💳 MC, V

KINLOCH HOUSE

DUNKELD RD., BLAIRGOWRIE

(01250) 884 237 | kinlochhouse.com

Surrounded by emerald meadows, this restaurant in the eponymous country house hotel a short distance from Pitlochry richly rewards a diversion. The cozy and traditional country manor prepares virtually every ingredient in-house. Chef Steve MacCallum's creative genius delivers mouthwatering dishes such as Arbroath lobster with fennel and citrus dressing, and loin of Perthshire lamb with gratin potatoes, mashed swede and carrot, roast garlic, and rosemary sauce.

£££ P 🕐 Closed second half of Dec. 🔗 All major cards

LOCH FYNE RESTAURANT & OYSTER BAR

LOCH FYNE, CLACHAN, CAIRNDOW
(01499) 600 482 | lochfyne.com

This seafood eatery spawned a nationwide chain, but for many the original is by far the best. Sumptuous seafood, which includes the likes of langoustines, oysters, mussels, clams, crab, and lobster, makes its way onto the daily-changing menu. Quality is also the ethos behind the ingredients and cooking when it comes to the restaurant's meat dishes, with locally sourced Glen Fyne venison and steaks aged for 28 days a real treat.

£££ 🔗 AE, MC, V

TAMBURRINI & WISHART

CAMERON HOUSE, LOCH LOMOND
01389/312 210 | cameronhouse.co.uk

In 2023, Michelin-starred chef Martin Wishart partnered with fellow revered Scottish chef Paul Tamburrini and metamorphosed Wishart's former restaurant at Cameron House (see Travelwise p. 347) into a new fine-dining restaurant serving innovative contemporary dishes inspired by Scotland's natural larder. Treat yourself to a three-course lunch menu with such seasonal treats as braised ox-cheeks, crab and lemongrass velouté, and Pink Lady tart tatin.

££££–£££££ P 🕐 Closed Mon.–Tues. 🔗 All major cards

MHOR 84

75–77 BALQUHIDDER, LOCHEARNHEAD
(01877) 384 646 | mhor84.net

Run by the people behind Monachyle Mhor hotel (see Travelwise p. 347), this airy and cheerful café-restaurant in the MHOR 84 Motel draws devoted locals and tourists alike for its fabled eggs benedict, gourmet burgers, and fresh seafood dishes such as chowders, mussel bowls, and loch oysters.

££ 🕐 🔗 MC, V

PIERHOUSE SEAFOOD RESTAURANT

PORT APPIN, ARGYLL
(01631) 730 302 | pierhousehotel.co.uk

Soak up the sea views through large picture windows as you enjoy a lovely meal. Oysters plucked from the Lismore oyster beds, Loch Etive langoustine, and fresh lobster are among the highlights on a fish-heavy menu. Meat-eaters are well cared for with tender Scotch beef and local game dishes, and there are vegetarian options as well. Stay the night and enjoy the peaceful location, looking across to the islands of Lismore and Mull.

£££ P 🔗 MC, V

RESTAURANT ANDREW FAIRLIE

GLENEAGLES HOTEL, AUCHTERARDER
(01764) 694 267 | andrewfairlie.com

Foodies make a pilgrimage to taste the famous Scottish chef's two-Michelin-starred cuisine. Like the Gleneagles Hotel in which it is located (see Travelwise p. 349), the dining room is refined but contemporary, with smooth personal service. While Chef Andrew Fairlie passed away in 2019, his successors maintain his French culinary culture, infused with a cheeky Scottish flair. Both the à la carte and six-course degustation menus employ the finest Scottish produce like wild venison and Perthshire lamb.

£££££ P 🕐 Closed lunch 🔗 All major cards

Wooded glens, impressive mountains, captivating castles, Pictish relics, and a smattering of distilleries to enjoy a wee dram or two

EAST COAST

■ A Scottish bagpiper plays in the hills above Braemar.

EAST COAST

The East Coast may not have the majestic mountains that run down the edge of the West Coast, but the region is steeped in centuries of history and offers its own natural and man-made treasures. It is also home to a much larger population than that found on the West Coast, boasting the two bustling cities of Aberdeen and Dundee.

The natural beauty of Scotland's East Coast has only been enhanced by the addition of dramatic castles, grand country houses, vast abbeys, and a number of lively towns and cities to the landscape. The southern extremity of this region is also home to St. Andrews, known the world over as the "home of golf."

NOT TO BE MISSED:

The remarkably well-preserved heritage village of Culross 171

The university town of St. Andrews, spiritual "home of golf" 172–173

Picturesque Ballater, where many shops display their royal warrants as suppliers to the queen 184

Aberdeen, vibrant with street art, historic attractions, and a busy working port 191–195

Driving the postcard-pretty northeast coast, where stunning Dunnottar Castle perches on a cliff 196–197

The self-styled kingdom of Fife lies to the north of Edinburgh, just across the Firth of Forth. The region was once a power base for the Scottish kings, and the grand Falkland Palace and Dunfermline Abbey are fitting legacies. In the coastal resort town of St. Andrews, the massive ruined cathedral hints at the church's once mighty power. Of course, St. Andrews is now the headquarters for golf and home to Scotland's most famous course, in the shape of the Old Course.

Just across the River Tay lies the region of Angus, which is home to the underrated city of Dundee. Over the last millennium, Dundee has transformed from a humble fishing port into a bustling industrial hub, and it is now home to a string of both historic and cultural attractions—the latter part of an ongoing attempt to regenerate the city and shake off its depressed, post-industrial image.

Outside the city, the historic delights of Glamis Castle—one of Scotland's grandest castles—and the natural beauties of the scenic Angus Glens await. These glens offer everything from simple low-level walks that most people can enjoy to challenging Munros—mountains in Scotland that are more than 3,000 feet (914 m) high—where having the right gear can make the difference between life and death. On the Angus coast, Arbroath is swathed in history and is also a great place to buy and/or eat fresh seafood, while Broughty Ferry is Dundee's relaxed seaside escape.

The vast Cairngorms mountain range separates Angus from Royal Deeside—the charming area of lush

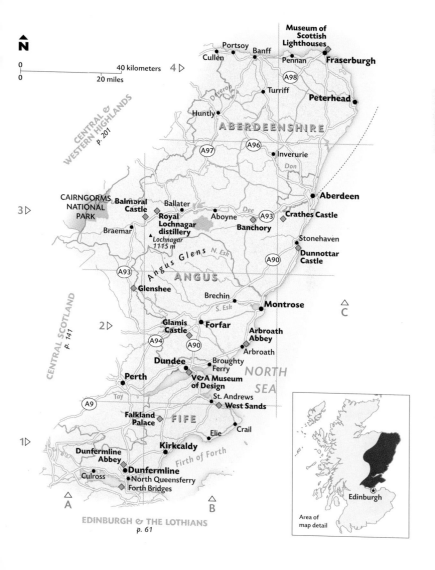

CENTRAL & WESTERN HIGHLANDS p. 201

CENTRAL SCOTLAND p. 141

EDINBURGH & THE LOTHIANS p. 61

valleys and forested hills where Queen Victoria chose to have her summer retreat, Balmoral, back in the 1840s. This is a land swathed in tartan and tradition, where the Highland Games were born. Today, tourists flock to this archetypal "shortbread tin" image of Scotland to spend time in pretty towns and villages like Braemar and Ballater.

On the coast east of Royal Deeside lies the "granite city" of Aberdeen—Scotland's third largest city. The once-sterile "oil capital of Europe" is reinventing itself as a showcase for public art. There's plenty of history and heritage landmarks, too, along with a sandy city beach and a surprising amount of green space. The port of Aberdeen also serves as a gateway to the islands in the north, with regular ferry services to and from both Orkney and Shetland.

The Aberdeenshire coast is a dramatic one, laced with sweeping sandy beaches, rugged cliffs, and attractive little fishing villages, such as Cullen and Portsoy, that are hidden away in the countless coves and bays. Then there are the busier ports, such as Peterhead and Fraserburgh, which bring home a bountiful deep-sea catch from the North Sea. Seafood lovers can enjoy the highlight on Scotland's East Coast—the world-class white fish—in many of the local restaurants. ■

■ **Sunset over Portsoy a fishing village in Aberdeenshire on the east coast of Scotland**

FIFE

Hemmed in by water on three sides—the Firth of Forth separating it from the Lothians to the south, the North Sea to the east, and the River Tay dividing it from Angus to the north—the kingdom of Fife feels like an island. This impression is reinforced by its strong sense of identity, variety of sights, and collage of landscapes.

Pittenweem typifies the fishing villages along the coast of Fife.

South Coast

Three towering **Forth bridges** (see pp. 85–86), monuments to Scottish engineering, are the main routes into Fife from Scotland's capital, Edinburgh. Each provides a fittingly grand entrance to the kingdom of Fife. Lying on the Fife flank of the Forth is former prime minister Gordon Brown's (1951–) hometown of **North Queensferry.** The relaxed village tumbles down to the water, where an old harbor and a sprinkling of pubs and restaurants await.

The main attraction here is the impressive aquarium, **Deep Sea World** *(Battery Quarry, tel 01383/411 880, deepseaworld.com, ££)*. A must for

Fife 167 A1–B1 **Forth Bridges** 167 A1 **Visitor Information** theforthbridges.org

children—and interesting for adults, too—the highlight is one of the world's longest shark tunnels, complete with huge sharks, billowing rays, and all manner of marine life.

The interior boasts myriad tanks laden with tropical fish and exotic species such as piranhas, while outside there are the more familiar seals.

Just to the north of North Queensferry is the ancient town of **Dunfermline.** While blighted by a clog of modern housing and a gaggle of faceless shops, it is still home to one of Scotland's most important abbeys. **Dunfermline Abbey** *(18 St. Margaret St., tel 01383/723 005, dunfermlineabbey .co.uk, closed Mon.–Fri. Nov.–Feb.)* was originally commissioned as a priory church by Queen Margaret (1045–

1093), who set up a ferry from South Queensferry to help pilgrims across the Forth. It opened in 1072, with her son, King David I (1085–1153), later developing it as an abbey to commemorate her. Today it is still an active place of worship. Seven kings of Scotland are buried in the abbey, including Robert the Bruce (1274–1329).

After visiting the abbey, check out what is very much a local secret, **Pittencrieff Park.** This lovely 76-acre (31 ha) green lung, with its main entrance off Dunfermline High Street, was a gift to the town by its most famous son, Andrew Carnegie (1835–1919)—once the richest man in the world, and one who had such a seminal influence on North America as well as his homeland. You can visit the **Andrew Carn-**

EXPERIENCE: Walk the Fife Coastal Path

The Fife Coastal Path is a long-distance path—the kind that Scots love and which opens up the country for visitors, too. The walk stretches for more than 117 miles (188 km), from the shadow of the Forth bridges at North Queensferry, east along the Firth of Forth coast, before turning north at the Fife Ness headland. It then follows the North Sea up past St. Andrews and on to the River Tay, where it ends at the Tay Bridge overlooking Dundee. Along the way are working fishing villages, castles and churches, nature reserves, and even the military air force base at Leuchars.

The organizers of the walk split it into seven bite-size stretches (see their excellent website, *fifecoastandcountryside trust.co.uk,* which also details attractions and handy transportation information). Some of these can be tackled as day trips—the section from the pretty fishing village of **Pittenweem** to **Fife Ness,** Fife's easternmost point, is ideal. At 8 miles (12.5 km), it skirts the coastline along some rough trails through attractive fishing villages, coves, and beaches, before reaching a dramatic finale at the headland.

egie Birthplace Museum, at the humble cottage where he was born. An adjoining exhibition hall sheds light on both his life, from bobbin boy to capitalist, and 19th-century Fife. West of Dunfermline, the most interesting settlement is Culross, a truly remarkable time capsule. Once a busy port that grew rich on the back of its salt and coal industries, Culross had slipped into decline by the 20th century. The National Trust for Scotland seized the opportunity to preserve this perfect piece of 17th-century Scotland and has worked tirelessly to do so. Highlights include the mustard-colored **Culross Palace** (1597), the **Townhouse** (1626), and the **Abbey Church,** parts of which date back to 1217. The streets have appeared many times in the television series *Outlander.*

East of Dunfermline, the interesting coastal towns and quaint villages include **Aberdour** (with its graceful town houses, castle mound, and sandy beach), **Kinghorn** (with a picturesque fishing harbor), and **Kirkcaldy**—birthplace of great 18th-century thinker Adam Smith (1723–1790). The latter's cultural hub is the refurbished **Kirkcaldy Galleries,** combining museum, library, art gallery, café, and children's areas. Wander their fine collection of art, including a large treasure trove of works by the Glasgow Boys.

Inland Fife

The Fife hinterland is a little-explored oasis of neat farmland, gently rolling hills, and quiet villages,

Andrew Carnegie Birthplace Museum ✉ Moodie St., Dunfermline ☎ (01381) 724 302 **carnegiebirthplace.com** • **Culross Palace** ✉ Culross ☎ (01383) 880 359 🕐 Palace closed Nov.–March, gardens open year-round 💲 ££ **nts.org.uk/visit/places/culross** • **Kirkcaldy Galleries** ✉ War Memorial Gardens, Kirkcaldy ☎ (01592) 583 206 **onfife.com/venues/kirkcaldy-galleries**

▪ Golfers head back to the clubhouse after a round on the Old Course at St. Andrews.

The Spiritual Home of Golf

Although locals in Leith claim to have pioneered the game, St. Andrews proudly proclaims itself to be the "home of golf" and is recognized by most of the world as such. Golfers used to drive balls around the land as far back as the 15th century, though King James II in 1457 famously banned the sport—he reckoned it interfered with his men's archery practice!

The august Royal and Ancient (randa.org)—golf's governing body—was founded in 1754 and still runs the town's most famous courses. This includes the iconic Old Course, which is on publicly owned land. So while you need to apply to play on the course (see p. 193), anyone can walk on the course and pose for pictures. Just be considerate of those playing.

dotted with less attractive towns that have suffered in recent years as the traditional heavy industries have flagged. The shining light is the expanse of **Falkland Palace,** 11 miles (18 km) north of Kirkcaldy. Built between 1450 and 1541 in a fold below the rambling walking country of the Lomond Hills, this was a refuge of the Stuart kings and queens in the days when they were genuine rivals to the Hanoverian dynasty Britain still has today. The lavish gardens are worth visiting, and the palace's 17th-century Flemish tapestries and captivating portraits of Stuart monarchs are a poignant throwback to what might have been.

A throwback to a different, but no less compelling, era is **Scotland's**

Secret Bunker. This sight, located off the B540 south of St. Andrews, is where Scotland would have been governed from 100 feet (30 m) down, in the event of a nuclear war with the former Soviet Union. The size of two soccer fields and spread across two floors, this time capsule hidden beneath an innocent-looking farmhouse perfectly conjures up the suspicion and fear of the Cold War, especially for Scottish visitors, who would have been left to their fate above while their leaders sought sanctuary far below the ground.

St. Andrews

If you visit only one town in Fife, make sure it is St. Andrews. The "home of golf" offers far more than

Falkland Palace 167 B1 ✉ Falkland, Cupar ☎ (01337) 857 397
🕐 Closed Nov.–Feb. 💲 ££ **nts.org.uk/visit/places/falkland-palace** •
Scotland's Secret Bunker ✉ Troywood, St. Andrews ☎ (01333) 310 301
🕐 Closed Nov.–Feb. 💲 ££ **secretbunker.co.uk** • **St. Andrews** 167 B2
Visitor Information ✉ 70 Market St.,St. Andrews ☎ (01334) 472 021
visitscotland.com

■ **West Sands Beach at low tide in the seaside town of St Andrews**

just the rich heritage of the game. It is a deeply historic place laden with sights, and with an active student population that helps imbue its old stone streets with a real energy. The setting is sublime, too, with the North Sea wrapped around its old town and stunning beaches spreading out in all directions.

Named for Scotland's patron saint, the site was allegedly founded when the custodian of the saint's relics was shipwrecked here. The **cathedral,** near the town center and dedicated to the saint's legend, is the main attraction. Once the mightiest religious building in the land, it was stripped of its altars and its statuary defaced during the Scottish reformation of the 1500s, and was abandoned. Townspeople used the cathedral stones to build their houses, and natural elements took their toll until the 1800s, when the ruin began to be protected. You can still climb up the tower of **St. Rule's Church,** for sweeping views of the town and the North Sea.

The other essential historical ruin is **St. Andrews Castle.** Dating from the 12th century, it is inexorably bound into the history of the cathedral, as another power base of the Scottish church. Exhibits shed light on the castle's history and gruesome past, but half the fun is ambling around the walls and conjuring up the days when men clashed swords against a majestic seascape backdrop

The sprawling **University of St. Andrews** owns many of the town's buildings and hosts numerous events. If you're visiting on a Sunday during term, head to the harbor below the cathedral around noon to watch the long-held tradition of red-robed students walking the pier after chapel.

The scenic coastline around St. Andrews attracts both golfers (see sidebar p. 172) and beach lovers. The most famous stretch is **West Sands,** a 15-minute walk from the town center. Watch out for the tides: The "beach" quickly turns into a sandbar, and then the sea. ■

St. Andrews Cathedral ☎ (01334) 472 563 ⏱ Museum & tower closed Oct.–March. 💲 £ **historicenvironment.scot** • **St. Andrews Castle** ✉ North St., St. Andrews ☎ (01334) 477 196 💲 ££ **historicenvironment.scot** • **University of St. Andrews** ☎ (01334) 476 161 **st-andrews.ac.uk**

DRIVE AROUND THE EAST NEUK OF FIFE FISHING VILLAGES

The East Neuk of Fife is within easy reach of Edinburgh, Glasgow, and Dundee but could not feel less urban—the pace of life seems to get slower every year as its once mighty fishing fleets dwindle away. Today, the picturesque whitewashed fishing villages house a modest sprinkling of hard-working fishermen with lobster pots sitting prettily by the harbors and an abundance of first-rate fish-and-chips restaurants.

Robust stone and whitewashed cottages line the harbor at St. Monans.

Organizing a Trip

This drive can be done as one long day out from St. Andrews and back. To get the most out of the trip, though, it is better to allow a night, preferably two, to really soak up the flavor of each village, which can seem very similar but reveal

NOT TO BE MISSED:

Elie • St. Monans • Scottish Fisheries Museum • Crail

0   4 kilometers
0   2 miles

START
St. Andrews Castle and Cathedral
St. Andrews ①
Brownhills
A917
A915
Pitscottie
Stravithie
FIFE
Kingsbarns
Craighead   *Fife Ness*
Lathones
Kingsmuir
⑤ Crail
Largoward
Kirkton of Largo
B941
Scottish Fisheries Museum
A917
Lower Largo
A917
St. Monans ③
④ Anstruther
A917
Elie ②
Earlsferry ②
Firth of Forth

North Sea

▲ N

🅝 See also area map p. 167
➤ St. Andrews
🕐 Choice of 1–3 days
↔ 33 miles (53 km)
➤ St. Andrews

their own distinct personalities the more time you devote to them.

It is popular to do much of the Elie to Crail section of this route as a walk, following the **Fife Coastal Path** (see sidebar p. 170), or you can take a few days to cycle the whole route.

Village Hopping

As the major tourist town in Fife, **St. Andrews** ① (see pp. 172–173) makes for an ideal starting point. Soon the town's beaches are left behind as you ease south on the A915 through the rural hinterland. Take the B941 south after Largoward, and the water quickly reappears, this time the Firth of Forth, with Edinburgh's dramatic

skyline looming beyond the southern bank.

As you approach the Firth, take the A917 south to the first of the small fishing villages, **Elie** ②. Here, the **Ship Inn** (see p. 199) is the heart of the community and great for a seafood meal or a pint of ale while catching up on the local gossip. In summer, watch for the inn's legendary cricket and boules games on the beach. In addition to the pretty harbor, lined with distinctive whitewashed houses with ocher roof tiles, there are gorgeous beaches to enjoy here.

Farther east along the A917, **St. Monans** ③, the smallest of the East Neuk villages, is something of a local secret. Wander the picturesque streets, then head out to the pier where the casual **East Pier Smokehouse** *(tel 01333/405 030, eastpier.co.uk, closed Nov.–March & other days rest of year)* serves up exceptionally tasty fish with sweeping views from its outside deck.

Another short hop along the A917 brings you to **Anstruther ❹**, a working fishing port that really feels authentic, and home to a brace of award-winning fish-and-chips restaurants, including the legendary **Anstruther Fish Bar** (see p. 198). The town also boasts the **Scottish Fisheries Museum** *(St. Ayles, Harbourhead, tel 01333/310 628, scotfishmuseum .org, closed Tues., ££)*, which reclines in a collage of deeply historic houses on the waterfront and fills visitors in on this coastline's fishing and whaling past. Warm up with the locals at friendly **Coast Coffee** *(13 Shore St., tel 01333/311 411)*, facing the scenic harbor.

The last of the East Neuk fishing villages along the A917 is picturesque **Crail ❺**. It tumbles down the hillside in a gaggle of stone houses, many populated by artists who find inspiration in the architecture, colorful people, and special light. Follow the signs to **Crail Pottery** *(75 Nethergate, tel 01333/451 212,crailpottery.com)*, jam-packed with items decorated in a variety of styles and sizes, making ideal hand-crafted souvenirs to take home. High Street has several welcoming pubs, but if you head to the informal wooden shack down by the water, you can kick back with some boat-fresh lobster and watch the fishermen at work. Here you can take in a scene that will live long in your memory before turning back north along the trusty A917, which flirts in and out of the rolling countryside along the coast all the way back to St. Andrews.

Elie Ness Lighthouse with sunset background

DUNDEE & ANGUS

Over the last millennium, Dundee has transformed from a humble fishing port into a bustling hub that is now Scotland's fourth largest city. This rise in status is in no small part due to its strategic location on the legendary banks of the River Tay, allowing trade to flourish with all corners of the globe. The surrounding Angus region boasts everything from the bucolic escape of the Angus Glens to a stretch of stunningly attractive coastline.

■ R.R.S. *Discovery*, docked in Dundee's Discovery Quay, took Ernest Shackleton and Robert Falcon Scott to Antarctica.

Dundee

Dundee's golden age began in the 14th century, when it prospered as a trading center and boasted a burgeoning wool industry that underpinned its economy for more than 200 years. Over time, however, a number of events conspired to undermine Dundee's fortunes. These included a 1548 fire started by the "Auld Enemy," the English; a lethal plague in 1607–1608; and further English attacks.

In 1878, the Tay Railway Bridge opened, linking the city with Fife to the south. Measuring almost 2 miles (3 km) long, it was the largest single-span bridge in the world at the time. Triumph soon turned to tragedy, however, and today's replacement crossing (still Europe's longest railway bridge) is one of Dundee's most poignant symbols. The remains of the old pier still haunt from the Firth of Tay and are an enduring reminder of the events of December 28, 1879. On that fateful night, the bridge collapsed; 75 passengers plunged to their deaths in the stormy river below.

For the best view over the Tay bridges (the road bridge was completed in 1966), as well as the river

INSIDER TIP:

Dundonian is a rich local dialect that is a mystery even to many Scots, but persevere and it is fascinating to listen to and not as impenetrable as it first sounds.

—LARRY PORGES
National Geographic author

and the coast beyond, head up to the **Mills Observatory,** which hangs 572 feet (174 m) over the city atop Balgay Hill. Britain's first purpose-built public observatory continues to stage regular planetarium shows.

Dundee's largely modern landscape is dotted with architectural gems that bring its colorful history to life, such as **St. Andrews Church** *(2 King St.),* completed in 1722; the early 20th-century **Caird Hall** *(City Sq., tel 01382/434 940, leisureand culturedundee.com/culture/caird-hall);* the historic town houses on **South Tay Street;** the **Malmaison Hotel;** and Dundee's oldest building, **St. Mary's Tower** (1480), located on Nethergate and more commonly

City of Discovery

The City of Discovery (named after Captain Scott of the Antarctic's vessel, *Discovery,* which is moored here) is on a grand new journey. Its run-down waterfront is being regenerated by the £1.6 billion (US$ 2 billion) Dundee Waterfront project *(dundeewaterfront .com).* The futuristic redevelopment includes a branch of the illustrious V&A Museum of Design *(Riverside Esplanade, tel 01382/411 611, vam.ac.uk/ dundee),* which opened in 2018 in a visionary building by Japanese designer Kengo Kuma. This massive 30-year undertaking is gradually unfolding, giving a tantalizing view of a city in the midst of innovation.

known as the Old Steeple. Built in the Gothic Revival style of 1867, the striking **McManus,** Dundee's premier gallery and museum, specializes in art from the 19th and 20th centuries.

Tourism has become a pillar of Dundee's economy. In 1986, the return of **R.R.S. *Discovery*—**the ship built for Capt. Robert Falcon Scott's 1901–1904 Antarctic voyage, during

Angus Visitor Information **visitangus.com Dundee** 🗺 167 B2 **Visitor Information** ✉ V&A Dundee, 1 Riverside Esplanade ☎ (01382) 527 527 🕐 Closed Tues.–Wed. **visitscotland.com • Mills Observatory** ✉ Glamis Rd., Balgay Park, Dundee ☎ (01382) 435 967 💲 £ **leisureandculturedundee .com/culture/mills • The McManus** ✉ Albert Sq., Meadowside, Dundee ☎ (01382) 307 200 **mcmanus.co.uk • R.R.S. *Discovery*** ✉ Discovery Point, Discovery Quay, Dundee ☎ (01382) 309 060 💲 £££ **dundeeheritagetrust.co.uk/attraction/discovery-point**

which he mapped swaths of previously unknown land and recorded more than 500 new kinds of marine animals, spiders, and shellfish—brought a new generation of visitors to the city's historic waterfront. Before boarding the elegant tall ship, join Captain Scott (1868–1912) on his groundbreaking expedition, detailed through enjoyable exhibits at the family-friendly **Discovery Point Visitor Centre.**

The city's other maritime relic is the **H.M.S. *Unicorn.*** Moored at Victoria Dock, this unrigged 1824 classic whisks you back to the days when Britain ruled the waves. Although never seeing action, she is one of the world's oldest surviving warships. The tour's highlights include the graceful unicorn figurehead and the huge cannon on the gun deck.

You can explore another aspect of Dundee's industrial age at **Verdant Works.** In the 1860s and 1870s, when Dundee's jute industry was in its prime, up to 50,000 workers—the total population of the city was around 90,000 at the time—produced the coarse fiber at more than 60 factories. This former mill employed 500 people. You can learn about every aspect of the production of jute and its many uses around the globe, before getting your hands on the more interactive exhibits.

Forward-Thinking City: While it has been inextricably shaped by its colorful past, Dundee is also a vibrant and forward-thinking city. A swath of investment in everything from the revamped **Overgate Shopping**

H.M.S. *Unicorn* ✉ Victoria Dock, Dundee ☎ (01382) 200 900 ⊕ Closed Mon. summer; Mon.–Tues. winter 💲 £ **frigateunicorn.org** • **Verdant Works** ✉ W. Henderson's Wynd, Dundee ☎ (01382) 309 060 ⊕ Closed Mon.–Tues. Nov.–March 💲 ££ **vundeeheritagetrust.co.uk/attraction/verdant-works**

▪ Caird Hall serves as Dundee's main concert and event venue.

EXPERIENCE: Walking in the Angus Glens

The Angus Glens stretch across Glen Esk, Glen Prosen, Glen Clova, Glen Isla, and Glen Lethnott. They are one of Scotland's secret walking treasures—a wild landscape tucked away in the foothills of the mighty Cairngorms. These rugged valleys feature spectacular mountains, fast, twisting rivers, and lush, green forests.

Easily accessible from Dundee, this stunning area is alive with heather, wild deer, and bountiful birdlife. As you watch a burn tumbling through the rocks, a dragonfly may dance in front of you. As you climb to the top of a Munro—a 3,000-foot-plus (914 m) peak—you may see the rare alpine flowers that thrive on the high ground. And if you are very lucky, you may spot a golden eagle soaring above the rocky outcrops where they nest.

The Angus Glens provide an ideal location for many outdoor activities such as fishing and hunting and, for the very adventurous, canoeing, rappelling, and climbing. The most popular activity is hill walking, with myriad routes to explore on your own (see *walkhighlands.co.uk/angus* for some recommended routes) or on guided walking or cycling tours.

Walkers looking for company should visit during the **Angus Glens Walking Festival** (*angus alive.scot/countryside-adventures*), in May or June. It incorporates more than 20 guided walks, for all ages and abilities, that are led by experienced local mountaineers, accompanied by countryside rangers and estate managers who share their knowledge of the area. It has not been held since the COVID-19 pandemic, but ANGUSalive, the charity that sponsors the festival, offers regular "health walks" and hikes.

Centre (*overgate.co.uk*) to the recent renovations along the lifeblood waterfront are testimony to Dundee's ongoing regeneration. New parks, hotels, restaurants, and even a leisure marina, and more are springing up on the coattails of the new V&A Museum of Design (see sidebar p. 178).

Immediately west of the city center, High Street becomes Nethergate and passes into the cultural quarter. Here, the **Dundee Rep Theatre** boasts a friendly café, a resident group of actors, and a contemporary dance company. Staging a string of daring productions, it has established itself as one of Scotland's premier venues. Here, too, **Dundee Contemporary**

Dundee Rep Theatre ✉ Tay Sq., Dundee ☎ (01382) 223 530 **dundeerep .co.uk** • **Dundee Contemporary Arts** ✉ 152 Nethergate, Dundee ☎ (01382) 432 444 **dca.org.uk**

The V&A Museum of Design in Dundee

Arts (DCA) is an avant-garde venue that stages everything from modern art exhibitions to art-house movies.

If the pace of sightseeing and shopping gets to be too much, go for a relaxing walk at the **University of Dundee Botanic Gardens**—one of the city's enjoyable green lungs. Alternatively, indulge in a treatment at **Yu Spa** at the Apex Hotel (see Travelwise p. 351).

Beyond Dundee

Dundee is surrounded by lush countryside, where the rolling hills of the **Angus Glens,** sweeping beaches, and historic fortifications number among its myriad attractions. The neighboring town of **Broughty Ferry,** 4 miles (6.5 km) east, charms visitors with its ruined castle and windswept beaches, as well as an appealing shopping district.

Arbroath Abbey, 17 miles (27 km) northeast of Dundee, is one of Scotland's most important historic sites. It was here that Robert the Bruce and other Scottish nobles signed the stirring Declaration of Arbroath (see p. 44). After its ruined sandstone abbey, Arbroath's other attraction is its smokies—strongly flavored smoked haddock. Buy some and enjoy them down by the harbor for a real Angus treat.

The area's must-see attraction is **Glamis Castle,** 12 miles (19 km) north of Dundee. Famous as the setting for the Shakespearean murder of King Duncan by Macbeth, it's said to be the most haunted castle in Britain. Following the tour, you can wander the gardens. ■

University of Dundee Botanic Gardens ✉ Riverside Dr. ☎ (01382) 381 190 💲 £ dundee.ac.uk/botanic • **Arbroath Abbey** 🏛 167 B2 ☎ (01241) 878 756 💲 £ historicenvironment.scot • **Glamis Castle** 🏛 167 B2 ✉ Glamis, Angus ☎ (01307) 840 393 💲 ££–££££ glamis-castle.co.uk

DEESIDE

Until the 19th century, Deeside—the region named for the River Dee—was a remote and rugged wilderness of craggy mountains, gushing rivers, and quiet villages. All that changed when British monarch Queen Victoria (1819–1901) decided to cement her love of the Scottish Highlands and buy the expansive Balmoral Estate. Her purchase instantly transformed the area into Royal Deeside. The estate is still a popular retreat for British royalty today.

The 17th-century turreted stronghold of Braemar Castle

The most dramatic approach into Royal Deeside descends from the dizzy heights of **Glenshee.** In winter, **Glenshee Ski Centre** is the portal to Scotland's busiest ski fields. In summer, it turns into prime walking territory. Tumbling down the slopes from rough, wild Glenshee, the first Royal Deeside town of **Braemar** emerges like another world, where nature is tamed with graceful granite buildings, reassuringly old hotels, and cozy tearooms. There are also

Glenshee 🄰 167 A2 • **Glenshee Ski Centre** ✉ Cairnwell, Braemar
☎ (01339) 741 320 💲 £££££ **ski-glenshee.co.uk** • **Braemar** 🄰 167 A3
Visitor Information ✉ **braemarscotland.co.uk**

many stores on hand to outfit you for cycling, skiing, and walking, as well as restaurants to offer refreshment both before or après ski.

INSIDER TIP:

Find a printed map. GPS and SatNav reception can be spotty, and local maps do a much better job at highlighting sights. When in doubt, ask a local!

—ZACK SOBCZAK
Assistant manager, operations,
National Geographic Books

The focus of much of the town's attention is on **Braemar Castle,** which the local community now owns and operates, including leading wonderful tours. The castle is expected to reopen in 2024 following a years-long restoration *(raisingthestandard.org.uk)* to return it to its former glory.

The main event in town is of course the annual **Braemar Gathering** (see pp. 189–190)—the world's most famous Highland Games—which attracts royalty and celebrities in equal measure.

If you are a serious hill walker, don't miss the hike up **Morrone** (2,818 feet/859 m), which starts just south of Braemar village center. This remarkable mountain opens up great views of the town, but also out toward the expanse of the Cairngorm Mountains to the north. As you overlook Braemar from this vantage point, close your eyes, then reopen them. Imagine the scene in 1715 when the hillsides echoed with the war cries of the Jacobite clans who gathered here to raise their standard in defiance of the united British government.

Balmoral Castle & Estate

The A93 east from Braemar crisscrosses the gushing **River Dee** all the way to Ballater (see p. 184)—another town that has thrived as a result of the royal connection. Watch for **Balmoral Castle** as it looms out of the stunning countryside. The grounds are open to the public year-round, and in summer, this holiday retreat for the British royal family allows a few visitors into a limited number of its palatial spaces. If you want to learn more about the castle's **estate,** dodge the tour buses and embark on an official **Expedition Tour** *(£££££)*. These luxurious tours by Land Rover start from the formal grounds but soon eke out into the wildly magnificent terrain that so entranced Queen Victoria all those years ago. Book ahead.

Braemar Castle ✉ Braemar ☎ (01339) 741 219 🕐 Closed Nov.–March & Mon.–Tues. April–June & Sept.–Oct. 💲 £ **braemarcastle.co.uk** • **Morrone walkhighlands.co.uk/cairngorms/morrone.shtml** • **Balmoral Castle** 🗺 167 B3 ☎ (01339) 742 534 🕐 Closed Aug.–March 💲 ££ **balmoralcastle.com**

Royal Seal of Approval

Queen Victoria, it can be argued, pretty much kick-started Scottish tourism after visiting Scotland in 1842 and falling in love with the countryside. After she had her palatial baronial home, Balmoral, built on Deeside (see pp. 182-188), other nobility followed suit. Now commonly known as Royal Deeside, the area even today hosts many businesses, such as butchers and bakers, who display distinctive plaques showing their Royal Seal of Approval, granted as a mark of recognition to those who have regularly sup-plied goods or services to the Royal Household.

Members of the current-day royal family typically visit Balmoral in September and early October, when it is closed to the public. Elsewhere in Scotland strong royal connections remain in evidence at Edinburgh's Palace of Holyroodhouse (the King's official Scottish residence) and Glamis Castle. Scots also take pride that the Prince and Princess of Wales (Prince William and Kate Middleton) studied and met in St. Andrews.

Whisky Country

Enter Deeside and you are also sneaking into serious whisky country, with the smells of Speyside almost discernible across the mountains. Continuing the royal theme, one of King Charles's famous tipples is the malt conjured up at **Royal Lochnagar Distillery** in Ballater. However, if you prefer working off calories rather than drinking them, try hiking up the 3,790-foot (1,115 m) Munro of **Lochnagar,** which is said to be King Charles's favorite mountain in Scotland.

The locals of the charming town of **Ballater** love the royals so much that even the bakers and the bus company that have received royal approval brandish their polished royal crests with great pride. The town center perfectly portrays what Royal Deeside is all about. Ballater is a neatly polished affair of trim stone houses, tourist-orientated coffee shops, outdoor activity operators, and everything that has a royal connection. The beloved **Ballater Royal Station** has been rebuilt after a 2015 fire, and once again hosts a visitor center and exhibits.

Ballater is also starting to push itself as a base for adventure sports fans. Queen Victoria loved the rugged, bleak mountain landscapes here,

(continued on p. 188)

Royal Lochnagar Distillery ⊠ Craithie, Ballater ☎ (01339) 742 700
💲 Tours: ££££–£££££ malts.com • **Lochnagar Munro** walkhighlands
.co.uk/munros/lochnagar • **Ballater** 🗻 167 B3 Visitor Information
⊠ The Old Station Sq., Ballater ☎ (01339) 755 306 visitscotland.com

THE TARTAN TRADITION

To put it simply, tartan is a crisscrossed pattern of horizontal and vertical threads whose various colors are woven together to create a dramatic and unique design. Tartan fabric is made up of colored threads woven at right angles to each other to form alternating bands of similar warp (length) and weft (width). The sequence of lines and squares formed by the weave creates a pattern known as the sett.

The first Scottish tartans, thought to have been made in the Highlands as far back as 600–500 B.C., were not as colorful as they are today. The oldest actual sample of a tartan, known as the Falkirk tartan, resides in the National Museum of Scotland in Edinburgh (see pp. 71–72) and dates from A.D. 300.

Some people call tartan "plaid," which to the Scots makes no sense. For them, plaid was originally the traditional name for a large sheet of woven material that men sculpted around their bodies or used as a blanket to keep warm. Only later did the shorter, neater kilt that we now know come into being, with a more elaborate ceremonial version today still being known as plaid.

To many Scots, tartan is more than just a design or fabric. It is a phenomenon that reaches deep into their history and has taken on semimythical status. Although many Scots think of tartan as being inexorably bound up with individual clans (or families), this was not always the case. Traditionally, the colors and patterns came from the country's regions, with the colors determined by the natural dyes that were available to the weavers in each area.

Weaving tartan is an art form.

EXPERIENCE: Playing Bagpipes

Another iconic Scottish tradition, the Scottish Highland bagpipe is essentially a woodwind instrument with enclosed reeds that are fed from a bag of air the player has to keep inflated. Key components include the chanter, which provides the melody, and the drone, the cylindrical reed-filled tube that sits above the bag. The origins of the bagpipe are hotly disputed—there are similar types of instruments in Ireland and Spain—but there is evidence that the Scottish variant has been around since at least the 1400s. Indeed, one surviving set of bagpipes is said to have been played at the landmark Battle of Bannockburn in 1314. Today, you can hear them played at Highland Games, competitions, and major sporting events and festivals.

If you want to learn how to play the bagpipes, the best way is to start with tunes on the chanter. The **National Piping Centre** in Glasgow (30–34 McPhater St., tel 0141/353 0220, thepipingcentre.co.uk, closed Sun.) sells all the necessary equipment and has a school that offers everything from individual lessons to extended courses. The center also has a museum (£) that delves into the history and culture surrounding Scotland's national instrument.

Showing Their True Colors

When the various clans piled into battle in support of Scotland's inspirational leaders, such as William Wallace and Robert the Bruce, they wore a blaze of different tartans, with myriad kilts/plaids. Sometimes a soldier would wear more than one tartan design in his garb. That all changed after the disastrous defeat at Culloden, when the British government butchered the tartan army where they lay and thrust through the heart of the traditional Highland way of life. Tartan and Highland dress were actually banned by the British government in 1746 by way of the Dress Act.

This ban was eventually rescinded in 1782. During the following century, tartan became popular again, although this time not as a pattern used in everyday dress, but more as a way of displaying traditions, heritage, and clan allegiance. Tartan became the national symbol that it remains very much today. Natural dyes were replaced by brighter, bolder, and more consistent artificial coloring. This trend reached its zenith during George IV's famous visit to Edinburgh in 1822, when Scots were encouraged by Sir Walter Scott to sport their tartan finery to impress the visiting British monarch.

Modern Tartans

There are thought to be more than 7,000 different tartans, with more designs being created every year. Most are linked to the various clans and regions. Others are

---

INSIDER TIP:

Don't be tempted by the cheap "kilts" in some of the tacky tartan tat shops on Edinburgh's Royal Mile. Go to a proper kiltmaker, who will measure you and supply a genuine quality garment that will probably outlast you.

—ALASTAIR GOURLAY
National Geographic contributor

---

purely constructed, such as Flower of Scotland or the tartan created for the Tartan Army—the fanatical followers of Scotland's national soccer team. Even then, only a small minority of them sport the "official" tartan, choosing to wear their own clan and regional tartans instead, much as their ancestors would have done centuries ago. Two of the most famous tartans in Scotland are the Black Watch and the Royal Stuart. The "official" British royal tartan is the Balmoral, designed by Prince Consort Albert in 1853 and commissioned by his wife, Queen Victoria, the British monarch who had a celebrated love of the Highlands.

Today, tartan is a global phenomenon—a design borrowed by fashion creators and celebrities and adored by Hollywood stars. Everyone from the 1970s punk band the Sex Pistols to Lady Diana (there is now a Lady Diana Memorial tartan) has embraced the traditional Scottish fabric. Tartan is now not limited to kilts and other items of Highland dress, nor confined to its country of origin, popping up throughout the globe in a far cry from its humble beginnings in the wild, windswept glens of the Highlands.

Isle of Skye tartan

■ Crathes Castle and its gardens

but if you prefer your mountain landscapes unadulterated with chairlifts and mountain huts, you will love the cycling and hill walking the region has to offer. Rent mountain bikes at one of two rental shops in town: Bike Station Ballater *(Station Sq., tel 01339/754 004, bikestationballater.co.uk)* or Cyclehighlands *(The Pavilion, Victoria Rd., tel 01339/755 864, cyclehighlands.com).* Trails cater to all biking levels.

Farther east, the A93 follows the River Dee into the lovely town of **Banchory,** which, in essence, marks the start of the Aberdeen overspill; an unmistakably urban feel creeps into the rural idyll. There are high-street stores and fast-food joints, but also plenty of graceful buildings, green spaces, and fine walks. The **Banchory Museum** interprets this lively little town with exhibits on the region's archaeological wealth as well as royal connections.

Deeside is also replete with grand country houses and castles. You can find your own favorite, but the 16th-century **Crathes Castle** offers an ideal introduction. The jeweled ivory Horn of Leys given to the Burnett family to mark the generous gift of land granted in 1323 by King Robert the Bruce, on which the family later built the castle, is prominently displayed in the Great Hall. Wander the gardens or view the estate from the Go Ape treetop playground *(£££££).* ■

Banchory Museum ✉ Bridge St., Banchory ☎ (0147) 536 544 ⊕ Closed Tues.-Thurs. *&* Sun. **livelifeaberdeenshire.org.uk/museums Crathes Castle**
🅰 167 C3 ✉ Near Banchory ☎ (01330) 844 525 ⊕ Closed Mon.–Wed. Oct.–March 💲 *££* **nts.org.uk/visit/crathes-castle**

EXPERIENCE: Braemar Royal Highland Gathering

The Highland Games are said to have originated in Royal Deeside during the reign of King Malcolm Canmore, so it is fitting that the most famous Highland Gathering today is held in Braemar. Attending this event offers a fascinating insight into Scottish heritage, class, and pageantry.

Scottish dancers twirl to the tune of bagpipes at the Braemar Gathering Royal Highland Games.

The Braemar Royal Highland Society began life as the Braemar Wright Society in 1815, changing its name to the Braemar Highland Society in 1826. In 1866, Queen Victoria, herself a big fan of the Highland Society Gatherings, decided that it needed royal patronage and the "Royal" was added to the society's name. It runs the games in this guise today, and a member of the royal family continues to award the winners prizes.

The Braemar Gathering is not the biggest, but that may be because it is so popular that spectator numbers are limited—unusual for Highland Games (see pp. 20–21). Held on the first Saturday of September, this lively event re-creates the Highland spirit in a style that those who turn up each year have become accustomed to. If you only go to one Highland Games, make it Braemar.

The highlight is the massed **drummers and pipers**, who impress the crowd with their sound reverberating around the heather-clad hills. The event's competitive aspect includes Highland dancing—in which tartan-clad dancers show off their graceful skills to traditional music—as well as "heavy" events and "track" events. The latter you may recognize as traditional athletics events, such as running, while the former includes traditional Highland sports, like tossing a long wooden pole called the caber. A titanic struggle also sees various branches of the British armed forces doing battle in a fiercely competitive tug-of-war.

More Fun

Other fun events include the children's sack race, always a laugh for children and spectators alike. The fit can tackle the tough hill race that sees the foolish and the brave sprint up and down the rugged mountain Morrone.

If you are in the region the fourth Saturday of August, the **Lonach Highland Gathering & Games** (lonach.org) in Aberdeenshire is also well recommended.

Tickets

Tickets for the grandstand are near impossible to come by, but visit the website (braemargathering.org) in February when they go on sale and to get tickets for the uncovered stand or the cheapest area—the ringside seats. If not, you can still buy a cheaper ticket to the beautiful 12-acre (5 ha) grounds, but seeing the main events properly from here can be a bit tricky.

Competitors take part in the fiercely contested tug-of-war competition during The Braemar Gathering.

ABERDEEN

Aberdeen is Scotland's third largest city (pop. 235,000), crisscrossed by the Don and Dee Rivers. With a historic center laden with granite architecture, bustling port, and sandy beach, this once-booming oil town is again attracting attention with its public art and craft beer culture.

The ubiquitous granite rock of much Aberdeen architecture is seen on Old Aberdeen High Street.

Given its strategic location in the middle of Scotland's East Coast, it is no surprise that by the 13th century Aberdeen had become a major trading hub. The 19th century saw its trading role grow, and the city followed suit with the coming of the oil industry, instigating another boom. Aberdeen still serves as the base for the massive North Sea oil industry, riding its economic waves of fortune.

Aberdeen is known to Scots as the "granite city," a moniker it well deserves. All of the city's most prominent

Aberdeen 167 C3 **Visitor Information** ✉ 23 Union St. ☎ (01224) 269 180 **visitscotland.com** & **visitabdn.com**

Aberdeen's Oil Industry

Scotland's oil and gas industry emerged after vast North Sea reserves were found off its east coast in the mid-20th century. As the closest city, and a coastal one at that, Aberdeen was perfectly positioned to become the "oil capital of Europe." Today it boasts the world's busiest heliport and a bustling harbor that caters to myriad offshore rigs. Production peaked in 2000, then declined precipitously, greatly impacting the city's economics Aberdeen began to future-proof itself by becoming a leader in the development of more sustainable energy.

The Aberdeen Renewable Energy Group (*aberdeenrenewables. com*) and government-sponsored Energetica (*energetica.co.uk*) energy corridor—a global showcase for renewable energy technology and sustainable industries development—are both based in the area, and Aberdeen University is also at the forefront of research into renewable energies.

However, while Westminster supported the oil and gas industry's efforts to develop new North Sea fields and reopen closed wells following Russia's invasion of the Ukraine in February 2022, Holyrood committed £500 million (US$612 million) over 10 years to help Scotland's coastal communities move away from carbon-based industries.

buildings are built in this solid stone, its main streets forming granite canyons that can take on an intimidating air when the North Sea storms howl in. Lately, the addition of public art has brought new life to some sterile spaces.

Union Square shopping center is one of the city's hubs, directly linked to the bus and train stations. Any English visitors who think that the name indicates a warm embrace of the 1707 Union might want to think again. The city's motto, "Bon Accord," comes from the night in 1306 when its citizens ransacked the

(continued on p. 194)

INSIDER TIP:

Don't miss the March of the Lonach Highlanders in late August, when hundreds, from several clans, march the winding roads of Aberdeenshire, stopping at each country house for a wee dram of hospitality from the local laird.

—LEON GRAY
National Geographic contributor

March of the Lonach Highlanders ✉ Bellabeg Park, Strathdon, Aberdeenshire 💲 ££ lonach.org

EXPERIENCE: Play a Round of Golf

With more than 550 golf courses dotted around the nation, Scotland is the world's number one golfing destination. Playing a round or two while you are here is obligatory for golf fanatics, while for less accomplished players the sport is a fascinating way of getting to the heart of the national psyche—not to mention experiencing some its most dramatic scenery.

The oldest golf course in the world lies in Musselburgh near Edinburgh (see p. 87). Documents show the game was played here as early as 1672, but there are tales that Mary Queen of Scots enjoyed a round in 1567.

Scotland is famous for its "links" courses, set along the coastal sand dunes. Most golfers with a reasonable handicap head for the grand courses that have hosted the British Open, such as **Muirfield** in East Lothian (see p. 87), **Royal Troon** and **Prestwick** in Ayrshire (see p. 116), **St. Andrews** in Fife (see pp. 172–173), and **Carnoustie** *(tel 01241/802 270, carnoustiegolflinks.com)* in Angus. Book in advance to play at one of these hallowed courses.

Many inland courses, like **Pitlochry** *(tel 01796/472 792, pitlochrygolf.co.uk)* in Tayside, are just as scenic and prestigious, though. Perhaps the most impressive golf resort does not even lie on the coast. Celebrating its golfing centenary in 2019, **Gleneagles,** with its grand hotel (see Travelwise p. 349), spreads across 850 acres (344 ha) of stunning Perthshire countryside, surrounded by woodland and hills. There are three full courses—the King's Course, the Queen's Course, and Jack Nicklaus–designed PGA Centenary Course—plus the nine-hole PGA National Academy course.

In Scotland, golf is very much the

A group hits the links at Gleneagles in Perthshire.

people's game. Many courses are open to the public, ranging from world-class links to modest courses within city boundaries. There are also simple nine-hole courses ideal for new players. Every year sees at least one new course open, with Jack Nicklaus' latest course design at **Ury Estate**, outside Aberdeen, scheduled to open in late 2024.

How you arrange to play golf in Scotland is up to you. Whether you want to hire one of the many golf tour operators to arrange games on famous courses, flying between them by helicopter, or just to play a quick game on a municipal course, see *visitscotland.com/things-to-do/outdoor-activities/golf* for all the information you need. However you choose to play, the experience is magnified by knowing that you are enjoying a round in the country where it all began.

English garrison and massacred its defenders.

Start your city tour at **Castlegate,** a square at the east end of Union Street, where the city's majestic castle once stood. Admire the 17th-century **Mercat Cross** here, once the focus of the city, with its intricate carvings. Farther west, at the start of Union Street, is the **Town House,** the city's dramatic council headquarters. The lavish 19th-century facade is wonderfully overblown. It conceals the earlier Tolbooth, now home to the **Tolbooth Museum** (temporarily closed at press time), which explores crime and punishment during its heyday as a jail in the 17th and 18th centuries.

A block north of Union Street is an even more dramatic creation—Aberdeen University's **Marischal College,** which is the second largest granite building in the world. This lavish building looks like someone has dripped granite all over a massive wedding cake.

Farther west on Union Street, with its entrance to the north on Belmont Street, is the recently revamped **Aberdeen Art Gallery.** This wonderfully eclectic collection boasts an impressive array of 19th- and 20th-century fine art, as well as early archaeological finds from ancient Greek and Roman periods. In addition, maritime exhibits shed light on the city's relationship with the North Sea. This creative space also stages many temporary exhibitions and concerts of everything from traditional

Tolbooth Museum ✉ Castle St., Aberdeen ☎ (03000) 200 293 **aberdeencity .gov.uk/AAGM • Aberdeen Art Gallery** ✉ Schoolhill ☎ (03000) 200 293 **aberdeencity.gov.uk/AAGM**

Aberdeen Beach hosts a popular amusement park.

Scottish ceilidh music to Indonesian gamelan.

Heading directly south from Castlegate, you will descend into the old **harbor.** Much of the modern working port is off-limits, and the buzz of the oil and gas industries has slowed as prices have fallen, but you will find activity, as well as a tumble of old stone cottages, cobbled streets, and warehouses. At the **Aberdeen Maritime Museum** you can learn about the city's long connection with the sea, from the days when fishing was the main maritime industry right through to today's massive oil and gas industry, with a fascinating scale model of an oil rig. The well-constructed and often interactive exhibits in this kid-friendly museum also cover shipbuilding and sailing ships.

North of the harbor lies **Aberdeen Beach,** where the whole city seems to flock on sunny days. This long stretch of sand is ideal for families, and there is a promenade that works well for strolls, which can be refreshingly bracing when the wind is coming off the sea.

The area has a good selection of cafés and restaurants, as well as arcades and amusement parks, and it is well set up for leisure activities. Chief among these is the **Beach Leisure Centre** (*Beach Promenade, Aberdeen Beach, tel 01224/507 739, sportaberdeen.co.uk, ££££*), with its swimming pool, wave machine, flumes, climbing wall, and other sporting activities. Also here, in 2022 the **Aberdeen Science Centre** emerged from a £6 million (US$7.5 million) transformation and enthralls adults and kids alike with scores of interactive exhibits across six themed zones spanning life zones to space.

This is an ideal attraction for active families on a wet day, which are all too common in this windswept, coastal city. To the southwest of the city, **Adventure Aberdeen Snowsports Centre** (*Garthee Rd., tel 01224/810 215, sport aberdeen.co.uk*) is perfect for rainy summer days with its dry ski slope, plus skiing and snowboarding lessons.

Aberdeen may be laden with gray granite, but real efforts are made to brighten it up with flower beds, which seem to pop up from every available pore. Of all the city's plentiful parks, the 44-acre (18 ha) **Duthie Park** (*Polmuir Rd.*) is a highlight. In summer, a number of play areas keep the children entertained, cricket is played, and special events such as Opera in the Park take place within the spacious grounds. Also in the warm weather, the boating lake opens to paddle boats, an enjoyable exercise opportunity for all ages. On colder days you can check out the park's **David Welsch Winter Gardens** (*open year-round*), where exotic species (including one of Britain's largest collections of cactuses) thrive in the artificially warm climate within huge greenhouses that replicate tropical and arid environments ∎

Aberdeen Maritime Museum ✉ 52–56 Shiprow ☎ (03000) 200 293 **aberdeencity.gov.uk/AAGM • Aberdeen Science Centre** ✉ 179 Constitution St. ☎ (01224) 640 340 💲 ££ (children £) **aberdeensciencecentre.org**

NORTHEAST COAST

The northeast coastline is renowned for its busy fishing ports. Fishing has been on the decline in recent years, but many of these picture-postcard villages still run small fleets. Atmospheric harbors are strewn with lobster pots and pretty stone fishing cottages, with thick walls built around them to protect their inhabitants against the biting North Sea winds.

■ Dunnottar Castle evokes a land of legend and myth far removed from modern times.

A good place to start exploring the fishing villages of this corner of Scotland is **Stonehaven,** south of Aberdeen. Visitors appreciate the great local fish and chips, the historic harbor, and its oldest building, the **Tolbooth,** which is now a volunteer-run museum that delves into the local fishing heritage. Boat trips are available in summer, and the best time to visit is during the folk festival in early July *(stonehavenfolkfestival.co.uk).*

A scenic path from the harbor leads 1.8 miles (3 km) to the area's best attraction (also reached by car via the Coastal Tourist Route), the dramatic **Dunnottar Castle** *(tel 01569/766 320, dunnottarcastle.co.uk, ££).* Set on an enormous flat-top outcrop, with the North Sea crashing below, Dunnottar was home to the Earls Marischal, a powerful Scottish family. It was here that a small garrison held firm against Cromwell's army for eight months, safeguarding

Stonehaven  167 C3 **stunningstonehaven.com • Tolbooth Museum**
✉ The Harbour, Stonehaven ☎ (07512) 466 329 🕐 Closed Tues.
& Nov.–May **stonehaventolbooth.co.uk**

the Scottish crown jewels until they were smuggled out in a pregnant woman's dress right past the English army. Although a ruin, there remains a lot to see here, with staircases, huge fireplaces, and a room for the Earl's pet lion to be explored. Stunning views abound.

The windswept castle is open all year, weather permitting, but be advised that the only access is by a series of steep steps down and back. To recover from your climb, stop by the concessions truck often parked by the entrance gate, which serves excellent soup as well as the obligatory fish and chips.

The landscape is much wilder north of Aberdeen, with stone villages set among sweeping sand dunes and looming sea cliffs. **Peterhead** is the biggest whitefish port in Europe and is worth a stop to feel the pulse of Scottish fishing and to try a slab of boat-fresh haddock at a local café.

Fraserburgh, at the tip of Aberdeenshire, is home to the **Museum of Scottish Lighthouses.** In addition to a tour of **Kinnaird Head Castle** and adjacent lighthouse building, you will learn about the family that designed many of Scotland's impressive lighthouses and gave birth to the literary talent of Robert Louis Stevenson.

Pennan, west of Fraserburgh, is the area's quintessential fishing village, sitting snug beneath huge cliffs with little more than a few houses set on one waterfront street. During storm tides, waves can wash over parked cars.

Just a few miles farther west, the twin settlements of **Crovie** and **Gardenstown,** less than a mile apart, get fewer tourists than Pennan but are also beguilingly pretty. Gardenstown is a great place to enjoy top-quality seafood.

Farther west again, **Portsoy** is one of the most complete fishing villages. Although quiet these days, you can still see the twin harbors and the voluminous old warehouses. The modest **Portsoy Salmon Bothy** (tel 01261/842 296, salmonbothy.org) tells the story of the town, with particular emphasis on commercial salmon fishing. **The Shore Inn** (49 Church St., tel 01261/842 831, facebook.com/TheShoreInn) is a cozy place to enjoy a pint and the tall tales of the local characters.

The trim little Moray village of **Cullen** is famous for "Cullen skink"— the delicious, creamy smoked haddock soup. The modern part of Cullen sits on a hilltop, with some grand civic buildings, cafés, and an ice-cream store, while down by the sea (under the old railway viaduct that sweeps around the village), the windswept harbor hints at former glories. ■

Peterhead 🄼 167 C4 • **Fraserburgh** 🄼 167 C4 • **Museum of Scottish Lighthouses** ✉ Kinnaird Head, Stevenson Rd., Fraserburgh ☎ (01346) 511 022 💲 £ lighthousemuseum.org.uk • **Pennan** 🄼 167 C4 • **Portsoy** 🄼 167 B4 portsoy.org

Where to Eat & Drink on the East Coast

PRICES

An indication of the cost of a three-course meal without drinks is given by **£** signs.

£££££	Over £50
££££	£40–£50
£££	£25–£40
££	£15–£25
£	Under £15

AMUSE

1 QUEEN'S TERRACE, ABERDEEN

(01224) 611 909 | amuse-restaurant.com

Opened in July 2022, award-winning chef Kevin Dalgleish's exquisitely furnished, fine-dining newcomer in a granite townhouse with a wood-burning oven earned instant Michelin recognition for its French-inspired Scottish cuisine, which is bursting with flavor. Other international flavors also find their way into dishes, such as the chicken liver parfait with toasted walnuts, raisin bread, and mango chutney.

£ 🕐 Closed Mon.–Tues.; Sun. dinner 💳 MC, V

ANSTRUTHER FISH BAR

43–44 SHORE RD., ANSTRUTHER

(01333) 310 518 | anstrutherfishbar.co.uk

This multi-award-winning chippy has been crowned the best in Scotland on numerous occasions. Here the fish is always fresh and the chips crisp. The sit-in restaurant and takeout menu feature more than just haddock and cod, with the likes of lemon sole, Pittenweem prawns, and hake, as well as the catch of the day, also on offer.

£ 💳 MC, V

BALGOVE LARDER

BALGOVE FARMHOUSE, STRATHTYRUM FARM, ST. ANDREWS

(01334) 898 145 | balgove.com

Situated just outside St. Andrews, in a very pretty setting, this appealing compound includes a farm shop, butchery, and café (try the cullen skink). A separate building, dubbed the Steak Barn, offers a fantastic introduction to local Angus beef as you perch on long wooden trestle tables. The shop is well stocked with a wide variety of Scottish deli meats and produce, much from Balgove itself. If you are a Scottish gin lover, you will be in heaven with the variety on offer here.

£–££ 🅿 🕐 Steak barn closed Mon.–Tues. 💳 MC, V

BREWDOG

17 GALLOWGATE, ABERDEEN

(01224) 631 223 | brewdog.com

Founded in 2007, BrewDog has exploded throughout the world, but nowhere as much as in Scotland. Owners James Watt and Martin Dickie opened their first bar in their hometown of Aberdeen, and the flagship location remains the favorite of many. Hang out here for a few hours, sampling myriad delicious beers while

■ **Fresh scones for sale at Balgove Larder**

🅿 Parking 🕐 Opening Hours 💳 Credit Cards

enjoying a game of Scrabble as the stresses of the day melt away.

£ MC, V

CAIRNIE FRUIT FARM TEAROOM
CAIRNIE, CUPAR

(01334) 655 610 | cairniefruitfarm.co.uk

If you've got kids in tow this is a great place to head for lunch. The café at this farm dishes up child-friendly staples like soup, sandwiches, and home-baked goods, as well as a handful of hot meals and locally made ice cream. What really wins the children over though is the play area that includes trampolines, mini-tractors, and a maze.

£ P Closed Mon.–Tues. & Nov.–Feb. MC, V

THE CELLAR
24 EAST GREEN, ANSTRUTHER

(01333) 310 378 | thecellaranstruther.co.uk

Diners have been heaping superlatives on this seafood restaurant for years. Happily, the accolades have continued under the new ownership of local lad turned top chef Billy Boyter, who has earned it a Michelin star. From premeal drinks right though to coffee, guests are treated to smooth but unobtrusive service. Foodies will swoon at the menu, and everyone will leave knowing they have experienced a special meal. Reservations required.

££££–£££££ Closed Mon.–Tues. MC, V

OLD BOATYARD RESTAURANT
FISHMARKET QUAY, ARBROATH

(01241) 879 995 | oldboatyard.co.uk

Panoramic views over Arbroath's atmospheric old harbor are reason enough to eat at the Old Boatyard Restaurant. Everything from seared scallops to whole lobster tempt from the largely seafood menu. For an authentic local taste, sample an Arbroath smokie (locally smoked haddock). A relaxed sofa area for pre- or postdinner drinks, a decent wine list, and friendly service complete the picture.

££ MC, V

THE PEAT INN
B940, PEAT INN, CUPAR

(01334) 840 206 | thepeatinn.co.uk

This Michelin-starred culinary oasis is beautifully run by husband-and-wife team Geoffrey and Katherine Smeddle and styles itself as a "restaurant with rooms." The food, which draws heavily on Scottish produce, is nothing short of superb, drawing diners from around the globe. Stay the night if you can; the eight luxurious and individually styled suites are much more than just rooms.

£££££ P Closed Sun.–Thurs. lunch, Mon.–Sun. dinner AE, MC, V

THE PIER
5–6 ESPLANADE, SEA BEACH, ABERDEEN

(01224) 374 490 | pieraberdeen.co.uk

With a menu featuring hearty breakfasts plus burgers, and more substantial mains like fish and chips, gumbo bowls, blackened cajun cod, and a wonderful selection of ice cream sundaes, this bright and cheerful seafront café has something for everyone.

£–££ MC, V

SHIP INN
ELIE, LEVEN

(01333) 330 246 | shipinn.scot

Pop into this upscale seaside watering hole–awarded the hospitality award for Scotland's "pub of the year"–for real ale and hearty food done well. There's a focus on local seafood, with daily specials chalked up on the blackboard. On summer weekends the pub often fires up its barbecue and its team plays cricket on the golden sand beach in front of the terrace. Six nice guest rooms are also available.

££ MC, V

Towering mountains, heather-clad hills, and deep primeval lochs (complete with monsters), plus winter sports and whisky galore

CENTRAL & WESTERN HIGHLANDS

The tranquil beauty of Loch Insh

CENTRAL & WESTERN HIGHLANDS

This wildly beautiful region has visitors agog at the sheer scenic splendor of it all, and making hasty plans to return before they have even left. Boasting world-famous lochs, the country's highest mountain, the U.K.'s largest national park, and top-notch adventure sports, this richly historic land is every bit as romantic as its legends suggest.

The central and western Highlands are Scotland at its best, a scenic and historic oasis that runs from coast to coast. Hulking mountain peaks rise up all around, while rugged passes slit through the glens and deep-blue sea lochs spread out like fjords toward the Atlantic Ocean.

The only city in the Highlands and the region's capital, Inverness, on the northeast coast, is developing at a rate that shows the area is finally recovering from the aftermath of the calamitous Battle of Culloden in 1746, an event that shaped the human and natural history of this region as much as any ice age. Currently one of Europe's

fastest growing cities, Inverness has become increasingly sophisticated and appealing for visitors, many of whom now often spend a few nights here rather than just passing straight through.

Aviemore, south of Inverness, is Scotland's busiest winter sports resort. It hangs in the shadow of the voluminous Cairngorms, a mountain range boasting some of the U.K.'s

highest peaks, including the mighty Ben Macdui, protected as part of Cairngorms National Park. The region is popular in summer with hikers and climbers who give way in winter to skiers and that particularly Scottish winter sport, curling.

On the foothills of the range sits the efficiently run Rothiemurchus, a forested sanctuary that has something for everyone, from fishing and mountain biking to wildlife-watching and dog-sledding to family activities and farm shop. Its well-maintained confines provide a neat condensed introduction to the charms of the area. Just east is Speyside, where some of the world's most famous whiskies are made, including Glenfiddich

NOT TO BE MISSED:

Learning about Scotland's most infamous battlefield at Culloden's eco-friendly visitor center 209

Loch Ness, Scotland's largest inland loch and home to the elusive monster, Nessie 220–222

Exploring Glen Coe, the most beautiful of the glens and laced with human tragedy 227–229

Glenfinnan, a magical glen with epic scenery, a profound sense of history, and Hogwarts Express of *Harry Potter* fame 226–227

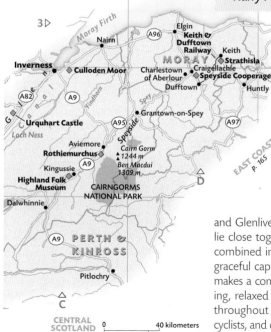

and Glenlivet. The major distilleries lie close together and can be easily combined into a tour. The region's graceful capital, Grantown-on-Spey, makes a comfortable base. This rolling, relaxed river valley is also busy throughout the year with walkers, cyclists, and canoeists.

On the opposite coast to Inverness, at the end of a 60-mile-long (100 km) series of glens (valleys) known as the Great Glen, is Fort William. The Great Glen encompasses four lochs, including Loch Ness, home to the world's most famous (and elusive) monster, Nessie. You can walk, cycle, canoe, or even take a boat between the two coasts. The remarkable Caledonian Canal, a wonder of 19th-century Scottish engineering, connects the quartet of lochs to the North Sea and the Atlantic Ocean, via the pretty town of Fort Augustus.

These days, Fort William serves as an adventure hub, offering easy access to the U.K.'s highest mountain, Ben Nevis, and the great Nevis Range that surrounds it, which is now a hotbed of mountain biking and skiing action. This region of the Highlands is also serious walking country, with trails to suit all levels of ability and experience.

Glen Coe, south of Fort William, may be the most attractive glen in the country, even if its name is inextricably linked with one of the most poignant Scottish tales of tragedy. West of Fort William you can take a train or drive the "Road to the Isles," seeking out the Atlantic Coast. It arrives having passed through a string of spectacular glens and unfurls in a sweep of starched white-sand beaches around the quiet villages of Morar and Arisaig.

The fishing port of Mallaig awaits at the end of the line, providing a gateway to the isles themselves, with Skye clearly visible across the water. The mainland north of Mallaig and Knoydart is as wild as anything found on Scotland's islands, and is again steeped in tragedy, resulting from the direct (and indirect) consequences of that defeat at Culloden—a battle that seismically shifted the Highland way of life forever and still fires the imagination and hearts of both locals and visitors today. ∎

Blackhouse Cottage, Glencoe

INVERNESS

The city of Inverness stands at the northern tip of the Great Glen, where the waters of Loch Ness flow down to Beauly Firth. Inverness is also at the crossroads between the Highlands and the Lowlands, and has seen many violent clashes over the centuries, from medieval clan warfare to the carnage of Culloden in 1746. Today it is the largest urban area in the Highlands, a dynamic modern city with a population of almost fifty thousand people.

■ Inverness's suspension footbridge links the busy center with the quieter side of the River Ness.

Inverness's population has grown in recent times, and it was formally proclaimed a city in 2000. It has also prospered thanks to its growing tourist industry, styling itself as the "gateway to the Highlands," and as a service center for the North Sea oil and gas fields

The main sight is **Inverness Castle** *(Castle St., invernesscastle.scot)*. The structure has been flattened on numerous occasions throughout its turbulent history, and the current red-hued sandstone building bears little resemblance to the original. Nonetheless, the ghosts of dead Highlanders, Mary Queen of Scots, and Robert the Bruce are never far away. As you stroll around the grounds look for the statue of Flora MacDonald, a tribute to the Scots woman who helped Bonnie Prince Charlie escape after his army's

Inverness 203 C2 **Visitor Information** ✉ 36 High St., Inverness
☎ (01463) 252 401 **visitscotland.com** & **visitinvernesslochness.com**

INSIDER TIP:

For a healthy dose of Highland hospitality and dry Scottish wit, stay with Richard and Jenny at Moyness House, just a few minutes' walk from the city center.

—JENNIFER SEGAL
National Geographic Development Office

defeat at Culloden. In recent years, the castle has been used as a courthouse. The castle is currently closed for conversion into a tourist venue, to open in 2025, with tours led by *seanchaidh* (storyteller) guides. Until then you can climb the north tower's **Viewpoint** *(£)*, offering 360-degree views of Inverness and beyond.

The Center

Just a block north of the castle, on Castle Wynd, is the **Inverness Museum and Art Gallery.** With free admission, it is well worth a visit, as it not only covers the history of the city but also delves into the past of the whole Highland region. Exhibits include

Moyness House ✉ 6 Bruce Gardens, Inverness ☎ (01463) 236 624 **moyness.co.uk • Inverness Museum and Art Gallery** ✉ Castle Wynd, Inverness ☎ (01349) 781 730 🕐 Closed Sun.–Mon. **highlifehighland.com/inverness-museum-and-art-gallery**

everything from brutal weapons and bagpipes to modern interactive displays that shed light on the traditional Highland way of life. Many of the paintings in the collection, meanwhile, show local history scenes. The curator's favorite piece is an old penny coin that was sculpted by an air force pilot into the shape of a plane to give to his sweetheart.

Pushing a short distance farther north brings you to the **Town House** (7 High St.). This building dates back to 1878 and is constructed in a Gothic style, which contrasts with much of the city center. The most famous gathering

EXPERIENCE:
The Calm of Ness Islands

A short stroll south of Inverness's busy center you'll find the Ness Islands, a park spread over a number of small river islands. Here the sounds of traffic are replaced by the swish of freshwater and the song of birds. The islands are linked by walkways, and, strolling along them on a sunny day, you will meet few other tourists, but will instead mix with locals walking their dogs or merely taking the air. Find the islands at the east end of the Infirmary Bridge; it's the first footbridge upstream from the main road bridge.

here was in 1921 when the first British cabinet meeting ever held outside London was rapidly convened as Ireland seceded from Britain. It is no longer open to the public. The city's **Mercat Cross** and the **Stone of Tubs,** where women used to rest their washing tubs en route to and from the river, are just outside. Legend has it that as long as this stone stays in place, Inverness will continue to thrive.

Crossing over Bridge Street to the north, the pedestrianized shopping heart of Inverness spills out to your left. It's a handy retail oasis selling everyday essentials that will come in useful for forays into the wild Highlands. There are also plenty of tourist-oriented "Scottish" shops, where half the fun is hearing all the myths and stories you will inevitably be told when asking about the merchandise.

Three blocks north, at 71 Church Street, is **Abertaff House.** Reputed to be the oldest building in the whole of Inverness, this protected structure dates back to 1593. Beyond the narrow entrance you'll find a small museum about 17th-century life. Along with the other buildings on and surrounding Church Street—including the 130–foot-tall (40 m) Georgian **Steeple** (2 Bridge St.) and the **Old High Church** (corner of Church St. & Friars' Ln.)—this remarkable house harks back to a very different era.

Abertaff House ✉ 71 Church St. 🕐 Closed Nov.–March **nts.org.uk/ visit/places/abertarff-house**

■ Cityscape of Inverness on a beautiful summer day

Across the River

Behind the Old High Church is a footbridge that crosses the River Ness to the quieter east bank. Turn immediately south and you will come to the **Highland House of Fraser** (4-9 Huntly St., 01463/222 781, highlandhouseoffraser.com), where you can buy a beautiful handcrafted kilt made by some of the most acclaimed kiltmakers in the world—or rent one out for a single-time use. They have hundreds of tartans to choose from, in a variety of price ranges. Be sure to pop upstairs to the **Scottish Kiltmaker Visitor Centre,** exploring the history of the tartan (see pp. 185–187). You can watch kiltmakers at work, ask questions, and be fitted for your own fashion statement. A hint: To save time, read the online guide to buying a kilt before visiting.

Easing south along the river you pass the most graceful of the city's bridges, the **Ness Bridge,** before the bulk of **St. Andrew's Cathedral** looms into view. This unheralded cathedral dates back only to the 19th century and, though it may not be highly rated architecturally, it makes a great photograph from across the River Ness on a sunny day. It has a relaxed, refined charm. Near the cathedral, the **Eden Court Theatre** (Bishops Rd., tel 01463/234 234, edencourt.co.uk) is an impressive cultural icon befitting a city on the rise. The theater

Moray Firth Dolphins

The large bottlenose dolphins that can often be seen flinging themselves out of the Moray Firth—the body of water connecting Inverness with the North Sea—or messing around in the wake of boats, are part of the most northerly pod in the world. They can occasionally be spotted from the shore, along with harbor porpoises and minke whales, but for a close look, you'll need to head out on the water as part of an organized boat trip. Try **Dolphin Spirit** (Inverness Marina, tel 07544/800 620, dolphinspirit.co.uk, ££££–£££££).

takes a multidisciplinary approach to its programming, with an eclectic roster of performances and activities—everything from interactive children's events and plays to classical music concerts, while art galleries host revolving exhibitions.

Three miles (5 km) west of the city center via the A862, **Craig Phadrig Hill** (forestryandland.gov.scot), the former stronghold of the Pictish King Brude, is home to an Iron Age fort and offers great views of the Moray Firth.

Culloden Moor

East of the city is an attraction that anyone with even a passing interest in Scottish history has to

St. Andrew's Cathedral ✉ 15 Ardross St. ☎ (01463) 225 553 invernesscathedral.org • **Culloden Moor** ⛰ 203 C2 ✉ About 4 miles (6.5 km) E of Inverness on the B9006 (Culloden Moor) ☎ (01463) 796 090 💲 ££ nts.org.uk/visit/places/culloden

visit. Mention Culloden to any Scot and you will always elicit a response, which can range from a recollection of something they have heard about at school to a fiery burn in the eyes that will make you feel that the seminal battle of Scottish history still rages in spirit.

The bleak moor occupies a sacred, painful place in Scottish history. It was here, in 1746, that the Jacobite rebels supporting Bonnie Prince Charlie met with the Duke of Cumberland's government army. After only an hour of fierce fighting, thousands of Highlanders lay dead on the boggy ground and the Jacobite rebellions (see pp. 47–48) were crushed once and for all. In the aftermath of the battle the Duke of Cumberland's men marched north through the Highlands, destroying communities and ending the traditional way of life forever.

For a long time, the battlefield was marked by little more than a small cairn and the musket balls and rusted weapons that were occasionally recovered from the ground. Now a state-of-the-art **visitor center** on the moor has time lines, a film, and superb exhibits to help recount the events from both the Jacobite and the government points of view, using historical accounts and archaeological evidence. The "battle immersion" room vividly brings the horrific fighting to life. Docents in period costume demonstrate traditional handicrafts. Pick up the self-guided audio tour as you leave the museum; it really helps you get more from your walk around the battle lines. ■

■ **The infamous battlefield at Culloden**

AVIEMORE & THE CAIRNGORMS

Some 30 miles (45 km) southeast from Inverness, perched on the edge of the mighty Cairngorms—and almost a thousand feet (300 m) up—is the Scottish ski resort of Aviemore. With long, snow-filled winters not always guaranteed, this Highland gateway has done much to diversify its appeal. The slopes and ski lifts are ready for when Scotland gets a decent dump of snow, but there's now much more to keep the whole family active all year long.

The Cairngorms provide skiers with readily accessible slopes—but snow is unpredictable.

Aviemore

Aviemore is clearly serious about its redevelopment and repositioning. VisitCairngorms has set the goal of transforming Aviemore and Cairngorms National Park—the U.K.'s largest—into a year-round destination. They are well on their way.

A good way to get a feel for Aviemore and its surrounds is on the Cairngorm Mountain Railway, a funicular which spirits you up to Munro height. There's a viewing terrace and restaurant at the top where you can relax while watching walkers trudge past on their way to and from the lofty peaks all around. In winter the railway is jammed with skiers and snowboarders coming up to hit the slopes.

Aviemore 🗺 203 C2 **Visitor Information** ✉ 7 The Parade, Grampian Rd. ☎ (01479) 810 930 **visitcairngorms.com** • **Cairngorm Mountain Railway** ✉ Aviemore ☎ (01479) 861 261 💲 ££££ **cairngormmountain .co.uk & visitscotland.com**

In the center of town, Aviemore's **Victorian railway station** (*Dalfaber Rd.*) is a charming old gem—timber-built and redolent of a bygone era when trains were not just a way of getting from A to B. The **Strathspey Steam Railway** is a wonderful throwback to the great days of steam travel and offers some stunning views of Cairngorms National Park as it rattles off on a route from Aviemore through Boat of Garten to Broomhill. You can travel third class, or treat yourself to first.

(continued on p. 214)

Strathspey Steam Railway ✉ Aviemore Station, Dalfaber Rd., Aviemore ☎ (01479) 810 725 💲 ££££ **strathspeyrailway.co.uk**

EXPERIENCE: Enjoying Winter Sports

Every year thousands of Brits jet off on expensive trips to Europe and farther afield in search of winter sports adventures, even though world-class winter sports are available right here in Scotland. The resorts may not be as glitzy, nor the operations as slick, as the jet-set retreats in the European Alps, but if you are here in winter and love the outdoors, there is a wealth of activities, which really open up the landscape in a way a car journey or bus tour never could.

Perhaps Scotland's most famous winter sport is curling. This Olympic discipline (Scotland has produced Olympic champions numerous times in both the women's and men's events) takes place on an ice rink. The 40-pound (18 kg) granite stones, used by competitors from all over the world, come from just one place—the dramatic rock stack of Ailsa Craig on Scotland's west coast. The four-person team event is highly tactical. One member of the team slides or "curls" the stone along the ice, while the other three use brushes to speed it up, slow it down, or change its direction. You'll find the game being played throughout Scotland at ice rinks, and occasionally outside during particularly severe winters. Contact the **Royal Caledonian Curling Club** (*tel 0131/333 3003, scottishcurling.org*) for details of curling venues and competitions.

More conventional winter sports on offer include skiing and snowboarding at Scotland's five ski centers (see Travelwise p. 373). The snow can be unreliable, but on a good day the skiing is excellent, even if most of the runs are of a beginner or intermediate level. If you don't feel like doing all the hard work yourself, you can always go dog sledding at the **Bowland Trails** (*Netheraird of Glasclune, Blairgowrie, tel 07775/435 181, bowlandtrails .com*).

A CAIRNGORM WALK: CAIRN GORM & BEN MACDUI

Until the start of the 20th century, many people thought that Ben Macdui, and not Ben Nevis, was Scotland's highest peak. It's certainly a huge mountain, a 4,296-foot (1,309 m) monster at the heart of the massively wild Cairngorms. Ben Macdui sits on a mountain plateau that provides an unforgiving but truly breathtaking escape from the pressures of the modern world.

In the spring and summer Aviemore makes a good base for tackling Ben Macdui. The Cairngorm Plateau is not recommended for inexperienced hikers, and it is best avoided altogether in winter unless on an official guided trip. You'll need to be prepared with proper outdoor clothing, plenty of food and drink, a map and compass, and someone in the party who knows how to use both.

Start at the **parking lot ❶** at the Cairngorm ski center, where the temptation is to set off to tackle the steep scree-strewn corries (bowl-shaped gullies) that protect the plateau. Don't be tempted—instead follow the much safer and easier-to-follow path that curls off to the southwest.

Walking far below the mighty rockmonsters of the Cairngorms is a humbling and challenging experience. At least you won't have to tackle the mountain burns, as the path has **stepping stones ❷** to ford the waterways draining Coire an t-Sneachda and—farther along the walk—Coire an Lochan. Coire an t-Sneachda itself is a stunning place with imposing rock walls.

The long, chunky ridge of **Miadan Creag an Leth-Choin ❸** is your access point onto the plateau. Be patient and steady with your movements now, and your thighs and calves will thank you later. Gaze east right down the throat of **Coire an Lochan** to its chill waters, if the clouds part long enough.

The rich forests around Aviemore are now replaced with testing bog. Watch for wild ptarmigans—snow-white in winter and equally well camouflaged in their brown plumage in summer. As you edge deeper across the plateau, conditions become ever harsher with the only sign of life coming in the form of little shrubs on the approach to Lochan Buidhe. The summit of **Ben Macdui ❹** (4,296 feet/1,309 m) is a rubble of stones with a simple stone shelter where you can enjoy your lunch out of the gales that sweep in with little or no notice.

Retrace your steps back down to **Lochan Buidhe ❺.** You can follow the same route back, but a more interesting choice is to cut northeast from

NOT TO BE MISSED:

Miadan Creag an Leth-Choin • Lochan Buidhe • Ben Macdui • Cairn Gorm

the lochan toward Cairn Gorm itself. Avoid getting too close to the sheer edge of the plateau, however, always a risk in poor visibility. The views from the summit of **Cairn Gorm ❻** (4,081 feet/1,244 m) are even more impres- sive than Ben Macdui. If the **funicular,** just below the summit, is open, you can take the quick way down (£££). Alterna- tively, the ski-slope-scarred **Corrie Cas ❼** awaits, or the longer, more scenic **Fiacailla Choire Chais.**

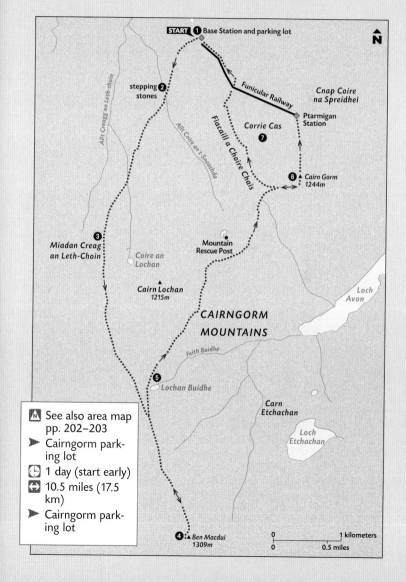

START ❶ Base Station and parking lot

stepping ❷ stones

Funicular Railway

Cnap Coire na Spreidhei

Ptarmigan Station

Corrie Cas ❼

Allt Creags an Leth-choin

Allt Coire an t-Sneachda

Fiacaill a Choire Chais

❻ ▲ Cairn Gorm 1244m

❸ Miadan Creag an Leth-Choin

Coire an Lochan

Mountain Rescue Post

Cairn Lochan 1215m

Loch Avon

CAIRNGORM MOUNTAINS

Feith Buidhe

❺ Lochan Buidhe

Carn Etchachan

Loch Etchachan

🄰 See also area map pp. 202–203

➤ Cairngorm park- ing lot

🕐 1 day (start early)

↔ 10.5 miles (17.5 km)

➤ Cairngorm park- ing lot

❹ ▲ Ben Macdui 1309m

0   1 kilometers

0   0.5 miles

Ospreys at Abernethy

In the 1950s the graceful osprey (or fish hawk, as it is also known) was thought extinct in Britain. Then a pair popped up out of nowhere at Loch Garten, just north of Aviemore. Conservationists jumped at this incredible opportunity and set up the **Loch Garten Osprey Centre** (*Aviemore, tel 01479/831 476, rspb.org.uk/loch garten*), which covers the loch and its forested surrounds. Their efforts have borne fruit, and there are now thought to be more than three hundred pairs of ospreys nesting throughout Scotland. The best time to see them is from April to late August. A visitor center opens during this period, offering telescopes and guided walks to help you make the most of the experience.

Aviemore's **Spey Valley Golf Course,** just to the north of the town, is one of Scotland's most exciting newer golf facilities. It is a tough course, laden with thick heather and tight fairways, but, even if your shots are going awry, you can still enjoy views of the famous River Spey and the surrounding hills and mountains.

Keen mountain bikers can head farther south to Laggan where the **Wolftrax** mountain bike course awaits (*tel 01528/544 366, lagganforest.com*). One of the best courses in the United Kingdom, it offers a comprehensive range of green, orange, red, and black trails. The reds provide a particularly stern test with scary rock drop-offs and tight single tracks winding through the forests. An easier option is the "wilderness trail," which follows old drovers' roads deep into wild country.

INSIDER TIP:

Never treat walking in Scotland's hills and mountains lightly or it may be the last thing you do.

—LARRY PORGES
National Geographic author

Rothiemurchus

The 24,000-acre (9,710 ha) area known as Rothiemurchus is set right on the edge of the remarkable Cairngorms mountain massif, just east of the town of Aviemore. This is one of the best places in Scotland to enjoy indigenous Caledonian woodland, with swaths of Scots pine, birch, and juniper trees draped around a brace of lochs.

Spey Valley Golf Course ✉ Aviemore ☎ (01479) 812 920
macdonaldhotels.co.uk • **Rothiemurchus** ⬛ 203 C2 ✉ Off the B970
near Aviemore ☎ (01479) 812 345 💲 £ **rothiemurchus.net**

■ **Mountain biking along the banks of Loch an Eilein is just one way to explore Rothiemurchus.**

Wildlife abounds on the route—watch for everything from red squirrels and crossbills to capercaillies (grouse) and pine martens.

The main parking lot has an **information center** with bikes available for rent. If you are short on time, a bike is the best way of getting around the estate. Even if you have a couple of days, it's a good idea to cycle one day, and then walk back to the areas you like best the next. You can also take a pony-trekking ride, which is great fun for older children.

Perhaps the prettiest part of the estate is **Loch an Eilein.** The "loch of the island" is named for the small islet that nestles in the middle of the silvery blue water, which is topped by a photogenic abandoned castle. A busier stretch of water is **Loch Morlich** on the edge of Rothiemurchus. A popular water sports center*(tel 01479/861 221, lochmorlich.com)* borders the loch, which, on a clear day, boasts stunning views of the Cairngorms. Next to the center are a beach and a campsite.

If you prefer what comes out of the water, rather than messing about on it, fishing is also a popular activity in Rothiemurchus. There are many options, from idly angling for rainbow and brown trout in the lochs to the more adrenaline pumping challenge of catching a wild salmon on the **River Spey.**

Once you've finished sampling Rothiemurchus's numerous attractions, retire to its café-restaurant, which utilizes fresh produce from the estate. You can also stock up on all manner of goodies at the farm shop, including excellent Highland cattle beef steaks.

Kingussie & Newtonmore

Those in search of a more authentic and relaxed location from which to explore the Cairngorms should head farther south, beyond Aviemore and Rothiemurchus and into

■ **The whisky selection at the Quaich Bar is legendary.**

the upper reaches of the Spey Valley. Here the attractive villages of Kingussie and Newtonmore provide a warm and welcoming atmosphere, largely untouched by the modern development that dominates Aviemore. Visitors can stay in one of the villages' several excellent family-run guesthouses and wander the local shops.

If your itinerary doesn't include a trip to the Outer Hebrides, don't miss the **Harris Tweed Shop** *(B9150, Newtonmore, tel 01540/670 188, harristweed shop.com)* for a chance to finger bolts of the famous woven fabric (see sidebar p. 291), and perhaps ship home an item or two.

Just outside Newtonmore, and often used as a set for the hit television series *Outlander,* is the **Highland Folk Museum.** Permeated by smoke from peat fires, exhibits include a traditional farmhouse, a working waterwheel-powered sawmill, a sweetshop, and interpreters in many locations.

Looming high above the villages on a hill south of the river is the imposing ruin of **Ruthven Barracks** *(on the B970 1 mile/ 1.6 km S of Kingussie),* one of the few remaining examples of the military posts established by the English to subdue the rebellious Highlanders and suppress their culture after the 1715 uprising.

Highland Folk Museum ⚐ 203 C2 ✉ Kingussie Rd., Newtonmore
☎ (01540) 673 550 ⏱ Closed Nov.- Mar. **highlifehighland.com**

INSIDER TIP:

Perhaps the most classic looking distillery in Scotland is Strathisla, with pot stills a few centuries old tucked snug into the old wooden stillhouse. The tour is extremely well done.

—JIM RICHARDSON
National Geographic photographer

If you hanker for a day on the water head to lovely **Loch Insh,** a 1-mile by 1.5-mile (1.6 km by 2.5 km) stretch of freshwater hemmed in by hills and heather just south of Aviemore, where ospreys roam wild. It is home to the family-run **Loch Insh Outdoor Centre,** which supplies canoes (both open and kayaks), sailing dinghies, mountain bikes, and more, as well as equipment for snow sports in winter. The center is ideal for families as it offers courses for all ages, all year long. A restaurant and accommodations are also available. You can paddle down the River Spey all the way from Loch Insh to Aviemore, a lovely adventure that really opens up the beauty of the region and affords some stunning views of the Cairngorms.

Also south of Aviemore, off the A9 near Kincraig, the **Alvie and Dalraddy Estates** *(tel 01540 651255, alvie-estate .co.uk)* offer places to stay as well as activities for all ages and abilities, from stag feeding to archery to clay pigeon shooting and much more.

Seven miles (11 km) south of Aviemore is the Royal Zoological Society of Scotland's **Highland Wildlife Park** *(B9152, tel 01540/651 270, highland wildlifepark.org.uk, ££),* where snow leopards, European bison, Japanese macaque, and more roam in designated areas.

Loch Insh Outdoor Centre ✉ Kincraig ☎ (01540) 651 272 **lochinsh.com**

EXPERIENCE: Shinty in Kingussie

High in the Spey Valley, away from the distillery tours and ski slopes, it is still possible to catch a glimpse of a Highland tradition that has changed little since the days when it was known as the "perfect exercise for a warrior people." Shinty—a game that resembles a faster moving, rougher version of field hockey—is still played in Newtonmore and Kingussie, whose respective teams dominate the Highland leagues. You can watch matches in either town during the summer, but the highlight of the season comes when the rival towns play each other and both towns turn out to cheer on their side. To find out when the teams are playing, and soak up the atmosphere with partisan onlookers, check *shinty.com*.

Speyside

The highest concentration of whisky distilleries in Scotland can be found in Speyside, where the cool, clear waters of the salmon-rich River Spey help conjure up first rate whiskies at more than 50 distilleries. This scenic region is ideal for touring by car, bike, or even on foot. There's a particularly appealing route from Aviemore to Speyside on the A95 that passes through graceful **Grantown-on-Spey.** Grand Georgian buildings abound in this relaxed town where you can enjoy a stroll down by the Spey, or explore the busy main street with its cafés and bars. In August the big event is the Grantown-on-Spey Highland Games (tel 01479/873 237) Pushing farther northeast, the A95 follows the Spey on its journey to the sea. Numerous distilleries line its banks forming part of the official **Malt Whisky Trail** (maltwhiskytrail.com), which encompasses 70 miles (112 km) and no fewer than nine of the most visitor-friendly distilleries.

One of the trail's most appealing whisky towns is **Charlestown of Aberlour.** Home of Aberlour whisky, Aberlour, as it is more commonly called, is also the birthplace of the world-famous **Walkers Shortbread.** First produced in town in 1898 by Joseph Walker, this delicious treat can be picked up in the factory store on High Street. The stately main street is replete with solid granite buildings, and a relaxed park reclines down by the banks of the River Spey.

A railway once ran through Aberlour, and the old station building now houses an information center dedicated to the **Speyside Way** (speyside way.org), a hiking trail that runs by the station. This 65-mile (105 km) trail is a great way of exploring whisky country if you can spare the time.

Just a couple of miles along the Speyside Way to the east is **Craigellachie,** a lovely little village that is, of course, home to its own distillery. It also boasts what may be the nation's finest whisky bar, the **Quaich Bar,** at the landmark **Craigellachie Hotel** (see p. 235 & Travelwise pp. 352–353). It's laden floor to ceiling with whiskies of all kinds—a dram from one of the rarest bottles could set you back more than £400! Half the fun here is browsing the massive whisky list and chatting with the knowledgeable bar staff.

The village's other main attraction is the cast-iron **Craigellachie Bridge,** built by the renowned and prolific Scottish engineer Thomas Telford (1757–1834) in the early 19th century.

Another 5 miles (7.5 km) south over rugged mountain scenery brings you to **Dufftown,** the self-styled "world capital of whisky," and this imposing granite-clad town

Speyside Visitor Centre ✉ Old Station Building, Aberlour ☏ (01340) 881 724 🕐 Closed Nov.–Mar. **speysidevisitorcentre.scot** • **Walkers Shortbread** ✉ Aberlour House, Aberlour ☏ (01340) 871 555 🕐 Closed Sat.–Sun. **walkersshortbread.com**

really does seem to almost burst at the seams with whisky distilleries. Find out about the local festival and more from the friendly folk at the tiny **Dufftown Whisky Museum & Heritage Centre,** then head over to the **Speyside Cooperage** *(reservation required)* which offers intriguing insight into a key part of the industry—the making of the famous barrels.

Visiting at least one distillery is practically obligatory in Speyside. Many offer excellent visitor facilities. **Strathisla** *(Seafield Ave., Keith, tel 01542/783 044, maltwhiskydistilleries .com/Strathisla, tour: ££££-£££££, closed Sun.–Tues. Nov.–Dec.)* in nearby Keith is one of the best. Having first opened in 1786, Strathisla claims to be the oldest distillery in the Highlands, and produces many of the whiskies that are used to make the famous blended brand of Chivas Regal. In summer a vintage train runs across the countryside along the **Keith & Dufftown Railway,** a fun way of arriving. The "Whisky Line" train—a retired British Rail Derby Class diesel—departs Dufftown, curves around the Glenfiddich Distillery and beneath Balvenie Castle, and continues for 11 miles (18 km) to Keith Town via the woodsy Scaut Hill and the scenic Isla Valley. ∎

Dufftown Whisky Museum & Heritage Centre ✉ 10 Conval St., Dufftown ☎ (01340) 820 507 🕐 Closed Nov.–March **whisky.dufftown .co.uk** • **Speyside Cooperage** 🅰 203 D2 ✉ Dufftown Rd., Craigellachie ☎ (01340) 871 108 💲 ££ 🕐 Closed Fri.–Sun. **speysidecooperage.co.uk** • **Keith & Dufftown Railway** 🅰 203 D3 ✉ Dufftown Station, Dufftown ☎ (01340) 821 181 🕐 Closed Mon.–Thurs. & Oct.–March 💲 ££ **keith-dufftown-railway.co.uk**

■ An aerial view of the town and the castellated tower bridge at Craigellachie

THE GREAT GLEN

The Great Glen is the mighty geological fault line that cuts around 60 miles (97 km) southwest from the North Sea down to the Atlantic Ocean in a swath of rugged mountains and scenic lochs, connecting two of the Highlands' biggest tourist hubs, Inverness and Fort William.

■ **Urquhart Castle stands high above the famous Loch Ness.**

Caledonian Canal

Four lochs stretch between the North Sea and the Atlantic—Ness, Oich, Lochy, and Linnhe—and these are in turn connected by the Caledonian Canal, one of the most remarkable canal systems in the world. Sailing is the best way to really appreciate the canal's grandeur. You can rent boats in Laggan through **Le Boat Laggan.** A week will give you enough time to traverse the entirety of the canal in both directions. **The Great Glen Way** *(highland.gov.uk/greatglen way)* takes walkers on a 79-mile (127 km) route alongside the canal. It is also popular with cyclists, though in the peak season some of the traffic-clogged roads can be slow going.

Another great way to see the area is by canoe. Although facilities are currently fairly limited, the **Great Glen Canoe Trail** *(Scottish Canoe Assoc., tel 01463/725 500, greatglencanoetrail.info)* provides a network of free campsites and canoe-friendly docks along the length of the Caledonian Canal.

The history of the Caledonian Canal dates back to the early 19th century. Striking a waterway from coast to coast was seen as a way of opening up the Highlands, as well as cutting out the arduous sea voyage up around the treacherous northern reaches of Scotland.

Legendary Scot Thomas Telford was the brains behind the plan to link the North Sea at Inverness with the Atlantic at Fort William via a series of canals and locks that would connect the Great Glen's quartet of freshwater lochs. The sheer scale of the engineering involved is staggering. Twenty-nine locks help boats climb from sea level to over 100 feet (30 m) before descending again to sea level.

Loch Ness

The most dramatic section of the canal is Loch Ness. The small

Caledonian Canal 🗺 202–203 B1–C2 **scottishcanals.co.uk** • **Le Boat Laggan** ✉ Laggan Locks ☎ (01809) 501 234 or (800) 734 5491 ⏰ Closed Sun. 💲 £££££ **leboat.com**

tourist town of **Fort Augustus** at the southern end of the loch is a relaxed place with a selection of bars, cafés, and restaurants lining the banks of the canal. There is little to do bar idling by the canal, strolling down to Loch Ness, looking at the beautiful exterior of **Fort Augustus Abbey** (now transformed into luxury holiday apartments and not open to the public), or setting off for a walk in the surrounding hills.

Cruise Loch Ness in Fort Augustus offers boat tours that not only open up the superb scenery of Scotland's longest inland loch, but also cater to the monster-spotting set, providing live underwater 3-D imaging as you go, which gives you the chance to search for the submarine lair of the world's most famous monster, Nessie. Loch Ness unfurls for 23 miles (37 km). If you spend long enough scanning every corner of a loch that ripples with large waves and dark shadows, you might start seeing mysterious creatures too.

Urquhart Castle looms over the west side of Loch Ness, north of Fort Augustus. A fun way to get here is via a boat tour from Inverness or Fort Augustus, which allows time ashore,

but you can also drive up the winding A82. This romantic ruin is very much the stereotypical Scottish castle, a ramble of 13th-century stonework tumbling down the hillside toward the shimmering loch amid a welter of history and myths. It looks its best when floodlit at night, when you almost expect to see Robert the Bruce patrolling the ramparts, but you can clamber over it and feel the history of the place at any time. Exhibits and an evocative film inside the visitor center give context to the ruins, as well as the enormous catapult replica aimed directly at the castle outside.

The nearest settlement to the castle

BOAT TOURS TO URQUHART CASTLE: Jacobite *(Tomnahurich Bridge, Glenurquhart Rd., tel 01463/233 999, jacobite.co.uk, £££–£££££)* offers tours from Inverness; and Cruise LochNess (see above) offers tours from Fort Augustus.

In Search of a Legend

Thousands of tourists flock to the banks of Loch Ness (surely the most famous loch in the world) every year hoping to catch a glimpse of Nessie (surely the most famous monster in the world) and snap the unique photo that will make their fortune. Everyone—well, almost everyone—understands there is no monster at all and it's all a tourist gimmick, but few can resist a peek in hopes of seeing the monster just in case! And, even without any mysterious creature, the loch itself is stunning. It's at its most impressive at Urquhart Castle, where the ruined castle watches over the chill waters.

Fort Augustus 🅰 202 B2
visitscotland.com • Cruise Loch Ness ✉ Fort Augustus ☎ (01320) 366 277 💲 *£££*
cruiselochness.com • Urquhart Castle 🅰 203 C2 ✉ North bank of Loch Ness, on the A82 from Inverness ☎ (01456) 450 551 💲
££ **historicenvironment.scot**

is **Drumnadrochit,** where Nessie fans will be in tall-tale heaven. Best for small children is **Nessieland** *(A82 at A831, tel 01456/450 342, nessieland.co.uk).* Just up the road the **Loch Ness Exhibition Centre** *(tel 01456/450 573, lochness .com, £)* offers an immersive experience, looking at the mystery of the monster with an appreciative, if skeptical, eye.

Ben Nevis & the Nevis Range

At 4,413 feet (1,344 m), Ben Nevis is the highest mountain in the British Isles. Known to many Scots simply as "The Ben," this colossal rock

giant can be seen from hundreds of other mountain peaks across the nation. It forms the heart of the Nevis Range, a chunky hulk of mountains that have together become one of the United Kingdom's top adventure sports destinations in recent years.

If you were to take a hike up Ben Nevis, you would be tackling the mountain from sea level and would no doubt feel every one of those steps on the ascent. Never treat Ben Nevis lightly, no matter how sunny and warm a day it is at the base in Fort William

EXPERIENCE: Glen Affric

It may only be a short drive from Loch Ness, but remarkable Glen Affric feels a million miles away from the modern world. A snaking road takes you into the east end, while on its other three impenetrable flanks is a whole lot of nothing.

Many Scots consider Glen Affric the finest glen in the land, and it is easy to see why. It is bordered by rugged mountains and split by a loch dotted with picturesque islands. The path that skirts around the shores of the loch is ideal for walkers, while the wider track on the south bank is gaining popularity with adventurous mountain bikers. You may need to ford the burns (if it is safe to do so) to get all the way around. The path itself is surrounded by Scots pines and fringed by swaths of heather, with a treasure trove of the native vegetation that the aftermath of the Highland Clear-

ances destroyed throughout so much of Scotland. Even in summer Glen Affric never overflows with visitors, and in winter you will probably see more stags than people.

One epic hike takes you along Loch Affric from east to west and then deep into the mountains where you can climb high over the **Five Sisters of Kintail** (see sidebar p. 251) before dropping down to finish at the **Glenshiel Campsite** *(Kyle of Lochalsh, 01599/511 221, glenshielcampsite .co.uk)* on the banks of Loch Duich. A remote youth hostel *(Alltbeithe, Glen Affric, 0345/293 7373, hostellingscotland.org.uk)* makes an ideal base from which to explore the area. More sedentary souls can drive to the eastern fringes of Glen Affric from Cannich and have a picnic to get a little flavor of this unique and wild region.

(see pp. 224–227). Snow can linger on through the summer around the summit, and visibility can drop to zero in minutes, suddenly turning a nice summer's day out into a life-or-death struggle to navigate yourself around the lethal gullies to safety. Almost as many people die on Ben Nevis every year as on Mount Everest, so beware. If you are in any doubt before you head off, check the conditions at the **Glen Nevis Visitor Centre** *(01397/ 705 922, ben-nevis.com)* in Fort William, where the most popular route starts, or just content yourself with enjoying the views from down below.

Having said that, if you are properly equipped and fit, you should be able to make it up and down with few problems—more than 100,000 people a year do, although it is a tough slog taking between five and seven hours. More experienced climbers, and particularly those who have no fear of heights, can tackle the alternative descent following the knife-edge ridge of Càrn Mòr Dearg Arête and coming back down to Torlundy.

The Nevis Range breaks east of Ben Nevis and has been opened up by a gondola system that whisks anyone who doesn't fancy the 2,000-foot-plus (600 m) hike up from its base in Torlundy to the year-round **Nevis Range Mountain Experience** resort center on Aonach Mor, with snow sports in winter and ceilidh evenings in summer. Walking is the most popular activity during the warmer months. The easier

■ **The snowcapped summit of Ben Nevis looms over the landscape of Loch Linnhe.**

walks are signposted from the center.

The steep and rocky trails that wind down the mountainside make the Nevis Range one of the best mountain-biking venues in Europe. Many trails are not for beginners, but inexperienced riders can hire an instructor to teach them how to handle the terrain. **Nevis Cycles** *(Lochy Crescent, Fort William, tel 01397/705 555, nevis cycles.com)* has bikes for rent and offers more information on biking in the area.

Every year thousands come to watch the world's finest riders tackle the famous **World Cup Downhill** course—a death-defying hurl down the mountain that sees riders descend 1,800 feet (555 m) in about 5 minutes. But the Nevis Range is not just about serious biking. A variety of longer, and much less steep, trails snake off all around. These gentler forest routes are known as the "Witches' Trails." And when the snow batters down, skiers and snowboarders flock to enjoy Scotland's highest ski center. ■

Nevis Range Mountain Experience ✉ Nevis Range, Torlundy, Aonach Mor ☎ (01397) 705 825 💲 Gondola: £££ **nevisrange.co.uk**

THE WEST

The western portion of the Highlands is a deeply romantic and wildly beautiful oasis laden with history. This is where Bonnie Prince Charlie both raised his standard and fled Scotland forever. It is also a corner that boasts some of the country's finest white-sand beaches, some of its prettiest glens, and a plethora of outdoor activities at all times of year.

The Corpach shipwreck, Fort William

Fort William

One of the largest settlements in the area, Fort William is an oft-derided transportation hub blighted with some ill-conceived architecture, a busy two-lane road that dominates its waterfront, and scores of decidedly average places to eat and stay. It does, however, boast handy transportation connections, including a direct overnight sleeper train service to London and buses to many points north, south, and east, as well as plenty of tourist facilities.

In town, Fort William's **High Street** has a swath of tacky tartan souvenir shops, but it is also a good place to stock up on any outdoor gear needed for a foray up Ben Nevis or out on the Nevis Range. The main sight is the **West Highland Museum.** Its collection delves into the history of the surrounding region and includes

Fort William 🗺 202 B1 **Visitor Information** ✉ 27 High St., Fort William
☎ (01397) 701 801 **visitscotland.com** • **West Highland Museum**
✉ Cameron Sq., Fort William ☎ (01397) 702 169 🕐 Closed Sun.
westhighlandmuseum.org.uk

the likes of old military medals won by local regiments, preserved wildlife such as golden eagles, and weaponry from throughout the ages.

The United Kingdom's highest mountain, **Ben Nevis** (see pp. 222–223), looms over Fort William. The long climb from the town to the mountain's base takes you through the idyllic and quintessentially Scottish landscape of **Glen Nevis,** where many scenes from the Hollywood blockbuster *Braveheart* were filmed. Development around Fort William has been kept to a minimum, and, reclining in the shadow of "The Ben," the steep forested slopes of Glen Nevis are used for a variety of outdoor activities.

Fort William is also the far western end of the **Caledonian Canal** (see pp. 220–221). Just 3 miles (4.5 km) north of town, **Neptune's Stair-case,** the United Kingdom's largest staircase lock, is the site of the canal's most dramatic set piece. The boats here climb an impressive 64 feet (19 m) from sea level, passing through eight locks. It takes a boat an hour and a half to complete the whole series of locks. You can sit and watch the action, or take a stroll or bike ride along the towpath, while you enjoy the views of Ben Nevis and the Nevis Range. The **Old Boat of Caol** shipwreck leans on the beach of Corpach, at the mouth of the Caledonian Canal, drawing photo enthusiasts hoping to snap a perfect shot of the hulk with Ben Nevis looming behind.

On the shores of beautiful Loch Linnhe, with a necklace of mountains all around, Fort William's setting could scarcely be more spectacular. A good way to appreciate it is to take one of the boat trips that leave from the

EXPERIENCE: Tracing Your Scottish Roots

The Highland Clearances led to a mass exodus of people to the Americas and even farther afield to Australia and New Zealand. Coupled with earlier and later economic migration, the Scots diaspora around the world now runs into the millions. If you think you might have Scots blood coursing through your veins, then you can trace your ancestry. Many family names hint at Scottish roots, most obviously those starting with "Mac" or "Mc" (in Scottish Gaelic meaning "son of"). You could start searching at Register House and the National Archives in Edinburgh, where a wealth of official documents are archived, or dig into the 1911 census and other resources online at *scotland.org/ about-scotland/our-people/ancestry.* The National Records of Scotland can also help you compile your family tree (*nrscotland.gov.uk/research/family-history*). A wealth of information plus a free ancestry e-book are available at *visitscotland .com/things-to-do/research-your-ancestry*

■ A train steams its way over the Glenfinnan Viaduct, part of the West Highland Line.

town pier. The trips, run by **Crannog Cruises** *(tel 01397/700 714, crannog .net, closed Oct.–Apr., ££),* ease along the sea loch. You may spot some seals, and the views are superb, with Ben Nevis on one side and the rough terrain of the Moidart Peninsula on the other.

Fort William's train station used to be the terminus for the West Highland Line from Glasgow and it still welcomes and sends off sleeper trains all the way south to the bright lights of London. The West Highland Line runs on a circuitous route from Glasgow to Mallaig on the west coast, running across mountains and glens at a relaxed pace. From its grand Victorian viaducts and bridges it offers breathtaking views of the Highland landscape and is widely considered the most beautiful railway route in Europe.

In summer, the **Jacobite Steam Train** operates between Fort William and Mallaig on the West Highland Line. The seven-decades-old train—famous as "Hogwart's Express" in *Harry Potter* movies—climbs out of Fort William with a grand puff of steam that takes you right back to the golden age of rail travel. The old-fashioned carriages are part of the attraction, and you can wind the windows down to take photographs. High tea, champagne, or artisan cheese may be ordered ahead for an even more luxurious experience. The most stun-

Jacobite Steam Train 🅼 202 A1–A2, B1 ✉ Fort William Railway Station, Station Sq., Fort William ☎ (0844) 850 4685; reservations (0333) 996 6692 🕓 Closed Nov.–April, although some special trains run off-season 💲 £££££ **westcoastrailways.co.uk**

INSIDER TIP:

Take a ride on the Jacobite Steam Train from Fort William to Mallaig. Book ahead to be sure of a seat in the Harry Potter carriage, where movie scenes of the Hogwarts Express were filmed.

—JENNIFER SEGAL
*National Geographic
Development Office*

ning viewpoint for photographing the train as it passes (April–October) is the curving, 21-arch **Glenfinnan Viaduct,** made famous in the *Harry Potter* films. Get there early to park by the visitor center (see p. 229) and hike to one of the hillside viewing areas to stake your spot among the throng of like-minded visitors.

Glen Coe

Located just a short drive south of Fort William, Glen Coe is one of Scotland's most famous glens. The unassuming village of Glencoe is dwarfed by the huge mountains that rise up toward the glen proper. Descending into the glen from the south is the rural equivalent of walking into St. Peter's Cathedral in the Vatican. Your jaw drops at the sheer scale of it all. It's a world of deadly crags and killer mountains that appear all but unconquerable. Humans here feel very small indeed.

Glen Coe is extremely popular with both walkers and serious climbers looking to test their skills, and even risk their lives, on its savage peaks and knife-edge ridges. Their hub is the village's legendary **Clachaig Inn** (see p. 234), a hearty oasis with its own "boots room" for drying your gear, chunky Scottish food, and Scots ales on tap. Here all the

Glen Coe ⛰ 202 B1 **Visitor Information** ✉ 1 mile S of Glencoe village off A82 ☎ (01855) 811 307 💲 Exhibition: £ **nts.org.uk/visit/places/glencoe**

Bonnie Prince Charlie on the Run

The wildly beautiful western Highlands were the perfect setting for Bonnie Prince Charlie's much romanticized flight from Scotland. He originally landed on the Scottish mainland at Loch Nan Uamh near Arisaig in 1745. After Culloden, with a huge reward on his head, he was saved by the still loyal Highlanders who spirited him from hiding place to hiding place. After a stint in the Outer Hebrides, and a bizarre boat crossing to the Isle of Skye during which he dressed as a woman to evade capture by the English redcoats, the would-be British king left Scotland for the last time from Borrodale. He sailed out through the Sound of Arisaig on a French ship, passing his ghost from a year earlier as he went.

■ Reenactment of Bonnie Prince Charlie's arrival, Glenfinnan

chatter is of the day's walking adventures and future grand plans. It's a great place to meet other like-minded souls if you are on your own.

A sign at the entrance to the Clachaig Inn harks back to 1692 and the darkest day in the glen's history. It warns "No Hawkers or Campbells." This is a reference to the Campbells, a clan that was then working for the British government, who committed the most horrendous breach of the traditional Highland clan hospitality code imaginable. After having enjoyed a fortnight being fed and watered by the MacDonalds of Glen Coe they—acting on government orders—set upon their hosts as they slept, massacring 38 in cold blood. Another 40 women and children were left to perish in the chill winter snows after their villages had been burned to the ground. Just south of the village off the A82, a moving exhibit at the **Glen Coe Visitor Centre** reaches into the darkness of those

INSIDER TIP:

Glenfinnan is perhaps my favorite setting for a Highland gathering. Surrounded by mountains, it sits close by the beach where Bonnie Prince Charlie came ashore to rally the Highlanders.

—JIM RICHARDSON
National Geographic photographer

days and explains how the glen has been shaped since.

Heading back north to Fort William, most people just continue on up the "Road to the Isles," but cast your eyes west across Loch Linnhe and the vision of the area referred to as **Ardnamurchan** soon begins to appear. The most westerly point on the British mainland feels very much like an island, and you can catch a ferry over from Corran Ferry, just south of Fort William, or from the Isle of Mull to the south. Ardnamurchan is an impressively wild place. The main population centers of Salen, Kilchoan, Glenborrodale, and Strontian are tiny outposts that function for visitors as little more than bases for setting out on walking or cycling trips. This beautiful oasis of abandoned beaches, ghostly lost villages, and mourning hills has never really recovered from the Highland Clearances (see p. 252).

If you find it a bit too wild, try one of the guided walks run by the **High Life Highland Countryside Rangers** service. Otherwise, just lose yourself in an area that lies at the heart of what the locals call the "Rough Bounds."

Road to the Isles

On the "Road to the Isles," which continues from Fort William west in search of the sea at Mallaig, **Glenfinnan** is an essential stop. This is the epically beautiful and deeply evocative spot where Bonnie Prince Charlie raised his standard back on August 19, 1745. For much of the day it looked like the prince may have miscalculated, but as the afternoon wore on the skirl of bagpipes over the hills heralded the arrival

of more and more soldiers, as the Highland clans rallied in anger for what was to be one last heroic, but ultimately tragic, time.

Fittingly, the elevated figure standing atop the 60-foot-tall (18 m) **Glenfinnan Monument** that today pins the shore of Loch Shiel is not the prince himself, but just an ordinary Highlander, the kind of man who fought and died for the cause, or perhaps fought, lost, and found his way of life changed forever. Climb up the tower for a superb panoramic view. Across the road the **Glenfinnan Visitor Centre** depicts the events leading up to the raising of the standard and attempts to conjure up the drama of the day, as well as examining the ensuing events. Guided tours of the site are available on occasion; ask ahead.

To the south of Glenfinnan, away from the well-trodden Road to the Isles, lies the mountainous and empty **Morvern Peninsula.** This area is deserted even by the standards of the Rough Bounds—only around 300 people living in an area the size of Washington, D.C. While the interior of Morvern is bleak, the villages along the Sound of Mull are worth a visit. The largest of the coastal villages, **Lochaline,** has the friendly **Lochaline Hotel,** an

(continued on p. 232)

High Life Highland Countryside Rangers ☎ (01349) 781 700 **highland.gov.uk/outdoorhighlands** & **highlifehighland.com/rangers** • **Road to the Isles** roadtotheisles.com • **Glenfinnan Monument** Visitor Information ✉ Glenfinnan, Lochaber ☎ (01397) 722 250 💲 £ **nts.org.uk/visit/places/glenfinnan-monument** • **The Lochaline Hotel** ✉ Lochaline, Movern ☎ (07900) 240 227 💲 £ **lochalinehotel.com**

EXPERIENCE: Exploring Remote Knoydart

This stunning and brutally remote corner of Scotland is one of Europe's last great wildernesses. Even few Scots are lucky enough to ever make it out here. Sandwiched fittingly between what the Gaels called the lochs of Nevis (heaven) and Hourn (hell), this otherworldly retreat has taken on a near-mythic appeal for adventurous Scots.

The lonely, isolated settlement of Knoydart

In many respects this is not a natural wilderness, as most visitors today believe. In fact, it was once home to a thriving crofting and fishing community. Before Culloden, Knoydart (visitknoy dart.co.uk) was home to more than a thousand clanspeople. Legend has it that Bonnie Prince Charlie sought refuge here after the battle, although there is no proof to back these claims. Whether he did or not, Culloden nonetheless had huge ramifications for the area, with the then thriving local community forced off their land during the Highland Clearances. Today only around a hundred people live in this remote peninsula.

Unless you are keen on the 16-mile (26 km) walk to Knoydart from Kinloch Hourn (staying in a rudimentary shelter on the way) the only way to arrive is on the **Knoydart Western Isles Ferry** (Harbour Rd., Mallaig, tel 01687/462 233, western islescruises.co.uk, ££££) from the small port of Mallaig, which drops you off by Britain's most remote pub, the **Old Forge** (Inverie,

Knoydart, tel 01687/462 358, the-oldforge.co.uk), and Knoydart's hotel-restaurant, the **Creag Eiridh** (Inverie, Knoydart, tel 01747/852289, creageiridh.co.uk). There are no trains, buses, or planes, and only one tiny and fairly pointless road on the Knoydart Peninsula, which leaves walking the main way of getting around. Knoydart's hiking trails are rewarding with low-level mountain passes for the inexperienced and an impressive trio of Munros (peaks in excess of 3,000 feet/ 914 m) for more serious adventure types to tackle. Hospitals and friendly mountain rescue services are a long way off in these parts, so take all the usual precautions.

For all the foreboding nature of the history and weather, the Knoydart story has, however, taken on a far more positive note over the last decade. The **Knoydart Foundation** (tel 01687/462 242, knoydart.org) is a charity that consists of enterprising locals working together for the community. In 1999 the foundation took over a large area of the peninsula from landowners who previously used it as an exclusive hunting and fishing retreat. They are now trying to develop the economy of the area without decimating the breathtaking landscapes and rich natural resources that attracted people to this peninsula in the first place.

A view of Invrie, Knoydart

excellent diving center (see sidebar opposite), and the **Whitehouse Restaurant** (see p. 235), for an extraordinary meal.

Beyond Glenfinnan the tarmac and railway Road to the Isles now finally lives up to its billing. Heading west, you catch fleeting glimpses of the Atlantic Ocean before some of Scotland's prettiest beaches appear—white strips of sand set against translucent waters that gaze out dreamily over the Hebrides.

Arisaig is a trim little village on the water. The beaches aside, there is little to visit here bar 28-acre (11 ha) **Larachmhor Gardens,** renowned for its spectacular displays of rhododendrons in spring and early summer; and the **Land, Sea & Islands Centre** *(tel 01687/450 771, arisaig info.org.uk).* This modest but fun

museum has eclectic displays spanning crofting, local marine wildlife, fishing, weaving, and even wartime espionage training, plus the various movies that have been filmed locally, including the popular *Local Hero.*

The old blacksmith's has been renovated and is also on display. Boat tours run from Arisaig in summer; these will take you to see a local seal colony or out to the surrounding islands.

A necklace of white-sand beaches stretches north for some 8 miles (12 km) to the quiet village of **Morar,** which hit the headlines when the beach scenes from *Local Hero* were filmed here. There are campsites right by the sand for adventurous travelers, or hotels and bed-and-breakfasts available in Arisaig and Morar for those who prefer their comforts.

Arisaig arisaiginfo.org.uk • Larachmhor Garden larachmhor.co.uk

■ **Fishing boats crowd the harbor at the west coast port of Mallaig.**

Inland from Morar is an often ignored loch that many Scots rate as one of the country's prettiest. **Loch Morar** is Scotland's deepest inland loch (indeed, it is the United Kingdom's deepest stretch of freshwater) with parts of it delving down to a chilly 1,017 feet (310 m). This perhaps explains why it is also home to its own monster legend. Morag is said to be Nessie's "sister," but pleasingly here there are no cheesy tours or over-the-top visitor centers, so you'll just have to leave it all up to your imagination—unless, of course, you see her. You can rent a boat, but most people who do so are trying to catch much smaller prey with their rods. Scotland's shortest river, the River Morar, gushes from the loch back out to Morar, and there's a quintet of islands sprinkled around the expansive loch.

The West Highland Railway line and the tarmac Road to the Isles both come to an abrupt halt at **Mallaig.** From here there are ferries to the isle of Skye, visible from the dock, as well as other locations. Right next to the railway station, the modest **Mallaig Heritage Centre** tells the history of Mallaig, once Europe's main herring port. The waterfront is a great place to sit with fish and chips from one of the town's excellent "chippies" as you watch the busy fishing fleet. Seagulls will be squawking overhead as you look for nosy seals, who like to keep an eye on what you are doing in a part

EXPERIENCE:
Diving in the Sound of Mull

Lochaline's **Highland Basecamp** (*Lochaline, tel 07824/541 901, highlandbasecamp.com*), formerly Lochaline Dive Centre, is the perfect base from which to explore the mysterious wrecks hidden in the cold, clear waters of the Sound of Mull. Those new to diving can take an introductory course with the camp's two experienced instructors, while experienced divers can charter one of two equipped dive ships from **Lochaline Boat Charters** (*Lochaline, tel 07967/419 025, lochaline-boats .co.uk*). The exceptionally clear waters around Lochaline are home to a fascinating and diverse range of underwater landscapes and aquatic wildlife, including dolphins, porpoises, and basking sharks in the summer. In addition to the natural sights, the Sound of Mull, with its treacherous rocks and fierce winter storms, has more than its share of shipwrecks including the cannon-strewn wrecks of the 17th-century warships *Swan* and *Dartmouth*.

of Scotland where the divide between man and nature is as thin as anywhere in the country. ■

Mallaig Heritage Centre 📷 (01687) 462 085 🕐 Closed certain days (check the website for details) 💲 £ **mallaigheritage.org.uk**

Where to Eat & Drink in Central & Western Highlands

ANDERSON'S RESTAURANT

BOAT OF GARTEN

(01497) 831 466 | andersonsrestaurant.co.uk

A few miles away from the hubbub of busy Aviemore, this small bistro serves quality fare in an upscale environment. A seasonal menu shows their commitment to using local Scottish produce in season. While the vibe here is sophisticated, Anderson's makes it clear that children are welcome and serves half-portion sizes. Drivers will especially appreciate the nonalcholic cocktail of the day.

£££ 🅿 🕒 Closed for L. & Mon.–Tues. 🖾 MC, V

THE BOAT INN

CHARLESTON RD., ABOYNE

(01339) 886 137 | theboatinnaboyne.co.uk

This casual restaurant, situated within an 18th-century coaching inn right on Aboyne's riverfront, serves Scottish classic comfort foods with flair. Whether you want something creative and modern or something traditional and hearty, this gem comes through. Of particular note are the superb soups. Should you be passing in the early hours, the inn's excellent breakfast is open to all.

££ 🅿 🖾 MC, V

CAFÉ 1

75 CASTLE ST., INVERNESS

(01463) 226 200 | cafe1.net

Situated opposite the castle in the center of Inverness, Café 1 supplies consistently excellent meals with a combination of European and Scottish standards. Emphasis is on fresh and local ingredients—some from the café's own croft—impeccably served. Thoughtfully, young guests are offered their own "wee menu" catering to their palate.

£££–££££ 🕒 Closed Sun. 🖾 MC, V

CLACHAIG INN

GLENCOE

(01855) 811 252 | clachaig.com

Busy with walkers and tourists, the Clachaig Inn serves the same varied menu in its three bars, although each location has its own atmosphere to suit your mood. Traditional Scottish favorites like haggis and leek and potato soup pop up alongside hearty burgers and more unusual dishes, such as wild boar sausages and burritos. The boozy hot chocolate is recommended.

££ 🅿 🖾 MC, V

CRANNOG RESTAURANT AT GARRISON WEST

4 CAMERON SQUARE, FORT WILLIAM

(01397) 701 873 | garrisonwest.co.uk

Although not offering the loch views of its now closed Crannog Restaurant at the Pier, diner's can still feast on fresh west coast seafood. The menu changes according to the daily catch, with blackboard specials offered along the likes of mussels, caramelized scallops, salmon, halibut, and the like. This friendly and casual spot is popular, so book ahead, particularly on weekends.

££–£££ 🅿 🕐 Closed L. Mon.–Tues. 🌐 MC, V

LOCH LEVEN SEAFOOD CAFÉ
ONICH

(01855) 821 048 | lochlevenseafoodcafe.co.uk

Dining on fresh seafood in this bright informal eatery is an enjoyable experience whatever the weather, but on a warm sunny day the outdoor terrace, with its views over the eponymous loch, is hard to beat. The café's seafood platter is legendary; lobster, langoustines, and other shellfish also feature on the changing monthly menu alongside the daily catch.

££–£££ 🅿 🕐 Closed Nov.–mid-Feb. 🌐 MC, V

MOUNTAIN CAFÉ
111 GRAMPIAN RD., AVIEMORE

(01479) 812 473 | mountaincafe-aviemore.co.uk

This lovely, family-friendly café bustles throughout the day, serving from about 8:30 a.m. to 5 p.m. The creative menu features everything from healthy or hearty breakfasts and zucchini pancakes to beef-steak baguettes and mouthwatering home-baked goods. Good coffee and views over the Cairngorms are an added bonus.

£ 🕐 Closed Wed. 🌐 MC, V

THE MUSTARD SEED
16 FRASER ST., INVERNESS

(01463) 220 220 | mustardseedrestaurant.co.uk

Housed in a former 19th-century church, this riverside restaurant has a lot of character. It also has plenty of choice, with a menu that offers such mains as sirloin steak, grilled tuna loin, and lamb chops. Outside, balcony tables offer lovely views over the River Ness.

££–£££ 🌐 AE, MC, V

QUAICH BAR
VICTORIA ST., CRAIGELLACHIE

(01340) 881 204 | craigellachiehotel.com

This destination bar (see p. 216) within the well-known Craigellachie Hotel offers a mesmerizing wall of whiskies to choose from. Happily, the friendly staff, and your fellow customers, are ready to help you make some wise choices. The hotel's adjoining Spey Inn restaurant serves farm to fork fare.

££–£££ 🅿 🌐 MC, V

THE WHITEHOUSE RESTAURANT
LOCHALINE

(01967) 421 777 | thewhitehouserestaurant.co.uk

While it may not look like much from the outside, dinner here may well become your favorite meal in all of Scotland. Try the four- or six-course tasting menu and put yourself in the hands of a masterful chef. Locally sourced ingredients are inventively prepared and beautifully presented.

££££–£££££ 🕐 Closed Sun.–Mon., L. Tues. 🌐 MC, V

WINKING OWL
123 GRAMPIAN RD., AVIEMORE

(01479) 812 356 | thewinkingowl.co

Friendly service, tartan-covered seat cushions, live music, and a plentiful supply of their own Cairngorm Brewery ales (as well as others), "the Winky" is a great casual option after a day outdoors. Choose from one of the tasty light bites or tuck into a full hearty meal, but save room for "pud" (pudding, aka dessert).

£–££ 🅿 🌐 MC, V

Dramatic snowcapped peaks, sweeping white-sand beaches, shimmering lochs, and charming centuries-old villages

NORTHERN HIGHLANDS

A tumbling burn (stream) just north of Ullapool

NORTHERN HIGHLANDS

Many Scots never explore the northern reaches of their country, so it is perhaps unsurprising that comparatively few travelers make it here either. Those who do are rewarded with a magnificent and varied natural landscape, rising from the rolling hills and sea cliffs of the east to the wild and barren mountains of the west.

A land where the people were brutally evicted to make way for sheep farming during the Highland Clearances, Scotland's far north can sometimes seem a quiet and lonely place. The region's most populated town, Thurso, and settlements such as Gairloch and postcard-perfect Plockton bring a welcome touch of humanity. They also boast plenty of places to eat and drink, with top-notch seafood often the order of the day.

One of the most accessible parts of the Northern Highlands, the Black Isle Peninsula has a rich Pictish history, as well

◾ **Good fishing for mackerel and pollack can be had from sea lochs around Guinard Bay.**

as a wealth of natural and man-made attractions that can easily be reached from the Highland capital, Inverness.

In the north, the attractive coastal town of Dornoch, with its beautiful beach and grand architecture, is a popular stop, as is John O'Groats, in Scotland's far northeast corner. Considered the most northerly settlement of mainland Great Britain, it marks the start/end point of the United Kingdom's longest trek, the mighty 874-mile (1,407 km) route to Land's End in southwest England.

The Great Outdoors

Nature and the outdoors are the main draw for most visitors to these parts. There are myriad opportunities for outdoor activities, ranging from bird-watching and walking along near-deserted beaches to gorge-scrambling and riding the waves at some of the globe's top surfing spots.

There are also plenty of mountains to explore, including the iconic Suilven and Stac Pollaidh on the northwest coast. The vaulting Torridon Mountains, also in the west, are one of Scotland's great wilderness playgrounds. Here visitors can ascend the lofty heights of Liathach and Beinn Eighe. The challenging ascent of An Teallach, meanwhile, tempts from Dundonnell. The National Trust for

NOT TO BE MISSED:

Dornoch's elegant Edwardian buildings, cathedral, and beach 240

The scenic and unspoiled beaches of Sandwood Bay 243

Scotland's Route 66, the stunning North Coast 500 244–245

The shortbread-tin pretty village of Plockton 253–254

The spectacular cinematic setting of Eilean Donan Castle 254

Scotland *(tel 0131/385 7490, nts.org .uk)* can put you in touch with knowledgeable local guides to help you tackle the climbs and other outdoor activities.

And if all that sounds far too energetic, this is also a great region for a driving holiday, whether taking on the sensational North 500 route or simply making your way along winding roads that skirt the windswept coastline, and enjoying spectacular and seemingly endless views of the sea with only an abundance of seabirds for company. ∎

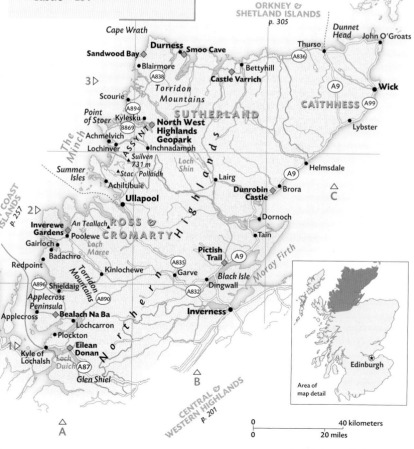

EAST COAST

Northeast of Inverness, the gentle rolling hills, fertile plains, and low sea cliffs that characterize the landscape in this part of Scotland come as a surprise to many visitors, who often associate the Highlands with the vaulting mountains and sea lochs that dominate the west.

■ Dunrobin Castle is the most northerly of Scotland's great houses and the largest in the Northern Highlands.

Black Isle & Tain

Leaving Inverness on the A9, visitors find themselves crossing the **Black Isle** (see sidebar opposite), not an island at all but a peninsula sandwiched between the Cromarty, Moray, and Beauly Firths. Farther north, in Tain, the **Tain Through Time** exhibition teaches you about this handsome borough's past—it claims to be the oldest Royal Burgh in Scotland. For whisky aficionados, Tain is also home to one of the country's most prestigious distilleries, **Glenmorangie,** offering tours and tastings.

The Fearn Peninsula east of Tain makes a worthwhile diversion, including the pretty coastal settlement of **Portmahomack** and the Pictish standing stones at **Hilton** and **Shandwick.**

Throughout this region, the well-signposted **Highland Pictish Trail** *(highlandpictishtrail.co.uk)* marks the distinctive carved stones and other sights relating to those who lived here from the third to the 9th centuries A.D.

Dornoch

Farther up the A9, Dornoch is the most charming settlement in the northeast Highlands, and it claims to be Scotland's sunniest town. At its center, the **Dornoch Cathedral** is a 13th-century beauty popular for celebrity weddings. Across the square, the revitalized **Carnegie Courthouse** holds a visitor center, as well as a deli, tearoom, and whisky shop. Dornoch is also home to one of the country's most prestigious golf courses, the **Royal Dornoch,** a links course that is as challenging as it is scenic. Non-golfers can enjoy the epic sweep of golden sand at **Dornoch Beach.**

Another essential stop is **Dunrobin Castle** *(Golspie, tel 01408/633 177, dunrobincastle.co.uk, closed Nov.–March, ££),* home to the Duke of Sutherland. With its

Tain Through Time ✉ Tower St., Tain ☎ (01862) 894 089 💲 £
🕐 Closed Sun.–Mon.; Nov.–March **tainmuseum.org.uk** • **Glenmorangie**
✉ Glen Morangie, Tain ☎ (01862) 892 477 💲 Tour: £–£££££ **glenmorangie.com**

INSIDER TIP:

At Dunrobin Castle, take time to marvel at the falconry show in the lower gardens, where birds of prey fly close overhead.

—MARY NORRIS
National Geographic contributor

towering conical spires, the castle seems inspired by a fairy tale. Dating from the 14th century, it is one of the oldest of Scotland's grand houses to be continually inhabited. It hosts falconry displays.

Wick

From Dunrobin the A9 continues along the coast to Wick, past the hulking **Sutherland Monument** atop Ben Bhraggie (1,302 feet/397 m), a 100-foot (30 m) memorial to the first Duke of Sutherland, notorious for his role in the Highland Clearances. The town's former heyday as a thriving fishing village is retold in the **Wick Heritage Museum,** where you can also learn about the harsh Highland Clearances (see p. 252) that drove crofters from the land to become fishermen. ∎

Dornoch ⚠ 239 B2 **Visitor Information** ✉ Dornoch Hub, Argyll St., Dornoch ☎ (07341) 284 405 **visitdornoch.com** • **Dornoch Cathedral** ✉ High St., Dornoch ☎ (01862) 842 263 **dornoch-cathedral.com** • **Royal Dornoch Golf Club** ✉ Golf Rd., Dornoch ☎ (01862) 810 219 💲 ££££ **royaldornoch.com** • **Wick Heritage Museum** ✉ 18–27 Bank Row, Wick ☎ (01955) 605 205 💲 £ **wickheritage.org**

EXPERIENCE: Visiting the Black Isle

Gently rolling hills and green pastures are the characteristics of the Black Isle—a hidden corner of the region's east coast where you can stroll through pretty villages, spot dolphins swimming in Cromarty Firth, or visit its prehistoric monuments. Measuring 23 miles (37 km) at its longest point and 9 miles (14.5 km) at its widest, the peninsula is home to a broad array of sights that most people never see as they rush past on the A9.

One of the best places to get a feel for the area's Pictish history is at the **Groam House**

Museum (*High St., Rosemarkie, tel 01381/620 961, groamhouse .org.uk, closed Nov.–March, £*). Here you can admire a unique display of 15th-century carved standing stones and watch a short film about the region's Picts.

Alternatively, why not commune with today's Scots on a tour of the **Black Isle Brewery** (*Old Allangrange, Munlochy, tel 01463/811 871, blackislebrewery .com*), or make new friends at the **The Singleton of Glen Ord Distillery** (*Old Rd., Muir of Ord, tel 01463/872 004, malts.com, £–££*).

TOP OF SCOTLAND

Many of the visitors who make the journey to the top of Scotland are on a pilgrimage to John O'Groats—a place famous simply for being the "end of the road," the most northeasterly point on mainland Britain's road network. You can also keep going along the scenic North Coast 500 loop (see pp. 244–245) to enjoy more of the wild and rugged beauty of Scotland.

■ Duncansby Head epitomizes the rugged, sea-battered beauty of Scotland's northern coast.

Northernmost Points

Visitors usually make the trip to far-flung **John O'Groats** to say they've been to one end of the longest distance between two inhabited points on the British mainland (Land's End, in Cornwall, being the other). An irresistibly photogenic signpost marks the distance: 874 miles. This is also one of the best places to see Atlantic puffins during their breeding season (roughly May to July).

John O'Groats Ferries operates guided wildlife cruises, as well as ferries to Orkney. Or simply enjoy a walk along the rugged coastline of **Duncansby Head. Dunnet Head,** 11 miles (18 km) west of John O'Groats, is the actual northernmost point on mainland Britain, with dramatic views of the coast. Here **Dunnet Head Lighthouse,** the work of world-famous engineer Robert Stevenson, is worth a visit.

Thurso

Many visitors pass through unassuming Thurso, about 10 miles (16 km) farther west, on their way to catch the Orkney ferry in Scrabster. Those into board-based water sports, however, know **Thurso East** to be one of the best surfing spots in Europe *(thessf.com)*. Non-surfers can explore the **Thurso Art Gallery** in the town library *(Davidson's Ln., tel 01847/896 357, closed Thurs. & Sun.)*.

Continuing west along the coast takes you past Dounreay as well as the remote beaches of Melvich and

John O'Groats ⚠ 239 C3 • **John O'Groats Ferries** ✉ John O'Groats
☎ (01955) 611 353 🕐 Closed Oct.–April 💲 £££ **jogferry.co.uk**
• **Thurso** ⚠ 239 C3 Visitor Information **visitscotland.com**

Strathy and on to **Bettyhill,** site of the pristine white sands of Torrisdale Beach and Farr Bay. In town, the small **Strathnaver Museum** sheds light on the clan tradition and the Highland Clearances. The hilltop ruins of **Castle Varrich,** 12 miles (19 km) farther west in a stunningly scenic location overlooking the hamlet of **Tongue,** is worth a detour. If you're hungry, stop for a fine meal at the restaurant within the **Tongue Hotel** *(tel 01847/611 206, tonguehotel.co.uk).* Nearby, **Ben Loyal** (2,506 ft/764 m) offers great views from dramatic cliffs.

Durness & Cape Wrath

This wild beauty continues as you travel to **Durness** *(durness.org),* Scotland's most northwesterly village. Here **Balnakeil Craft Village** *(balnakeilcraftvillage.weebly.com)* hosts various independent artists selling their craft within a disused nuclear early-warning base from the 1950s.

A visit to the 200-foot (61 m) **Smoo Cave,** 1 mile (1.6 km) east of town, is a must and, from May to September, visitors should consider tackling the 11-mile (18 km) excursion to **Cape Wrath,** reached by a ferry *(tel 07719/678 729 capewrathferry.wordpress .com)* across the Kyle of Durness and then along a rough road via minibus *(tel 07534/591 124, visitcapewrath.com, ££).* Highlights include the steepest cliffs on mainland Britain, the 620-foot (189 m) **Clo Mor,** and another Robert Stevenson creation, **Cape Wrath Lighthouse.** Cape Wrath is a special protection area for birds, including fulmars.

Heading south through the northwestern Highlands, you could be forgiven for bypassing **Sandwood Bay,** as the trip involves a 4-mile (6.5 km) hike over moorland from Blairmore. Yet those who make the walk are well rewarded. Flanked by cliffs, its impressive sand dunes and sweep of unspoiled pink sand make it a contender for the U.K.'s best beach. ∎

Strathnaver Museum ✉ Clachan, Bettyhill ☎ (01641) 521 418
🕐 Closed Nov.–March 💲 £ **strathnavermuseum.org.uk**

Robert Stevenson's Lighthouses

Traveling around Scotland's coast, you'll quickly become familiar with the name Robert Stevenson (1772–1850). Following in the footsteps of his stepfather, the renowned engineer Thomas Smith (1752–1815), the Glasgow-born Robert was recruited by the Northern Lighthouse Board in 1797. Over the course of the next 47 years he would design 18 lighthouses for Scotland, including those at Dunnet Head and Cape Wrath (both at the top of Scotland). Even after his death, the Stevenson family continued to play a pivotal role in the design of Scotland's lighthouses, with no fewer than eight members of the family engineering a grand total of 97 lighthouses over a period of 150 years.

DRIVE THE NORTH COAST 500

The wild and remote North Highlands is a world-class venue for a road trip, but it was only in 2015 that a prescribed route was launched. The North Coast 500 (aka NC500)— a 500-mile (805 km) round-trip from Inverness—is an unremitting dramatic journey that passes glistening lochs, glacial valleys, and rugged mountains, taking in the regions of Wester Ross, Sutherland, Caithness, Easter Ross, the Black Isle, and Inverness-shire.

The NC500 website (northcoast500 .com) and mobile app make it easier for travelers to find hotels, campsites, and eateries that match their budget and needs.

Start by heading west of Inverness on the A832, which together with the A890 sweeps from the North Sea to the Atlantic. On this inland section of the drive, the bustle of the highland capital is soon replaced by loch-laden glens, heather-clad hills, gushing rivers, and Caledonian forest. You'll soon come to the legendary **Bealach na Ba ❶**, a steep mountain pass that rises from sea level to 2,054 feet (626 m) in a series of steep gradients and switchbacks with panoramic views over the Western Isles. Drop down to the picturesque village of **Applecross ❷**, where boat-fresh seafood awaits at the legendary **Applecross Inn** (seep. 255). Continue north from Applecross along the unnamed coast road, and enjoy sweeping views over to Skye before joining the A896 at the whitewashed village of **Shieldaig**, an excellent place to stop for lunch—**Nanny's** (Shieldaig, tel 01520/755 787, nannys shieldaig.com) offers simple seafood.

Then continue east along the southern shore of Loch Torridon with epic views of the vaulting Torridon mountains. At Kinlochewe follow the A896

NOT TO BE MISSED:

• Applecross • Shieldaig • BeinnEighe Nature Reserve • Ullapool• Inverewe Gardens • Coigach and Assynt Peninsulas • Summer Isles• John O'Groats • Dunrobin Castle

toward Ullapool, stopping at **Beinn Eighe Nature Reserve ❸** (nature. scot/enjoying-outdoors/nnrs-and-nature-reserves-visit-our-nature-reserves) to stretch your legs along the Woodland Trail. At **Ullapool ❹**, an active fishing fleet dishes up seafood to the area restaurants. Sample a local ale (or coffee for those driving) at the **Ferry Boat Inn** (tel 01854/612 431, fbiullapool.com), then enjoy the blooms of **Inverewe Gardens** (see sidebar p. 247).

Continue on the A835 north and then take the minor road to **Achiltibuie,** a great base for the **Coigach and Assynt Peninsulas ❺**, arguably the most scenic part of the NC500 with the sweep of coastal scenery and beaches around **Achmelvich,** as well as the rock monoliths of **Stac Pollaidh** and **Suilven.** From May through September catch a boat cruise with **Summer Isles Sea**

Tours *(tel 07927/920 592, summerisles-seatours.co.uk, reservation essential)* out to the sprinkling of **Summer Isles** ❻ to see this rugged Highland scenery from a different perspective, along with myriad species of seabirds.

Head north on the A894 and the A838 to the isolated village of **Durness** ❼, where vaulting cliffs front the ocean. In addition to visiting some excellent local beaches, the vast **Smoo Cave** is a must to explore. **John O' Groats** ❽, renowned as the most northerly village on the British mainland, is reached via yet more jaw-dropping scenery on the A838 and the A836. Stop in **Scrabster** at the **Captain's Galley** (see p. 255) if you crave world-class seafood. The scenery changes as you sweep south down

the A99 and the A9, with the panorama of Highland peaks and islands replaced by the vast peaty moors of "flow country." **Dunrobin Castle** ❾ (see pp. 240–241) should be visited for the chance to see how the gentry in these parts have lived for generations.

Your last stop before continuing on the A9 back into Inverness is **Dornoch** ❿, known for its small 13th-century cathedral and one of Scotland's finest golf courses as well as beautiful beaches.

🗺 See also area map p. 239
▶ Inverness
🕐 6-plus days
🔁 500 miles (805 km)
▶ Inverness

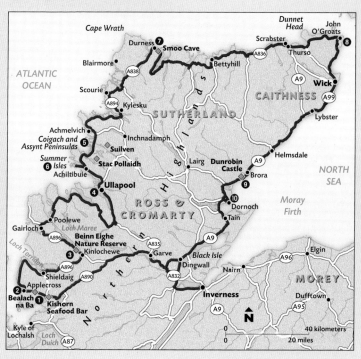

THE NORTHWEST

This rugged region of snowcapped peaks, looming medieval castles, and gnarled, weather-battered sea cliffs has its more serene side, as represented by great sweeps of white-sand beach, tiny villages perched on the edge of lochs, and even a garden of tropical flowers.

■ Framed by mountains, the resplendent Eilean Donan Castle guards the chill waters of Loch Duich.

Assynt

Scotland boasts a treasure trove of mountains, but there is something special about the peaks of Assynt Parish and those on the neighboring Coigach Peninsula. Unlike the Cairngorms, they are not part of a big massif but stand defiantly alone, each one rising like rugged giant sugarloafs from miles of inhospitable moorland. For many, a visit to Assynt is all about tackling these mountains, although the area also offers plenty of low-level walks and a clutch of pretty beaches.

South of Blairmore, the curving sweep of white sand at **Scourie Bay** is a dramatic location for a bracing stroll or a relaxed picnic. On a good day you can make a detour to Tarbet, where small boats leave for the offshore island of **Handa,** home to one of the largest colonies of seabirds in northern Europe.

While few venture as far north as Scourie, more visitors find their way to the sleepy village of

Assynt 🗺 239 A3–B3 **discoverassynt.co.uk**

Kylesku, home to a great pub-restaurant, the **Kylesku Hotel** (see p. 255), and a colony of seals. **Kylesku Boat Tours** *(tel 017821/441 090, north westseatours.co.uk, ££££)* offers trips of Loch Glencoul between March and October, when sightings of seals are nigh on guaranteed. Some boat trips also take in Britain's highest waterfall, **Eas a'Chual Aluinn,** nowhere near as impressive as it might sound. This trip is weather dependent, so call ahead.

The massive UNESCO **North West Highlands Geopark** takes in some 772 square miles (2,000 sq km) of mountain, peatland, beach, forest, and coastline across west Sutherland and on to the north coast. Its hub, just south of the Kylesku Bridge, is the **Rock Stop Café** and **visitor center** *(Unapool, Kylesku, tel 01971/488 765, nwhgeopark.com).*

From Kylesku, the B869 runs west to **Point of Stoer** and its eponymous lighthouse, another Stevenson creation (see sidebar p. 243), which has beamed out across the Minch since 1870 and is now a guesthouse *(stoerlighthouse .co.uk).* On the head, a rough ramble leads to cliffs overlooking the **Old Man of Stoer,** a distinctive 200-foot-high (61 m) rock plug sitting alone in the surf. You can stare out toward the top of Scotland and Handa, while to the south the distinctive peaks of Assynt rear into view.

Pushing south toward Lochinver, it is worth taking the detour to **Ach-melvich** where an idyllic white beach, backed with impressive dunes, slips down to a lovely little cove. **Lochinver** is a good place to stock up on supplies in these remote parts and also boasts the **Culag Woods** *(culagwoods.org.uk),* where a series of family-friendly trails take in sea and mountain vistas and lead down to a pretty pebble beach.

There are some terrific mountain-walking opportunities in this region. **Stac Pollaidh**, or Stac Polly, makes a powerful first impression—a Tolkien-evoking weirdness of crags and pinnacles that looks different from every angle—and presents a few scrambling challenges on the way to its summit. While this can be covered in a half

(continued on p. 251)

Inverewe Gardens

His contemporaries may have found the idea of importing exotic plants and flowers from around the globe to Wester Ross bizarre, but it seems Osgood MacKenzie, founder of Inverewe Gardens (*Poolewe, tel 01445/712 952, nts.org.uk/visit/ places/inverewe, ££, closed Nov.– March; see p. 244*), knew what he was doing. Although the garden lies farther north than Moscow, the warm currents passing through the loch from the Gulf Stream create ideal conditions for Inverewe's foreign blooms. Visitors can tour the house, join guided ranger walks, amble along the paths that crisscross the extensive woodland (which contain both native and exotic trees), and even enjoy a meal in one of the two on-site cafés.

Lochinver ⚠ 239 A3

DRIVE THE APPLECROSS PENINSULA

The drive from the Torridon Mountains around the Applecross Peninsula to Lochcarron takes in a swath of Europe's most dramatic scenery. The dizzying twists and turns of Scotland's highest road, the Bealach Na Ba, deter some, but stunning loch and mountain views and fine seafood reward those who make the journey.

Ben More Assynt rises above the NC500 near the northwest tip of Scotland.

This drive can be completed in a day, but to truly appreciate the wild beauty of the peninsula, an overnight stay in Applecross is recommended. This gives travelers opportunities both to get out and about in this stunning natural environment, and to feast on delicious boat-fresh fish and shellfish.

With its myriad walking routes, including an ascent of the mighty Liathach (3,461 feet/ 1,055 m), the **Torridon Mountains** make an ideal starting point. From the **Loch Torridon Community Centre** ❶ *(Torridon, tel 01445/791 361, loch torridoncentre.co.uk)* ease southwest along the A896 through the tiny

> **NOT TO BE MISSED:**
>
> Applecross • Bealach Na Ba• Kishorn Seafood Bar

settlement of Annat and on to **The Torridon** ❷ (see Travelwise p. 355). This grand country house on the banks of Loch Torridon serves good food and a range of single malt whiskies. It also offers gorge-scrambling and mountain hikes up Beinn Damph (2,960 feet/902 m), just south of the estate, through **Torridon Outdoors** *(tel 01445/791 242, thetorridon.com/ torridon-outdoors)*.

A short hop along the A896 brings you to a **viewpoint** ❸ on the right-hand side of the road, which delivers startling elevated vistas over Loch Torridon and the mountains beyond. After passing though Balgy, the road continues onto **Shieldaig** ❹. If you are hungry, turn off the A896 and head to the bar at the **Tigh an Eilean Hotel** (see Travelwise pp. 355–356), which serves wonderful seafood. Leaving Shieldaig, the A896 heads south toward Lochcarron. Take the first road on the right, which skirts the coast of the Applecross Peninsula, winding dizzily along the shore of Loch Torridon before turning south along the **Inner Sound,** which opens up dramatic vistas over the Inner Hebrides islands of Rona and Raasay.

You pass through the hamlets of **Cuaig** ❺ and **Lonbain,** and as the road sweeps alongside a pretty sandy cove, you will know you have arrived in **Applecross** ❻. This whitewashed village has an inn and a clutch of quaint cottages. Stop here to take in its stunning location and first-rate seafood served up in the **Applecross Inn** (see p. 255). The village is also an

A See also area map p. 239
▶ Loch Torridon Community Centre
🕑 Choice of 1–2 days
↔ 50 miles (80 km)
▶ Lochcarron

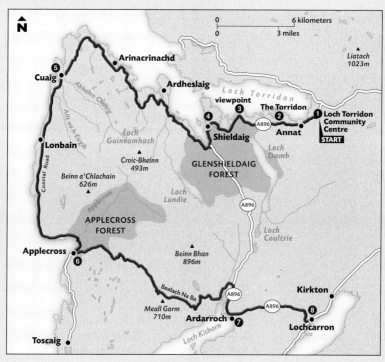

ideal base for walking and has a good campsite.

The most exhilarating part of the drive comes next. From Applecross, the infamous **Bealach Na Ba** road winds east, then southeast, as it rises in search of the A896. You will pass several viewpoints on the climb, with the highest located at 2,053 feet (626 m). From here, things get really exciting. If you thought ascending around hairpin bends on a single-lane road was challenging, then wait until you begin the steep descent to sea level along a snake of stomach-testing turns that feel akin to a roller-coaster ride. At the foot of the Bealach Na Ba, turn right onto the A896; the village of **Ardarroch** ❼, at the head of Loch Kishorn, is just a short hop away. Reward yourself with mouthwatering shellfish at the **Kishorn Seafood Bar** (see p. 255), then head west on the A896 to **Lochcarron** ❽. This whitewashed village, spread out on the northern shore of Loch Carron, is a great place to unwind, with bicycles and kayaks available for rent, as well as a nine-hole golf course. **Lochcarron Weavers** (tel 01520/722 212, lochcarron .co.uk), 2 miles (3 km) west of the village, boasts a working loom and beautiful tartans.

Road up to Bealach na Ba mountain pass with Loch Kishorn and Sgurr A Chaorachain and Meall Gorm mountains

day, the most famous peak here, **Suil-ven,** is a more serious proposition. It's a mighty mountain, 2,398 feet (731 m) high, that makes for a big day out, involving a 4.5-mile (7 km) walk just to get to its base. The epic views over Assynt and out to the Outer Hebrides make it worthwhile, but be sure to take full precautions.

For those heading south to Ull-apool (see p. 253), taking a detour along the winding single-track road toward Achiltibuie provides stunning scenery. This dramatic stretch of road, flanked by mountains and running alongside a burn, culminates at a T-junction. Taking the right fork brings you to what is arguably Assynt's most dramatic beach, **Achnahaird,** an epic stretch of cotton-white sand and turquoise waters. To one side lie rocks and rock pools, while to the other rear up the region's distinctive mountain

peaks. Just a few miles away is **Achilti-buie,** a tiny village that is the improbable home to the **Summer Isles Hotel**, with its renowned restaurant and great informal seafood bar. Tides willing, from May to September **Summer Isles Sea Tours** (*Old Dorney Harbour, Achiltibuie, ttel 07927/920 592, summerisles-seatours.co.uk*) travels to the Summer Isles. Note that reservations are essential.

> **INSIDER TIP:**
>
> Nobody goes by Eilean Donan Castle without stopping to take a picture. It is the quintessential castle. Catch it at dawn or dusk for best results.
>
> —JIM RICHARDSON
> *National Geographic photographer*

Achiltibuie 239 A2

Five Sisters of Kintail

Anyone driving on the A87 between Glen Shiel and Loch Duich cannot fail to notice the five steeply pointed peaks blocking the horizon. These are the Five Sisters of Kintail, which together provide one of the most popular ridge walks in Scotland. The walk involves tackling three mountains over 3,000 feet (914 m) high, known as Munros in Scotland: Sgurr na Ciste Duibhe (3,369 feet/1,027 m), Sgurr na Carnach (3,287 feet/1,002 m), and Sgurr Fhuaran (3,501 feet/1,067 m). As such, it's not recommended for the inexperienced or fainthearted, as you will have to make steep ascents on rocky ground and scramble along narrow ridges. (There are two other slightly lesser peaks.) The best place to start the walk, which takes 8 to 10 hours, is at the pull-in off the A87 between the two sections of forest.

THE HIGHLAND CLEARANCES

Many visitors are struck by how sparsely populated the northern Highlands are. This is not just a result of their remoteness, nor flagging economies with little industry to employ people, or even the harsh winter climate. Instead, this emptiness is largely a legacy of the brutal Highland Clearances of the 18th and 19th centuries.

This destruction of the traditional clan system—the allegiance to specific tribes, based loosely on ancestry—and eviction of people from their land took more than a century to complete. It was done in the name of agricultural progress and as a punishment for Bonnie Prince Charlie's heroic (some would say reckless) attempt to recapture the British throne, which culminated in the fateful 1746 Battle of Culloden (see pp. 208–209).

Brutal Evictions

The early Clearances, which were largely confined to the northern Highlands, are regarded by many historians as the most brutal. They involved forcing Highlanders from their lands to the wind-lashed coast, where they were allowed to live on a small piece of land, known as a croft, in return for which they had to pay their landlords rent, often a substantial sum. As a result, these Highlanders cum crofters were forced into collecting kelp (the large iodine-rich seaweed used in the manufacture of soap) or fishing in order to survive. The landlords then replaced the people with large flocks of sheep, taking advantage of the huge profits that wool then commanded.

For visitors today, the idea of relocating the population and giving them somewhere to live and a new trade doesn't sound that bad and the true awfulness of the Clearances can be hard to grasp. But the gentry who owned the land didn't politely ask the Highlanders to leave, nor did they serve them with timely eviction notices. Instead, they hired sheep farmers from the Borders and Moray to terrorize the people from their homes, including ripping roofs off houses or setting them on fire, while still occupied.

Exodus to the Coast

For a people used to an inland, agricultural way of life, starting again on the coast was not easy. Most had no experience fishing or kelping, and earning a living this way proved tough. The demise of the kelping industry during the early 19th century made life even harder. Their income dwindled, while the demand for rent did not. As landlords began clearing the coastal settlements to graze yet more sheep, crofters were forced to leave for foreign lands. Although their departures were often disguised by landlords as sponsored emigration schemes, with no political representation and no money, the Highlanders really had no choice.

Wester Ross

When thinking about Scotland, people often conjure up images of dazzling lochs, rugged mountains, quaint villages, and sandy beaches. For many, the region of Wester Ross is perhaps the epitome of this romantic idyll.

Ullapool is Wester Ross's most populous urban settlement. This old fishing port, reclining prettily on the shore of Loch Broom, is integral to Highland history. Many of those exiled during the Clearances set sail for North America, Australia, and New Zealand from here. Today, ferry passengers travel only as far as the Isle of Lewis, and many people quickly pass through. But Ullapool has a lot to recommend, including cozy pubs and the area's premier performance venue, **The Ceilidh Place** (see p. 255). It also makes a great base for forays into the Assynt peaks. You can delve deeper into the history and heritage of the area at the **Ullapool Museum** *(tel 01854/612 987, ullapoolmuseum .co.uk, £)*, housed in an early 19th-century church by Thomas Telford.

Continuing south toward the dramatic Torridon Mountains, the A835 passes **Inverewe Gardens** (see sidebar p. 247) on its way into the pretty village of **Poolewe.** From here you can also walk to one of Scotland's most attractive lochs, **Loch Maree.**

Gairloch, on the shores of Loch Gairloch, boasts some lovely sandy beaches. Following the B8021 on the

■ **A simple cottage of the type used by crofters in the wake of the Highland Clearances**

north side of the bay presents drivers, cyclists, and walkers with dramatic coastal scenery. It leads to a headland dominated by the **Rua Reidh lighthouse** *(tel 01445/771 263, stayatalighthouse.co.uk),* now a guesthouse. Southwest, a single-track road takes you past classic loch and glen scenery, through the village of **Badachro,** home to a great pub, the **Badachro Inn** *(badachroinn.com)* with a waterfront terrace. The next village is **Redpoint,** its expansive pink-sand beach a stunning spot for a walk with views of the Hebrides.

Plockton

Some 60 miles (97 km) south of Gairloch, wrapped around the shores of Loch Carron with views

Ullapool 🗺 239 A2 **Visitor Information** ✉ Argyle St., Ullapool ☎ (01854) 612 486 **visitscotland.com**

■ **The silhouette of the Applecross mountains looms beyond the lochside village of Plockton.**

over the Applecross mountains, is the postcard-pretty village of Plockton. One of the best ways to view the dramatic area is to take to the sea. A boat trip with the gregarious Calum of **Calum's Plockton Seal Trips** offers fine vistas back over the whitewashed cottages and the haunting Cuillin Hills of Skye beyond. It also guarantees seal sightings (or your money back) and, if you're lucky, dolphin, otter, and porpoise sightings too. Landlubbers, meanwhile, can savor the panorama and boat-fresh "Plockton prawns" (langoustines)

from the loch-side garden at the **Plockton Hotel** (see Travelwise p. 355).

A half-hour drive southeast of Plockton, the A87 opens up to reveal one of Scotland's most beautiful castles, **Eilean Donan.** This fortress dates from the 13th century, but was destroyed by the English, who exploded the magazine, in 1719. It lay in ruins for almost 200 years until it was restored in the early 20th century. The castle's setting is breathtaking, overlooking Loch Long, Loch Alsh, Loch Duich, and the Five Sisters of Kintail (see sidebar p. 251). ■

Calum's Plockton Seal Trips ⊠ 32 Harbour St., Plockton ☎ (01599) 544 306 🅂 ££ **calums-sealtrips.com** • **Eilean Donan** 🅼 239 A1 ⊠ Dornie ☎ (01599) 555 202 🕓 Closed Jan. 🅂 £ **eileandonancastle .com**

Where to Eat & Drink in Northern Highlands

APPLECROSS INN

SHORE ST., APPLECROSS

(01520) 744 262 | applecrossinn.co.uk

This lovely inn is legendary in Scotland, not least for the hair-raising car ride over the Bealach na Ba (see p. 250) to get there. Then there is its stunning waterfront setting. The real reason to make the pilgrimage, though, is the sumptuous and simply cooked seafood that is dished up every day.

££–£££ P Closed Tues. MC, V

BOATH HOUSE

AULDEARN

(01667) 454 896 | boath-house.com

Set within a charming Regency hotel is one of Scotland's best restaurants, the holder of a Michelin star and four AA rosettes. The pièce de résistance is the six-course fine-dining menu, featuring game, meat, poultry, and seafood.

£££££ P Closed Mon.–Tues. AE, MC, V

THE CAPTAIN'S GALLEY

THE HARBOUR, SCRABSTER

(01847) 894 999 | captainsgalley.co.uk

Everything about this seafood restaurant is spectacular, from its exposed brickwork walls to smooth service and a menu that showcases the diversity of Scotland's natural larder.

££££–£££££ Closed Tues., & L Mon. & Wed. MC, V

THE CEILIDH PLACE

14 W. ARGYLE ST. MAIN ST., ULLAPOOL

(01854) 612 103 | theceilidhplace.com

Plenty of local bonhomie combine with refined décor and superbly executed Scottish and fusion fare at this homey inn's restaurant—an Ullapool institution for local artsy types and crusty salts-of-the-earth alike. Live music adds to the good cheer. The seasonal menu might include pier-fresh baked cod with white bean, sundried tomato, and chorizo cassoulet, or wild mushroom risotto with truffled hazelnut, thyme oil, and parmesan.

£–£££ P MC, V

KISHORN SEAFOOD BAR

KIRSHORN

(01520) 733-240 | kishornseafoodbar.co.uk

The seafood at this modest eatery located along the scenic North Coast 500 (see pp. 244–245) is allowed to speak for itself. Langoustines, scallops, mussels, oysters, lobsters, crab, and locally smoked salmon are just some of the mouthwatering local seafood on the menu. Sunny days lure diners to the outside tables for views across the sea to the Isle of Skye

££ P Closed D Sun–Wed. May–June, Sat.–Sun.. July–Aug., & Sep.–April MC, V

KYLESKU HOTEL

KYLESKU

(01971) 502 231 | kyleskuhotel.co.uk

Lochinver haddock, west coast mussels, and wild venison are just some of the dishes on the bar menu at the lochside Kylesku Hotel. With its use of local produce, the meals served are superior to those in the average pub.

££ Closed Dec.–mid-Feb. MC, V

Colorful villages and smoky whiskies on a patchwork of spectacular islands stretching from the Scottish coast to the wild North Atlantic

WEST COAST ISLANDS

The colorful town of Tobermory, on the island of Mull

WEST COAST ISLANDS

While many visitors dream of visiting the Isle of Skye, a land shrouded in romantic history and misty mountains, few realize that Scotland has more than 800 islands, of which almost 100 are inhabited. Scotland's West Coast islands are diverse both in their geography and landscapes, as well as in their wildlife and cultures.

The most easily accessible of Scotland's islands include Bute and Arran, whose proximity to Glasgow have made them popular with the vacationing masses since Victorian times. The island of Arran is enjoying something of a renaissance. It is home to boutique hotels and many great places to eat, as well as a number of local businesses that offer outdoor adventures, local produce, and information on the island's history and wildlife.

For whisky aficionados, the Inner Hebridean Isle of Islay needs little introduction. Not only do its nine distilleries produce some of the country's finest whisky, they also enjoy extremely scenic locations, on an island dotted with sandy beaches and whitewashed villages. For most, the Isle of Jura provides a dramatic mountainous background to an Islay trip. This rugged island, whose deer population far outnumbers its human population, offers bountiful rewards for hill walkers, wildlife enthusiasts, and those who are simply looking to get away from it all.

A short ferry trip away from the bustling west coast port of Oban, the island of Mull has long been popular with Scottish and other vacationers, who come to relax in its colorful capital Tobermory and enjoy the picturesque mountains and stunning sandy beaches. Mull is also a good base for forays onto some of the smaller isles, including the deeply religious Iona, a place of pilgrimage for centuries, as well as Eigg, Rum, Canna, and Muck.

Those who want to travel farther afield can spend time walking, cycling, or just relaxing on the improbably beautiful and empty beaches of the isle of Coll, from where views of the Western Isles (also called the Outer Hebrides) and

NOT TO BE MISSED:

Comparing the smoky whiskies at the nine distilleries on the wildly beautiful isle of Islay 261

Sampling the delicious Scottish produce and adventure sports on the isle of Arran 263, 266–267

Visiting the Benedictine abbey on the faith-filled isle of Iona 272–273

Hiking the Trotternish Peninsula to the fantastical rock formations of the Quiraing on the misty Isle of Skye 281–283

Exploring the extraordinarily scenic Isle of Harris 290–293

Edinburgh

Area of
map detail

NORTHERN HIGHLANDS p. 237

CENTRAL & WESTERN HIGHLANDS p. 201

CENTRAL SCOTLAND p. 141

0   40 kilometers
0   20 miles

N

6▷

Port of Ness

Dun Carloway
Broch
Stornoway
Callanish ◇
Lewis

The Minch

← St. Kilda

Harris

Tarbert
Leverburgh

ROSS &
CROMARTY

Berneray

5▷

North
Uist

Lochmaddy

Skye Museum
of Island Life ◇
Quiraig

Gairloch

Benbecula

Dunvegan
Castle ◇
Dunvegan

Stein
Uig

Portree
A87

Raasay

4▷

South
Uist

Lochboisdale

Eriskay

Barra
Castlebay

INVERNESS-SHIRE

Skye

Kyle of
Lochalsh

Sleat
Peninsula

Canna

Kinloch Castle ◇
Rum

Armadale
Mallaig

Inner
Hebrides

Eigg
Muck

Coll

3▷

Arinagour

Tobermory
Calgary

Mull

Tiree

Staffa
Iona

Craignure
Duart Castle ◇

Oban

ARGYLL
&
BUTE

Firth of Lorn

Ardfern

2▷

Colonsay

Lochgilphead

Argyll Islands

Jura

Port Askaig

Craighouse

Rothesay

Port
Charlotte

Bowmore

Islay

Port Ellen

Sound of Jura

Kennacraig

Bute
Lochranza

Goatfell
819 m ▲
Arran

Kintyre

Brodick

Firth of Clyde

1▷

Campbeltown

Mull of
Kintyre

△
B

△
C

ATLANTIC OCEAN

Inner Hebrides unfold. Neighboring Tiree, meanwhile, enjoys the dual honor of being the sunniest spot in Britain, as well as host to an important global windsurfing event, the Tiree Wave Classic.

To the north, the Inner Hebridean island of Skye is a vast natural playground, complete with challenging hill walks for the experienced mountaineer, attractive whitewashed villages, and miles of breathtaking scenery. Ferries leaving from the port of Uig in the north of the island link Skye to the Outer Hebrides via Lochmaddy on North Uist and Tarbert on the Isle of Harris.

A string of causeways links the isles of North Uist, Benbecula, South Uist, and Eriskay, and together these islands offer a rich, scenic web of azure lochs, small lochans, and sprawling swaths of sandy beach backed by the delicate machair ecosystem (see sidebar p. 293). At the southern end of this chain, the Isle of Barra is just a short ferry hop away, but the most memorable way to visit this island is by plane, though beach landings are subject to change depending on the tide.

In the north of the Outer Hebrides, the island of Harris and Lewis (one island, but two very different destinations) tempts with its looming mountains and paradisiacal beaches. No matter which west coast islands you visit, taking the ferry and getting out and about in the great outdoors is all part of the fun, with everything from gentle coastal walks and flat cycling to technical climbing and sea kayaking on offer through an increasing number of adventure operators and outdoor centers. ■

I ARGYLL ISLANDS

Venturing west from the Scottish mainland by ferry brings visitors to the offshore Argyll Islands, part of the archipelago that makes up the Inner Hebrides. There is something for everyone here, from Bute's Victorian charms, Arran's culinary delights, and Jura's unspoiled natural beauty to Islay's whisky distilleries and Mull's dramatic castles and colorful villages.

■ The Caledonian MacBrayne ferry, Kyles of Bute, Argyll

Bute

It may measure just 15 miles (24 km) by 5 miles (8 km) at its widest and longest points, but the isle of Bute has much to offer visitors. Located in the Firth of Clyde, Bute celebrated its heyday in the 19th century, when it was a popular vacation destination for Glaswegians who came "doon the watter" aboard the traditional paddle steamers (see sidebar p. 114).

A pervading sense of faded grandeur fills the main town of **Rothesay,** which boasts Victorian architecture, a seafront promenade, and the fully functional, magnificent **Victorian Toilets** *(Rothesay Pier).* You can learn more about the natural history of the island at the **Bute Museum** *(7 Stuart St., tel 01700/505 067, butemuseum.org.uk, £, closed Dec.–Jan.),* or venture into the 14th-century **St. Mary's Chapel** *(High St.),* where Napoleon's niece, Stepha-

Argyll Islands 259 B1–B2, C1 **Visitor Information** ✉ 3 North Pier, Oban ☎ (01631) 563 122 **visitscotland.com**

GETTING TO THE ARGYLL ISLANDS:
Caledonian MacBrayne *(tel 0800/066 5000, calmac.co.uk)* serves the Argyll Islands. You can also fly (Loganair *&* Hebridean Air Services), drive, ortake ScotRail.

Bute 259 C1–C2 **Visitor Information** ✉ Victoria St., Rothesay
☎ (01700) 507 043 **visitscotland.com**

nie Hortense Bonaparte, is interred. Its most impressive sight, though, is the 800-year-old ruin of **Rothesay Castle** *(Castlehill St., tel 01700/502 691, historicenvironment.scot, £),* the imposing home of several Scottish kings from the 13th through the 16th centuries, now with ducks on the moat. It was closed for repairs at press time.

As you break away from the town, more of the island's heritage unfolds.

A short hop south brings you to **Mount Stuart,** a decadent Victorian Gothic mansion, arguably the most impressive in the United Kingdom, and home to the third Marquess of Bute. Its 300 acres (121 ha) of woodland gardens boast horticultural collections of global significance, while the house features a stunning art collection amassed by the Third Earl of Bute in the 18th century. Like its

Mount Stuart ✉ Rothesay, Bute ☎ (01700) 503 877 💲 ££ **mountstuart.com**

EXPERIENCE: Islay Whisky

If you are looking for a quality whisky experience, then a visit to the island of Islay is a must. It is home to no fewer than nine whisky distilleries. **Laphroaig** *(laphroaig.com),* Lagavulin, and Ardbeg are the island's three southern dames that produce some of the smokiest flavors in the whisky world. They also offer excellent tours and shops.

For a laid-back distillery tour head to **Lagavulin** *(malts.com),* where you can sample a wee dram in the comfort of an armchair. The most impressive visitor experience is at **Ardbeg** *(ardbeg.com),* with its numerous tour options and superb Old Kiln Café, where many of the dishes are whisky infused.

The island capital of **Bowmore** has an eponymous distillery *(bowmore.com),* itself home to a £100,000 (US$127,000) bottle of whisky. Notably, 25 percent of the barley is melted on-site.

Out to the west, **Bruichladdich** *(bruichladdich.com)* has been using traditional equipment and methods since reopening in 2001. On Islay's east coast, **Caol Ila** *(malts.com)* and **Bunnahabhain** *(bunnahabhain.com)* pour a lot of their malt into blends, but they have recently started selling more single malt expressions. And **Ardnahoe** *(ardna hoedistillery.com)*—the first new distillery in 15 years—opened in April 2019, with gorgeous views over the Sound of Islay.

Last but certainly not least is the island's smallest distillery, **Kilchoman** *(kilchomandistillery .com),* featuring a "100 percent Islay" whisky made using only barley grown on the island and malted on-site. Stay to dine at the café, where dishes are made with fine local produce.

Making the Most of Arran's Food Renaissance

Green and fertile Arran is an island that takes food provenance seriously, something that shines through in its impressive food and drink production scene. Key players in the island's culinary landscape include **Arran Fine Foods** (The Old Mill, Lamlash, tel 1770/600 118, facebook.com/arranfinefood skitchenshop), renowned for the quality of its preserves, jams, and sauces, as well as its melt-in-the-mouth shortbread.

The **Island Cheese Company** (Home Farm, Brodick, tel 01770/302 788, arranscheese shop.co.uk) has, by infusing cheddars with the likes of garlic, claret, and whisky, created some 15 first-class cheeses. The perfect accompaniment for these delectable cheeses is, of course, a **Wooleys of Arran** oatcake (Invercloy, Brodick, tel 01770/302 280, wooleys.co.uk).

There is also an ice-cream maker, **Arran Dairies** (Market Rd., Brodick, tel 01770/302 374, arranicecream.co.uk); a chocolatier, **James of Arran** (Invercloy, Brodick, tel 01770/302 873, jamesofarran.com); and the **Isle of Arran Brewery** (Brodick, tel 01770/302 353, arranbrewery .co.uk) and **Seagate Brewery** (Seagate, Lamlash, tel 01770/600 110, seagatebrewery.co.uk), both making artisanal real ales. Most of these venues offer tours.

In the west, the **Arran Butcher** (Harbour View, Blackwater foot, tel 01770/860 354, thearranbutcher.com) has developed a range of island haggis and black pudding. Blackwaterfoot is also home to the **Blackwater Bakehouse** (behind the Kinloch Hotel, tel 07827/816 273, facebook.com/bakehouseblack water), fabled for its wonderful breads and cakes. Ask for these products or visit them direct.

southwestern neighbor Arran, Bute is an island that is divided into highland and lowland areas by the Highland Boundary Fault. In the north, the seismic activity of millennia past has thrown up peaks, like **Windy Hill** (913 feet/278 m), the island's highest, to tempt visiting hill walkers. The south of the island, in contrast, is characterized by verdant farmland and sandy beaches, among which **Kilchattan Bay** and **Scalpsie Bay** (perfect for viewing the local seals) are highlights.

Located just over 2 miles (3 km) from Bute's southern tip, Kilchattan Bay also marks the beginning of the **West Island Way** (westislandway .co.uk)—a walk that provides some stunning views. Covering about 30 miles (48 km), the route does a small loop in the south of the island before striking north to Rhubodach and then heading south to Port Bannatyne on the east coast. A highlight is the 12th-century ruin of **St. Blane's Chapel.**

■ The Machrie Moor standing stones on Arran

Arran

With seven golf courses, dramatic castles, picturesque villages, a whisky distillery, a first-rate seafood restaurant, and a flurry of local food producers, it is easy to see why the 20-mile-long (32 km) isle of Arran is dubbed "Scotland in miniature." Then there are Arran's natural attractions—the rugged mountains of the north and the rolling hills of the south, as well as its sandy beaches.

Brodick is the island's main town, with a ferry terminal, hotels, bars, cafés, shops, a sandy beach, and a crazy golf course. Its major attractions, though,

are located on its northern fringe. Housed in an early 20th-century cottage, the **Isle of Arran Heritage Museum** delves into the island's social history. A few miles farther on is the grand **Brodick Castle, Gardens & Country Park,** with its stately rooms and expansive landscaped gardens, where 600 years of history unfold. The main path up Arran's highest peak, **Goatfell** (2,866 feet/874 m), whose mighty hulk dominates the island, starts behind the **Isle of Arran Brewery** in Brodick (see sidebar opposite). From the summit, on a clear day, you can see a dramatic panorama

(continued on p. 267)

Arran 259 C1 **Visitor Information** The Pier, Brodick, Arran (01770) 302 774 **visitscotland.com • Isle of Arran Heritage Museum** Rosaburn, Brodick (01770) 302 636 £ **arranmuseum.co.uk • Brodick Castle, Gardens & Country Park** Brodick, Arran (01770) 302 202 Closed Nov.–March ££ **nts.org.uk/visit/places/brodick-castle**

CRUISING SCOTLAND

Few people associate Scotland with cruising, but the nation's spectacular western coastline is crowded with more than 800 islands and bountiful wildlife, with a broad sweep of tempting attractions en route. Queen Elizabeth II regularly chartered the M.V. *Hebridean Princess* to cruise these epic waters, and it is easy to see why a growing number of savvy travelers are following suit.

National Geographic Expeditions' *Lord of the Glens* explores Scotland's lochs and inland waterways.

Why Is Scotland So Good for Cruising?

Scotland is easily one of the world's most dramatic cruise destinations. It boasts more than 10 percent of Europe's coastline and a seashore three times larger than England's, and that's not even including its islands. This abundance of waterways allows a diverse cruising experience, from sailing to remote islands set adrift miles out in the Atlantic to

visiting charming island villages and mountainous isles. The main cruising areas are the relatively sheltered Firth of Clyde and the Inner Hebrides, although some ships take on the rougher waters around the Outer Hebrides.

Scottish waters are alive with numerous species of porpoise and dolphins, as well as bountiful whales—including killer whales—and hulking basking sharks. Seabirds flock here

INSIDER TIP:

Scotland is a rainy, misty land, which makes for great photos but wet equipment. Remember to keep your camera and lenses dried and safely stored.

—JEFF MAURITZEN
*National Geographic
Traveler photographer*

in summer, with the undeniably cute multicolored puffins perhaps the most famous visitors. The majestic sea eagle also flourishes in Scotland. On land look out for the ubiquitous red deer—the largest land mammal in the British Isles. The culture and heritage of the coast is compelling too, as this is a land awash with the ghosts of the Celtic Gaels and the Norse Vikings. Indeed, the Gaelic language is still spoken on some of the islands and in many parts of Scotland's west coast. Add in standing stones, mysterious broch forts, ruined castles, and traditional croft villages and the human history is as compelling as the natural.

Cruising Options

A number of dedicated cruise ship operators now serve Scotland's west coast, rather than just cruise ships that pass through as part of a longer itinerary. Easily the most famous is the **Hebridean Princess** (hebridean .co.uk); the British royal family charters her regularly. This brilliantly reinvented old passenger ferry hosts a maximum of 50 passengers, making it feel like a very exclusive country house party, with superb fine dining, single malt whiskies, and wine to match. Year-round itineraries include the Inner and Outer Hebrides, the lochs of Argyll, and ports along the Firth of Clyde.

National Geographic Expeditions (nationalgeographic.com/ expeditions) and Lindblad Expeditions together explore Scotland's famed lochs and inland waterways aboard the M.V. *Lord of the Glens*. This teak-lined motor yacht sleeps 48 guests and is nimble enough to navigate the eight narrow locks of Neptune's Staircase, as well as the windswept Hebridean seas, Loch Ness, and the Isle of Skye. The sleek, rugged 148-passenger *National Geographic Explorer* will brave the Orkneys and Shetlands Isles, plus the Faroes and Iceland.

Plus, Scotland is included on various other itineraries, such as "Ancient Isles: England, Ireland, and Scotland" (with visits to the Inner and Outer Hebrides, the Orkney islands, the Shetlands, as well as Aberdeen and Edinburgh), aboard the *National Geographic Explorer*.

Charming and family-run, **The Majestic Line** (themajesticline.co.uk) made its name through its characterful conversion of two old fishing vessels, the *Glen Tarsan* and the *Glen Massan*. Majestic's latest additions, the *Glen Etive* and *Glen Shiel*, have stabilizers that enable them to tackle the rougher seas to St. Kilda and the Outer Hebrides. All Majestic

■ **Passengers view the powerful whirlpool in the Gulf of Corryvreckan from a safe distance.**

Line vessels sleep a maximum of 12 passengers in some comfort, serving superb local produce with wine inclusive with meals.

In 2015, Iain Duncan, a former skipper on the Majestic Line, jumped ship to start **Argyll Cruising** (argyll cruising.com) around the Firth of Clyde and Hebrides. On board his wee vessel, the M.V. *Splendour,* things are very much family-run. Inside space is at a relative premium, but she is cozy and very welcoming. Duncan is an expert skipper who knows these waters intimately, thus bringing his passengers to some superb hidden anchorages.

Hebrides Cruises (hebridescruises .co.uk) is another family-run cruise business. Flexible skipper and qualified scuba diver (known to dive for king scallops for dinner) Rob Bar-

low is at the helm of the 12-berth *Elizabeth G.* and her sister vessel, the 10-berth *Emma Jane,* and the company recently added the luxury 4-berth *Lucy Mary.* They offer an expedition cruise, which means that the itinerary is often more adventurous, landings are often by zodiac (dinghy), and berths are compact.

Several reputable tour operators, such as **Abercrombie & Kent** (abercrombiekent.com) and **Tauck** (tauck.com), charter these or other, usually larger, vessels for Scottish-themed cruises. Experts on Scottish history, geography, culture and/or wildlife usually offer lectures. These are ideal for those who want the stability of a bigger vessel with more facilities, as well as passengers interested in learning.

of craggy mountains and sparkling lochs that stretches to Ireland in the southwest and Ben Lomond on the mainland.

Lochranza, at the northern tip of the island, is home to the 11-hole pitch-and-putt **Lochranza Golf Course** *(tel 01770/830 273, arran campsite.com/golf, ££££)* and the **Isle of Arran Distillers** *(tel 01770/830 264, arranwhisky.com, £),* where you can learn all about this superb single malt in a slick visitor center experience. However, it is the dramatic 13th-century ruin of **Lochranza Castle** *(closed Nov.–March, historic environment.scot)* that etches itself most in the memory in these parts. A rich history has seen the castle used by the MacSween family and Oliver Cromwell. There are even reports that Robert the Bruce landed here in 1306 when he returned from Ireland in order to claim the Scottish throne.

Snaking down Arran's west coast, the coastal road passes through **Catacol,** whose beautiful whitewashed cottages have been dubbed the "Twelve Apostles." They were built in the mid-19th century to house people cleared from the land, whose hardship has earned the cottages the alternative moniker "Hungry Row."

Older history unfurls at **Machrie Moor** *(historicenvironment.scot),* whose chief attraction are its six Neolithic **standing stones.** These range from circles with a single stone slab left standing to ambitious double circles

that, although they are now reduced to granite boulders, hint at the ambition of this ancient site. The **King's Cave** *(forestryandland.gov.scot/visit/ kings-cave)* outside **Blackwaterfoot** also has historic connections, as it claims to be the place where Robert the Bruce, inspired by a spider patiently attempting to rebuild its web, found the courage to avenge his early defeats.

The nearby villages of **Lagg, Kilmory,** and **Torrylin** run into one another, giving the impression that they are all one village. This part of Arran is worth exploring for ancient monuments like the Neolithic **Torrylin Cairn** and **Torr a'Chaisteal Dun** (also known as Corriecravie Dun), a fortified farmstead from around A.D. 200.

In recent years, a range of adventure activities has added to Arran's traditional charms. Mountain biking, gorge walking, and sea kayaking are all available from **Arran Adventure Company** *(Auchrannie Rd., tel 01770/302234, auchrannie.co.uk/ adventure.html)* at the full service Auchrannie Resort.

Jura

One of Scotland's best-kept secrets, Jura is a stunning island spanning some 142 square miles (368 sq km) where nature rules. Its most defining landmark is the Paps of Jura—three majestic mountains that dominate the island and can be seen from Islay and Argyll's west coast.

Jura 259 B2 **isleofjura.scot**

Jura is pleasantly devoid of roads and traffic (it has just one road that hugs its southern and eastern shoreline), allowing for thriving wildlife. Here, ornithologists can spot grouse, snipe, and even golden eagles. Its deer population is reckoned to extend to some 5,000, while only about 200 people call this rugged island home. Centuries ago Jura was called Dy Oer (Joora), meaning "deer island."

While Jura does have some attractions, such as the **Isle of Jura Distillery** *(tel 01496/820 385, jurawhisky .com),* in **Craighouse,** Jura's only real village, the main reason to visit is to get out and about in the great outdoors and simply enjoy the tranquility.

For hill walkers and climbers, the **Paps of Jura** are the main attraction. Beinn an Oir, or "mountain of gold," is the highest. Standing 2,576 feet (785 m) above sea level, it is classed as a Corbett (mountains over 2,500 feet/ 762 m tall). To the east rises Beinn Shiantaidh (2,477 feet/757 m) and to the southwest is Beinn a'Chaolais (2,407 feet/734 m). The former translates as "sacred mountain," the latter as "mountain of sound." The coastline, dotted with beaches, cliffs, and caves stretching out more than 115 miles (185 km), provides myriad opportunities for walks, while inland walkers might uncover ancient **standing stones,** ruined **hill forts,** and the ruins of **Aros Castle** and **Claig Castle.**

If hiking isn't your thing, why not swim the infamous **Gulf of Corryvreckan,** home to a 100-foot (30 m) whirlpool? You can visit it via tall ship as part of a week-long **SwimTrek** tour of the Inner Hebrides, or visit via one of the myriad boat operators (see sidebar p. 271). Do not under any circumstances try to tackle the dangerous whirlpool on your own.

Islay

With nine whisky distilleries (see sidebar p. 261) and a string of stunning beaches on one wildly beautiful island, Islay should be deluged with tourists. Yet such is the remoteness of this Hebridean isle that the hordes have yet to descend on this paradise, leaving the locals to get on with the impressively self-sufficient life they have been savoring since the days when the legendary Lords of the Isles ruled whole swaths of the Scottish Highlands and islands from their Islay stronghold.

Covering an area of around 239 square miles (619 sq km), Islay has an airport and two ferry terminals. Beyond the ferry services to the islands of Jura and Colonsay, as well as Kennacraig on the mainland, **Port Askaig** in the northeast of the island offers a popular pub with stunning views in the family run **Port Askaig Hotel** *(tel 01496/840 245, portaskaig .co.uk).* Those arriving at **Port Ellen** in the south should keep a lookout for

SwimTrek ✉ 6 Hove Manor, Hove St., Brighton & Hove ☎ (01273) 739 713 💲 £££££ **swimtrek.com • Islay** 🗺 259 B1–2 **Visitor Information** ✉ The Square, Bowmore, Islay ☎ (01496) 305 165 **visitscotland.com**

the **Carraig Fhada Lighthouse.** This striking 19th-century settlement also boasts a long-defunct distillery, which now operates as a malting house for other distilleries, and one of the island's prettiest beaches, the **Singing Sands.** East of the village, the road to Claggan Bay passes by three distilleries, the ruined **Dunyvaig Castle,** and the spectacular **Kildalton Cross**—one of the best examples of an early Christian cross in Scotland—as well as the ruined **Kildalton Chapel.**

Heading west brings you to the wild and windswept **Oa peninsula** (The Oa), home to the **American Monument,** a monolith that looms out over the Mull of Oa in commemoration of two U.S. ships that were sunk back in 1918. To the north, the road passes the sweep of sandy beach at **Laggan Bay** on its way into Islay's capital, **Bowmore.** Famous for its eponymous **distillery,** the second oldest in Scotland, it's also known for its round church and picturesque Loch Indaal views.

To the southwest, the **Rhinns of Islay,** once a separate island, has a distinctive Gaelic culture and is dotted with stone crosses, standing stones, and other ancient monuments. Here, you'll also find the island's prettiest village, **Port Charlotte,** with white-washed houses and a quaint harbor on the shores of silvery Loch Indaal. The settlement is also home to two attractions: the **Museum of Islay Life,** with a strong emphasis on history, and the **Natural History Centre,** focusing on

Bowmore Distillery ✉ School St., Bowmore, Islay ☎ (01496) 810 441 💲 £ **bowmore.co.uk** • **Museum of Islay Life** ✉ Port Charlotte, Islay ☎ (01496) 850 358 🕐 Closed Sat.–Sun., & Nov.–March 💲 £ **islaymuseum.org** • **Natural History Centre** ✉ Port Charlotte, Islay ☎ (01496) 850 288 🕐 Closed Sat.–Sun. & Oct.–March **islaynatural history.org**

▪ The isle of Jura is home to about 6,000 deer.

■ A puffin on the cliffs of Treshnish Isle, Inner Hebrides

the island's animals and birds.

A short hop away are the twin villages of Portnahaven and Port Wemyss. In **Portnahaven** there is little to do but relax on the water-front and enjoy the world-class view over the tranquil harbor as you ease yourself into the gentle pace of local life. Attractive cottages (whitewashed or in pastel hues) also fringe the **Port Wemyss** seafront, from where your gaze is drawn more to Laggan Bay and the Mull of Oa to the east. Islay has its own **woolen mill,** a family-run business known for its traditionally woven fabrics. The north is also dotted with old churches, Celtic crosses, sandy bays, and memorials to shipwreck victims. **Loch Finlaggan** is home to an ancient settlement and was once a power base for the Lord of the Isles all those centuries ago.

Islay also has its own golf club, **The Machrie Hotel & Golf Links** *(Port Ellen, tel 01496/302 310, themachrie .com),* with some of the most dramatic scenery of any course in Britain. One of Islay's biggest charms is how little it has been tainted by tourism. Old industries like fishing and weaving remain an important part of local life. Visiting during a festival—whisky in May, music and malt in June, jazz in September—can be a wonderful way to experience this island.

Mull

With the CalMac ferry from Oban to Craignure taking just 50 minutes, the isle of Mull is one of Scotland's most accessible islands (alternative routes connect Lochaline to Fishnish and Kilchoan to Tobermory). During the summer months, the

Islay Woollen Mill ✉ Bridgend ☎ (01496) 810 563 **islaywoollenmill .co.uk • Mull** ⛰ 259 B2–B3 **Duart Castle** ✉ Mull ☎ (01680) 812 309 🕐 Closed mid-Oct.–March 💲 £ **duartcastle.com**

piers are thronged with visitors keen to explore an island that is far from undiscovered. Even at the height of summer, though, the island is big enough never to feel crowded. To get the most out of Mull, spend more than a day on the island.

Easing toward the island from Oban, Mull's appeal is obvious as its looming peaks rear out of the water and the craggy outline of **Duart Castle**—with its great hall and clan exhibit—hints at the island's alluring history.

The north tip of the east coast holds Mull's primary settlement, **Tobermory.** Originally fashioned as a fishing port, its main business today is undoubtedly tourism, with plenty of places to stay, eat, shop, and drink, many of which come wrapped in lovely multicolored stone buildings on the waterfront. Local culture is alive and well here with the creation of **An Tobar and Mull Theatre** *(Druimfin, tel 01688/302 211, antobarandmulltheatre .co.uk)*, with three venues providing multiuse arts space for live theater, music, visual arts, and creative learning.

In the south, the **Ross of Mull,** with its dramatic cliffs and sandy beaches, separates Craignure from Fionnphort, where boats leave for the isle of Iona. In the summer months, Staffa Tours *(tel 07831/885 985, staffatours.com)* and Staffa Trips *(Tigh na Traigh, Iona, tel 01681/700 755, staffatrips.co.uk)* organize boat trips from here to Staffa (see p. 273).

For most, a visit to Mull is all about its scenery, with the highlight the coastal road, at its best from Salen to Calgary. As you descend toward the Atlantic from Salen, views of Ben More open up with a whole host of other peaks and ridges. **Calgary** itself is the island's best beach and one of the finest in Scotland. This sweep of white sand is neatly hemmed in by rugged hillsides on three flanks. There is a designated wild camping site where you can pitch a tent by the dunes, with toilets and picnic tables, all for free. Those with more time might also want to hop over to **Ulva** *(on-demand passenger ferry operates from Ulva Ferry Apr.–Oct., tel 01688/500 226, facebook.com/theulvaferry, £).*

Gulf of Corryvreckan

The Gulf of Corryvreckan, a narrow strait separating the isles of Jura and Scarba, is also home to a 100-foot (30 m) whirlpool, the world's third deepest. The Corryvreckan whirlpool is created by an underwater mountain, whose peak lies close to the surface, and tidal changes. You can lookdown on the whirlpool, and it is possible to visit by boat. Operators include **Farsain Cruises** *(tel 07880/ 714 165, farsain-cruises.business .site)* in CraobHaven, near Lochgilphead; **Seafari Adventures** *(Ellenabeich, Easdale, tel 01852/300 003, seafari.co.uk);* and **Sealife Adventures** *(Dunaverty, Easdale, tel 01631/571 010, sealife-adventures.com).*

Ulva ulva.scot

For walkers, Mull offers everything from the heights of **Ben More** (3,169 feet/966 m) and challenging coastal walks to easy, low-level strolls.

Iona

This tiny island, measuring just 3 miles (5 km) by 1 mile (1.6 km), is the island where St. Columba set about trying to convert the Picts to Christianity. The island's main sight is its magnificently restored Benedictine **abbey,** founded in the 12th century. To make the most out of a visit, join one of the free guided tours or invest in the excellent audio tour. For those with more time, the flat, windy island offers a number of easy walks, notably to its sandy northern beaches or the pebble-strewn Port a'Churiach, St. Columba's Bay. Artists abound on Iona as well, with interesting shops to explore.

Iona 🗺 259 B3 **Iona Abbey** ✉ Iona ☎ (01681) 700 404 💲 £

■ A Celtic stone cross on the Isle of Islay

Islay's Great Geese Migration

Even those not into bird-watching cannot fail to be impressed by the huge flocks of migrating geese that descend on Islay in the winter months. Keen ornithologists will know that these magnificent birds come from different places. Beginning in late September flocks of barnacle geese arrive from Greenland to the Loch Indaal and Loch Gruinart mudflats, where they stay until April. Dusk is the prime time to see the geese as they head for their roosts. From September to November, you will also see flocks of greylag geese and pink-footed geese. In spring, watch for wading birds, including snipe, redshanks, and curlews.

The best place for geese-watching is **Loch Gruinart Nature Reserve** (tel 01496/850505, rspb.org.uk/days-out/reserves/loch-gruinart) in northwest Islay.

INSIDER TIP:

My favorite golf course is Machrie on Islay. It's right by the sea, with waves crashing close to the fairways and grass growing 3 feet (0.9 m) high in the roughs.

—JIM RICHARDSON
National Geographic photographer

Staffa

If you visit only one of Scotland's uninhabited islands, make it Staffa, which has been impressing travelers with its row of giant black basalt columns—formed millions of years ago by a volcanic eruption—since the days of the Vikings, who called it "pillar island." Staffa entered mainstream culture in 1772 when it was painted by Joseph Mallord William Turner (1775–1851). Felix Mendelssohn's (1809–1847) Hebrides Overture (Die Hebriden), also known as Fingal's Cave (Die Fingalshohle), really popularized it in the 19th century, when even Queen Victoria visited. In the summer visitors still flock here to visit **Fingal's Cave,** with its stunning natural acoustics. In spring and summer, hundreds of seabirds alight here, most notably the colorful puffins, for whom this is a favorite breeding spot. Seals and other sea life can also be spotted from your tour boat.

Coll

The CalMac ferry trip from Oban to the far-flung Inner Hebridean oasis of Coll is all part of the fun. On a journey just shy of three hours, the Clansman treats passengers to jaw-dropping views of the Ardnamurchan Peninsula, the Isle of Mull, the Isle of Skye, the Small Isles, and even the distant Outer Hebrides before berthing

Staffa 259 B3 • **Coll** 231 B3 **visitscotland.com**

■ The entrance to the famous Fingal's Cave is hidden among Staffa's colonnade of black basalt polygons.

at **Arinagour.** From the sea, Coll looks a bit disappointing—flat, rocky, and fairly featureless. First impressions, though, could not be more wrong, and with its sandy beaches, this little-known Scottish island gives the others a run for their money.

The best base for exploring the island is the **Coll Hotel** (see Travelwise p. 356–357) in Arinagour, the only real village on a tiny island that is just 12 miles (19 km) long and 4 miles (6 km) wide at its broadest points. Here a clutch of whitewashed cottages skirt the pretty bay of Loch Eatharna and savor sea views over the Treshnish Isles and the peaks of Mull.

Coll's main attraction is its more

than 20 beaches—puffy white strips of sand that are definitely worth seeking out. Hogh Bay and Crossapol are among the best, but whichever stretches of sand you visit you will be unlikely to meet any other people, even at the height of the summer.

Virtually traffic free, Coll is also great for cycling and walking, with bicycle rental available from the **An Acarsaid** gift shop and post office. The ascent of 341-foot (104 m) Ben Hogh, the island's highest point, is a good option for walkers. The summit commands distant vistas of the Paps of Jura and a panorama that encapsulates whole swaths of the Inner and Outer Hebrides.

Coll doesn't have any slick tourist attractions, but if you have a car

An Acarsaid ✉ Arinagour Post Office, Coll ☎ (01879) 230 329
🕐 Closed Sun.

it is worth viewing the island's two "castles," although neither is open to the public. Both are in the south of the island. The older **Breachacha Castle** dates from the 15th century and includes a circa-1750 Georgian mansion recently restored as luxury rental accommodations (*breachacha castle.com*) while nearby the mansion house, or "New Castle," was built in the mid-18th century. In addition to the wildlife easily observed throughout the island, areas of Coll are also protected as nature reserves (*rspb .org.uk),* without tourist facilities, just walking trails.

Tiree

A 55-minute hop aboard the CalMac ferry takes you from Coll to the Isle of Tiree (the island also has an airport). The most westerly of the Inner Hebrides, this compact island—measuring 12 miles (19 km) by 3 miles (5 km)—is now host to the annual world-class windsurfing competition, the Tiree Wave Classic, a contest that hints at the windy conditions on this flat isle (see sidebar below).

Tiree also stakes a fair claim to being the sunniest place in the British Isles. Throw in the moderating effects of the Gulf Stream and visitors can often enjoy warm and balmy summer days, with plenty of white-sand beaches on which to unwind. Indeed, it has often been called a "raised beach" for its low-lying terrain.

This is also a superb spot to gaze at the night sky; with little light pollution the stars are brilliant.

A haven for birdlife, Tiree also attracts ornithologists, while walkers who don't want to scale the dizzy heights of Scotland's Munros appreciate the gentle slopes of the island's three hills: **Ben Hynish** (463 feet/141 m), **Beinn Hough** (390 feet/119 m), and **Kennavara** (338 feet/103 m) ■

Tiree 259 A3 **isleoftiree.com**

EXPERIENCE: Windsurfing on Tiree

Stunning sandy beaches, offshore breezes, and Atlantic swells combine to make Tiree Scotland's leading wind sports destination. The island has established itself as a world leader within the windsurfing arena, as competitors from around the globe descend for the annual **Tiree Wave Classic** (*tireewaveclassic.co.uk*). Held in October each year, this eight-day event is a spectacle to behold. The enthusiastic staff members at **Wild Diamond** (*wilddiamond.co.uk*) will give you expert instruction (whether you are a novice or expert windsurfer) throughout the year. You can also rent equipment from them. If you have more advanced skills, it is better to visit during the island's windiest months (March–June or Sept.–Oct.), when the conditions are more exciting.

THE SMALL ISLES

South of Skye is a cluster of islands—Muck, Eigg, Rum, and Canna. Known collectively as the Small Isles, they are tranquil natural oases where few people live and few tourists venture. As such, they are low on tourist trappings, have limited accommodations, and offer no public transportation.

Walking on the An Sgurr, Eigg, with Rum island in the background

Muck

Muck, the smallest and most southerly of the Small Isles, is just 2 miles (3 km) long by 1 mile (1.6 km) wide, with little to do but kick back and watch the wildlife or admire the stunning scenery. The island has a craft shop, a tearoom, and a hotel, the **Gallanach Lodge** (tel 01687/462 365, galla nachlodge.co.uk), but its population of about 40 is heavily outnumbered by seals. Mull is also famous for its white Highland ponies, sired by a single stallion called "Strathmashie Seumas Mhor." **Mull Pony Trekking** (tel 07748/807 447, facebook .com/killiechronanponytrekking), in Killiechronan, offers rides, including along white-sand beaches.

Eigg

North of Muck, Eigg is the most distinctive of the Small Isles. A

Muck 259 B3 **isleofmuck.com** Eigg 231 B3–B4 **isleofeigg.org**
GETTING TO THE SMALL ISLES: Caledonian MacBrayne Ferries (calmac.co.uk) sail from Mallaig to Rum, Eigg, and Canna. The M.V. Sheerwater (arisaig.co.uk) offers wildlife trips from Arisaig to Rum, Eigg, and Muck.

landmass measuring just 5 miles (8 km) by 3 miles (5 km), it is dominated by the hulk of **An Sgurr** (1,289 feet/393 m), pitchstone lava sitting atop the basalt plateau. This striking geological formation dates back some 58 million years, and golden eagles are sometimes seen soaring high above, while hen harriers swoop over the boggy foothills.

The hike to the top, which begins at the pier where boats arrive from Mallaig on the mainland, is relatively straightforward. It is marked by cairns and takes around two hours. The island also captivates visitors with its beautiful Singing Sands beach.

Rum

The largest of the Small Isles, Rum has an area of more than 38 square miles (100 sq km) and is designated as a national nature reserve—one of the largest in Britain. **Rum National Nature Reserve** (tel 0131/314 4181, nature.scot/enjoying-outdoors) offers its very own mountain range, Rum Cuillin (whose highest peak, Askival, soars at 2,664 feet/812 m high), as well as low-level walks. It is also an

Rum 259 B4 isleofrum.com

The Islands' Newest Castle

Kinloch Castle, on Rum, was built between 1897 and 1900 by George Bullough, the eccentric son of a British textile magnate. He spared no expense in its construction, importing 250,000 tons (270,000 tonnes) of soil so he could have formal gardens and a private golf course on this windswept island. It was the first home in Scotland to have electricity—provided by a small hydroelectric dam near the castle—which was used for lighting and powering a giant mechanical music box called the "Orchestrion." The castle went into decline after World War I and eventually, in 1957, Bullough's widow sold the island and castle, to Scottish Natural Heritage for £1 an acre. In 2018 a fundraising campaign was launched to save this Edwardian time capsule from demolition. Tours, timed to the ferry, may resume in 2024.

---

ornithologist's paradise, where the once extinct white-tailed eagles can now be spotted. Nearby is the red sandstone **Kinloch Castle** (see sidebar p. 277), with its grand Edwardian interiors dating from the early 1900s. Cycling, fishing, and water sports are also popular throughout the island.

Canna

Birders, walkers, and those seeking solitude visit the tiny island of Canna, which measures just 5 miles (8 km) by 1 mile (1.6 km).

Bring your binoculars—the entire island is a National Trust for Scotland property *(tel 0844/493 2100, nts.org.uk/visit/places/canna)* and is run as a farm and bird sanctuary. While not exactly overrun with tourist facilities, it does have a café, guesthouse, and campsites. Walk along the coastal cliffs for dramatic views of nearby Skye and Rum. For travelers with an interest in botany, Canna has a special appeal: It is spectacularly carpeted with orchids in early summer. ■

Kinloch Castle 259 B4 ✉ Rum ☎ (01687) 462 026 ⏱ Closed Nov.–March Ⓢ £ • **Canna** 259 B4 **theisleofcanna.com**

White horses on a beach on the Isle of Muck

SKYE

Ever since the days when Flora MacDonald spirited Bonnie Prince Charlie away from his English pursuers "over the sea to Skye," the "isle of mist" has held a special place in the Scottish imagination. Approaching the island from Kyle of Lochalsh to the east, it is hard not to be impressed by the view that unfolds.

■ The ruin of Castle Moil provides a romantic backdrop for Kyleakin harbor, on the Isle of Skye.

Skye is renowned as a paradise for walkers and climbers. There are 12 Munros to choose from (11 of which are on the rugged Cuillin ridge), ranging in difficulty. For avid climbers, the highlight is the island's highest peak, **Sgurr Alasdair** (3,257 feet/993 m). To tackle the aptly named "inaccessible pinnacle," you will need the right gear including ropes. You don't have to be Sir Edmund Hillary, though, to enjoy yourself on Skye, which offers dozens of great treks dotted all over the island, including forest trails and pretty bay walks. The largest of the Hebridean islands, with an area of 639 square

Skye 259 B4–B5 **Visitor Information** Bayfield House, Bayfield Rd., Portree (01487) 612 992 **visitscotland.com & isleofskye.com**

GETTING TO SKYE: Now that the Skye Bridge is open, there is no need to hop aboard a ferry. But for those wanting to take a boat, the main route is via Caledonian Macbrayne *(calmac.co.uk/destinations/skye)* between Mallaig and Armadale.

INSIDER TIP:

On the isle of Skye, take
time to drive the scenic
route along the east coast
from Portree to Uig. Pre-
pare to stop often for one
stunning photo opportunity
after another.

—NICOLE ENGDAHL
*National Geographic
Development Office*

miles (1,656 sq km), Skye also
boasts a wealth of historic monuments and more modern tourist
attractions. In the days when the
ferry sailed from Kyle of Lochalsh
to **Kyleakin,** the latter was a bustling little tourist village. Today
most visitors just skip by after they
cross over the bridge (see sidebar
right).

Portree & the Trotternish
Peninsula

As the A87 travels north toward
the island's capital, Portree, it passes
through **Broadford.** This is a good
place to stock up on local crafts;
it is also well endowed with tourist amenities like accommodations,
grocery stores, adventure tour
operators, and gas stations.

Portree is a reasonably charming
town, whose harbor—framed by colorful cottages and rugged cliffs—is one of
the most attractive in Scotland. Here
you will find a pier by Thomas Telford

Portree 259 B4

and some good places to eat, drink,
and stay. The rest of the town bustles
with bars, cafés, souvenir stores, outdoor specialists, and, a real highlight,
Skye Batiks *(The Green, Portree, tel
01478/613 331, skyebatiks.com),* where
colorful Celtic batiks are used to make
everything from T-shirts to tablecloths.

A visit to the Trotternish Peninsula,
extending north from Portree, is nigh
essential. In addition to having some
of Skye's most distinctive scenery, it is
also bathed in romantic and ancient
history. An adventure playground of
tumbled boulders, bizarre rock formations, and dramatic cliffs, the **Quiraing** (see pp. 281–283) and the **Old
Man of Storr** should be on every

(continued on p. 284)

Skye Bridge

The Skye Bridge (actually two
bridges that connect on the tiny island of Eilean Ban) opened
in 1995, bringing with it
24-hour access to the mainland for islanders and quicker
journey times. Rather than celebrating the freedom that it
gave them, many islanders felt
that it stopped Skye from being an island at all. For most
the objections were financial.
The bridge toll was based on
the old Kyle of Lochalsh to
Kyleakin ferry fares, meaning
this 1-mile (1.6 km) structure
was initially the most expensive toll bridge in Europe. Happily, it has been toll-free since
December 2004.

A WALK ON THE TROTTERNISH PENINSULA: THE QUIRAING

With most of the high-level walks on Skye demanding technical skills, it can be hard for many walkers to know where to start. Fortunately, the Quiraing (a collection of fantastic rock formations, not a single peak) comes to the rescue in the form of a largely moderate 4-mile (7 km) hill walk that offers breathtaking views, including out to the Western Isles and myriad offshore islets. Note that it does involve some scrambling, and a head for heights is essential, as well as the usual walking gear.

The Needle in the jumble of rock formations in Quiraing, Skye

Organizing a Trip

This circular walk—which may be done in either direction—starts and finishes at the parking lot on the Quiraing road, about 2 miles (3 km) northwest of Staffin. It is a moderate walk that climbs around 1,115 feet (340 m) and can be accomplished in three to four hours, depending on how

NOT TO BE MISSED:

The Table • The Needle • The Prison

much time you spend absorbing this weird and wonderful scenery of crags, rocky pinnacles, and bizarre rock formations. The paths are generally good, but some of the ascent is quite steep. Take full Scottish walking precautions and don't start out if the weather looks poor.

Making the Ascent

From the **parking lot ❶** on the Quiraing road, set out on the footpath signposted to Flodigarry. After a few hundred yards, hike up the grassy hillside (take a zig-zag line to make this easier) until you reach the high-level path that will lead you northeast across the slope.

Eventually you will reach a **gated fence ❷**. Go through the gate and follow the path that branches off to the right. This path quickly opens up stunning views as you gaze down over the area from the cliff edge above. From here you can see Staffin Bay to the east, the Atlantic Ocean, and the Torridon Mountains back in Wester Ross on the mainland.

- See also area map p. 259
- ➤ Parking lot on Quiraing road
- 🕓 3–4 hours
- ↔ 4 miles (7 km)
- ➤ Parking lot on Quiraing road

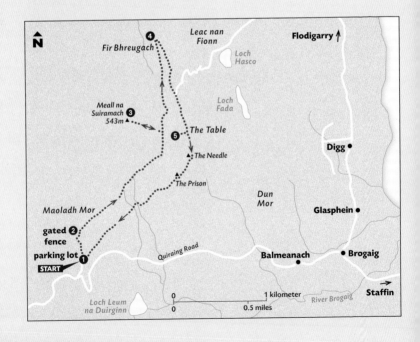

The cliffs don't get much higher, so you have done the hard work; although one possible detour, to the west of the path, takes you to the summit of **Meall na Suiramach** ❸ (1,781 feet/543 m). Back on the main path, sticking close to the cliff's edge, walk around a few gullies and then follow the path as it descends into **Fir Bhreugach** ❹, the col (lowest part of the ridge) connecting the peaks of Sron Vourlinn and Meall na Suiramach.

To continue your descent, follow the path as it zigzags down from the eastern side of the col. As you go, take time to enjoy the stunning views north over **Kilmaluag Bay.** Once you have finished the descent, turn right onto the path below the cliffs. This pathway will lead you back to your starting point. From the path you will see a collection of small pinnacles, as well as two of the Quiraing's most iconic rock stacks.

The thin jagged finger of **The Needle** is one of the Quiraing's most easily distinguished landmarks. Nearby, **The Prison** boasts a dramatic triple summit, which the more imaginative can make resemble a castle from the correct angle. To see The Needle from the best vantage point, scramble up to **The Table** ❺. This steep climb over loose scree is best avoided by those lacking experience. Return to the clear path and follow it back to the parking lot. The path is relatively easy to follow, but you will need to use your hands to cross a small gully.

▶ The Quiarang, Isle of Skye

reasonably fit visitor's hit list. The latter, a needle-like pinnacle amid a dramatic landscape of unusual rock formations, is perhaps Skye's most iconic symbol. Allow at least one hour to ascend the mountainside trail for a breathtaking panorama from above the pinnacle. Farther along the east coast, **Lealt Falls** carves a canyon to the shore, while **Mealt Falls** forms a dramatic cascade tumbling 180 feet (55 m) into the sea from atop **Kilt Rock** cliffs. Beside the A855 immediately inland of Kilt Rock, is the **Staffin Dinosaur Museum** *(tel 01470/562 321, staffin dinosaurmuseum.com, £)*, which houses an impressive collection of fossils found in the area, most notably dinosaur fossils. Call ahead to book a guided walk by the curator of the collection, Dugald Ross, who started the museum when

a teenager. Staffin itself is home to the largest and best-preserved dinosaur tracks—said to be 165 million years old—ever found in Scotland.

On Trotternish's west coast awaits the engaging **Skye Museum of Island Life** *(Kilmuir, tel 01470/552 206, skyemuseum.co.uk, closed Sun., £)*. This collection of impressively preserved traditional blackhouses provides a fascinating insight into island life just over a century ago. The views that it commands of the Isle of Harris are also magnificent. If you have more than a passing interest in the life of Flora MacDonald and her role in helping Bonnie Prince Charlie flee after his devastating defeat at Culloden, head up to the cemetery behind the museum, where you will find the heroine's grave.

Dunvegan Castle 259 B4 W of Portree in Dunvegan (01470) 521 206 Closed mid-Oct.–March £££

EXPERIENCE: Loch Coruisk Cruise

Situated in the jagged Cuillin mountain range, Loch Coruisk is a strong contender for the title of Scotland's most isolated and breathtaking loch. This lake is about 2 miles (3 km) long and a few hundred yards wide. With two operators—**Bella Jane** *(tel 01471/866 244, bellajane.co.uk, ££££)* and **Misty Isle** *(tel 01471/866 288, mistyisleboat trips.co.uk, ££££)*—running boat trips to the loch from Elgol from Easter through September, you can plan the experience you

want once you reach the loch. Choose a nonlanding trip or take advantage of early-bird sailings to give you more time ashore and longer to walk in the Cuillins. Most visitors opt for about 90 minutes ashore.

The loch's shore is relatively easy terrain for walking (though you should wear walking boots). If you are a seasoned walker or climber with the right gear you can also plan a one-way trip and make your own way through the mountains to Sligachan or back to Elgol.

■ The Fairy Pool on the Isle of Skye

Durnish, Vaternish, & Minginish Peninsulas

West of Portree **Dunvegan Castle** beckons. The Clan MacLeod have held sway over this historic castle since the 13th century, although much of the fortress that you see today dates from the mid-19th century. Those expecting opulent grandeur might be disappointed; however, the castle is worth visiting for its dramatic lochside setting, attractive gardens, and chance to see the treasures of the clan, including a Fairy Flag said to hold magical properties. Seal-watching cruises also leave from outside the castle. From Dunvegan, incursions onto the **Duirnish Peninsula** to the west or **Waternish** to the north bring their own rewards, not least swaths of dramatic scenery. Here you can find a warm welcome at the **Stein Inn**, with tasty meals and comfy beds, as well as live music some nights. A five-minute walk uphill leads to **SkyeSkyns,** where you can witness sheepskins being made in time-honored fashion downstairs in the tannery, by all manner of sheepskin products in the upstairs showroom, and savor hot teas or cappuccinos and scrumptious desserts in the yurt cafe. The island's western extremity, **Neist Point,** has its eponymous lighthouse, dramatic sea cliffs, and Western Isles views.

SkyeSkyns ✉ Waternish ☎ (01470) 592237 **skyeskyns.co.uk**

Near Dunvegan, the **Colbost Croft Museum** (*closed at press time for repair*) gives insight into crofting on Skye, including a restored illicit whisky still. Learn more about illegal whisky making and the production of the island's own (legal) single malt with a tour of the **Talisker Distillery** on the rugged Minginish Peninsula. The peninsula itself is a good base for lower-level walks when the mist settles in on the mighty Cuillin to the east. Tackling this seemingly impenetrable mountain range may be a no-no for non-climbers and less experienced walkers, but it is possible to immerse yourself in the dramatic scenery without making any much effort. A well-maintained trail leads to **Fairy Pools,** a series of exquisite cascades and jade-colored pools at the base of the Cuillin mountains. Or take a boat trip from Elgol out to **Loch Coruisk** (see sidebar p. 284), a thin glacial loch flanked by the Cuillin peaks.

Sleat Peninsula

Once-sleepy Sleat, the most southern of Skye's many peninsulas, has been discovered, as evidenced by a few new luxury hotels and the **Torabhaig Distillery** (*Teangue, tel 01471/833 447, torabhaig.com, ££–££££*), which has tours by reservation. The CalMac ferry from Mallaig docks at **Armadale.** To the west you'll find sandy beaches, whitewashed cottages, and great views of Skye's mountains. From Isleornsay to the north, it is possible to walk out to the **Ornsay Lighthouse** (engineered by David and Thomas Stevenson) at low tide, but do make sure you check the tide times first.

Sleat also has a must-see attraction in the form of **Clan Donald Skye**—a multilayer and family-friendly attraction that includes **Armadale Castle,** its extensive gardens, woodland walks, and the **Museum of the Isles.** The latter, complete with clashing sword sound effects and battle songs drifting through the display rooms, explores the history of the medieval period when the MacDonald family (Clan Donald) were the Lords of the Isles.

Sleat remains the seat of the Clan Donald family today. Those who want to meet the current laird and lady should visit **Kinloch Lodge** (*Sleat, tel 01471/833 333, kinloch lodge.co.uk*); they have turned their sumptuous old hunting lodge into a welcoming hotel, complete with excellent dining in its Michelin-starred restaurant, cooking classes, spa treatments, and tours. ∎

Colbost Croft Museum ✉ Colbost ☎ (01470) 521 296 $ £ **dunveganmuseums.co.uk** • **Talisker Distillery** ✉ Carbost ☎ (01478) 614 308 $ £–£££ **malts.com** • **Armadale** ▲ 259 B4 • **Clan Donald Skye** ✉ Armadale, Sleat ☎ (01471) 844 305 ⏱ Closed Nov.–March $ ££ **armadalecastle.com**

OUTER HEBRIDES

Located in the far north, across The Minch from the Isle of Skye, Lewis and Harris are often thought of as two islands, but they are in fact one landmass that forms the core of the Outer Hebrides, one of the most remote outposts of Europe. These islands, sometimes referred to as the Western Isles, have played home to Highland clansmen, Jacobite rebels, and even Vikings. The Gaelic language is also alive and well throughout the Outer Hebrides.

■ Blackstone Village, Isle of Lewis

Lewis

The obvious place to start an exploration of the Isle of Lewis is in its main town, and the island's transportation hub, **Stornoway.** With a population of more than 6,000 people, Stornoway is the closest that the Western Isles get

to a city, so while you are there take the chance to stock up on groceries and gas, and even enjoy a meal out. You may wish to linger to take in one of the offerings at the **An Lanntair Art Centre** *(Kenneth St., tel 01851/708 480, lanntair .com),* a contemporary arts venue

Outer Hebrides visitouterhebrides.co.uk • Stornoway 259 B6 **Visitor Information** ✉ 26 Cromwell St., Stornoway ☎ (01851) 703 088 **visitscotland.com**

Stone Circles in Lewis

They may be the most visually impressive and therefore the most visited, but the Calanais stone circles (see below) are by no means the only standing stones in Lewis. Many are not that inspiring; eroded over the centuries they can be small with just one or two stones left.

There are, of course, exceptions. The largest standing stone in Scotland, Clach an Trushal, lies about 12 miles (20 km) north of Stornoway, rising a mighty 20 feet (6 m) tall. The Steinacleit Cairn and Stone Circle, a little farther south, is another site worth seeking out.

whose eclectic role varies from showcasing temporary exhibitions to hosting Celtic music concerts and regular cinema screenings.

Watching over the town from across the bay is the imposing and newly refurbished Victorian **Lews Castle** (tel 01625/416 430, lews-castle .co.uk), now offering posh accommodations in upstairs suites. Ground-floor public rooms are open for all,

---

INSIDER TIP:

Do not miss the ancient Calanais Standing Stones on Lewis. Visit the site early morning or late afternoon for the best light for photographs as well as far fewer crowds.

—JENNIFER SEGAL
National Geographic
Development Office

---

but don't miss the island's **Museum Nan Eilean** (tel 01851/822 746, closed Sun.–Mon.), housed in a new, modern wing. Exhibits here are informed by the museum's mission to share the culture and history of the Outer Hebrides. Of particular note are six of the world-famous Lewis Chessmen, carved from walrus ivory and whales' teeth in the 12th century and found on a beach at Uig in 1831. A café is also on hand.

Heading west out of Stornoway, the road crosses wild moorland littered with tiny salmon-laden lochans in search of **Callanish** (Calanais in Gaelic), whose awe-inspiring, 5,000-year-old stone circles make up the most visited tourist site in the archipelago, the **Calanais Standing Stones.** A visitor center explains the speculation surrounding this atmospheric site, and a welcoming café offers refreshment. The visitor center also has information on the lesser known stone circles on Lewis,

---

Calanais Standing Stones ✉ Callanish, Lewis ☎ (01851) 621 422 💲 £
calanais.org

■ Calanais Standing Stones, Isle of Lewis

such as those at **Na Dromannan,** a quarry just a mile (1.6 km) east of the Calanais stones. This collapsed circle is believed to be older than the world-famous Stonehenge, and the quarry is also thought to have provided some of the standing stones in the Calanais circle.

Slightly to the north, **Carloway** is home to another of Lewis's most important heritage sites, the **Dun Carloway Broch.** With its circular dry-stone walls, this is one of the best preserved of the hundreds of fortified towers that pepper Scotland's Atlantic coastline. The small **Doune Broch Centre** (tel 01851/643 338) sheds light on the mysterious origins of the brochs and tries to recall the days when people sought shelter in them.

Cross north from Callanish onto **Bernera,** the small island that has been linked to Lewis by a bridge since 1953, and you'll have a chance to learn more about the region's Pictish settlers at the reproduction **Bostadh Iron Age House** (tel 01851/612 314, visitouterhebrides.co.uk, £) on the site of a shoreline settlement thought to have been occupied from the sixth to ninth centuries. Signs of more recent periods also compel on Lewis. At the **Arnol Blackhouse Museum,** also located on the west coast, you can explore an old croft house, seeing how the local people lived with a smoky peat fire at the heart of their homes. Down the road (even closer to Callanish) in Carloway, a whole hamlet of thatched crofters houses,

• **Arnol Blackhouse Museum** ✉ Arnol, Lewis ☎ (01851) 710 395 ⏱ Closed Sun. April–Sep., Sun. & Wed. Oct–March 💲 £ **historicenvironment.scot**

■ **Individual crofters weave tweed on the isle of Harris.**

the **Gearrannan Blackhouse Village** *(tel 01851/643 416, gearrannan .com)*, has been preserved, including a demonstration of Harris Tweed weaving. You can amble between the nine homesteads as they tumble down the hillside to the Atlantic, and even stay overnight.

Lewis's landscape is one of vast bleak peat bogs, punctuated by austere settlements that are in keeping with the largely strict Presbyterian

way of life on the island. In stark contrast the island's coastline also boasts sandy beaches—most notably **Uig Sands**—and the sheer cliffs and stacks of the **Butt of Lewis**, pinned by a lighthouse at the northern tip of the isle, and the even more sublime stacks of **Mangersta.**

All this dramatic scenery lends itself effortlessly to outdoor activities. Surf lessons are available from **Hebridean Surf** *(The Welcome In Filling Station, Lower Barvas, tel 01851/840 343, heb rideansurf.co.uk)* and **Surf Lewis** *(Stornoway, tel 07920/427 194, surflewis .com)*. Cyclists are also catered to, through **Heb Holidays** *(6 Sand St., Stornoway, tel 07775/943 355, heb holidays.com)*, which rents kayaks as well as bicycles, and offers guided day trips and cycling tours.

A raft of sailing adventures from Lewis are provided by **Sea Trek Hebrides** *(Miavaig, tel 01851/672 469, seatrek.co.uk)*, with boat trips ranging from 12-hour excursions to St. Kilda to fishing trips to wildlife cruises through to fast-paced rides onboard a rigid inflatable boat (RIB).

Harris

South of Lewis, the landscape and name changes as you cross onto the Isle of Harris, one of the most naturally stunning places in the British Isles. Harris has it all: vaulting mountains that are among the highest in the islands, sweeping, white-sand beaches,

Harris ⚠ 259 A5–B5

Harris Tweed

Most people think of Harris Tweed in terms of an iconic brand, conveying durability and respectability through the colors of the Scottish landscape. But the fabric has much humbler beginnings. Originally called Clò-Mòr, the cloth was made at home by the islanders well before the industrial revolution brought manufactured cloth to the Outer Hebrides.

Members of the Scottish gentry began noticing the fine tweed by the mid-1800s, leading to efforts to promote it as a cottage industry. By the 1900s, the quality of this woven material, now known as Harris Tweed, brought a wider market. Cheap imitations soon followed, along with the necessity of a registered trademark to identify true Harris Tweed. The Orb Mark is still prominently used on labels today, certifying material handwoven by the islanders at their home in the Outer Hebrides and made from pure virgin wool dyed and spun in the Outer Hebrides. You can connect with these local artisans yourself by visiting the Harris Tweed Authority's fine website (harristweed.org/buy-harris-tweed), which has a list of the many independent weavers and mills.

and a smorgasbord of wildlife that encompasses everything from seals to bountiful birdlife. What really crowns the island's appeal, though, is that it is virtually untouched by tourism, even in the middle of summer.

Like Harris and Lewis themselves, Harris is divided into two distinct geographic halves. North of its main settlement, **Tarbert,** the island is impressively mountainous with rugged peaks and lofty ridges everywhere you look—a hill walkers' paradise. Much of the land is now owned by the community as part of the North Harris Trust, which redressed some of the legacies of the Highland Clearances and gave the community more control over its future.

Visitors can find the famous Harris Tweed being made throughout the Outer Hebrides (see sidebar above). A quantity of the beautiful cloth can be perused at the **Harris Tweed Shop** (Caberfeidh Rd., Tarbet, tel 01859/502 040, harristweedisleof harris.co.uk, closed Sun.).

Poised overlooking the ferry terminal, the **Isle of Harris Distillery**

Coexisting Religions

While islanders living in the Western Isles peacefully coexist, there is a distinct religious divide with those in the north (North Uist, Harris, and Lewis) following the Protestant church and those in South Uist and Barra largely adhering to the Catholic faith. In addition to the Church of Scotland there are other Protestant denominations in the Outer Hebrides. In their desire to maintain the purity of worship they ensure in these parts that Sunday really is the Lord's Day. Shops, pubs, businesses, and gas stations close. Even children's playgrounds are out of bounds. The Outer Hebrides have the highest level of church attendance in Scotland, and catching a fiery Gaelic sermon is a powerful experience.

opened in 2023 and produces "The Hearach" malt whisky and copper-still gin using kelp from local sea lochs.

Scooping over to South Harris, the scenery is completely different. Its eastern coast is home to a moonscape of weirdly shaped rocks and a scattering of craggy bays. Astonishingly this seemingly inhospitable land is where most of the residents in the south of the island live, after being relocated there during the Highland Clearances (see p. 252). These disjointed settlements are today linked by a winding route known colloquially as the Golden Road, a reference to how much it cost to build—the joke being that it may as well have been made of gold. While it serves some very remote communities, it also provides visitors with access to this surreal and mesmerizing coastal landscape.

On the west coast the scene is very different. Here there are sweeping beaches, some of the cleanest and most impressive in Europe. The crème de la crème is **Luskentyre Beach,** with a swath of white sand fringed by brooding and translucent water, framed by rolling hills and the distant shadowy mountains of North Harris.

Beyond Luskentyre, the equally gorgeous sands of Sgarasta Mhor merge into **Northton Salt Marshes**—Britain's largest sedge tidal marsh. Continue to the southern tip of Harris and **St. Clements** *(historic environment.scot),* a remarkably well-preserved medieval church that escaped defacement during the 16th-century Reformation.

Harris is otherwise relatively short on sights and wet-weather entertainment, but the main reason to come here is to get out and about in the great outdoors. Unfortunately, the

Isle of Harris Distillery ✉ Tarbert ☎ (01859) 502 212 🕐 Closed Sun.
💲 Tours ££££ **harrisdistillery.com**

COVID-19 pandemic forced many local tour operators to close, but newcomer **Wild Harris** *(3b Meavaig N., tel 07828/528 247, wildharris.co.uk)* showcases the wilds with bespoke

---

guided sea-kayaking, snorkeling, and wildlife and wilderness walks—from easy to challenging—led by experienced outdoor activity guides Daryll Brown and Kate Lewis. They also offer mountain bike guiding, but you'll need to bring your own bike. Or enjoy a personalized hill walk with Mike Briggs *(Bunabhainneadar, tel 01859/502 376)*, who can also formulate a tour for non-hikers. For days when you don't feel particularly active, the **Hebrides People Visitor Centre** in **Northton** offers the chance to delve into the rich history of the island.

In summer **Sea Harris** *(tel 01859/502 007, seaharris.co.uk)* and **Kilda Cruises** *(tel 01859/ 502 060,*

kildacruises.co.uk) offer tourists the chance to visit remote St. Kilda on a full-day boat trip from Leverburgh in South Harris. They also organize shorter trips to some of the other smaller Hebridean islands, as well as catch-and-release tuna fishing. **Isle of Harris Sea Tours** *(tel 01859/502 060, isleofharrisseatours.co.uk)*, in Tarbert, will also take you fishing or on explorations around the coast of Harris.

Sitting just west of Harris you find the island of **Taransay,** which briefly rose to fame in 2000 as the location of the BBC's *Castaway* fly-on-the-wall reality TV show. You can book a

Machair

Machair (a Gaelic word) is a term used to describe a long and low-lying fertile plain. Around half of Scotland's machair is located in the Outer Hebrides. This rare and delicate habitat is difficult to define, but generally speaking it stretches from the sand dunes through to the peaty soil farther inland, has a high shell content, and is characterized by the presence of marram grass. For those visiting South Uist, Barra, and South Harris in July and August this translates as a vivid and colorful carpet of rare wildflowers, including orchids. Myriad birdlife also thrives in the machair, including the ringed plover, the lapwing, and the rare corncrake.

• **Seallam! Visitor Centre** ✉
Northton, Harris ☎ (01859) 520 258 🕐 Closed Sat.–Sun. 💲 £
hebridespeople.com/visitor-centre

private charter boat from Leverburgh for a day trip to the island *(seaharris .com)*, which will also get you closer to Harris's sea mammals and sea-birds. When the wet weather sets in you can do worse than pop into the **Skoon Art Cafe** in **Geocrab** *(4 Geocrab, tel 01859/530 268, skoon .com)*, which dishes up lovely home-made fare and displays paintings by a resident artist, Andrew John Craig. On a clear day the café offers lovely views over The Minch.

North Uist

CalMac ferries *(calmac.co.uk)* travel south around the treacherous rocks from Leverburgh in Harris to the island of **Berneray**, itself con-nected to North Uist via a cause-way. This small island, measuring roughly 2 miles (3 km) by 3 miles (5 km), is worth exploring, as it is blessed with gorgeous dune-backed beaches and stunning views all around. To really get a feel for Berneray follow the marked walk that circles the northern part of the island—the posts are blue and the terrain is relatively easy.

The other main entry point in North Uist is **Lochmaddy** on the east coast, welcoming cars and their pas-sengers from Uig on the Isle of Skye. Lochmaddy has the best amenities on the island including the Uists' only tourist office, a bank, a general store, and a couple of eateries, so it is a good place to get your bearings. The highlight is **Taigh Chearsabhagh,** an arts center and museum at the heart of the island's cultural scene. A variety of events happen here year-round, and there is also a café and gift shop.

West of Lochmaddy, the North Uist landscape comes as something of a surprise. Gone are the mountains of Harris and in their place is a haunting landscape of bog and loch where deer and wild salmon outnumber humans. Some small settlements cling to the coastal roads, but the real tragedies are the people who are not here, their sor-rows played out in derelict crofts and deserted villages., victims of the High-land Clearances (see p. 252). Walking, cycling, or driving around the island is the best way to appreciate its beauty. Keep an eye out for the **Barpa Langais** burial cairn, the three **Na Fir Bhreige** standing stones, and the **Pobull Fhinn** stone circle. These Neolithic sights are remarkable more for the history they tell than their appearance today. In the island's northwestern corner the castle-like folly that is **Scolpaig Tower** enjoys a scenic spot on an islet in the epony-mous loch. The RSPB nature reserve at **Balranald,** a short hop south of the tower, is a good place to stretch your legs with lovely coastal views and the chance to see (or at least hear their *kerrx-kerrx* call) one of Britain's most rare birds, the corncrake.

North Uist 259 A5 **explore-western-isles.com** • **Taigh Chearsabhagh** ✉ Lochmaddy, North Uist ☎ (01870) 603 970 🕐 Closed Sun. 💲 £ **taigh-chearsabhagh.org** • **Balranald** ✉ 3 miles (5 km) W of Bayhead; turn for Hougharry off the A865 ☎ (01876) 569 287 **rspb.org.uk**

■ Two common dolphins skirt through the waters at Barra Head.

South Uist

Unlike Harris and Lewis, the Uists are actually two distinct islands, linked by causeways via the small island of **Benbecula,** home to an airport, hospital, library, and other amenities, as well as the ruins of **Borve Castle** and **Teampull Mhuire.** South Uist differs from North Uist not just in its appearance, but also in outlook. The prominence of Catholicism can be keenly felt, with Madonnas popping up by the roadside.

The South Uist landscape is characterized by hills and mountains in the east and golden-sand beaches on its exposed western shore. Tackling the highest peak, **Ben More** (2,034 feet/620 m) is a popular pastime with hill walkers. From its summit views over the Hebridean islands unfold to reward those who have made the steep ascent. This vantage point also allows you to fully appreciate how many lochs and lochans dot the Uists. **Hecla** (1,988 feet/606 m) yields similar views.

Back at sea level, the island's Atlantic coastline is backed up by machair, sand dunes that in spring explode with a stunning collage of wildflower blossoms. The landscape in between is also dotted with old crofting villages and a wealth of lochans. Keen ornithologists or those who enjoy low-level walks can also visit **Loch Druidibeg Nature Reserve** *(Stilligarry, tel 07747/455 978, rspb.org.uk).* A marked trail leads

into the reserve from Stilligarry,
where this Site of Special Scientific
Interest (SSSI) incorporates machair
strewn with colorful flowers, moorland, and lochans. The fauna is at
its best in July, while the late spring
and early summer months also provide the chance to see wading birds,
wildfowl, and corncrakes.

South Uist's indoor attractions
are limited, with the **Kildonan
Museum,** situated on the main
A865, the highlight. Here assorted
artifacts shed light on island life
over the centuries; the collection's
prized possession is the Clanranald
Armorial Stone, dating from the
16th century and adorning the coat
of arms of the clan that held sway
over the island for more than 450
years.

Those moved by the tales of
Bonnie Prince Charlie and Flora
MacDonald might be interested to
know that Flora lived in South Uist
as a child, with a cairn marking the
spot a short distance south of the
Kildonan Museum. The tragic Stuart
history is continued on the beautiful and untouristy island of Eriskay,
linked to South Uist by a causeway.
Charles Edward Stuart reputedly
arrived here in preparation for the
1745 Jacobite rebellion.

Despite sweeping white-sand
beaches and the eponymous Eriskay ponies grazing the hills, most
people just pass through on their
way to the Barra ferry.

• **Kildonan Museum** ✉ Kildonan, South Uist ☎ (01878) 710 343
🕐 Closed Nov.–March 💲 £ **kildonanmuseum.co.uk**

Flying to Barra

Traveling by boat is the usual form
of travel to Barra, but a thrilling
alternative is to fly in. As your
flight swoops in over the sea, Barra "airport" appears amid a rum-
ble of hills overlooking the sands
of Cockle Bay. There is a tiny terminal building, but no runway. The
plane tugs around for its final approach, drops down onto the
beach, and then bounces along to
the terminal. The Barra service
must be one of the few in the
world whose timetable includes
the caveat "subject to tides," and
the dramatic beach landing makes
an indelible imprint. Flights to Barra airport depart twice daily from
Glasgow and can be booked
through Loganair *(loganair.co.uk).*

■ Small plane on the sandy runway of Barra Airport

Barra

Located at the southern end of the Outer Hebrides, the Isle of Barra is instantly appealing. It may be only 8 miles (13 km) long and 5 miles (8 km) wide, but what it lacks in size it makes up for in diversity. Here you'll find the vaulting hulks of Ben Tangaval and Heaval giving way to rambling glens, bright machair flowers, moors, rolling hills, and pristine, white-sand beaches.

The capital of **Castlebay** is a good place to start exploring. First up should be the **Barra Heritage Centre,** which delves into the local Gaelic culture and stories of the island's people. The town's most unmissable sight, literally, is **Kisimul Castle**—which, as it has its own freshwater spring, is able to stand alone in the water, casting a dramatic presence over the wide bay. The striking fortification is also testimony to the Clan MacNeil family who ruled Barra for much of the island's history. The 45th clan chief, Robert MacNeil, who was an American architect, bought the castle back in 1937 and made it his life's work to rebuild one of Europe's oldest castles. The reconstructed fortress houses a museum whose intriguing artifacts include British army weapons that date back to the 1746 Battle of Culloden. In 2023 it was closed for repairs (check the website for updates).

Barra  259 A4 **visitouterhebrides.co.uk/our-islands/barra • Barra Heritage Centre** ✉ Castlebay, Barra ☎ (01871) 810 413 Closed Sat.–Sun. 💲 £ **barraheritagecentre.com • Kisimul Castle** ✉ Barra ☎ (01871) 810 313 🕐 Closed Oct.–March 💲 £ **historicenvironment.scot**

One of the best perspectives of the fortification is from the water aboard a kayak; the local company **Clearwater Paddling** (*Castlebay, Barra, tel 07960/217 168, clearwater paddling.com*) rents kayaks or organizes fantastic trips across the bay that culminate by Kisimul. Castlebay is also at the island's cultural heart, regularly hosting folk bands and the island's annual **Fèis Bharraigh** (*feisean.org/en*) children's music, drama, and Gaelic language festival in July.

Outside Castlebay, much of the island is easily accessible on foot, though cycling is also a good way of getting around. **Barra Bike Hire** (*tel 07876/402 842, barrabikehire .co.uk*), on the north end of Castlebay, will get your whole family going, with bikes of all sizes and drop-off service available. Barra abounds with spectacular scenery, with highlights including the sandy stretch of Halaman Bay, with its soaring Atlantic surf, and the scattering of beaches that lead north from Halaman.

The island's most unusual attraction is **Barra Golf Club** (*Cleat, Barra, tel 01871/810 419, isleofbarra .com/barragolfclub.htm, ££*). This unique course would stump the likes of Sandy Lyle and Tiger Woods. It may have only nine holes, but it contains tricky hazards such as the "largest bunker in the world" (a giant Atlantic beach) and fences built around the greens to keep out the cows. (They have the same effect on golf balls!) Fairways are little more than rock-strewn hillsides, and many players consider themselves lucky to lose only one ball a hole. Still, it has to be one of the most scenic courses in the world.

Elsewhere around the island, layers of history reveal themselves through sights like the **standing stones of Brevig Bay** and the **Dun Cuier** complex. Then there is the **Dun Bharpa** cairn, where the dead were laid to rest in Neolithic times. **Barra Island Tours** (*tel 01871 810 255, barraislandtours.co.uk*) offers guided excursions.

Evacuation of St. Kilda

The way of life on St. Kilda was rudimentary and some even think Utopian, as there was no money and no government, with the Gaelic-speaking people all just pitching in to help each other and do what work needed to be done. This self-sufficiency became hard to maintain, with the emigration of 36 residents to Australia in 1852, accompanied by a greater reliance on imported food and goods. Acute food shortages in 1912, an influenza outbreak in 1913, the influence of tourism, and the ramifications of World War I sounded the final death knell for island life, with the remaining 36 islanders evacuated in 1930.

■ **A village house on Hirta, St. Kilda, west of the Outer Hebrides**

Between Barra and the Isle of Eriskay to the north is a stretch of water famous around the world. In 1941 the S.S. *Politician* ran aground here and her cargo of 24,000 bottles of whisky was "lost." The enterprising locals intervened to lend a hand, and by the time customs officials arrived, much of the whisky that had gone down with the ship had mysteriously disappeared. Compton Mackenzie's book *Whisky Galore* vividly recalled the tale and it was made into a movie in 1949 (released as *Tight Little Island* in North America). In 2017, husband and wife, Michael and Katie Morrison, launched **Barra Distillers** *(isleofbarradistillers.com)*, producing award-winning gin distilled from local seaweed in their home and plans to expand to whisky production in a purpose-built distillery and visitor center.

St. Kilda

The remote and mystical islands of St. Kilda lie in the Atlantic 40 miles (66 km) west of the Outer Hebrides. For many Scots St. Kilda has something of the holy grail about it, with many dreaming of one day visiting this World Heritage–listed outpost. Few, though, manage to conquer the Atlantic and land on the islands. Those who do make the sometimes stomach-churning journey discover an oasis swirling in myths, legends, and the echoes of a long-lost way of life.

Getting to St. Kilda is all part of the challenge. Not for those who suffer from sea sickness, it is a stomach-testing 16- to 18-hour cruise from Oban, or a 4- to 6-hour trip from the Outer Hebrides. The difficult journey, though, is quickly forgotten

St. Kilda △ 259 A5 ☎ (01463) 732 635 **visitouterhebrides.co.uk/ourislands** & **nts.org.uk/visit/places/st-kilda**

as the unique landscapes of this archipelago rear into view, a sight unlike anything else in the British Isles. St. Kilda was never tamed by the smoothing actions of glaciers, and the jagged sheer rock faces and towering *stacs* (Gaelic for "sea stack") that shudder out of the Atlantic to puncture the horizon have more in common with Iceland or the Faroe Islands than Scotland. There are several islands and stacs in the chain, with the main islands Hirta, Boreray, Soay, and Dun.

In a land where man definitely plays second fiddle to nature, wild-life abounds. With around a million birds nesting in St. Kilda, the islands are an ornithologist's dream. Highlights include the tens of thousands of impossibly cute puffins that occupy the cliffs and, on Boreray, the world's second-largest gannet population, with around 60,000 nesting pairs (Bass Rock, off the east coast of Scotland, is now the first). On land the scraggy soay sheep are a form of primitive sheep that are unique to the islands. The National Trust for Scotland administers St. Kilda as a National Nature Reserve, in partnership with the Ministry of Defence.

A Unique Way of Life: For hundreds of years man eked out an existence on St. Kilda. In spring and summer, the "bird men" clung with prehensile toes as they clambered barefoot down the steep cliff faces on ropes to hunt birds and collect eggs for food.

The main island of the St. Kilda group is **Hirta,** and this was the only one to have been permanently inhabited. Standing forlornly back from the shore is the island's old residential street, whose old stone and traditional blackhouses stretch along the hillside. A visit to the small **museum** at number 3 on "the street" provides thorough insight into the history of the island and is an essential stop. A fascinating heritage walk weaves through the village, further illuminating how the locals once lived.

Hanging omnipresent above the village is **Conachair,** a 1,411-foot

■ Hebridean Smokehouse, North Uist

(430 m) peak with Britain's highest sea cliff dropping off, which offers stunning views of the islands and back east toward the Outer Hebrides. The steep hike to the top is pretty arduous, even though a road travels part of the way up. The biggest difficulty is avoiding the great skuas, the hulking brown birds that swoop down to buzz walkers in a bid to keep them away from their nests. The rewards, though, far outweigh the effort involved. After all, how many people can say that they have been to the highest point in St. Kilda? On a clear day the views are phenomenal. Atop the plateau you'll find a lonesome radar tracking station, ungainly amid the pristine beauty.

Although Hirta is relatively easy to land on and to get around, landing on the other isles is much more problematic. The majority of visitors, therefore, have to content themselves with the view from the sea. Taking a boat around **Boreray** as 40 percent of the world's gannet population swirls around the hulking rock island and its protective stacs is a stunning experience.

A number of companies organize boat trips out to St. Kilda from the Outer Hebrides, including **Go St Kilda** *(Waternish, Skye, tel 07789/914 144, gotostkilda.co.uk),* **Sea Harris** (see p. 293; *seaharris.com*), Kilda Cruises (see p. 293; *kildacruises.co.uk*), and **Clearwater Paddling** *(Castlebay, Barra, tel 07960/217 168, clearwater paddling.com),* which offers week-long sea-kayaking trips of St. Kilda using the tall ship, *The Lady of Avenel.*

If you prefer, you can spend longer on the islands as a volunteer with the National Trust for Scotland. Details can be found on the St. Kilda World Heritage website *(nts.org.uk/visit/ places/st-kilda/).* ■

■ **A gannet soars above Scottish sea waters.**

Where to Eat & Drink in West Coast Islands

BRAMBLES SEAFOOD AND GRILL

AUCHRANNIE RD., BRODICK, ARRAN

(01770) 302 234 | auchrannie.co.uk/brambles-seafood-grill.html

Simply cooked food that is allowed to speak for itself, contemporary surrounds, and friendly service combine to make this resort restaurant a good bet for guests and nonguests alike. Shetland mussels cooked in Arran ale, hand-dived Hebridean scallops, and famous chunky fish cake (using smoked salmon and haddock) are just some of the highlights on a menu that makes the most of local ingredients. Scotch beef hung for 21 days makes the steaks (which come in rib eye, fillet, or sirloin cuts) a perennial favorite.

£££ P 🌐 AE, MC, V

CAFÉ KISIMUL

MAIN ST. CASTLEBAY, BARRA

(01871) 810 645 | cafekisimul.co.uk

On the harborfront, this venerable café-restaurant is now staff-owned and run, but the menu stays true to its traditional focus on Scottish, Indian and Italian cuisine with fresh seafood at its heart. Daily specials might include hand-dived scallop pakoras, and slow-cooked local venison with garlic mash and spiced carrots, perhaps washed down with a pint of Skye Gold.

££ 🔲 P 🕐 Closed L. Sun. 🌐 MC, V

CASTLEBAY HOTEL

CASTLEBAY, BARRA

(01871) 810 233 | castlebay-hotel.co.uk

An easy walk from the ferry, Castlebay's high-quality food and cooking make it the Isle of Barra's best dining option. A seasonal menu makes the most of the fresh seafood and shellfish that is landed daily in Barra, with local scallops the highlight. Meat-eaters are also well catered for by the likes of island lamb, Scotch beef, venison, hare, and wild boar. These are backed by a number of vegetarian options. Good bar food is also served.

££ P 🌐 MC, V

COLL HOTEL

ARINAGOUR, COLL

(01879) 230 334 | collhotel.com/#eat

An island gathering place, this hotel restaurant offers great food and hospitality overlooking the harbor. On a ridiculously good menu in these remote parts are the likes of a local seafood platter with fresh salmon, lobster, plump scallops, and crab, and Malaysian sweet potato and Coll butternut squash curry. The changing daily menu is a real delight and the sort of treat you could spend every day on Coll dreaming of.

££–££££ P 🌐 MC, V

LOCHBAY RESTAURANT

1 MACLEODS TERRACE, STEIN, SKYE

(01470) 592 235 | lochbay-restaurant.co.uk

A talented chef, attentive service, and a warm, picturesque setting combine for a memorable meal. Evening diners at this small and inviting restaurant choose between a three- or six-course menu, including such options as Salt Herring and Mussel Nibbles, Short Rib and Tongue of Beef, and Loch Bay Bourride (fish, lobster, prawn, and oyster). Lunch is also offered.

£££ 🕐 Closed L & Sun.–Mon.; Sun.–Tues. Nov.–mid-Dec.; mid-Dec.–April

---

P Parking 🕐 Opening Hours 🌐 Credit Cards

PRICES

An indication of the cost of a three-course meal without drinks is given by £ signs.

£££££	Over £50
££££	£40–£50
£££	£25–£40
££	£15–£25
£	Under £15

PORT CHARLOTTE HOTEL

PORT CHARLOTTE, ISLAY

(01496) 850 360 | portcharlottehotel.co.uk

This hotel's elegant restaurant is widely considered to be the best on Islay. A constantly evolving menu offers diners the chance to enjoy fresh local meat and game, as well as seafood caught by the local fishermen. Highlights on a typical menu might include Islay lamb, or Indian spiced monkfish. A refined wine list and a relaxed dining room with exposed brick walls and modern furniture provide the finishing touches. A bar supper menu plus packed lunches are available, and live music with Gaelic singing is a highlight.

£££–£££££ P MC, V

SCARISTA HOUSE RESTAURANT

SGARASTA BHEAG, HARRIS

(01859) 550 238 | scaristahouse.com

It may not offer much choice but the set dinner menu at this lovely B&B, open to outside diners, works wonders with fresh local produce, much of which is organic. A typical meal might include Highland lamb, Sound of Harris langoustines, and local Scottish cheeses that pair well with the extensive wine list. A lot of the vegetables and herbs come from the hotel's kitchen garden, and the breads, cakes, jam, yogurt, and ice cream are all homemade.

££££ P AE, MC, V

THE THREE CHIMNEYS

COLBOST, SKYE

(01470) 511 258 | threechimneys.co.uk

Despite its remote location in a tiny village in the northwest of Skye, this intimate restaurant housed in a converted stone croft has won plaudits from around the globe. Their pride in Scottish cuisine shines through at every corner. Fresh local produce, including Lochalsh beef and world-class seafood, like crab sourced in Colbost itself, expertly cooked by head chef Scott Davis and his team, lies at the heart of its success. This is one case where the quality of the food matches the spectacular scenery. Reservations are essential.

£££–£££££ P Closed mid–Dec.–mid–Jan. AE, MC, V

Seabirds soaring over craggy sea stacks and sandstone cliffs on far-flung islands, and ancient secrets emerging from windswept sand

ORKNEY &
SHETLAND ISLANDS

The prehistoric stone tower of Mousa Broch dominates the island of Mousa in the Shetland archipelago.

ORKNEY & SHETLAND ISLANDS

Plowing through the rough seas from the Scottish mainland's northern tip to the remote Orkney and Shetland Islands is no ordinary ferry ride. The journey transports you back to the islands' Norse heritage and then to the prehistoric days of mystical stone circles, mysterious hilltop monuments, and the lost village of Skara Brae, a remarkable netherworld that sheds light on daily life in this area five millennia ago.

NOT TO BE MISSED:

Prehistoric Orkney

Skara Brae is just one of the sites dating back to 3000–2000 B.C. that prompted UNESCO to place the Heart of Neolithic Orkney on its World Heritage List in 1999. The archipelago's other must-see sights—valued because of the extraordinary exemplars of Neolithic life and the achievements of these ancient peoples in northern Europe—are Maeshowe, the Stones of Stenness, and the Ring of Brodgar, alongside many as yet unexcavated sites.

Orkney's more recent history, centered around the vast natural harbor of Scapa Flow (one of the world's leading scuba dive venues), and its natural environment, are also remarkable. South of Orkney Mainland, the island of Hoy awaits with its rugged, mountain-tossed scenery and the iconic Old Man of Hoy rock stack. The rest of the outlying islands, in common with the Mainland, are blessed with rolling hills rather than hulking mountains. The land is generally smooth and fertile, one of the factors contributing to the prosperous life the islanders have lived, largely unruffled by the machinations of mainland Britain, for thousands of years. Wildlife has thrived here, too, especially in the archipelago's nature reserves.

Destination Scorecard survey—conducted by *National Geographic Traveler* magazine—rated Shetland

Green Shetland

Ask many British people to point out the Shetland Islands on a map and they may struggle. Even the BBC weather forecasts have often been a bit reluctant to place this most faraway of northern island archipelagos. In recent years, however, Shetland's green tourism credentials have started to come to the fore, finally placing it on the global map. A fourth annual

as one of the most appealing island destinations in the world (it had the fourth highest score).

The island rated highly on criteria such as "environmental and ecological quality," "condition of historic buildings and archaeological sites," and "outlook for the future." An expert panel member described Shetland as having "everything with bells on," which conveys just how special this spectacular northern eco-oasis is, where Mother Nature is firmly in charge.

This protected environment of pristine white beaches, vaulting sea cliffs, and rugged islands also makes for some of the most impressive wildlife-viewing opportunities in Europe. In summer, legions of puffins flutter around the sea cliffs while the mammoth great skuas put humans firmly in their place by dive-bombing anyone foolhardy enough to venture into their territory. Almost all the varieties of seabird found in the United Kingdom grace Shetland. And the water itself is alive with seals (common and grey), porpoises, otters, dolphins, and whales, with orcas one of the most spectacular visitors.

Shetland is also home to some stunning historical sites, where conservation has been paramount. At Jarlshof, you can ramble among remarkably preserved Iron and Bronze Age houses and conjure up the days when Viking longships patrolled these waters. ■

■ **Alone Shetland Pony on a Scottish Moor on the Shetland Islands**

ORKNEY ISLANDS

For most visitors, both practicalities and time limit their Orkney island discovery to the Mainland. However, the archipelago is actually made up of 70 or so islands and smaller rock skerries, of which 17 are currently inhabited. Together, the islands cover an area of more than 347 square miles (900 sq km), with the archipelago about 53 miles (85 km) from north to south and 23 miles (37 km) from east to west.

Bird-watching at Yesnaby, in the Orkney Islands

Mainland

By far the biggest and most populous of the Orkney Islands, the Mainland supports a thriving community of more than 17,000 people who are concentrated around the centers of Kirkwall and **Stromness**.

The latter is Orkney's picturesque ferry port, which boasts graceful stone buildings. Here, the **Pier Arts Centre** *(Victoria St., Stromness, tel 01856/850 209, pierartscentre.com, closed Sun.–Mon.)* showcases British modernism. Then learn about the island's natural history at the **Stromness Museum** *(52 Alfred St., tel 01856/850 025, stromness museum.org.uk, £),* a short stroll away. At the end of May, the town is awash in

GETTING TO ORKNEY: Loganair *(tel 0344/800 2855, loganair.co.uk)* operates flights from major British airports. For ferry information, contact Orkney Ferries *(tel 01856/872 044, orkneyferries .co.uk)*, NorthLink Ferries *(tel 800/111 4422, northlinkferries.co.uk)*, John O'Groats Ferries *(tel 01955/611 353, jogferry.co.uk)*, or Pentland Ferries *(tel 01856/831 226, pentlandferries.co.uk).*

Orkney Islands 307 A1–A2, B1–B2 **Visitor Information** West Castle St., Kirkwall (01856) 872 856 **visitscotland.com & orkney.com**

St. Magnus Cathedral

Founded in 1137 by the Viking Earl Rognvald, Kirkwall's magnificent St. Magnus Cathedral is also known as the "Light of the North." Over the centuries, erosion has taken its toll on the soft red and yellow sandstone used in the church's construction. The cathedral's ornate exterior is largely medieval in appearance, the work of master stonemasons who are believed to have also worked on England's Durham Cathedral. Come to a Sunday morning service (11:15 a.m.), schedule a tour, or stop in for one of the regular concerts. If you're able, time your visit for the St. Magnus International Festival in June, when all of Kirkwall is full of performances. (Check *stmagnus.org* or *stmagnus festival.com* for listings.)

traditional music, with concerts, pub sessions, a fiddler's rally, and more during the lively **Orkney Folk Festival** *(orkneyfolkfestival.com).*

On the outskirts of town, the **Ness Battery** *(tel 07759/857 298, nessbattery.co.uk, £)* once defended Scapa Flow against enemy attack. This important relic of Orkney's wartime heritage is now open for a fine guided tour.

Heading due east, the A965 takes visitors to the Orkney capital, **Kirkwall,** where you can peruse local crafts shops or stop by the Kirkuvagr gin **Orkney Distillery**. Most important for all visitors is the magnificent **St. Magnus Cathedral** *(Broad St., Kirkwall; see sidebar above)*. To understand the history of these islands, the **Orkney Museum** is helpful. On the town's outskirts, slightly peaty single malts (among Scotland's finest) await at the **Highland Park Distillery** *(Holm Rd., tel 01856/874 619, highland parkwhisky.com, tour £–£££££).*

Signs that humans have been living on Orkney for thousands of years emerge at every turn. Spread across the islands are upright stones and burial cairns, some of which archaeologists have investigated, but many of which remain a mystery.

West Mainland has many mustsee sights besides the amazing **Skara Brae** (see pp. 316–317)—the website for Historic Environment Scotland *(historicenvironment.scot)* has details on each. The standing **Stones of Stenness,** located about 5 miles (8 km) northeast of Stromness on the B9055, were originally a circle of 12 rock slabs. Today, only four continue to defy the elements, and chances are you will be alone at this bleak and romantic spot.

Nearby is one of the best-preserved

Orkney Distillery ✉ Ayre Rd., Kirkwall ☎ (01856) 875 338
💲 Tours ££–££££ April–Oct. **orkneydistilling.com** • **Orkney Museum**
✉ Tankerness House, Broad St., Kirkwall ☎ (01856) 873 191
🕐 Closed Sun. **orkneydistilling.com**

Neolithic burial chambers in Europe, **Maeshowe** (tel 01856/851 266, historic environment.scot, ££), dating back more than 3,000 years. Tours, which must be booked in advance, leave from the new visitor center in Stenness.

Also nearby is the **Ring of Brodgar,** one of Orkney's most dramatic sights. Of all the islands' standing stones, this one is closest in appearance to Stonehenge in England. It is estimated that the circle originally had 60 stones when it was erected over four and a half millennia ago. Today 36 remain. Open for tours in July and August while the dig is active is the intriguing **Ness of Brodgar** (nessof brodgar.com), a fairly recent archaeological effort.

To learn more about Orkney's Viking heritage, head to Orphir, where the **Orkneyinga Saga Centre** (Gyre Rd., £) brings the violent invasion of the northern isles to life.

On the north coast of the island lie the well-preserved ruins of the **Broch of Gurness,** an ancient fortified settlement dominated by a circular stone tower. The structure that you see today is believed to date from somewhere around 200–100 B.C., with low walls dotting the site that are actually the remnants of the village that was built around the broch. With a good dose of imagination and a look at the exhibition in the visitor center, you can

Italian Chapel

Ingenuity and determination led hundreds of Italian prisoners of war to construct the ornate chapel on Orkney's Lamb Holm from two Nissen huts during World War II (they also built the Churchill Barriers). Their attention to detail is staggering. Notable in the interior are Christian frescos, stained-glass windows, and intricate ironwork. Sadly, several priceless panels were lost to vandalism and theft in 2014, but the church remains open and worth a visit.

conjure up a vivid picture of Iron Age life on Orkney.

Lamb Holm, Burray, & South Ronaldsay

While Orkney's prehistory is certainly captivating, its more recent history is also worth exploring. Heading south from the Mainland, it is possible to drive on to the uninhabited island of Lamb Holm, home to the fantastic legacy that is the **Italian Chapel** (see sidebar above) and World War II bunkers, to Burray, and then on to South Ronaldsay.

The four causeways connecting the islands, known as the **Churchill**

Broch of Gurness ✉ Evie 🕐 Closed Oct.–March ☎ (01856) 715 414 💲 £ **historicenvironment.scot** • **Lamb Holm, Burray, & South Ronaldsay** 🗺 307 A1 **orkney.com/explore/burray-south-ronaldsay** • **Italian Chapel** ✉ Lamb Holm ☎ (01856) 781 580 💲 £ **orkney.com/ listings/the-italian-chapel**

■ A grey seal pup with its mother on the shores of the Pentland Firth in Hoy

Barriers, were erected on the orders of the British Prime Minister Winston Churchill (1874–1965) between 1940 and 1945, to improve the defenses of the vast natural harbor of **Scapa Flow** (see sidebar p. 314). Close to the causeways, the capsized and rusting ships were deliberately sunk as blockships to protect against attack from German U-boats, a practice carried out during both World War I and World War II.

Families in particular enjoy the **Orkney Fossil and Heritage Centre** on Burray, with its fossils and "glow room" that reveals the fluorescent colors of the rocks on display. A tearoom, run by local volunteers, offers a relaxing chance to discuss the day's finds.

For those hankering after more archaeological sites, **South Ronaldsay** is home to one of Orkney's most impressive, the **Tomb of the Eagles,** also known as the Isbister Chambered Cairn. The dramatic coastal location of this Bronze Age burial mound adds to the appeal. At press time, it was closed (check the website for updates).

Also on South Ronaldsay you can explore the unexpected **Olav's Wood** (*off the A961, olavswood.org .uk*), planted in the 1970s and 1980s to bring woodland to the mainly treeless Orkneys.

Orkney Fossil and Heritage Centre ✉ Viewforth, Burray ☎ (01856) 731 255 🕐 Closed Oct.–April. 💲 £ **orkneyfossilcentre.co.uk** • **Tomb of the Eagles** ✉ Liddle, St. Margaret's Hope, South Ronaldsay ☎ (01856) 831 339 🕐 Closed Nov.–Feb. 💲 £ **tomboftheeagles.co.uk**

Hoy

The second largest of the Orkney Islands, Hoy also boasts dramatic scenery, with mountain peaks that rise up to 1,577 feet (479 m) and vertical cliffs. It is also home to one of the archipelago's most iconic sights, the **Old Man of Hoy**—a fabled sea stack that is high on the wish list for many Scottish climbers wishing to tackle the technically tricky challenge. The island has as much to offer nature lovers as it does walkers, with its thriving populations of mountain hares and birds of prey.

If scaling a vertical stack adrift in the Atlantic isn't for you, you can still get some thrills by following the refurbished cliff-top path to **St. John's Head,** where the 1,136-foot (346 m) cliff is dizzyingly high—note, this is not for those who are afraid of heights. Alternatively, climbing the island's highest peak, **Ward Hill** (1,577 feet/479 m), is not technically difficult and offers panoramic views out over all of the islands.

Orkney's military history comes to the fore once again on Hoy's eastern shore, with the **naval cemetery** in Lyness and its **Scapa Flow Visitor Centre** (see sidebar p. 314), both worth a visit. Don't miss the expansive collection of photographs that shed light on island life during the two World Wars and the assortment of old military vehicles and weapons.

INSIDER TIP:

As you gaze from the cliff top out to the towering sea stack known as the Old Man of Hoy, you'll realize it was well worth negotiating the logistics of the ferry from Orkney's Mainland and the ensuing hike.

—LARRY PORGES
National Geographic author

On the shores of Scapa Flow the small team at the **Scapa Distillery** (*St. Ola, Kirkwall, 1856/873 269, scapawhisky.com, closed Nov.–May, tours £££–£££££*) craft a highly regarded, honeyed single malt. Tours are available by reservation.

Across a narrow causeway from the tip of Hoy awaits the small island of South Walls, home to one of Orkney's best hotels and restaurants, the **Stromabank Hotel** (see Travelwise p. 359). Here, too, are the impressive defenses of the **Hackness Battery** and the sandstone **Hackness Martello Tower,** both dating from the Napoleonic Wars. At Brims, on the southern shore of Scapa Flow, the **Longhope Lifeboat Museum** honors the brave volunteer crews of the RNLI lifeboats, including the eight

Hoy 🗺 307 A1 **orkney.com/explore/hoy-graemsay • Scapa Flow Visitor Centre** ✉ Lyness, Hoy ☎ (01856) 791 300 🕐 Closed Sun. & Jan. **orkney.com/listings/scapa-flow-museum • Longhope Lifeboat Museum** ✉ Brims, South Walls 🕐 Closed Sat.–Tues. **longhopelifeboatmuseum.org** • **Westray** 🗺 307 A2 **orkney.com/explore/westray**

EXPERIENCE: Reliving History at Scapa Flow

During World War I and World War II, Orkney's Scapa Flow was a major naval base, with more than 100 warships moored in the bay at any one time. This military past has left an indelible mark on the harbor; even today, visitors can see the blockships that were sunk to try and protect it from attack by German U-boats while the surrounding hills are dotted with gun batteries.

At the end of World War I, 74 captured German ships were also moored in this vast natural harbor. When the Germans learned that peace terms meant they would have to hand over their ships, the German commander ordered that the fleet be scuttled and all 74 were sunk before the Allies could intervene.

The majority of the vessels didn't stay where they were sunk, and those that were washed ashore were quickly salvaged. In 1920, one of the biggest salvage operations ever attempted by the British began, and, in the interwar period, the majority of the wrecks were removed. Some of the vessels, however, including three battleships and a U-boat, are still wedged on the floor of the deep waters of Scapa Flow.

One of the early naval casualties of World War II, the *Royal Oak*, was sunk by a German U-boat in 1939, with more than half of her 1,400-strong crew losing their lives. Today the wreck of the *Royal Oak* is protected as a war grave, with an annual service held on October 13 to commemorate this tragic event.

The ship-strewn harbor is now firmly established as one of Europe's most popular scuba-diving sites. However, wet suits are required and the dangerous nature of the wrecks means that only experienced divers should delve below the waters. Even then, local advice should be sought beforehand—every year there are casualties in Scapa Flow. **Halton Charters** (*17 Graham Place, Stromness, tel 01856/851 532, clasina.co.uk*) offers guided dives. Browse the listings on *orkney.com/things/leisure/diving* for other dive companies.

Those venturing to Hoy can visit the **Scapa Flow Visitor Centre** (see p. 313), which delves into the harbor's role in both world wars.

locals who lost their lives in 1969 while attempting to rescue the crew of the S.S. *Irene,* which ran aground farther up the South Ronaldsay coast.

North of the Mainland

Each of the inhabited islands north of the Mainland has something to recommend it, from prehistoric sights and lighthouses to dramatic sandstone cliffs and nature reserves.

Westray sustains a community of around 600 people. In the main settlement of Pierowall, you can learn about island life in the **Westray Heritage Centre.** Elsewhere, the ruined 16th-century **Noltland Castle,** the dramatic **Noup Head** sea cliffs, and the **Castle o'Burrian** sea stack, home to nesting puffins, are worth seeking out.

Getting to Westray's smaller sibling, **Papa Westray,** located in the far northwest of the Orkney archipelago, is all part of the fun, whether you arrive by ferry *(orkneyferries.co.uk)* or on board the world's shortest scheduled flight (it takes around two minutes; *loganair.co.uk*) from Westray. Papay, as it is known locally, is mentioned in the *Orkneyinga Saga*—a semi-mythical history of the Viking Earls of Orkney written in the early 13th century—and it has a strong religious heritage. Legend has it that the "priest isle" (as it literally translates) was so named after it became a pilgrimage center dedicated to Saint Tredwell. Countless pilgrims came here seeking miracle cures for their eyes, although the chapel once dedicated to her is little more than rubble today. Still standing is the sensitively restored **St. Boniface Kirk,** where Pictish stones in the graveyard indicate a church on this site since the 7th century.

Papa Westray's most impressive attraction is **Knap of Howar** *(historic environment.scot).* In an atmospheric spot overlooking the sea, this Neolithic farmstead is every bit as evocative as Skara Brae on the Mainland. Experts reckon it dates back to 3500 B.C., making it one of the oldest still existing in Europe, if not the oldest.

Papa Westray also has a lot to offer wildlife enthusiasts, from waters rich in seals and otters to myriad seabirds. **North Hill RSPB Nature Reserve** is a birding highlight—and it is also home to the rare Scottish primrose.

The hilly island of **Rousay** has been dubbed the "Egypt of the North" for its numerous archaeological riches, with some 160 sites to explore, many along the mile-long (1.6 km) **Westness Heritage Walk.** A heritage center at the ferry terminal provides more information. Close to Rousay's eastern shore, **Egilsay** is notable for the ruins of the 12th-century round-towered **St. Magnus Church;** a memorial nearby signifies the spot where the saint was murdered around 1116. You can spot seals from the small nearby isle of **Wyre,** another island with Norse heritage.

Stronsay, once a bustling hub of herring fishing, is now mainly visited for its dramatic coastal vistas. **Sanday,** along with numerous archaeological sites, is best known to tourists for its white sand beaches. Birds of a feather flock to **Shapinsay,** where the wetland of **Mill Dam Nature Reserve** *(rspb.org. uk)* teems with whooping swans, geese, and other wildfowl. To the north lies the island of **North Ronaldsay,** also revered by ornithologists as a place to check off rare migratory birds. ∎

Westray Heritage Centre ✉ Pierowall, Westray ☎ (01857) 677 414 🕐 Closed Oct.–April, except Wed. or by appointment 💲 £ **westrayheritage.co.uk** • **Papa Westray** 🅰 307 A2 **papawestray.co.uk & orkney.com/explore/papa-westray** • **North Hill RSPB Nature Reserve** ✉ Papa Westray ☎ (01856) 850 176 **rspb.org.uk** • **Rousay** 🅰 307 A2 **orkney.com/explore/rousay-egilsay-wyre** • **Shapinsay** 🅰 307 A1 **orkney.com/explore/shapinsay**

PREHISTORIC ORKNEY

Until 150 years ago, the sparse landscape of Skara Brae on remote Orkney lay as it had for thousands of years. Few people, let alone tourists, ever ventured to this bleak, inhospitable bay that takes the full brunt of the Atlantic breakers and chill winds accompanying them. Yet buried beneath the sand was an ancient secret, uncovered one stormy night, that brought man face-to-face with his prehistoric ancestors.

On that night in 1850, the sand miraculously cleared away, unearthing the fishing and farming village of Skara Brae, Europe's most complete and best-preserved Neolithic village. It soon became clear that this was no normal archaeological dig when it came to light that the remains of Skara Brae dated back as far as 5000 B.C., making them much older than young upstarts like the Colosseum in Rome and even more ancient than the Egyptian pyramids and England's Stonehenge.

Today "Scotland's Pompeii," as it has been eulogized, has been recognized by UNESCO as part of the Heart of Neolithic Orkney World Heritage site and has become a mecca for historians, archaeologists, and travelers. The location itself is spectacular, as Skara Brae occupies a wide, sandy bay where the chill waters of the Atlantic Ocean tumble onto the unspoiled sands. There have been concessions to the tour bus crowd, like a visitor center and a reconstructed house, but the site really does possess a magical sense of the timeless and speaks for itself.

Visiting Skara Brae

The visitor center is tastefully done and provides some information, or rather speculation, on the people who once inhabited the village. We know that they were farmers and fishermen and that they built their homes below the earth to survive the harsh climate, but we are still not certain what forced them to abandon their homes around 4500 B.C., only 500 years after the foundation of the community. Was it a war with a rival village or maybe a savage storm like the one in 1850 that uncovered the village, or was it something more sinister?

The reconstructed house gives a good idea of the conditions that the original people lived in all those millennia ago, but walking around the actual village is the main attraction. It is no longer possible to get right into the houses—they were closed due to fears that they would be damaged by tourists. Today, looking down from the walkways above, there are numerous clues as to how those prehistoric people lived and many recognizable features that you do not need a guide to tell you about. Carved out of stone slabs are dressers, cupboards, shelves, hearths, and even beds, offering a unique insight into a prehistoric life that was not as different from our own as you might have imagined.

Skaill House

In the warmer months, the Skara Brae admission ticket also buys access to Skaill House *(skaillhouse.co.uk)*. Once home to the Laird of Skaill, the grand house was built in 1620 and today you can walk around its stately rooms and terraced gardens, and witness daily falconry displays *(skaillhousefalconry.co.uk)*. You can even book an apartment in the North Wing. A fascinating exhibit is the crockery that belonged to Capt.

James Cook, who set in place the chain of events that led to the founding of modern Australia. His dinner service was given to the Laird of Skaill when the ships *Discovery* and *Resolution* docked in Stromness in 1770 during Cook's Third Voyage.

Visitor Information

Skara Brae is located 18 miles (30 km) northwest of Kirkwall, Orkney, on the B9056. Historic Environment Scotland *(tel 01856/841 515, historicenvironment.scot)* looks after the site *(£)*. It's open daily year-round, with tasty fare available in the on-site café, although hours may be restricted in winter.

Daily Life in Neolithic Skara Brae

The well-preserved site of Skara Brae gives us many clues as to the daily lives of the people who lived here 7,000 years ago. The signs point to a close-knit farming and fishing community, with its houses arranged in a uniform manner. Some historians believe this architectural uniformity indicates that Skara Brae was an egalitarian society, whereas others think it is simply the result of a tried-and-true homogenous design that dealt successfully with the area's harsh conditions.

Each house consisted of one room with a central hearth and no windows, so that the only interior light would have come through a smoke hole in the roof above the fireplace. Due to the lack of wood

in the area, the furniture was made of stone, including a tank for storing limpets, thought to be used for fishing bait or as emergency food.

Animal bones found on the premises show that the inhabitants kept sheep and cattle—and hunted the nearby red deer and wild boar—for food. They also used the bones to make tools and the skins for clothing and blankets. Shells and seeds were also discovered here, indicating that the residents harvested fish and shellfish, along with wheat and barley as crops.

Houses were linked by a network of sheltered, insulated passageways so that people could travel around the village comfortably during the long, cold winters.

SHETLAND ISLANDS

If the Orkney Islands seem remote, then the Shetland Islands may as well be, as far as many Scots are concerned, on the moon. They are, in fact, nearer to the Norwegian city of Bergen than they are to Aberdeen on the Scottish mainland. The locals in these far-flung islands know Orkney as the "South," never mind the Scottish mainland or the unimaginable foreign outpost of London.

■ Modern-day Vikings celebrate the Up Helly Aa festival by setting their longboat alight.

Those who make the considerable effort to travel this far north will be richly rewarded, by dramatic scenery, abundant wildlife, and ancient monuments in this archipelago of a hundred islands, islets, and beaches.

One of the highlights of the Shetland year is the **Up Helly Aa** fire festival *(uphellyaa.org)*, when a Viking longboat is ceremonially burned. This

GETTING TO SHETLAND: Loganair *(tel 0344/800 2855, loganair.co.uk)* operates flights from major British airports. For ferry information, contact NorthLink Ferries *(northlinkferries.co.uk)*.

Shetland Islands 🅜 307 B3–B4, C3–C4 **Visitor Information** ✉ Market Cross, Lerwick, Mainland ☎ (01595) 693 434 **visitscotland.com & shetland.org**

ritual connects the past and the present in a land where reality and myth merge. The main one takes place in Lerwick on the last Tuesday of January; nine others are held around the islands from January through March. If you do visit in January, be prepared for cold, short days. These long and gloomy winters are compensated for by glorious summers—from June to September, it never really gets dark. This is a truly magical time.

Mainland

Whether you arrive by boat or fly into Sumburgh Airport in the south of the Mainland, it is likely you will spend some time in the archipelago's capital, **Lerwick.** This attractive waterfront town, with an old harbor, is the center of commercial life in the islands and is often referred to locally as just "the town." With some good accommoda-

INSIDER TIP:

A sprinkling of the old fishing böds have recently been opened up as rudimentary, but deeply romantic and historic, places to spend the night.

—LEON GRAY
National Geographic contributor

tions to choose from, as well as some of the islands' best dining options, Lerwick makes a good base from which to visit some of the outlying islands, many of which can be tackled as a day trip. It also has a few tourist attractions, including the elevated views from the reconstructed **Fort Charlotte,** an artillery fort that was built in the 18th century, and the 19th-century **Town Hall.** Look to the latter for stained-glass

(continued on p. 322)

Fort Charlotte ✉ Harbour St., Lerwick, Mainland **historicenvironment.scot**
• **Town Hall** ✉ Hill Ln., Lerwick, Mainland ☎ (01595) 744 511 **shetland .gov.uk/lerwick-town-hall**

Oil & Gas on Shetland

When vast oil and gas reserves were found in the Brent and Ninian fields in the 1970s the Shetland Islands Council saw a huge opportunity. They lobbied to have the oil shipped through the islands and to secure their own cut. Over the last four decades the massive Sullom Voe terminal (able to fill up to four 1,312-foot/400 m tankers simultaneously) has shipped billions of dollars worth of oil, and the islands have prospered thanks (at least in part) to the levy imposed on oil landings. Further untapped reserves remain, but the collapse of the oil price globally in the past decade has reined in development and had a negative impact on the local economy, including local government spending cuts and less employment in the oil industry.

ESHA NESS CIRCULAR WALK

On these rugged islands, bashed into existence by volcanic forces and then shaped by the mighty Atlantic and battering winds, one of the biggest joys is walking in a land where man plays second fiddle to nature.

Esha Ness Lighthouse beams out over the basalt cliffs.

One of the most geologically diverse and scenic areas in the Shetland Islands—indeed, in all of Great Britain—is the Esha Ness Peninsula, located on the remote northeast coast of the Mainland.

This circular walk begins and ends at the parking lot at Esha Ness Lighthouse. The 4-mile (6.5 km) circuit climbs just 164 feet (50 m), so any reasonably fit adult should be able to complete the walk without difficulty in three to four hours. Dramatic natural scenery that incorporates volcanic cliffs, Atlantic Ocean views, and abundant seabirds make this walk popular with locals and visitors alike. If you begin at the information board in the parking lot, you can also learn more about Esha Ness's remarkable geology.

> ### NOT TO BE MISSED:
> **Esha Ness Lighthouse • Calder's Geo • Grind o' Da Navir • Loch of Houlland**

Views From the Cliff Tops

Before setting out from the Esha Ness parking lot, take time to admire the **Esha Ness Lighthouse** (*nlb.org.uk/lighthouses/esha-ness*) ❶. Engineered by David and Charles Stevenson, the lighthouse itself enjoys a dizzyingly spectacular setting, hovering near the edge of the black volcanic cliffs. In 2005, the Shetland Amenity Trust (*shetlan -damenity.org*) restored the property for self-catering rental accommodations, but it no longer served as such at press time. Check the website for current updates.

Following the dramatic cliff top north, but keeping a safe distance from the edge, you quickly reach the head of **Calder's Geo ②**. This narrow and deep cleft in the cliff was gouged out by the Atlantic at a point of weakness in the cliff rock.

Keeping with the line of the cliffs as they continue to wind north, you soon see **Moo Stack ③**. This massive sea stack, seemingly set adrift from the Mainland, has a sheer face and narrow ledge pitted with ridges and caves. It is a great place to see nesting fulmars and kittiwakes—be sure to watch the seabirds as they surf on the air currents above the Atlantic swell. From here, you can also see the Loch of Houlland to the east.

As the cliff-top "path" leads toward the Head of Stanshi, you have to climb over a number of fences. Rising from the ocean to the west down you'll see Dore Holm island, with its dramatic **Natural Arch ④**, carved out of the rock by marine erosion. Atlantic storms have also left an indelible mark at the spectacular **Grind o' Da Navir ⑤**. Here the cliffs appear to have an enormous vertical gateway, the result of a raging storm that smashed a huge hole in the cliff and hurled tons of rock inland. In turn, the boulders have trapped a small loch between them.

Just beyond the Grind o' Da Navir, the **Head of Stanshi ⑥** is a dramatic spot where the waves pound the cliffs and craggy volcanic rocks below. From here this "circular" walk takes you back south along the cliff tops toward the

Loch of Houlland. Just before you come to the loch, on the left-hand side, you will pass the **Holes of Scraada**—a subterranean stream that forms an underground passageway from the loch to the sea. Once the **Loch of Houlland ⑦** comes into view, head over the stile and onto the loch's western shore. Keep to the western side of the water as you continue to make your way south. Looking out over the loch, you will see a small causeway that leads to a small islet. The rocks strewn over the surface of this grassy mound are the remains of an **Iron Age broch.**

After leaving the loch shore behind, you will need to cross a dry-stone wall with a ladder stile. Then continue south until you reach the **cemetery** and the paved road that heads northwest to Esha Ness Lighthouse and the end of the walk.

🅜 See also area map p. 307
▶ Esha Ness Lighthouse
🕘 3–4 hours
↔ 4 miles (6.5 km)
▶ Esha Ness Lighthouse

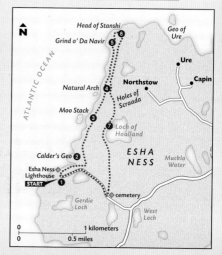

windows that tell Shetland's story and include many of its most famous faces.

The main attraction, though, is the **Shetland Museum & Archives**—a shining example of everything a family-friendly, modern museum should be. On its lower level, Shetland's story emerges from deep in the mists of time and travels right up to the 1800s. The upper levels cover the years since, with the open-plan nature of the museum allowing for a display of boats that have helped shape the island's history. Exhibits include everything from archaeological finds from the Stone and Iron Ages to the arrival of the oil industry in the 1970s (see sidebar p. 319), which radically changed the islands.

On the fringes of town, the **Clickimin Broch** (historicenvironment.scot), an ancient fortified tower, stands adrift on an island in Loch Clickimin. Along with the diminutive Shetland ponies, the island is also famous for its unique böds. The böds were small storehouses and dwellings located on the coast that were used on a seasonal basis by the islands' fishermen. One good example, the **Böd of Gremista,** now houses the **Shetland Textile Museum** (Union St., tel 01595 694 386, shetlandtextile museum.com, closed Sun.–Mon., Oct.–March , £), where you can watch locals demonstrating Fair Isle knitting, Shetland lace, and more. A shop tempts with work from the island's top craftspeople. In addition to the textile exhibits, this 18th-century böd has a small display illuminating the life of Arthur Anderson, who was born here and went on to be the co-founder of global shipping company P&O.

The long, thin strip of land to the south of Lerwick, with its fertile fields, sandy beaches, and great sea views, has what is arguably the Mainland's most dramatic scenery. Heading all the way to the bottom not only brings

Shetland Museum & Archives ✉ Hay's Dock, Lerwick, Mainland
☎ (01595) 695 057 🕐 Closed Mon.–Tues. in winter 💲 £
shetlandmuseumandarchives.org.uk

Mousa's "Simmer Dim"

It may be tiny and uninhabited, but Mousa—reached from Sandwick on the Shetland Mainland—is one of the most engaging islands in the Shetland archipelago. It is home to Mousa Broch—the world's most complete ancient broch (prehistoric circular stone tower), which is over 40 feet (12 m) tall in places.

The island's wildlife, with its abundance of common seals and birdlife, including arctic terns and black guillemots, is another lure. The island is especially magical during the "simmer dim," when, after midnight, with the imposing bulk of Mousa Broch looming in the twilight, flocks of storm petrels fly noisily home.

■ Bright-beaked puffins take a break from diving for their favorite meal of sand eels on Fair Isle.

you to Sumburgh Airport but also the islands' most impressive archaeological attraction, **Jarlshof.** This remarkable place contains remnants of occupation across 4,000 years, from Bronze Age stone houses and an Iron Age broch to the Pictish art created before the Vikings descended on Shetland, plus the most extensive Viking remains left anywhere in the United Kingdom, a medieval farm, and a laird's house from the 1500s.

For more evidence of Iron Age occupation, head to the **Old Scatness Broch & Village,** discovered during construction of an airport access road. Next take a look at Britain's largest active **sand tombolo,** a result of waves approaching from opposite directions, which attaches the Mainland to **St. Ninian's Isle.** The latter is known for "St. Ninian's treasure," including jewelry, scabbards, and feasting bowls made in the second half of the 8th century. Now on display in the National Museum of Scotland (see pp. 71–73), they were found buried in a wooden box by a schoolboy helping with an excavation in 1958.

The carefully preserved **Croft-house Museum** (Boddam, Dunrossness, tel 01595/695 057, visit-unst.com

Jarlshof 🅰 307 C3 ✉ Sumburgh, Mainland ☎ (01950) 460 112 🕐 Closed Sun.–Mon., Oct.–March 💲 £ **historicenvironment.scot • Old Scatness Broch & Village** ✉ Sumburgh, Mainland ☎ (01595) 694 688 🕐 Closed Sat.–Mon. Sept.–April 💲 £ **shetland-heritage.co.uk/old-scatness**

shetlandmuseumandarchives.org.uk/visit/ crofthouse-museum, closed Oct.–April, £), inhabited from the mid-19th century until the 1960s, shows how an extended Shetland family lived in the 1870s.

Also of interest on South Mainland is the **Sumburgh Head Lighthouse,** a Stevenson Lighthouse (see sidebar p. 243) in continuous operation since 1821. A fine visitor center includes a marine life center and radar hut. The accessible seabird colonies are the focus of the surrounding RSPB nature reserve. For a unique experience, you can stay at the lighthouse keeper's cottage *(tel 01595/694 688, shetlandlighthouse.com).*

Other Islands

Only around 15 of the Shetland Islands are inhabited, with a network of ferries, planes, helicopters, and small boats providing transportation between them. Shetland can be a bleak place to visit in bad weather, and **Yell,** in the north, can be among the bleakest. Still, it is a great place to experience the archetypal Shetland scenery of unremitting peat bogs and brooding *voes* (sea inlets).

Its dark, earthy beauty gives it an end-of-the-world feel that helps you recharge. It is also one of the finest places in Europe to find otters, which splash around

the island's rugged coastline. Yell is also handy for ferry connections to neighboring **Fetlar,** a much more fertile island, as well as Unst.

At the top of the archipelago, **Unst** is home to Britain's most northerly **Shetland Reel** *(tel 01957/711 217, shetlandreel.com),* which offers tours *(££££)* if you book ahead. Unst also has one of the highest archaeological concentrations of Viking longhouses anywhere in the world. You can learn about them, as well as other elements of island history, at the **Unst Heritage Center** *(Haroldswick, tel 01957/711 528, closed Oct.–April , £).*

Like **Mousa** (see sidebar p. 322), all of the Shetland Islands are alive with wildlife, especially birdlife. To the east of Lerwick, the **Isle of Noss** is a real ornithologist's paradise. A skyscraper of rock bursts out of the sea and looms above the tumbling Atlantic surf. This protected nature reserve can be visited by ferry *(tel 0849/600 0449, north linkferries.co.uk)* from the neighboring island of **Bressay.** The cliffs and water are host to many kinds of birds, from diving gannets and puffins to soaring great skuas.

Although administratively part of the Shetland Islands, **Fair Isle** lies about halfway between Shetland and Orkney. Decimated by the Clearances in the 19th century it remains home to a vibrant and, by necessity, self-suf-

---

Sumburgh Head Lighthouse ✉ Sumburgh, Mainland ☎ (01595) 694 688 🕐 Closed Oct.–March. 💲 £ **sumburghhead.com** • **Mousa** 🗺 307 C3 • **Yell** 🗺 307 C4 • **Fetlar** 🗺 307 C4 **fetlar.org** • **Unst** 🗺 307 C4 • **Isle of Noss Nature Reserve** ☎ (01595) 693 345 **nature.scot** • **Fair Isle** 🗺 307 B2 **fairisle.org.uk**

■ The still active Bressay Lighthouse is a welcome landmark for visitors to the Shetland Islands.

ficient community. This is a walkers' and bird-watchers' haven (hundreds of species migrate through the islands), with a warm welcome waiting at the **Fair Isle Bird Observatory & Guesthouse** (closed for reconstruction through 2024).

For years the main industry in Fair Isle was the knitting of the famously patterned Fair Isle sweaters. The island crafts cooperative dissolved in 2011, so you will have to ask locally to secure one of these authentic and labor-intensive lifelong souvenirs from an artist.

The island's modest **George Waterston Museum** (*Ultra, tel 01595/760 244, facebook.com/ ShetlandHeritageAssociation, closed Oct.- April*) tells many colorful stories, including that of the 1588 sinking of *El Gran Grifon*. More than 50 shipwrecked sailors and soldiers died of starvation or exposure before locals arrived, took them prisoner, and provided care. ■

Fair Isle Bird Observatory & Guesthouse ✉ Fair Isle ☎ (01595) 760 258 **fairislebirdobs.co.uk**

Where to Eat & Drink in Orkney & Shetland Islands

THE DOWRY

98. COMMERCIAL ST., LERWICK

(01595) 692 373 | Facebook.com/TheDowryShetland

A simple yet airy and appealing café, The Dowry serves equally no-frills yet tasty and hearty fare, from eggs Benedict to soups and delicious fresh-baked cakes and scones. Or opt for a scrumptious Dowry burger, ranch chicken, or to-be-expected battered haddock 'n' chips. Kids will delight in the oversize ice cream servings. Plus, beverages include fresh-brewed local beer on tap.

£-££ ⊕ Closed Sun.

THE FOVERAN

ST. OLA, MAINLAND, ORKNEY

(01856) 872 389 | thefoveran.com

This "restaurant with rooms" establishment provides home-baked bread, warm and friendly service, and huge windows with great views across Scapa Flow and Kirkwall. The menu is based on fresh seasonal ingredients—local shellfish, fish, and cheese among them.

£££ P ▧ MC, V

HAMNAVOE RESTAURANT

36 GRAHAM PL., STROMNESS, MAINLAND, ORKNEY

(01856) 850 606 | hamnavoe-restaurant.co.uk

This relaxed and lively restaurant just off the main street in Stromness has quite a traditional menu that makes liberal use of the good stuff: cream sauces, whisky, haggis, and Scotch beef. Fish dishes provide a lighter option, with highlights including succulent Orkney scallops and daily specials such as lemon sole. Consistent cooking and competent service make this the town's most popular restaurant, so phone ahead to reserve a table in advance.

£££–£££££ ⊕ Closed L & Sun.–Tues.; Mon.–Thurs. early Dec.–Nov.; Mon.–Fri. Dec.–April ▧ MC, V

HELGI'S

14 HARBOUR ST., KIRKWALL, MAINLAND, ORKNEY

(01856) 879 293 | helgis.co.uk

Located near the busy Kirkwall harbor, where the ferry boats arrive, this welcoming pub takes its cue from the island's Viking past, with a slate floor and wood-panelled walls. This two-decades-old establishment is the place to try local ales or whisky among friendly company. Fare is of the comfort-food variety, with decent burgers, fish and chips, and the like, plus vegetarian and gluten-free options. Happily, they promise coffee and "homebakes" available all day, every day: Try the Beery Sticky Toffee Pudding.

£-££ ▧ MC, V

N°88 KITCHEN AND BAR

88 COMMERCIAL ST, LERWICK

(01595) 692 139 | no88shetland.com

Informal dining at its best, with

cheery décor, friendly service, and an eclectic, ever-changing menu that makes the most of locally sourced ingredients from producers that are as passionate about their produce as N°88 is about cooking it. Seafood chowder, delicious melt-in-the-mouth scallops, and braised Shetland lamb with goat-cheese curd, Swiss chard, and squash are typical temptations.

££–££££ 🕐 Closed L Mon.–Tues., D Sun.–Tues.

PIEROWALL HOTEL

PIEROWALL, WESTRAY, ORKNEY

(01857) 677 472 | pierowallhotel.co.uk

This small waterfront hotel has a dining room for its guests, with non-guests being treated to the same solid home cooking in the lounge bar. Food farmed and fished in Orkney is the order of the day; the shellfish and local beef both excel. Daily specials and home-baked goods also feature on the menu.

££–£££ 🅿 🗥 MC, V

SKERRIES BISTRO

ST. MARGARET'S HOPE, SOUTH RONALDSAY, ORKNEY

(01856) 831 605 | skerriesbistro.co.uk

This unpretentious glass-front café near the Tomb of the Otters is a recent standout in local dining. Enjoy stunning views over the sea as you peruse the menu, which focuses on fresh local fish and shellfish served with skill. Lunch available daily; dinner offered Monday, Wednesday, and Friday nights.

££ 🅿 🕐 Closed Oct.–mid-April 🗥 MC, V

A colorful Scottish shellfish platter

TRAVELWISE

■ Mountain bikers speed along a woodland track in Mabie Forest, Dumfries and Galloway.

PLANNING YOUR TRIP
When to Go
A raft of events and a varied climate —warm summers and cold Highland winters that have enough snow for skiing— make a visit to Scotland rewarding at any time of year. A busy cultural calendar that sees numerous festivals liven up the country's towns and cities means that July and August are two of the busiest months to visit. August, when the world-famous Edinburgh International Festival (see pp. 74–75) is in full flow, is peak season in the capital. These months also coincide with school holidays in Scotland and the rest of the United Kingdom, so

demand for accommodations is high, as are prices. All across Britain, Easter school holidays (March–April) are also a very popular time to visit, as is the festive period of Christmas and Hogmanay (New Year celebrations) at the end of December.

It is not just Scotland's urban centers that are busy during school breaks. Long sunny days and natural landscapes brimming with opportunities for outdoor activities ensure that rural areas are also popular July through September. Cheaper accommodations and mild weather make the months of May and June a good time to visit.

During the winter months, snow and subzero temperatures draw winter sports enthusiasts to the Highlands for ice-climbing or even skiing. As a general rule, the best time to visit Scotland's five ski resorts—Aviemore, Glenshee, Glencoe, the Nevis Range, and the Lecht—is from mid-January until the end of February. An unexpected cold snap can also see the resorts open in December and March.

October, November, and January to March compose the low season, when accommodations are less expensive. This can be a good time to cozy up in a local hostelry beside a roaring fire, or to make the most of quieter periods in the country's art galleries and museums. Scotland has a temperate climate, with rainfall reasonably evenly distributed throughout the year.

What to Take

Midsummer temperatures average around a comfortable 68°F (20°C); however, many days and places can be considerably cooler (or warmer). Sunscreen is essential, particularly for the summer's long days. Packing sunglasses, a sun hat, and breathable lightweight clothing (which can be layered if the weather turns cold) is also a good idea during the summer. In the cooler spring and autumn months a sweater and often a jacket are needed. Warm coats, scarves, gloves, and hats help keep the winter chill at bay. An umbrella or waterproof clothing might be needed at any time of year.

Smart or smart casual clothing is generally worn in more expensive restaurants. Elsewhere casual clothing is the norm. Specialist outdoor gear is essential for many activities and is widely available, but can be expensive, so try to bring your own.

It is advisable to bring (and store elsewhere in your baggage) photocopies of any important documents such as passports and travel insurance in case the originals get lost. For the same reason it is a good idea to make a note of any prescription medicines that you are taking. Travelers who wear contact lenses or glasses should pack spares. Although it is usually possible to buy replacements, it is a good idea to bring spare camera and cell phone chargers, digital photo memory cards, and travel plug adapters.

Insurance

It is advisable for all travelers to take out comprehensive travel insurance prior to their departure. This provides medical coverage and compensation for loss, cancellation, and delay. Policy wording should be checked carefully. For example, are medical costs paid by the policyholder and then claimed back or are they paid directly by the insurer? Many policies exclude activities deemed "dangerous" such as skiing, mountaineering, and other adventure sports. Preexisting health conditions may also be excluded under many policies.

Entry Formalities
Visas

Citizens of the United States, Canada, and many other countries can visit the United Kingdom for up to six months without a visa; the U.K. Border Agency provides details on its website (*gov.uk/browse/visas-immigra tion*). U.K. passport holders and those with passports issued in the EU, European Economic Area, and Switzerland plus Australia, Canada, and the U.S., do not currently need a visa to cross U.K. borders. The U.K. Border Agency lists nationals who need a visa to enter the U.K. on its website (see above). Any travelers requiring a visa must apply for and receive it before they arrive in the United Kingdom. The British Foreign, Commonwealth & Development Office (FCDO) website (*gov.uk/fcdo*) has a list of embassies and consulates where a visa application can be made.

British Embassies

United States
British Embassy
3100 Massachusetts Ave., NW
Washington, D.C. 20008
Tel (202) 588-6500
E-mail: britishembassy
enquiries@gmail.com
gov.uk/world/usa

Canada
British High Commission
80 Elgin St., Ottawa
Ontario, Canada K1P 5K7
Tel (613) 237-1530
E-mail: ukincanada@fcdo.gov.uk
gov.uk/world/canada

Customs

Travelers are currently permitted to bring an unlimited amount of most goods from other EU countries. When it comes to alcohol and tobacco the following criteria, however, must be met: The goods must be for personal use or for a gift, and tax and duty must have been paid in the country where they were purchased. In addition, owners must transport the goods themselves. The official individual allowances for these goods are available on the government website (gov .uk/bringing-goods-into-uk-personal-use). Be aware that if customs officials think goods are being transported for resale, they have the power to seize them and the vehicle they are carried in.

Travelers must also inform customs officials if they are carrying more than £10,000 (or its equivalent in alternate currency) in cash. Items such as stun guns, self-defense sprays, and bladed weapons will be confiscated even if stored in checked baggage. It is prohibited to enter the country with counterfeit goods or obscene materials. Travelers are allowed to bring their own prescription medicine with them, but should make sure they have the relevant paperwork.

HOW TO GET TO SCOTLAND
By Airplane

From North America it is possible to fly direct to Edinburgh (EDI; *tel 0844/448 8833, edinburghairport .com*) from New York's JFK and Newark, as well as Chicago, Philadelphia, Washington, D.C., and Toronto, and other cities on a seasonal basis. Glasgow Airport (GLA; *tel 0844/481 5555, glasgowairport .com*) is served by nonstop flights from Toronto, and by connecting flights via Edinburgh, London, and cities throughout Europe. Glasgow Prestwick Airport (PIK; *tel 0871/223 0700, glasgow prestwick.com*) is also well connected to Europe, with direct flights from Amsterdam, Berlin, Brussels, Copenhagen, Dublin, London, Madrid, Milan, Oslo, Paris, Rome, Vienna, and Zurich, among many others. Low-budget carrier Ryanair (*tel 531/582 5932 Ireland, 0127/935 8588 UK, ryanair .com*) flies in and out of Prestwick. It is also possible to fly direct to Inverness (INV; *tel 01667/464 000, hial.co.uk/inverness-airport*), Aberdeen (ABZ; *tel 0844/481 6666, aber deenairport.com*), and Dundee (DND; *tel 01382/662 200, hial.co.uk/dundeeair port*) from a growing number of U.K. and European cities including Amsterdam, Bergen, Birmingham, Dublin, Leeds, Liverpool, London, Manchester, Oslo, and Paris.

The majority of overseas visitors to Scotland still arrive at Edinburgh or Glasgow airports. Taxis from Edinburgh Airport into the city center cost about £25–30 and take approximately 20 minutes depending on traffic. With a station directly outside the airport, the smooth Edinburgh tram (*edinburghtrams .com*) is well worth the £7.50 fare, with stops along the 30-minute ride to Waverley Station, just below the Royal Mile. Bus (*tel 0131/555 6363, lothianbuses.co.uk)* options include the swift Airlink 100 bus, which leaves the terminal every 10 minutes; services take 25 minutes and cost £5.50 for a single journey or £8 return. Bus numbers 200, 300, and 400 also run into the city every 20 to 30 minutes and cost less, but are much slower than the Airlink, taking around an hour. The N22 night bus also runs to Edinburgh Airport. This leaves every 30 minutes and costs £3.

Taxis from Glasgow Airport into the city cost £20–£25. The Glasgow Airport Express *(tel 0141/ 420 7600, firstbus.co.uk/greater-glasgow/routes-and-maps/glasgow-airport-express)* costs £10 single or £16 return. Journeys take 15 to 25 minutes and buses leave every 10 minutes. The easiest way to buy your ticket is to download and use the First Bus App, and show it to the driver.

Both airports are modern and amenities include ATMs, money changing facilities, car rental desks, cafés, restaurants, bars, and shops.

By Boat

Stena Line *(stenaline.co.uk)* ferries run from Belfast in Northern Ireland to Cairnryan. P&O Irish Sea *(poferries .com)* ferries run between Cairnryan and Larne. Scotland also features on cruise ship itineraries. Among those who operate cruises that include Edinburgh are Royal Caribbean, Princess Cruises, Cunard, Windstar, and Celebrity Cruises. Ports at Aberdeen, Lerwick (Shetland), Stornoway (Lewis), Greenock (Glasgow), Portree (Skye), Ullapool, Invergordon, Peterhead, Oban, Scrabster, and Fort William also welcome cruise ships.

By Bus

National Express *(tel 0871/781 8181, nationalexpress.com)* operates one of the United Kingdom's biggest bus networks. From London there are direct services to Aberdeen, Dundee, Edinburgh, Glasgow, and Inverness, among others. Stagecoach *(tel 0345/241 8000, stagecoachbus.com)* offers a low-cost bus service between London and Scotland.

By Car

An extensive network of paved and well-maintained motorways (freeways), dual carriageways (divided highways), and single carriageways (highways) make it easy to drive to Scotland from England and Wales. Those traveling from mainland Europe can travel directly to Scotland by ferry, or cross to ports in England or Wales before driving north. Another way of reaching Scotland from the Continent is to travel via Eurotunnel *(tel 08443/353 535, eurotunnel.com)* from Calais to Folkstone in southeast England and then head north.

By Train

London North Eastern Railway *(tel 03457/225 225, lner.co.uk)* operates services from London to Edinburgh, Glasgow, Aberdeen, and Inverness. CrossCountry trains *(tel 03447/369 123, crosscountrytrains .co.uk)* connect Edinburgh, Glasgow, Dundee, and Aberdeen to destinations throughout England. CrossCountry (see above) and West Midland Railways *(tel 0333/311 0039, westmid landsrailway.co.uk)* link Birmingham to Edinburgh and Glasgow. The Caledonian Sleeper *(tel 0330/060 0500, sleeper.scot)* has overnight rail service from London Euston on five routes serving Edinburgh, Glasgow, Aberdeen, Fort William, and Inverness, with stops at other Scottish destinations en route. For complete timetables and fare information, contact National Rail Enquiries *(tel 08457/484 950, nationalrail.co.uk)*.

GETTING AROUND
By Airplane

It is often quicker to access some of Scotland's more remote areas via an internal flight. Highlands & Islands Airports *(tel 01667/462 445, hial.co.uk)* operate airports in:

Barra *(tel 01871/890 212)*
Benbecula *(tel 01870/602 051)*
Campbeltown *(tel 01586/553 797)*
Dundee *(tel. 01382/662 200)*
Inverness *(tel 01667/464 000)*
Islay *(tel 01496/302 361)*
Kirkwall *(tel 01856/886 210)*
Stornoway *(tel 01851/702 256)*
Sumburgh *(tel 01950/461 000)*
Tiree *(tel 01879/220 456)*
Wick *(tel 01955/602 215)*

Flights to these airports mainly leave from Glasgow or Edinburgh, but check the authority's website for full details. Scotland boasts one of the shortest plane journeys in the world—a two-minute hop from Westray to Papa Westray in Orkney. Loganair *(tel 0344/800 2855, loganair.co.uk)* operates Scotland's inter-isle services.

By Bus

Local and national bus connections are good in Scotland. The main long distance provider is CityLink *(tel 0141/352 4444, citylink.co.uk).* Local bus services accept cash (with fares typically ranging between £1.50 and £4) and bus passes. In bigger towns and cities like Edinburgh and Glasgow it is also possible to buy a day ticket that gives you unlimited bus travel in a single 24-hour period. Longer distance coach travel should be paid for in advance, either online or at a ticket office. More than 200 companies offer local or national bus service *(travelinescotland.com/bus-coach-operators).*

By Car

Driving is on the left. A well-maintained and extensive network of paved roads makes Scotland a good driving destination. Outside of city centers and away from main routes the roads can be quiet but twisting. Tourists traveling north on the A9 should take extra care. This road switches between single and dual carriageway frequently and is an accident hot spot due to frustrated drivers taking risks in order to overtake slower vehicles. Scotland also has numerous narrow one-lane, or "single-track" roads, on which traffic drives in both directions; here passing places (indented pull-overs on the side of the road) are used to keep traffic flowing. Be courteous and give way as needed.

Visitors from North America in particular may not be familiar with roundabouts, which are plentiful in Scotland and take the place of intersections. Traffic already on the roundabout has the right of way and cars have to give way to vehicles on their right.

Speed limits in Scotland are 30 mph (48 kph) in built-up areas, 60 mph (96 kph) on single-carriageways, and 70 mph (112 kph) on motorways and dual carriageways, unless otherwise indicated. Forty mph (64 kph) and 50 mph (80 kph) speed limits are also common. It is illegal to use hand-held cell phones while driving or waiting at traffic lights. Minor speeding offenses and parking violations often incur a fine. The legal blood alcohol limit for driving is 80 mg of alcohol per 100 mL of blood or 0.08 percent, the same as that of the United States. It is much safer for drivers to avoid drinking alcohol altogether.

By Ferry

One of the easiest and cheapest ways to navigate the jagged coastline of western Scotland and its scattered islands is by ferry. Ferries, such as those operated by Caledonian MacBryne *(tel 0800/066 5000, calmac.co.uk),* run frequently and operate vessels capable of carrying cars. The northern isles are served by NorthLink Ferries *(tel 0800/111 4422, northlinkferries.co.uk).* In addition to these simple everyday ferries, there are many smaller companies, some offering a more exotic experience such as a trip on a Clyde steamer (see sidebar p. 114). Ask locally as you travel.

By Subway

Glasgow has a single subway route operated by Strathclyde Partnership for Transport *(tel 0141/332 6811, spt.co.uk).* Many of the city's key attractions are within easy walking distance of a station. Fares are the same regardless of distance traveled, with a single journey costing £1.80. Purchasing a seven-day pass, can be good value for those staying in Glasgow for several days. Day tickets are also available for £4.30.

By Taxi

In larger towns, black cabs can be hailed on the street and journeys are metered. Tariff regulations in black taxis are also clearly displayed. Private rental taxis (minicabs), such as Uber *(uber.com),* tend to be cheaper, but must be reserved by telephone. Minicabs rarely have meters, so it is essential to agree on a price in advance. Minimum charges apply, with short hops costing in the region of £3.50 to £6 and a 20-minute journey coming in at around £20. Longer distance fares should be negotiated, for example Edinburgh to Glasgow would cost in the region of £75.

By Train

ScotRail *(tel 0344/811 0141, scotrail .co.uk)* operates throughout Scotland, with special offers, tickets, and a live network map on its easy-to-navigate website. The rail network is extensive, reaching Wick in the north, Aberdeen in the northeast, Mallaig in the west, and Stranraer in the south. Rail travel in Scotland can be expensive, particularly if tickets are purchased immediately prior to travel. Advance purchase tickets can be much cheaper, with the Trainline *(thetrainline.com)* portal being a good place to buy these.

ScotRail also sells rover passes as well as special holiday packages for those planning to explore Scotland by train (various rates and conditions apply). The ScotRail website has full details.

PRACTICAL ADVICE
Communications
Post Offices

Post offices are located in every city and town. They are also commonly found in rural villages on the same premises as a general store. Buy postage stamps here. One price sends a letter to all European destinations outside of the United Kingdom. Rates to the United States are a little more. Within Britain, first class arrives the next day, second class takes two or three days. Post offices also sell prepaid international phone cards as well as credit for prepaid cell phones.

Mailboxes

Mailboxes are red and may be freestanding or attached to a wall. Details of collection times are displayed on the mailboxes.

Telephones

Public telephones generally accept coins and phone cards. Some phones also take credit card payments. Outside of city centers and busy shopping malls, pay phones can be hard to find. Visitors should consider buying a pay-as-you-go cell phone, or buy a SIM card to use in an existing unlocked cell phone.

The main phone operator in Scotland and the United Kingdom is BT *(bt.com).* The main cell phone providers are 3 *(three.co.uk),* O$_2$ *(O2.co.uk),* Sky

Mobile (sky.com/shop), T-Mobile (T-Mobile .co.uk), Virgin (virginmedia.com/mobile), and Vodaphone (vodafone.co.uk).

Useful Telephone Numbers
Operator: 100
International Operator: 155
U.K. directory inquiries: 118 500
International directory inquiries: 118 505
Country code: 44
City codes start: 01
Local rate calls start: 0845
National rate calls start: 0870
Toll-free calls start: 0800 or 0808

Using the Telephone
To telephone Scotland from the United States, dial 011, the U.K. country code 44, then drop the first 0 of the area code, followed by the number. When making calls within the U.K., include the "0."

To telephone abroad from Scotland, dial the international code 00, then the national code (1 for the U.S. and Canada, 61 for Australia, 64 for New Zealand, etc.), then the area code (minus any initial 0), followed by the number.

Numbers prefixed by 0800 and 0808 are free calls. Other 08 number prefixes may indicate expensive calls (the situation varies). These include 0845 and 0870. Numbers prefixed by 09 are certain to be expensive. You can search for any number on the British Telecom website (thephonebook.bt.com).

Internet Access
Wi-Fi is increasingly available in cafés, bars, hotels, and other public spaces, sometimes free of charge.

Conversions
Scotland uses the metric system with two notable exceptions. Road distances are measured in miles and some alco-holic drinks are still served by the pint or half pint. In situations where the imperial system is still used, it should be noted that some British measures are not exact equivalents of U.S. standard measures. For example, an imperial pint (568 mL) is considerably larger than a U.S. pint (473 mL)—something to bear in mind when drinking at a pub or restaurant.

Electricity
Scotland uses 240V, 50HZ. Outlets have three holes and only accept flat pin plugs. Your appliances, including chargers, will require a voltage converter (unless dual capable) and an adapter.

Etiquette &
Local Customs
Scots observe normal courtesies such as shaking hands and greeting people with the appropriate good morning, good afternoon, or good evening. In formal meetings smart dress is normally required and business cards are often exchanged. In social situations if someone includes you in a round of drinks it is polite to buy a round in return. The kilt is often worn for formal events such as weddings.

Liquor Laws
Strict licensing laws mean that it is illegal for anyone under the age of 18 to buy alcohol. It is also illegal to purchase alcohol for minors. In general alcohol can be sold in shops only between 10 a.m. and 10 p.m. The Scottish government is trying to discourage binge drinking, and, as a result, many cheap drinks promotions have disappeared.

Media
Newspapers
Scotland has three dedicated national newspapers—The Daily Record (daily record.co.uk), The Scotsman (scotsman .com), and The Herald (heraldscotland.com).

Larger towns and cities also frequently have their own local papers. Scottish editions of U.K. papers include *The Scottish Daily Mail*, *The Scottish Daily Express*, *The Scottish Daily Mirror*, and *The Scottish Sun*. U.K. broadsheets like *The Times*, *The Independent*, and *The Guardian* are also widely available in Scotland. Sunday papers on sale in Scotland include *The Sunday Post (sundaypost.com)*, *The Sunday Herald (heraldscotland.com)*, *The Sunday Mail (dailyrecord.co.uk /allabout/sunday-mail)*, and *Scotland on Sunday (scotsman.com)*. Scottish and U.K. editions of the U.K. Sunday papers are also widely available.

Radio

All of the BBC's national radio stations *(bbc.co.uk/sounds)*–BBC Radio 1, BBC Radio 2, BBC Radio 3, BBC Radio 4, and Five Live–are available in Scotland, as are the country-specific BBC Radio Scotland *(bbc.co.uk/ radioscotland)* and the Gaelic language BBC Radio nan Gaidheal *(bbc .co.uk/radionangaidheal)*. More stations are available via the Internet and digital radio. There are also many local community radio stations.

Television

Scotland has its own BBC Scotland services, BBC One Scotland and BBC Two Scotland *(bbc.co.uk/ scotland)*, as well as other regional stations through the STV group *(stv.tv)*. Hundreds of other channels of all sorts–terrestrial, digital, free, and subscription–are the same as those watched throughout the United Kingdom, although local news broadcasts may well take a Scottish slant.

Money Matters

Scotland's currency is the British pound sterling (£), divided into 100 pence (p). It comes in bills of £50, £20, £10, and £5, although many places won't accept £50 bills. Coins come in £2, £1, 50p, 20p, 10p, 5p, 2p, and 1p denominations. Scottish banknotes differ from those of England and Wales, but all are used interchangeably in Scotland. The best places to exchange money are post offices, banks, or dedicated exchange offices. Larger hotels will also frequently change money, but at a poorer exchange rate or with higher commission charges. The most easily converted currencies are the euro and the U.S. dollar.

Most major credit cards are accepted in main centers and larger hotels, but always carry some cash with you, especially in the more remote areas and smaller towns. ATMs are found inside and outside banks, at transportation terminals, in shopping malls, at gas stations, and outside shops. Fees charged for ATM withdrawals will vary depending on the terms and conditions at your own bank and which machine you use.

National Holidays

Banks, offices, and most shops, restaurants, museums, and attractions close on national holidays, also known as public or bank holidays. Note if a public holiday falls on the weekend, then the following Monday becomes a holiday in lieu of this date:

January 1–New Year's Day
January 2–Additional New Year holiday
March/April–Good Friday
First Monday in May–May Day
Last Monday in May–Spring Bank Holiday
First Monday in August–Summer Bank Holiday
November 30–St. Andrew's Day (not universally observed)
December 25–Christmas Day
December 26–Boxing Day
Other days of national celebration in Scotland, when places generally do not close, are:

January 25–Burns Night
November 5–Bonfire Night
December 31–Hogmanny

Opening Times
Business hours may vary from place to place, but a general indication is given below:

Banks–generally open 9 a.m. to 5 p.m. Monday to Friday. Some are also open on Saturday or on Saturday morning.

Offices–generally 9 a.m. to 5 p.m. Monday to Friday.

Shops–9 a.m. to 6 p.m. Monday to Saturday, although this can vary. Many shops in larger towns, cities, and malls are open later on Thursdays (usually closing somewhere between 7 p.m. and 9 p.m.) and on Sundays. Typical Sunday opening hours are 11 a.m. to 5 p.m., but in the Highlands and islands, most shops and gas stations close.

Supermarkets–typically 8 a.m. to 10 p.m. daily, and some are open 24 hours.
Pharmacies–typically open 8 a.m. to 6 p.m. Monday to Saturday.

Pubs–generally 11 a.m. to 11 p.m. Monday to Saturday, and Sunday 12:30 p.m. to 2:30 p.m. and 6:30 p.m. to 11 p.m.

Places of Worship/ Religion
The majority of Scots (around two-thirds) identify as Christian, although fewer than 10 percent of the population regularly attends any kind of religious service. That said, in some areas, such as the Outer Hebrides, communities are still firmly religious. The Protestant Church of Scotland is the country's national church, but Catholicism and other Christian faiths also have a significant following. Scotland is a multicultural society so the other major world faiths, Islam, Judaism, Buddhism, Sikhism, and Hinduism, are also practiced. Visitors are welcome to services in churches, mosques, and temples throughout the country.

Time Differences
Scotland is on Greenwich Mean Time. From the last Sunday in March to the last Sunday in October it operates on British Summer Time (GMT+1).

Tipping
Tipping can be a confusing issue in Scotland. Where paying for service is optional some locals simply add a little extra onto the bill, others diligently add an additional 10 percent, while others don't tip at all. As a general guide, add 10 to 15 percent for good service in a café or restaurant. Tipping is not expected in a bar; however, you may hear the bar person being told to buy one for themselves; when this happens they will usually add the price of a drink to the bill and take this as a tip. For taxi fares it is usual to round the fare up to the nearest pound or to add on a couple of pounds.

Travelers With Disabilities
Facilities for travelers with disabilities are reasonable, with many hotels, cafés, and restaurants having rooms and restrooms with wheelchair access. Many buildings also have elevators that can accommodate wheelchairs. Public buses often have drop down ramps to allow wheelchair users to board, and trains have wheelchair spaces. This said, the very nature of some of Scotland's historic streets and ancient buildings means that they are not wheelchair friendly. Hearing-impaired travelers will find audioloop facilities where the ear logo is displayed.

Visitor information centers can advise on local conditions. Online, Tourism for All (tourismforall.org.uk) is a good resource.

Visitor Information

Scotland's national tourist office is VisitScotland *(tel 0131/472 2222, visitscotland.com)*. It provides a wealth of useful information about accommodations, sightseeing, and activities throughout Scotland via its excellent call center and website. Most cities and towns also have walk-in tourist information offices, where you can pick up helpful brochures, maps, and leaflets; learn about local tours; and book accommodations. Many, but not all, local tourist offices have redirected telephone inquiries to the VisitScotland call center.

Several additional websites provide a wealth of information:

Historic Environment Scotland—covering many historic sights *(historic environment.scot)*.

The List—a guide to what's on throughout Scotland *(list .co.uk)*.

The Scottish Government—official website *(gov.scot)*.

Traveline Scotland—useful for planning journeys throughout Scotland *(travelinescotland.com)*.

EMERGENCIES

Crime & Police

Scotland is a relatively safe country to visit, with low levels of crime reported against tourists. Travelers should take the usual precautions to keep themselves safe, such as carrying handbags slung diagonally across the chest and keeping clasps and openings facing inward; not carrying wallets, cell phones, or other valuables in pockets; keeping cameras inside a bag when they are not in use; and removing valuables from vehicles. Some visitors might also like to consider carrying money beneath their clothing in a money belt, although locals don't do this. Falling prey to a pickpocket is the most serious crime suffered

by most tourists. In order to maintain personal safety, visitors shouldn't walk alone in dark places and should try to avoid confrontations with anyone who appears high on alcohol or drugs. Scotland suffers from its fair share of poverty, and some parts of Glasgow, Edinburgh, and other big cities should be avoided (such as high-rise housing estates). Binge drinking is also a problem in Scotland, and alcohol-related violence occasionally spills out onto the streets. The police are usually on hand to deal with this, so there is no need to be unduly concerned.

The police are generally helpful and will take any complaints made seriously. Most insurance policies require proof from victims of crime that the incident has been reported to the police: This involves visiting a police station, where the police will provide a crime reference number to victims if they are going to seek financial compensation.

Embassies/Consulates

U.S. Consulate General
3 Regent Terrace
Edinburgh EN7 5BW
Tel (0131) 556 8315
uk.usembassy.gov

Canadian Consulate
By appointment
edinburgh@international.gc.ca
travel.gc.ca/assistance/embassies-consulates/united-kingdom

Emergency Telephone Number

Emergency services (police, ambulance, and fire) 999

What to Do in a Car Accident

In the event of a car accident involving another vehicle, a stationary object (such as a street lamp), or an animal, it is imperative to stop and see if anyone/anything is injured or damaged. Once the driver has stopped they must remain near their vehicle to provide anyone else involved (either directly, such as another driver, or indirectly, for example the owner of an injured dog) with their details. The information that needs to be given includes the driver's name and address, the name and address of the vehicle owner (if different) or rental company, the car registration number, and the insurance company. If personal injury hasn't been sustained and details have been exchanged, then nothing further needs to be done.

In the event of causing injury to someone else, the driver must also report the accident to the police and provide their insurance details. Drivers not in possession of their insurance details must provide them to the police within 24 hours. Driving without insurance is a criminal act.

Lost Property

If you lose something, check with any hotel, café, restaurant, bus, train, or taxi company that you have used since you last saw it. If your property isn't relocated, you need to report it at the local police station. Most travel insurance policies require policyholders, if they are going to make a claim, to report any lost property within 24 hours. Travelers who lose their passport should report this to their embassy or consulate, which will help with organizing a replacement. Photocopies of important documents (passports, travel insurance, etc.) can help in the event of loss.

Health

Scotland has an extensive network of National Health Service (NHS) hospitals, clinics, and doctors. Private health care facilities also exist. The standards of care are generally high. Pharmacies (or chemists) sell over-the-counter medicines such as painkillers, cold remedies, and antihistamines. For prescription medication visitors will need to see a doctor.

EU nationals currently benefit from free emergency medical care in the United Kingdom if they are in possession of a valid European Health Insurance Card (EHIC). The EHIC does not cover the cost of non-urgent medical attention or emergency repatriation. Some non-EU countries also have reciprocal health care arrangements with the United Kingdom; check if this is the case before your journey. Some services, such as accident and emergency visits to a hospital or general practitioner (GP), are free to everyone, if determined to be urgent by an attending clinician. Non-emergency care will normally be charged for, even if the patient is seen by an NHS doctor, and visitors should be sure to have travel or health insurance that covers the duration of their trip.

No vaccinations are officially required to enter Scotland, and tap water is safe to drink throughout the country.

FURTHER READING
Nonfiction
Culture & Miscellaneous

A Night Out with Robert Burns: The Greatest Poems by Robert Burns and Andrew O'Hagan (2022)
Malt Whisky Yearbook 2019: The Facts, the People, the News, the Stories by Ingvar Rande (2018)
Pipers: A Guide to the Players and the Music of the Highland Bagpipe by William Donaldson (2005)
Single Malt: A Guide to the Whiskies of Scotland by Clay Risen (2018)
Tartan: Romancing the Plaid by Jeffrey Banks and Dora De La Chapelle (2015)
The World History of Highland Games by David Webster and L. Boland Richardson (2010)

History & Archaeology

A History of Scotland by Neil Oliver (2011)
Before Scotland: A Prehistory by Alistair Moffat (2023)

The Highland Clans by Alistair Moffat (2013)

The Highland Clearances by Eric Richards (2016)

Independence or Union: Scotland's Past and Scotland's Present by T.M. Devine (2016)

Scotland: A History from Earliest Times by Alistair Moffat (2017)

Scotland Archaeology and Early History: A General Introduction by Graham-Ritchie and Anna Ritchie (2001)

Scotland's Forgotten Past: A History of the Mislaid, Misplaced and Misunderstood by Alistair Moffat (2023)

Scotland: The Story of a Nation by Magnus Magnusson (2003)

Nature

RSPB Handbook of Scottish Birds by Peter Holden (2018)

Scotland's Wildlife by Niall Benvie (2004)

Outdoors

101 Best Hill Walks in the Scottish Highlands and Islands by Graeme Cornwallis (2009)

The Munros: Scotland's Highest Mountains by Cameron McNeish (2006)

Rivers and Lochs of Scotland: An Angler's Complete Guide by Bruce Sandison (2013)

Scotland: Where Golf Is Great by James W. Finnegan (2010)

Scotland Mountain Biking: The Wild Trails by Phil McKane (2012)

Scotland's Mountain Ridges: Scrambling, Mountaineering and Climbing—The Best Routes for Summer and Winter by Dan Bailey (2009)

Scottish Canoe Classics: Twenty-five Great Canoe and Kayak Trips by Eddie Palmer (2015)

Travel

Caledonian, the Monster Canal by Guthrie Hutton (2009)

Clanlands: Whisky, Warfare, and a Scottish Adventure Like No Other by Sam Heughan and Graham McTavish (2022)

Hebrides by Peter May (2015)

Iron Roads to the Isles: A Travellers and Tourists Souvenir Guide to the West Highland Lines by Michael Pearson (2009)

Made in Scotland: My Grand Adventures in a Wee Country by Billy Connolly (2018)

Outlander's Scotland by Phoebe Taplin (2018)

Scotland: A Literary Guide for Travellers by Garry MacKenzie (2016)

The Southern Upland Way: Official Guide by Roger Smith (2005)

West Highland Way (British Walking Guides) by Charlie Loram (2019)

Fiction

At the Loch of the Green Corrie by Andrew Greig (2010)

The Collected Poems of George Mackay Brown by George Mackay Brown, Archie Bevan, and Brian Murray (2006)

Complete Sherlock Holmes by Sir Arthur Conan Doyle (2008)

The Cone Gatherers by Robin Jenkins (1989)

Harry Potter and the Philosopher's Stone by J. K. Rowling (1997)

Kidnapped by Robert Louis Stevenson (1886)

Outlander by Diana Gabaldon (1991)—and others in this series Saints of the Shadow Bible by Ian Rankin (2013)—and the author's other Rebus novels Trainspotting by Irvine Welsh (1994)

The Wasp Factory by Iain Banks (1992)

Waverley by Sir Walter Scott (1814)

Whisky Galore by Sir Compton MacKenzie (1947)

HOTELS & RESTAURANTS

Scotland has a diverse range of places to stay and eat. The selection in this book is limited to some of the best or most interesting choices. Many other places are also excellent and a lack of listing does not mean that you should not stay or eat there.

Places to Stay

In Scotland you can stay anywhere from a youth hostel or a campsite, to guest houses offering a bed-and-breakfast or a luxurious five-star hotel. Inns (pubs with rooms) and restaurants with rooms are also common. More unusual places to stay include country house hotels, castles, and lighthouses. Wild camping is also legal in Scotland, so if you have a tent you can pitch it (as long as you abide by the rules) without spending any money at all.

This variety means that there is something to suit every budget. Even at the lower end of the scale hotels are usually clean if basic. Many hotels and guesthouses have formal accreditation (a star-rating) from VisitScotland (visitscotland .com). Five-star accommodations are considered to be of exceptional quality, four-star excellent, three-star very good, two-star good, and one-star acceptable.

Guest rooms are commonly double or twin rooms, the former have one big bed and the latter two single beds. Many places have family rooms, with one double and up to two single beds. Rollaway beds for children and baby cribs are often available. Some places charge extra to accommodate children in their parents' room. Additional charges also depend on age, with a lot of places charging an adult rate for children older than 12. Some hotels have interconnecting rooms.

It is advisable to make advance reservations during the peak holiday season, particularly in July, August, and around Christmas and New Year. In August almost all hotels and guesthouses in the capital increase their prices to coincide with the Edinburgh Summer Festival. Reservations can be made by phone, or e-mail; online; and through travel agents. Internet booking agencies often quote much lower prices than the rack rate, but some hotels offer breaks such as free breakfast if you book directly with them, and you also have the opportunity to request a room with a view.

In the summer some bed-and-breakfast (B&B) establishments will not take reservations for one night. Similarly some hotels may also specify a minimum stay of two nights at busy times or on weekends.

In the summer it can be hard to get a double room in Edinburgh for less than £110, especially during festival season in August, with prices in five-star hotels often exceeding £300. Outside Edinburgh double occupancy rooms in a bed-and-breakfast start at around £50 and rise to more than £100. Hotels of all grades tend to be cheaper outside the capital.

Organization & Abbreviations

Accommodations are listed by chapter, then by price, then in alphabetical order.

Abbreviations used: AE (American Express), MC (Mastercard), V (Visa).

PRICES

ACCOMMODATIONS

An indication of the cost of a double room in peak season is given by £ signs.

£££££	over £300
££££	£200–£300
£££	£120–£200
££	£80–£120
£	Under £80

▶ EDINBURGH & THE LOTHIANS

EDINBURGH

SOMETHING SPECIAL

🏨 BALMORAL
🍴 *£££££*

1 Princes St.
Tel (0131) 556 2414
roccofortehotels.com

This grand old dame offers a slice of Old World luxury, with opulent public spaces and elegant guest rooms. Added extras include a top-notch health spa and **Number One,** a Michelin-starred restaurant (see p. 97). For a real treat check into one of the suites, with sweeping views out over the city.

🛈 188 🅿 🚭 ❄ 🏊 🏋 📶 Free
🅰 All major cards

🏨 APEX WATERLOO
🍴 *££££-£££££*

23-27 Waterloo Place
Tel (0131) 523 1819
apexhotels.co.uk

Within a restored 1819 Georgian hotel at the base of Calton Hill, this trendy option boasts a stylish chic, splashes of bright, bold colors, plus king beds, robes, and slippers. Its elegant Elliot's restaurant with deliciously eclectic menu is a bonus.

🛈 148 🚭 🛜 ❄ 🏊 🏋 📶 Free
🅰 AE, MC, V

🏨 THE BONHAM
🍴 *££££-£££££*

35 Drumsheugh Gardens
Tel (0131) 226 6050
thebonham.com

This classically modern hotel in Edinburgh's west end retains its Old World charm. Room no. 1, a superior double, houses a fabulous old copper bath, while suite 100, with its four-poster bed, has a shower that blasts water from all angles.

🛈 49 🅿 🚭 ❄ 📶 Free
🅰 All major cards

🏨 GLASSHOUSE
££££

2 Greenside Pl.
Tel (0131) 525 8200
theglasshousehotel.co.uk

Spacious rooms and stylish décor, not to mention the private rooftop garden and floor-to-ceiling windows, make this suave remake of a 19th-century church a top choice.

🛈 77 🅿 🚭 ❄ 📶 Free
🅰 All major cards

🏨 FRASER SUITES
🍴 *£££-££££*

12–26 St. Giles St.
Tel (0131) 221 7200
frasershospitality.com

The Edinburgh branch of this serviced-apartments chain offers suites in a variety of sizes fitted into a grand Victorian building. It's in a fantastic location, just off the Royal Mile and above Waverley Station. Most of the spacious, well-appointed rooms also have great views of the city.

🚭 Nonsmoking ❄ Air-conditioning 🏊 Indoor Pool 🏊 Outdoor Pool 🏋 Health Club 🅰 Credit Cards

(i) 75 ⮀ 🚭 🐾 📶 Free
💳 All major cards

🏨 MALMAISON
£££–££££
1 Tower Pl.
Tel (0131) 285 1478
malmaison.com
This contemporary hotel has resurrected a neglected 19th-century seamen's mission down by Leith docks. Its bright and breezy rooms and public areas are what make the pages of design magazines.
(i) 100 🅿 ⮀ 🚭 📺 📶 Free
💳 All major cards

🏨 THE RUTLAND HOTEL
🍴 **£££–££££**
1–3 Rutland St.
Tel (0131) 229 3402
therutlandhotel.com
The rooms at this suave hotel boast lots of character. The restaurant is also excellent, and its buzzing bar offers informal food and serves as the venue for breakfast. Eight luxury apartments are also available.
(i) 20 ⮀ 🚭 🐾 📺 📶 Free
💳 AE, MC, V

🏨 EDINBURGH HOLYROOD
🍴 **HOTEL**
£££
81 Holyrood Rd.
Tel (0131) 528 800
marriott.com
The Holyrood manages to tread the fine line between tartan tack and modernity with understated "Scottish" décor in guest rooms, and traditional touches in the contemporary themed restaurant and public areas.
(i) 157 🅿 ⮀ 🚭 🐾 📡 📺
📶 Free 💳 AE, MC, V

🏨 OROCCO PIER
🍴 **££–£££**
17 High St., South Queensferry
Tel 0130 331 1298
oroccopier.co.uk
Stylish guest rooms and an equally chic restaurant and café-bar enjoy one of the most stunning settings in Scotland, overlooking the Firth of Forth and its iconic Forth Bridge.
(i) 17 🚭 🐾 📶 Free
💳 All major cards

🏨 ALBYN TOWNHOUSE
££
16 Hartington Gardens
Tel (0797) 314 6210
albyntownhouse.co.uk
Housed in a Georgian town house, this elegant B&B wows guests with its fine guest rooms, friendly service, and high standards.
(i) 8 🅿 🚭 📶 Free 💳 MC, V

THE LOTHIANS

🏨 MACDONALD MARINE
🍴 **HOTEL & SPA**
£££
Cromwell Rd., North Berwick
Tel (0844) 879 9130
macdonald-hotels.co.uk
Graceful guest rooms, a relaxing spa, and a restaurant serving first-rate Scottish and international dishes are all compelling reasons to check into this seaside hotel. Then there are the golf course, the nearby beach, and the sea views over Bass Rock and North Berwick Law from the turret suites.
(i) 83 🅿 🚭 📡 📺 📶 Free in public areas 💳 AE, MC,

▶ **GLASGOW &
AYRSHIRE**

GLASGOW

SOMETHING SPECIAL

⊞ **BLYTHSWOOD SQUARE**
¶ £££–£££££
Blythswood Sq.
Tel (0141) 248 8888
kimptonblythswoodsquare.com
Blythswood Square delivers subtle
luxury and muted hues in spacious
and comfortable guest rooms. A
contemporary restaurant, an opulent
health spa, and two pools help ease
guests through their stay.
ⓘ 100 ⓟ ⇄ Ⓢ Ⓔ 🛜 Free
Ⓒ All major cards

⊞ **ABODE**
¶ £££
129 Bath St.
Tel (0141) 221 6789
abodeglasgow.co.uk
Its central Glasgow location, cozy
restaurant, and chic modern guest
rooms within an Edwardian town
house are all compelling reasons
to stay.
ⓘ 59 ⇄ Ⓢ Ⓔ 🛜 Free
Ⓒ AE, MC, V

⊞ **APEX CITY OF GLASGOW HOTEL**
££–£££
110 Bath St.
Tel (0141) 357 3333
apexhotels.co.uk
Located close to restaurants and
shops, this elegantly hip hotel offers
up-to-date amenities along with
good-size guest rooms and unusual
slanting cruise ship–style windows
leaning over the rooftops.

ⓘ 104 ⇄ Ⓢ 🛜 Free
Ⓒ All major cards

⊞ **HILTON GARDEN INN**
¶ ££–£££
Finnieston Quay
Tel (0141) 240 1002
hilton.com/en/brands/hilton-
garden-inn
Reclining on the banks of the River
Clyde, rooms in this modern hotel
may be a little on the small side, but
they are impressively well equipped. The restaurant is wonderful
on warm spring and summer days,
when alfresco tables make the most
of the waterfront locale.
ⓘ 164 ⓟ ⇄ Ⓢ Ⓔ 🛜 Free
Ⓒ All major cards

⊞ **RADISSON BLU**
¶ ££–£££
301 Argyle St.
Tel (0141) 204 3333
radissonhotels.com/en-us/
destination/united-kingdom/
glasgow
Inside what looks like a spaceship
next to the railway's Central Station, the Radisson delivers three
styles of guest rooms, many with
floor-to-ceiling windows from
which to admire the city skyline,
as well as an excellent restaurant,
health club, and spa treatments.
ⓘ 247 ⇄ Ⓢ Ⓔ Ⓐ 🎖
🛜 Free Ⓒ All major cards

⊞ **GRASSHOPPERS**
¶ £–££
87 Union St.
Tel (0141) 222 2666
grasshoppersglasgow.com
Located right next to the train station,
this one-floor hotel in an old Scottish
Rail building offers clean, cozy, and
comfortable rooms at bargain prices.

Ⓢ Nonsmoking Ⓔ Air-conditioning Ⓘ Indoor Pool Ⓐ Outdoor Pool 🎖 Health Club Ⓒ Credit Cards

A warm welcome, top breakfast, and complimentary cupcakes add to the experience. Surprisingly quiet for its location.

🚪 30 🔲 📶 Free
💳 All major cards

OUTSIDE GLASGOW

🏨 CROSSBASKET CASTLE
🍴 £££££

Stoneymeadow Rd., High Blantyre
Tel (01698) 829 461
crossbasketcastle.com

Exuding luxurious elegance, this landmark crenellated country house turned hotel set in sprawling grounds on the banks of the River Calder offers individually designed guest rooms lavishly adorned with antiques, including canopied beds. The renowned **Baillie Room** restaurant serves traditional French dishes using seasonal Scottish produce.

🚪 9 🅿 🔲 🔳 📶 Free
💳 AE, MC, V

🏨 NEW LANARK MILL HOTEL
🍴 £££

South Lanarkshire
Tel (01555) 667 200
newlanarkhotel.co.uk

Housed in a former 18th-century cotton mill, this characterful hotel has elegant guest rooms, all of which enjoy great views over the River Clyde or its adjacent conservation area. The health and fitness center has spa packages, an indoor pool, and a decent restaurant; eight self-catering cottages are next door in the New Lanark World Heritage site.

🚪 38 🅿 🔄 🔲 🔳 🏊 🔳
📶 Free 💳 All major cards

PRICES

ACCOMMODATIONS

An indication of the cost of a double room in peak season is given by £ signs.

£££££	over £300
££££	£200–£300
£££	£120–£200
££	£80–£120
£	Under £80

AYRSHIRE

🏨 GLENAPP CASTLE
£££££

Ballantrae
Tel (01465) 831 212
glenappcastle.com

Secluded amid woodlands and extensive gardens, this country house hotel is a superb example of 19th-century Scottish baronial grandeur. Period furniture, including canopy beds, evoke a warm Victorian-era ambience, and suites are truly palatial. Gourmet cuisine, an all-weather tennis court, and falconry displays are added draws.

🚪 17 🅿 📶 Free
💳 All major cards

▶ SOUTHERN SCOTLAND

DUMFRIES & GALLOWAY

SOMETHING SPECIAL

🏨 KNOCKINAAM LODGE
🍴 ££££–£££££

Portpatrick
Tel (01776) 810 471
knockinaamlodge.com

Those looking for a romantic hideaway need look no further. This small and intimate hotel delivers classical luxury in the form of individually styled rooms, a peaceful and welcoming ambience, and equally tranquil surroundings. The sea views available from some of the guest rooms and public areas are breathtaking. The hotel also serves excellent Scottish food (see p. 139).

🛈 11 🅿 🚫 📶 Free 🏧 AE, MC, V

🏨 BLACKADDIE COUNTRY 🍽 HOUSE HOTEL
£££–££££
Sanquhar, Dumfriesshire
Tel (01659) 50270
blackaddiehotel.co.uk
This restaurant with rooms and riverside cottages was recently refurbished with deluxe furnishings, but for that added luxury, splurge on the River Suite. The owner-chef, author Ian McAndrew, oversees gourmet cuisine.

🛈 11 🅿 🔄 🚫 📶 Free
🏧 AE, MC, V

🏨 THE CORSEWALL 🍽 LIGHTHOUSE HOTEL
£££–££££
Corsewall Point, Kirkcolm
Tel (01776) 853 220
lighthousehotel.co.uk
The former living quarters of the lighthouse keeper have been transformed into a unique place to stay. Rooms and suites are all individually styled, with extra space and sea views commanding a small premium. Splurge for the Lighthouse Suite, with its own private conservatory, or the Firth of Cromarty Room with its private terrace. The hotel also has a decent restaurant, and the full tariff includes dinner, bed, and breakfast.

🛈 11 🅿 📶 Free (some rooms & public areas) 🏧 All major cards

🏨 FRIARS CARSE COUNTRY 🍽 HOUSE HOTEL
££–£££
Dumfries
Tel (01387) 740 388
friarscarse.co.uk
Feel like the lord or lady of the manor at this 19th-century country house hotel. Anglers have exclusive access to the stretch of the River Ninth that runs through the hotel grounds, where they can fish sea trout, grayling, and salmon. Or explore the 45 acres (18 ha) of woodland, then head in to the **Whistle Restaurant**.

🛈 21 🅿 🔄 🚫 📶 Free
🏧 AE, MC, V

🏨 THE WATERFRONT HOTEL 🍽 & BISTRO
££–£££
Portpatrick
Tel (01776) 810 800
waterfronthotel.co.uk
This small and welcoming hotel is located on the harbor of the pretty village of Portpatrick. Guest rooms, like the hotel itself, are cozy, clean, and comfortable. Sea view rooms are well worth the extra fee. As you might expect in a fishing village, seafood dominates the menu in the hotel's elegant restaurant.

🛈 15 🚫 📶 Free 🏧 AE, MC, V

🏨 AIRDS FARMHOUSE B&B
£–££
Crossmichael, near Castle Douglas
Tel (07944) 765 108
airds.com
In addition to large, clean, and cozy guest rooms, this lovely B&B also boasts great views over farmland and Loch Ken below. The hearty break-

fasts are a taste sensation, and guests are welcome to use the conservatory, with its stunning views over the Galloway Hills.

🛈 5 🅿 🔄 🛜 Free 🆔 AE, V, MC

BORDERS

🏨 CRINGLETIE HOUSE
🍽 ££££–£££££
Edinburgh Rd., Peebles
Tel (01721) 725 750
cringletie.com

This lovingly restored 19th-century baronial mansion and its ornate grounds include an upstairs dining room. Guests at this excellent hotel receive the same tender care as Cringletie House itself, while in the restaurant an eclectic menu marries fine Scottish ingredients with French flair.

🛈 15 🅿 🔄 🛜 Free 🆔 AE, MC, V

🏨 SCHLOSSE ROXBURGHE
£££–££££
Heiton, Roxburghshire
Tel (01573) 450 331
schlosshotel-roxburghe.com

One of Scotland's finest country house hotels impresses guests with its stately guest rooms (recently refurbished with an elegant chic), first-rate restaurant, spa treatments, and golf course. Sleep like a king and book the Schloss Suite, with its open log fire and private balcony. Now owned by Hyatt, it features a new 58-room extension.

🛈 78 🅿 🔄 🛜 Free 🆔 AE, MC, V

🏨 MACDONALD CADRONA
🍽 HOTEL, GOLF & SPA
£££
Cardrona

Tel (0344) 879 9000
macdonaldhotels.co.uk/cardrona

Boasting its own golf course, Cardrona is ideal for golfers or those who want to indulge in a relaxing spa treatment and a first-rate meal. For cyclists the world-class mountain-biking trails of Glentress are just next door. Make the most of its dramatic River Tweed location with a ground-floor room where floor-to-ceiling glass doors open up onto an outdoor terrace.

🛈 99 🅿 🔄 🛜 Free 🆔 AE, MC, V

🏨 THE TOWNHOUSE
🍽 ££–££££
Market Sq., Melrose
Tel (01896) 822 645
thetownhousemelrose.co.uk

Owned by the same people behind Burt's Hotel across the road, but here the emphasis is on contemporary style, with bold patterns, contrasting colors, and plenty of space. Friendly staff and high-quality fare in both the brasserie and restaurant add to the pleasure.

🛈 11 🅿 🛜 🆔 All major cards

🏨 BURT'S HOTEL
🍽 ££–£££
Market Sq., Melrose
Tel (01896) 822 285
burtshotel.co.uk

This old Melrose institution is much more than just a hotel. It also boasts one of the town's best restaurants (see p. 139) and a lively bar stocked with single malt whisky. Newly elegant accommodations in this 18th-century building are individually styled.

🛈 20 🅿 🛜 Free 🆔 All major cards

🏨 Hotel 🍽 Restaurant 🛈 No. of Guest Rooms 🅿 Parking 🚇 Metro 🕐 Closed 🔄 Elevator 🛜 Wifi

▦ THE TONTINE
¶ ££
High St., Peebles
Tel (01721) 720 892
tontinehotel.com
This welcoming family-run establish-ment with smartly furnished guest rooms is located right in the center of town. There's also good food in its bistro and restaurant.

ⓘ 36 🅿 🚭 📶 Free 🄰 AE, MC, V

▶ CENTRAL SCOTLAND

STIRLING AREA

▦ DOUBLETREE BY HILTON DUNBLANE HYDRO
£££–££££
Perth Rd., Dunblane
Tel (01786) 822 551
doubletreedunblane.com
Rich colors and plush fabrics infuse luxury into the contemporary guest rooms of this stately hotel. Deluxe rooms are even more spacious and can be configured to sleep families, who also appreciate the intercon-necting rooms, children's menus, and a babysitting service (organize this in advance of your stay). Kids love the indoor swimming pool, while adults head to the sauna, steam room, and spa.

ⓘ 200 🅿 🚭 🄰 🚭 🛠 📶
📶 Free in public areas
🄰 All major cards

▦ MACDONALD INCHYRA
¶ HOTEL & SPA
£££–££££
Grange Rd., Falkirk
Tel (0344) 879 9044
macdonaldhotels.co.uk/inchyra
A swish spa, excellent Scottish steak-house restaurant, and proximity to the Kelpies and Linlithgow Palace are pluses at this former manor house nestled on a serene estate. Guest rooms—most newly refurbished—in older and newer wings have smart furnishings in calming autumnal colors.

ⓘ 100 🅿 🄰 🛠 📶 Free
🄰 AE, MC, V

THE TROSSACHS

SOMETHING SPECIAL

▦ CAMERON HOUSE HOTEL
¶ £££££
Loch Lomond
Tel (01389) 310 777
cameronhouse.co.uk
A golf course, state-of-the-art spa, elegant public spaces, and beauti-fully decorated guest rooms, cotta-ges, and apartments make Cameron House truly world class. Then there is the Lochside Boat House restau-rant with scenic views, plus a cinema perfect for rainy days.

ⓘ 132 🅿 🚭 🚭 🄰 🛠 🄲
📶 Free 🄰 All major cards

SOMETHING SPECIAL

▦ MONACHYLE MHOR
¶ ££££–£££££
Balquidder
Tel (01877) 384 622
monachylemhor.net
This chic hotel may be easy to get to from the central belt, but hid-den away down a quiet glen it feels a million miles away. Contemporary suites ease guests through their stay, and there's a romantic cabin and a wagon, but for many it is the leg-endary food that lures them here (see p. 163).

ⓘ 18 🅿 🚭 📶 Free in public areas 🄰 MC, V

🚭 Nonsmoking 🄲 Air-conditioning 🄰 Indoor Pool 🚭 Outdoor Pool 🛠 Health Club 🄰 Credit Cards

🏨 LAKE OF MENTEITH
🍴 HOTEL AND WATERFRONT
RESTAURANT
£££

Port of Menteith
Tel (01877) 385 258
lake-hotel.com

The hotel has been impressing locals and visitors alike with its pretty lakeside location and good food for a long time. For overnight guests, it also offers spacious and comfortable rooms, many with great views.

🛈 18 🅿 🚫 🛜 Free 🏷 MC, V

ARGYLL

SOMETHING SPECIAL

🏨 ISLE OF ERISKA HOTEL, SPA
🍴 & ISLAND
£££££

Isle of Eriska, Ledaig
Tel (01631) 720 371
eriska-hotel.co.uk

This luxurious retreat, which reclines on its own 300-acre (121 ha) private island, offers the Old World charm of the country house hotel with contemporary spa suites and two-bedroom cottage suites. Guests also have access to a fine-dining restaurant, well-stocked bar, small gym, indoor swimming pool, and spa. If this isn't enough there is also a six-hole golf course, croquet lawn, and tennis court.

🛈 23 🅿 🚫 🛎 🈂 🛜 Free
🏷 AE, MC, V

🏨 ARDANAISEIG
🍴 **£££–£££££**
Kilchregan by Taynuilt
Tel (01866) 833 333
ardanaiseig.com

This grand old dame reclining on the shores of Loch Awe has been hailed as one of Scotland's most romantic hotels, and justifiably so. The individually styled rooms all offer a slice of elegant luxury, with stately public rooms and a good restaurant its crowning glory. For a really special occasion book the cozy Boat Shed or former gatekeeper's cottage.

🛈 18 🅿 🛜 Free
🏷 All major cards

🏨 LOCH FYNE HOTEL & SPA
🍴 **£££**

Shore St., Inveraray
Tel (01499) 302 980
crerarhotels.com/lochfyne

Located right on the shores of the eponymous loch, this attractive hotel offers comfortable (if not always luxurious) guest rooms decorated in warm neutral shades, a swimming pool, spa treatments, and a decent restaurant. For a deluxe stay, reserve one of the mini suites with stunning loch views.

🛈 67 🅿 🛎 🚫 🈂 🛜 Free
🏷 AE, MC, V

🏨 STONEFIELD CASTLE
🍴 **£££**

Tarbert, Loch Fyne
TEL (01880) 820 836
stonefieldcastlehotel.co.uk

This is your chance to stay in an old castle in a dramatic lochside location. For a really memorable stay, book one of the suites, which benefit from big bathrooms, separate sleeping and sitting areas, and truly mesmerizing views over Loch Fyne.

🛈 36 🅿 🛎 🚫 🛜 Free 🏷 MC, V

🏨 OBAN BAY HOTEL & SPA
££–£££

Corran Esplanade, Oban
Tel (01631) 564 395
crerarhotels.com/oban-bay-hotel

Many of the rooms in the main

PRICES

ACCOMMODATIONS

An indication of the cost of a double room in peak season is given by **£** signs.

£££££	over £300
££££	£200–£300
£££	£120–£200
££	£80–£120
£	Under £80

building of this waterfront hotel enjoy sweeping views over the eponymous bay. The newly refurbished rooms fuse contemporary styling and yesteryear elegance. For a luxurious stay check into one of the junior suites and enjoy the small spa with its steam room, sauna, and massage chair, as well as an outdoor hot tub.

🛈 79 🅿 🚭 📶 Free
💳 AE, MC, V

PERTHSHIRE

SOMETHING SPECIAL

🏨 GLENEAGLES HOTEL
🍴 £££££

Auchterader
Tel (01764) 290 024
gleneagles.com

For most visitors, Gleneagles needs little introduction. This oasis of luxury in the heart of Perthshire hosts a championship golf course (one of Scotland's finest), opulent spa, and wonderful swimming pool. Graceful public spaces, a range of dining options—including renowned chef Andrew Fairlie's restaurant (see p. 163)—and activities ranging from shooting to horse riding keep guests

occupied. A playroom and a game room (the Zone) are also on hand for the kids. The pampering continues in the elegant and spacious guest rooms.

🛈 232 🅿 🚭 🚭 🚭 🏊
💳 📶 Free 💳 All major cards

🏨 ROMAN CAMP
🍴 £££–£££££

Callander
Tel (01877) 330 003
romancamphotel.co.uk

Nestled on the banks of the River Teith, this opulent hideaway is just off Callander's main street but feels miles from anywhere. Its large grounds, fine restaurant, classical rooms, and ornate public spaces all make for a romantic stay.

🛈 15 🅿 🚭 💳 All major cards

🏨 CRIEFF HYDRO
🍴 £££–££££

Crieff
Tel (01764) 655 555
crieffhydro.com

A firm family favorite, Crieff Hydro offers a wide range of accommodations, from standard double rooms to family rooms and suites in the main hotel and self-catering cottages. Rooms are comfortable rather than luxurious. Crieff's real appeal lies in the diverse raft of activities, including quad biking and an 18-hole golf course, two swimming pools, a game room, and child care facilities. Evening entertainment includes ceilidhs and quizzes, and there are a number of dining options.

🛈 213 🅿 🚭 🏊 💳 📶 Free
💳 AE, MC, V

🏨 LANDS OF LOYAL HOTEL
£££–££££

Aylth, Blairgowrie
Tel (01828) 633 151
landsofloyal.com

This charming Victorian mansion impresses guests with its fine period décor, personal service, and huge log fire in the main hall. Relax in the public areas or head to the beautiful terraced garden to soak up romantic rural views.

🛈 17 🅿 🚭 🛜 Free
💳 AE, MC, V

🏨 🍴 ROYAL HOTEL
£££–££££

Melville Sq., Comrie
Tel (017640) 679 200
royalhotel.co.uk

This classically luxurious hotel is housed in a historic building, where Queen Victoria was once a guest (hence the name). Individually styled rooms plus elegant public rooms and a restaurant and lounge bar await.

🛈 11 🅿 🚭 🛜 Free in public areas 💳 AE, MC, V

🏨 🍴 PARKLANDS
££–£££

2 St. Leonard's Bank, Perth
Tel (01738) 622 451
theparklandshotel.com

This relaxing hotel has to be the best located in Perth, perched prettily on a hill overlooking South Inch Park. Individually styled guest rooms are comfortable and spacious, some with views over the park.

🛈 15 🅿 🚭 🛜 Free 💳 MC, V

▶ EAST COAST

FIFE

SOMETHING SPECIAL

🏨 🍴 OLD COURSE HOTEL, GOLF RESORT & SPA
£££££

St. Andrews
Tel (01334) 260 300
oldcoursehotel.co.uk

Palatial rooms enjoy views out onto the golf course and the sea beyond. The hotel's golf stewards can help guests organize a round of golf on one of the local courses. This glorious five-star dame also embraces indulgences at the opulent Kohler Waters Spa. A handful of decadent restaurants offer everything from good pub food (at the Jigger Inn) to fine dining.

🛈 144 🅿 🛗 🚭 📶 📺 🛜 Free 💳 All major cards

🏨 🍴 FAIRMONT ST. ANDREWS
££££–£££££

St. Andrews
Tel (01334) 837 000
fairmont.com/st-andrews-scotland/

The welcome and service at the Fairmont St. Andrews is exemplary. This five-star resort boasts top service, modern amenities, and spacious guest rooms, many with views across the golf courses to the sea. The hotel's other big drawcards are its two championship golf courses, indoor swimming pool, and spa.

🛈 211 🅿 🛗 🚭 📶 📺 🛜 Free 💳 All major cards

🏨 THE SHIP INN
£££

ELIE., FIFE
Tel (01333) 330 246
shipinn.scot

🏨 Hotel 🍴 Restaurant 🛈 No. of Guest Rooms 🅿 Parking 🚇 Metro 🕒 Closed 🛗 Elevator 🛜 Wifi

Amiable hosts Rachel and Graham Bucknall run a tight ship at this lovely beachfront inn, where individually styled, light-filled guest rooms (four with sea views) have nautical-meets-tartan-themed décor. Then, of course, there's the renowned gastro-pub restaurant (see p. 199) and the chance to indulge in some on-the-sands cricket.

🏠 6 🅿 🔇 📶 Free 💳 MC, V

🏨 STRAVITHIE CASTLE B&B
££–£££

Off the B9131, St. Andrews
Tel (01334) 880 251
standrews-bb.co.uk

Three spacious, comfortable rooms, hearty breakfasts, and the attractive 18th-century fortified manor itself—complete with moat, drawbridge, and expansive grounds—make this one of the St. Andrews area's most impressive guesthouses.

🏠 3 🅿 🔇 📶 Free 💳 MC, V

DUNDEE

🏨 APEX CITY QUAY HOTEL 🍴 & SPA
£££

West Victoria Dock Rd., Dundee
Tel (01382) 202 404
apexhotels.co.uk

This chic metropolitan hotel shows off the impressive new face of Dundee. The opulent spa offers a seemingly infinite number of treatments, while the fine-dining restaurant is a cut above the average hotel eatery. The city and river views from rooms on the top floors are superb.

🏠 151 🅿 🔄 🔇 🔆 🏊 💪
📶 Free 💳 MC, V

DEESIDE

🏨 AULD KIRK 🍴
££–£££

31 Braemar Rd., Ballater
Tel (01339) 755 762
theauldkirk.com

This B&B offers visitors the rare chance to stay in a former Scottish Free church. Guest rooms are comfortable without being fussy.

🏠 7 🅿 🔇 📶 Free 💳 MC, V

🏨 BURNETT ARMS HOTEL 🍴
£–££

25 High St., Banchory
Tel (01330) 538 725
burnettarms.co.uk

This historic coaching inn combines character with modern conveniences. Rooms are traditionally decorated, and guests can make use of the public bars and dining room, with the high tea popular with both guests and nonguests.

🏠 18 🅿 🔇 📶 Free 💳 AE, MC, V

ABERDEEN

🏨 THE MARCLIFFE HOTEL AND SPA
£££–£££££

North Deeside Rd., Pitfodels
Tel (01224) 861 000
marcliffe.com

Warm colors infuse the rooms and suites at the Marcliffe with understated luxury. Rooms are all individually designed and seamlessly blend old and new, mixing antique furnishings with more contemporary looks. In-room amenities include mini-bars and 24-hour room service. The hotel's spa and restaurant are on hand guests through their stay.

🏠 39 🅿 🔄 🔇 🔆 📶 Free in public areas 💳 All major cards

🔇 Nonsmoking 🔆 Air-conditioning 🏊 Indoor Pool 🏊 Outdoor Pool 💪 Health Club 💳 Credit Cards

🏨🍴 MACDONALD PITTODRIE HOUSE

£££–££££

Chapel of Gairoch, By Inverurie
Tel (0344) 879 9066
macdonaldhotels.co.uk/pittodrie-house

This grand country house hotel is a perennially popular wedding venue, and it is easy to see why. Comfortable rooms decorated in warm hues, turrets, and stone spiral staircases combine to give it a romantic feel. Wonderfully, the hotel is also set within a 2,000-acre (810 ha) private estate overlooking Mount Bennachie—perfect for walking or taking advantage of the outdoor sports on offer.

🛈 27 🅿 ⬆ Ⓢ 🛜 Charge
💳 AE, MC, V

🏨🍴 MACDONALD NORWOOD HALL HOTEL

££–£££££

Garthdee Rd., Aberdeen
Tel (01224) 868 951
macdonaldhotels.co.uk/norwood-hall

Nestled amid 7 acres (2.8 ha) of private woodland, this attractive 19th-century Victorian mansion has period furnishings and a classical elegance. For a really special stay, book a room in the original house. The restaurant is open every night.

🛈 73 🅿 ⬆ 🛜 Free
💳 All major cards

🏨 MALMAISON ABERDEEN

££–£££

49–53 Queens Rd.,
Tel (01224) 507 097
malmaison.com/locations/aberdeen/

The Malmaison chain of boutique hotels has become synonymous with affordable luxury in the United Kingdom. Its Aberdeen hotel takes this level of comfort a step further, adding a spa and a whisky snug. Spacious guest rooms have a modern vibe.

🛈 79 🅿 ⬆ Ⓢ 🍸 🛜 Free
💳 All major cards

▶ CENTRAL & WESTERN HIGHLANDS

INVERNESS

🏨🍴 ROCPOOL RESERVE HOTEL

£££–£££££

Culduthel Rd., Inverness
Tel (01463) 240 089
rocpool.com

The gracious Georgian exterior of this town manse hides a luxuriously chic, and vibrantly colorful, boutique interior. Four types of guest rooms are clad in chocolates and golds. The **Chez Roux** restaurant is renowned for its inventive gourmet fare using local ingredients.

🛈 11 🅿 🛜 Free
💳 All major cards

🏨🍴 LOCH NESS COUNTRY HOUSE HOTEL

£££–££££

Loch Ness Rd.
Tel (01463) 230 512
lochnesscountryhouse
hotel.co.uk

This palatial and elegant hotel is ideally situated between Inverness and Loch Ness. Lovely rural views, a cozy lounge with a roaring fire, a good restaurant, and 6 acres (2.4 ha) of attractive grounds that include a croquet court add to the appeal.

🛈 15 🅿 Ⓢ 🛜 Free
💳 All major cards

THE CAIRNGORMS

🏨 CRAIGELLACHIE HOTEL
🍴 £££–££££

Victoria St., Craigellachie
Tel (01340) 881 204
craigellachiehotel.co.uk
This country hotel was built in 1893, and the rooms and public areas, including the lovely drawing room, while modernized, remain sympathetic to the era. The renowned **Quaich Bar** (see p. 235) boasts one of the finest collections of single malt whiskies on the planet. The restaurant also has a deservedly good reputation.
🛏 26 🅿 🚭 📶 Free
🏧 AE, MC, V

🏨 THE BOAT COUNTRY INN
🍴 ££–£££

Deshar Rd., Boat of Garten
Tel (01479) 831 258
boathotel.co.uk
This welcoming hotel, located at the heart of Cairngorms National Park, offers comfortable guest accommodations. Rooms vary in size and style—those in the main hotel are traditionally elegant, while those in the Garden Wing enjoy more contemporary décor. The country pub and restaurant are equally friendly.
🛏 34 🅿 🚭 📶 Free
🏧 All major cards

🏨 COIG NA SHEE
GUEST HOUSE
££–£££

Fort William Rd.,
Newtonmore
Tel (01540) 670 109
coignashee.co.uk
Set in attractive grounds on the outskirts of Newtonmore, this Highland lodge has tastefully decorated en suite rooms, spacious common areas, and excellent views of the surrounding countryside.
🛏 5 🅿 🚭 📶 Free
🏧 All major cards

🏨 CULDEARN HOUSE
🍴 ££–£££

Woodlands Terrace,
Grantown-on-Spey
Tel (01479) 872 106
culdearn.com
A warm welcome, inviting public spaces, and good food await guests at this family-run hotel. The six guest rooms seamlessly blend the things that you would expect to find in an old country house—antique furnishings and period features—with modern décor. Enjoy a drink in front of the lounge's roaring fire, then head into the intimate dining room for good Scottish food.
🛏 6 🅿 🚭 📶 Free 🏧 MC, V

THE WEST

SOMETHING SPECIAL

🏨 INVERLOCHY CASTLE
🍴 HOTEL
£££££

Torlunday, Fort William
Tel (01397) 702 177
inverlochycastlehotel.com
Follow in the footsteps of Queen Victoria and enjoy the palatial public spaces and guest rooms at one of Scotland's most luxurious hotels. Dinner is sublime, too, at a hotel where you will leave feeling every bit like royalty.
🛏 17 🅿 🚭 📶 Free
🏧 All major cards

🚭 Nonsmoking 🅰 Air-conditioning 🏊 Indoor Pool 🏊 Outdoor Pool 💪 Health Club 🏧 Credit Cards

🏨 GLENFINNAN HOUSE
🍴 HOTEL
££–£££

Glenfinnan
Tel (01397) 722 235
glenfinnanhouse.com

This country house hotel, dating from 1755, extends a warm welcome to everyone, including guests traveling with dogs. At press time, guest rooms and public spaces were being refurbished to more luxurious standards under new owners. Its location on the banks of Loch Shiel is second to none. The hotel also serves bar meals and has a fine-dining restaurant.

🛈 11 🅿 🚫 🛜 Free
🪙 AE, MC, V

🏨 KNOYDART LODGE
££–£££

Knoydart
Tel (01687) 460 129
knoydartlodge.co.uk

Available on a private room basis with shared self-catering facilities, including a three-bedroom apartment, this retreat has a stunning natural setting in a very remote location (you have to take a boat there). You have access to the kitchen, as well as other areas, making this is a good communal option for large families or other groups.

🛈 5 🚫 🛜 Free 🪙 MC, V

🏨 COIRE GLAS GUEST HOUSE
££

Roy Bridge Rd., Spean Bridge
Tel (01397) 712 272
coireglas.co.uk

Owners Morven and Simon Hardiman take good care of guests at this cozy guesthouse set in a serene, woodsy garden with an excellent view south to Ben Nevis, best

admired from the breakfast room.

🛈 10 🅿 🚫 🛜 Free in lounge
🪙 MC, V

🏨 CLACHAIG INN
🍴 £–££

Glencoe
Tel (01855) 811 252
clachaig.com

Catering mainly to walkers and climbers, the Clachaig offers three types of accommodations. Rooms are fairly basic, but the location next to Glen Coe's Three Sisters is hard to fault. The inn serves hearty pub grub (see p. 234) and has a large drying-room, both of which are great after a day in the hills. Ask for a packed lunch to take with you as you roam.

🛈 23 🅿 🚫 🛜 Free in public areas 🪙 MC, V

▶ NORTHERN HIGHLANDS

EAST COAST

🏨 BOATH HOUSE
🍴 £££££

Auldearn
Tel (01667) 454 896
boath-house.com

Get away from it all at this country house hotel set on 22 acres (9 ha) of private land northeast of Inverness. The décor in the eight charming guest rooms ranges from contemporary to classically elegant. The hotel also boasts an award-winning restaurant (see p. 255), on-site fishing in the ornamental lake, *Outlander*-themed tours, and relaxing spa treatments.

🛈 8 🅿 🛜 Free 🪙 AE, MC, V

🏨 DORNOCH CASTLE HOTEL
🍴 ££££–£££££

Castle St., Dornoch
Tel (01862) 810 216
dornochcastlehotel.com

One of most distinctive buildings in the lovely town of Dornoch is also a great place to stay. Classically themed guest rooms feature soft floral prints, antique furnishings, and some even have four-poster beds. There is an impressive whisky bar and tasty food, served up in the restaurant overlooking the formal gardens or before a log fire in the former bishop's kitchen.

🛈 22 🅿 🚭 📶 Free 🀫 AE, MC, V

THE NORTHWEST

🏨 THE TORRIDON
🍴 ££££–£££££

Torridon, Wester Ross
Tel (01445) 791 242
thetorridon.com

Opulent guest rooms with enormous stand-alone baths, elegant public spaces, and a first-class restaurant impress guests. It is the magnificent mountain views, though, that are truly unforgettable. The hotel's whisky bar is a good place to learn more about the hallowed spirit. Adventure activities, luxury self-catering accommodations, and basic but much cheaper inn rooms are also available. The inn has a full-service bar.

🛈 18 🅿 🛏 🚭 📶 Free
🀫 AE, MC, V

🏨 THE OLD INN
🍴 £££

Gairloch
Tel 01445 712 006
theoldinn.net

The combination of simple but comfortable rooms, friendly service, and hearty local meat and seafood dishes make this traditional Highland coaching inn a good option for sleeping and eating.

🛈 17 🅿 🚭 📶 Free 🀫 MC, V

🏨 PLOCKTON HOTEL
🍴 £££

41 Harbour St., Plockton
Tel (01599) 544 274
plocktonhotel.co.uk

This charming waterfront hotel boasts an award-winning seafood restaurant, as well as a cozy pub. Guest rooms are clean and modern, and the best enjoy views over the bay—one of the prettiest in Scotland. The cottage annex is perfect for families.

🛈 15 🚭 📶 Free 🀫 AE, MC, V

🏨 THE CEILIDH PLACE
🍴 £–£££

14 West Argyle St., Ullapool
Tel (01854) 612 103
theceilidhplace.com

Famous for its superb restaurant and live music (see p. 255), this whitewashed inn is a sociable cultural haven for locals. Comfy guest rooms are simply furnished with pinewoods in contemporary fashion; some have shared bathrooms. An eight-room bunkhouse across the road serves budget travelers. A cozy lounge has plush sofas for snuggling on rainy days, when the inn's art gallery and bookshop come in handy.

🛈 13 🅿 🚭 📶 Free 🀫 MC, V

🏨 TIGH AN EILEAN HOTEL
🍴 £–£££

Shieldaig
Tel (01520) 755 251
tighaneilean.co.uk

🚭 Nonsmoking 🔆 Air-conditioning 🏊 Indoor Pool 🏊 Outdoor Pool 🏋 Health Club 🀫 Credit Cards

This whitewashed inn has cozy guest rooms with few modern conveniences (no TVs, although there is one downstairs) to allow guests to really enjoy the peace and quiet and the sea views. Guests also have access to two comfortable sitting rooms that look out over Loch Torridon and an honesty bar. The fine-dining restaurant and public bar both make the best use of local produce, especially seafood.

🛏 11 📶 🛜 Free 🅰 AE, MC, V

▶ **WEST COAST ISLANDS**

ARGYLL ISLANDS

🏨 AUCHRANNIE RESORT
££££–£££££
Brodick, Isle of Arran
Tel (01770) 302 234
auchrannie.co.uk

Two hotels, 30 self-catering lodges, three restaurants, and myriad activities comprise this resort. Accommodations are classically elegant in the main House Hotel; more contemporary rooms are in the Spa Resort. Great facilities for all the family include restaurants, swimming pools, spa, a fitness studio, and a sports hall. All guest rooms are spacious and can comfortably accommodate a family of four.

🛏 84 🅿 🔄 📶 🔲 🎞 🎯
🛜 Free 🅰 AE, MC, V

🏨 PORT CHARLOTTE
🍴 HOTEL
££££
Port Charlotte, Isle of Islay
Tel (01496) 850 360
portcharlottehotel.co.uk

Its location alone is enough to lure guests; however, this lovely old whitewashed hotel offers more than magnificent views across a sea loch and the Atlantic. Rooms are cozy, while the restaurant and welcoming bar (see p. 303) are favorites with locals and visitors alike. Live music evenings are regularly scheduled in summer.

🛏 10 🅿 📶 🛜 Free 🅰 MC, V

🏨 ROSLYN HOUSE
£££
Tobermory, Isle of Mull
Tel (01688) 302 030
roslynhousetobermory.co.uk

Graceful themed rooms, an elegant garden, and relaxing guest lounges (one includes an honesty bar) impress at this luxury B&B. In 2023, new owners began an ongoing refurbishment, gracing some rooms with canopy beds.

🛏 8 🅿 📶 🛜 Free 🅰 MC, V

🏨 ISLE OF MULL HOTEL & SPA
££–£££
Craignure, Isle of Mull
Tel (01680) 812 544
crerarhotels.com

With friendly service and an excellent location for touring the island, this seafront hotel belies its ungainly exterior. Many recently updated guest rooms (some with Jacuzzis) are appealingly furnished, and many rooms and the hotel's public areas enjoy sweeping views across the water. No elevator.

🛏 82 🅿 📶 🔲 🎞 🎯
🛜 Free 🅰 AE, MC, V

🏨 ISLE OF COLL HOTEL
🍴 ££
Arinagour, Isle of Coll
Tel (01879) 230 334
collhotel.com

This remarkable little retreat with newly refurnished guests rooms is the epitome of a family-owned establishment. Run by Kevin and Julie Oliphant for more than 25 years, not only is it a great place to stay but it also is the island's social hub with the fine **Gannet Restaurant** (see p. 302). Room Two boasts an old-fashioned bath and epic sea views.

ⓘ 6 🅿 🅢 🛜 Free 🅼 MC, V

SKYE

🏨 SKEABOST HOUSE HOTEL
🍴 *££££££*

Skeabost Bridge, Skye
Tel (01470) 532 202
sonascollection.com/our-hotels/
skeabost

A steeple-topped former Victorian hunting lodge with a fine country-hour-hotel pedigree, this grande dame checks of a long list of country pursuits, from fly-fishing to its own nine-hole course. Beyond the wood-paneled lounge with sumptuous leather sofas and armchairs, a range of seemingly mismatched guest rooms—some with sea views—all offer inspired décor and opulent furnishings. A conservatory restaurant dishes out equally spectrum-spanning fare, from beer-battered fish 'n' chips to aged ribeye steak.

ⓘ 20 🅿 🅢 🛜 Free 🅼 AE, MC, V

🏨 UIG HOTEL
🍴 *££–£££*

Uig, Skye
Tel (01470) 542 205
uig-hotel-skye.com

Overlooking Uig harbor, this old coaching Inn has magical views and makes a perfect base for exploring the nearby Quiraing or catching a morning ferry to the Outer Hebrides. Comfy guest rooms vary in size, and some are in a modern annex. The restaurant, popular with locals, serves fresh seasonal seafood and Scottish fare, washed down by draft real ales.

ⓘ 19 🅿 🅢 🛜 Free 🅼 MC, V

OUTER HEBRIDES

🏨 SCARISTA HOUSE
🍴 *££££*

Sgarasta Bheag, Isle of Harris
Tel (01859) 550 238
scaristahouse.com

This former Georgian manse oozes character, from its beautiful white-washed exterior and its cozy drawing room to its library stocked with books and CDs. Three of the guest rooms are in the main house and while they are quite small, they are comfortable. Three guest suites are located in the Glebe House, and all rooms enjoy views out over the lovely bay. The hotel also serves very good food at its restaurant; breakfast is included with room.

ⓘ 6 🅿 🅢 🛜 Free 🅼 MC, V

🏨 CASTLEBAY HOTEL
🍴 *££–££££*

Castlebay, Isle of Barra
Tel (01871) 810 233
castlebay-hotel.co.uk

Accommodations in this welcoming hotel come in various sizes and shapes, including standard and superior. All are clean, comfortable, and cozy and furnished with subtle Scottish tartan fabrics. Superiors benefit from extra space and lovely views of Kisimul Castle and Barra harbor, as does the light-filled restaurant serving seafood fresh from the harbor.

ⓘ 15 🅿 🅢 🛜 Free 🅼 MC, V

🅢 Nonsmoking 🅢 Air-conditioning 🏊 Indoor Pool 🏊 Outdoor Pool 🏋 Health Club 🅼 Credit Cards

SOMETHING SPECIAL

🏨 LEWS CASTLE
🍴 ££–£££
Stornoway, Isle of Lewis
Tel (01625) 416 430
lews-castle.co.uk
This gothic-revival style 19th-century castle, while open to the public below, now dedicates its upper floors to crisp-white contemporary-styled suites and self-catering apartments, many offering sweeping views of Stornoway harbor. Comfy, rather than deluxe, is the watchword. **The Storehouse Café** serves breakfast and light lunch, and the nearby downtown offers plenty of dining options.
🅿 🚫 🔆 🔌 Free 🖎 AE, MC, V

🏨 POLOCHAR INN
🍴 ££–£££
Polochar, South Uist
Tel (01878) 700 215
polocharinn.com
This 18th-century inn on the tip of South Uist was once used by passengers waiting for the ferry to Barra. Today it is a peaceful retreat that stands right on the water's edge and enjoys views to the islands of Eriskay and Barra. Rooms have been refurbished to a high standard, but the wow factor comes in the form of their sea views. The inn is also known for the quality of its food, particularly fish and shellfish.
🛈 11 🅿 🚫 🔌 Free 🖎 MC, V

▶ ORKNEY & SHETLAND ISLANDS

ORKNEY ISLANDS

🏨 ALBERT HOTEL
🍴 ££–£££
Mounthoolie Ln., Kirkwall
Tel (01856) 876 000
alberthotel.co.uk
Immaculately clean guest rooms, with large well-kept bathrooms, make this hotel a good option. Large beds, flat-screen televisions, and complimentary tea- and coffee-making facilities add to the basics. The popular Bothy Bar and hotel restaurant also offer meals.
🛈 19 🚪 🚫 🔌 Free 🖎 AE, MC, V

🏨 KIRKWALL HOTEL
🍴 ££–£££
Harbour St., Kirkwall
Tel (01856) 872 232
kirkwallhotel.com
Within a fine old Victorian building, chic contemporary rooms have everything most guests need for a comfortable stay, and the superior rooms look out over the harbor and have plenty of space. The on-site **Harbor View Restaurant** features locally-caught seafood and local meats.
🛈 37 🚫 🔌 Free 🖎 MC, V

🏨 SANDS HOTEL
🍴 ££–£££
Burray, Orkney
Tel (01856) 731 298
thesandshotel.co.uk
Set in the peaceful village of Burray, this solid stone inn—built in 1860 as a herring store—is particularly popular among divers to Scapa Flow. Family rooms offer extra space. The busy restaurant serves tasty meals with

stunning views, at reasonable prices.

[i] 8 **[S] [wifi]** Free **[cc]** MC, V

🏨 STROMABANK HOTEL
££–£££

Longhope, Hoy
Tel (01856) 701 494
stromabank.co.uk

With just four rooms the Stromabank is a lovely and relaxing B&B hotel. Rooms are big enough to accommodate children on foldaway beds, and the service is friendly and personal. Highlights of a stay, though, are the wonderful location and the delightful conservatory restaurant.

[i] 4 **[P] [S] [wifi]** Free **[cc]** MC, V

🏨 BURNSIDE FARM B&B
£–££

A965, Stromness
Tel (01856) 850 723
burnside-farm.com

Visitors can stay at this working dairy farm, which supplies milk for the island's Orkney Mature Cheese. It's just a 10-minute stroll to the center of Stromness, but you may find yourself wanting to stay in this cozy spot, enjoying home cooking, a cozy ambiance, and fantastic views.

[i] 3 **[P] [S] [wifi]** Free **[cc]** MC, V

SHETLAND ISLANDS

🏨 BALTASOUND HOTEL
££–£££

Baltasound, Unst
Tel (01957) 711 334
baltasoundhotel.co.uk

This remote Shetland bolt-hole stakes a claim to being the most northerly hotel in Britain. There is more to recommend the hotel, though, than its stunning waterside location. Modest but comfortable

accommodations are available in the main house or in the garden log cabin–style chalets. Local seafood, ales, and more are served in the simple restaurant or lounge bar. A special welcome is made to walkers, with advice on circular routes from the hotel and back.

[i] 24 **[P] [S] [cc]** MC, V

🏨 BUSTA HOUSE HOTEL
[restaurant] ££–£££

Brae, Shetland
Tel (01806) 522 506
bustahouse.com

Individually styled rooms at this 16th-century hotel have fittingly traditional décor, with stunning views over the bay or attractive gardens. The hotel's online gallery lets you choose from among the 22 rooms (all named after Shetland islands) prior to booking.

[i] 22 **[P] [S] [wifi]** Free
[cc] All major cards

🏨 SCALLOWAY HOTEL
££–£££

Main St., Scalloway
Tel (07747) 138 932
scallowayhotel.scot

Given a chic post-pandemic reboot by new owners, this charming harborfront guesthouse now boasts enhanced comforts and style, plus such mod-cons as flat-screen TVs in guest rooms. The pub-restaurant has outdoor seating for better enjoying the superb sunset views.

[i] 10 **[wifi]** Free **[cc]** MC, V

SHOPPING

Both in and outside of its urban centers, traditionally Scottish souvenirs—haggis, Scottish produce, pottery, handicrafts, wool textiles, Celtic jewelry, tartan, and Harris tweed—are widely available. Many visitors to Scotland are keen to take home a bottle of single malt Scotch whisky, which can be purchased in specialty stores and direct from the distilleries.

For those who enjoy shopping, Scotland's cities offer designer and boutique stores alongside chain stores. But your most memorable buys will likely come from a wee shop in a small village, presided over with pride by locals who are happy to share their knowledge with interested visitors. Happy hunting!

Arts & Crafts

House of Bruar
Blair Atholl, Perthshire
Tel (0845) 136 0111
houseofbruar.com
Freestanding building housing a collection of shops selling country crafts, Scottish knitwear, art, and Scottish food.

Iona Craft Shop
Isle of Iona, Argyll
Tel (01681) 700 001
ionacraftshop.com
Quality handmade woven items, clothing, and gifts.

Jail Dornoch
Castle St., Dornoch
Tel (01862) 810 500
jail-dornoch.com
Upscale department store–style shop selling art, ceramics, toiletries, clothes, and more.

Jamieson's of Shetland
93 Commercial St., Lerwick, Shetland
Tel (01595) 693 114
jamiesonsofshetland.co.uk

Family business specializing in wool from Shetland sheep.

Nairn Wool Shop
106 High St., Nairn
Tel (01667) 452 423
facebook.com/NairnWoolShop
Selling wool and yarn as well as goods made by local artisans.

National Trust for Scotland (NTS)
Tel (0131) 458 0200
nts.org.uk/shop
The gift shops at NTS properties throughout Scotland often stock a varied selection of local arts and crafts.

Clothing

Harvey Nichols
32–34 St. Andrew Sq., Edinburgh
Tel (0131) 524 8388
harveynichols.co.uk
Prestigious department store selling designer goods.

House of Fraser
45 Buchanan St., Glasgow
Tel (03439) 092 025
houseoffraser.co.uk
Landmark department store that still retains its grace and charm.

Food

Arran Gift Box
Shore Rd., Brodick

(01770) 303 556
thearrangiftbox.com
Online retailer of produce from the
Isle of Arran.

House of Bruar
Blair Atholl, Perthshire
Tel (0845) 136 0111
houseofbruar.com
Collection of shops selling coun-
try crafts, Scottish knitwear, art, and
Scottish food.

I. J. Mellis Cheesemonger
30A Victoria St., Edinburgh
Tel (0131) 226 6215
mellischeese.net
This renowned cheesemonger supplies
many of Edinburgh's leading restaurants, including great Scottish cheeses.
Also at:
330 Morningside Rd., Edinburgh,
tel (0131) 447 8889
6 Bakers Pl., Edinburgh,
tel (0131) 225 6566
78 Albion St., Edinburgh
(0131) 661 9955
492 Great Western Rd., Glasgow,
tel (0141) 339 8998
149 South St., St. Andrews,
tel (01334) 471 410

Harris Tweed
Harris Tweed Authority
harristweed.org/buy-harris-tweed
This website lists all the authentic
independent weavers plus the three
operating mills, along with their
contact information for a visit.

Harris Tweed and Knitwear
Drinishader, Isle of Harris
Tel (01859) 502 505
harristweedandknitwear.co.uk
Traditional Harris tweed and knit-
wear, with an exhibition center.

Harris Tweed Shop
Tarbet, Isle of Harris

Tel (01859) 502 040
harristweedisleofharris.co.uk
Selling tweed produced on the island.
Weaving demonstrations can be ar-
ranged.
Also at:
6-8 Inglis St., Inverness
Tel (01463) 240 378

Jewelry
Heathergems Visitor Centre
22 Atholl Rd., Pitlochry
Tel (01796) 474 391
heathergems.com
Visitor center and factory outlet
of renowned jewelry and silver
crafts specialist made with natural
Scottish heather as part of design.

The Longship
7–15 Broad St., Kirkwall, Orkney
Tel (01856) 888 790
thelongship.co.uk
The only retail outlet of a leading
British jewelry producer, Ola Gorie,
who is known for her Celtic and
Norse designs.

Skye Silver
The Old School, Colbost,
Isle of Skye
Tel (01470) 511 263
skyesilver.com
Beautiful gold and silver Celtic jewel-
ry in a stunning location.

Pottery
Borgh Pottery
Fivepenny House, Borgh, Lewis
Tel (01851) 850 345
borghpottery.co.uk
Porcelain and stoneware pottery
made by Alex and Sue Blair.

Crail Pottery
75 Nethergate, Crail
Tel (01333) 451 212

crailpottery.com
Cheerful family-run pottery shop.

Edinbane Pottery
Edinbane, Isle of Skye
Tel (01470) 582 234
edinbane-pottery.co.uk
Wood-fired and salt-glazed pottery in stunning designs.

The Meadows Pottery
11A Summerhall Pl., Edinburgh
Tel (0131) 662 4064
themeadowspottery.com
Lovely hand-thrown stoneware.

Tain Pottery
Aldie, Tain
Tel (01862) 894 486
tainpottery.co.uk
See craftspeople at work and buy stoneware at one of the country's largest potteries.

Tartan & Kilts
21st Century Kilts
59 High St., Edinburgh
Tel (07774) 757 222
21stcenturykilts.com
Designer Howie Nicholsby's store sells kilts in a wide variety of modern styles and fabrics.

Geoffrey Tailor
57–59 High St., Edinburgh
Tel (0131) 557 0256
geoffreykilts.co.uk
One of Scotland's best kiltmakers, Geoffrey Tailor's stocks all the clans as well as its own range of ancestral and contemporary kilts.

Slanj Kilts
604 Duke St., Glasgow
Tel (03333) 201 977
slanjkilts.com
This tailoring workshop and shop also sells all the essential true Scot accouterments.

Also at:
30 St. Enoch Sq., Glasgow
Tel (03333) 201 977

Toiletries & Cosmetics
Arran Aromatics
The Home Farm, Brodick,
Isle of Arran
Tel (01770) 302 595
arran.com
Brand synonymous with quality and luxury.

Highland Soap Company
North Rd., Fort William
Tel (01397) 719 186
highlandsoaps.com
Family-run maker of handmade soap and other toiletries, with a new visitor center at its Fort William headquarters, and a shop on nearby High St. Also shops in Aviemore, Oban, Pitlochry, and St. Andrews.

Sheepskins & Woollens
Dunedin Cashmere
2 Hunter Sq., Edinburgh
Tel (0131) 608 1882
dunedincashmere.co.uk
Lovely cashmere garments, from scarves to sweaters, by celebrated designers and brands. Also at eight other locations in Edinburgh.

Edinburgh Woollen Mill
Tel (0808) 202 0242
ewm.co.uk
Selling woolen and cashmere knits alongside more contemporary fashion. With almost 30 outlets across Scotland.

Fair Isle Knitwear
Nedder Taft, Fair Isle, Shetland
Tel (01595) 760 255
mativentrillon.co.uk
Carrying on the tradition of Fair Isle

knitwear with limited-edition designs by gifted crofter-designer Mati Ventrillon.
Contact for more info.
Joyce Forsyth
21 Station Rd., Edinburgh
Tel (0131) 333 5403
scottishdesignerknitwear.co.uk
Colorful knitwear from a creative Scottish designer.

SkyeSkyns
Waternish, Isle of Skye
Tel (01470) 592 237
skyeskyns.co.uk
Sheepskins, footwear, cushions, and other woollen wear and sheepskin products direct from the tannery's impressive showroom.
Also at:
5 The Green, Portree
Tel (01470) 592 237

ENTERTAINMENT

Scotland's main cities are brimming with theaters and music venues that stage everything from opera and ballet to live music and exciting new plays. Edinburgh's summer festivals (see pp. 74–75) are at the heart of the country's cultural calendar, when everything from stand-up comedy shows to controversial political plays are staged in the city.

High culture is well established in Scotland, and the country has its own opera, ballet, and orchestras, as well as myriad theaters. Scotland celebrates its burgeoning movie industry with the Edinburgh International Film Festival (edfilmfest.org.uk). The country also has a strong tradition of folk music and dance. Folk musicians are in local pubs, town halls, and community centers. Scotland's biggest winter music festival, Celtic Connections (celticconnec tions.com), is a prestigious celebration of Scottish music taking place in Glasgow every January.

Ballet
Scottish Ballet
Tramway, 25 Albert Dr., Glasgow
Tel (0141) 331 2931
scottishballet.co.uk
Touring ballet company.

Ceilidh
These social gatherings, where traditional Scottish music is played, are a common occurrence in the inns and pubs of rural Scotland, especially in the Highlands. Ask as you travel.

Cinema
Cameo
38 Home St., Edinburgh
Tel (0871) 902 5747
picturehouses.com/cinema/the-cameo
Art-house and mainstream films.

DCA Cinema
152 Nethergate, Dundee
Tel (01382) 432 444
dca.org.uk
A great venue for watching bigger budget movies.

Dominion
18 Newbattle Terrace, Edinburgh
Tel (0131) 447 4771
dominioncinema.co.uk
This independent cinema shows mainstream movies.

Glasgow Film Theatre
13 Rose St., Glasgow
Tel (0141) 332 6535
glasgowfilm.org
Mainstream and offbeat movies.

Highland Cinema
Cameron Sq., Fort William
Tel (01397) 609 696
highlandcinema.co.uk
Small boutique cinema with a chic café-bar.

Vue Cinema
Eastfield Way, Inverness
Tel (0345) 308 4620
myvue.com
Seven screens offer something for everyone.

Concert Venues
Aberdeen Music Hall
Union St., Aberdeen
Tel (01224) 641 122
aberdeenperformingarts.com

Recently redeveloped state-of-the-art venue.

Barrowland Ballroom
244 Gallowgate, Glasgow
Tel (0141) 552 4601
barrowland-ballroom.co.uk
Widely regarded as the best place to see a live band in Glasgow.

Caird Hall
City Sq., Dundee
Tel (01382) 434 940
leisureandculturedundee.com/culture/caird-hall
From pop bands to orchestras.

Center for Contemporary Arts
350 Sauchiehall St., Glasgow
Tel (0141) 352 4900
cca-glasgow.com
Host to experimental music, art-house films, and visual art.

City Halls
Candleriggs, Glasgow
Tel (0141) 353 8000
glasgowlife.org.uk/whats-on/glasgow-life-tickets
Classical and world music.

Edinburgh Corn Exchange
11 Newmarket Rd., Edinburgh
Tel (0131) 477 3500
academymusicgroup.com/o2academyedinburgh
Venue attracts big-name bands.

Glasgow Royal Concert Hall
2 Sauchiehall St., Glasgow
Tel (0141) 353 8000
https://www.glasgowlife.org.uk/whats-on/glasgow-life-tickets
Celtic Connections festival hub.

King Tut's Wah Wah Hut
272a St. Vincent St., Glasgow
Tel (0141) 846 4034
kingtuts.co.uk
Up-and-coming bands.

The Lemon Tree
5 W North St., Aberdeen
Tel (01224) 641 122
aberdeenperformingarts.com
New talent and bands, plus dance, comedy, and theater.

O$_2$ ABC
330 Sauchiehall St., Glasgow
Tel (0141) 332 2232
academymusicgroup.com
Nightclub and live music venue.

O$_2$ Academy Glasgow
121 Eglinton St., Glasgow
Tel (0141) 418 3000
academymusicgroup.com/o2academyglasgow/
Bands of the moment and breakthrough artists.

The Queens Hall
85–89 Clerk St., Edinburgh
Tel (0131) 668 2019
thequeenshall.net
Wide range of musical acts.

Royal Conservatoire of Scotland
100 Renfrew St., Glasgow
Tel (0141) 332 5057
rcs.ac.uk
Music and drama venue.

SEC Armadillo
Exhibition Way, Glasgow
Tel (0141) 248 3000
sec.co.uk
Massive venue for massive bands.

St. Giles' Cathedral
Royal Mile, Edinburgh
Tel (0131) 226 0677
stgilescathedral.org.uk
Regular concerts in grand setting.

Usher Hall
Lothian Rd., Edinburgh
Tel (0131) 228 1155
usherhall.co.uk
Eclectic array of music.

Folk Music
Hootananny
67 Church St., Inverness
Tel (01463) 233 651
hootanannyinverness.co.uk
One of the country's best places for
traditional Scottish music.

The Royal Oak
1 Infirmary St., Edinburgh
Tel (0131) 557 2976
royal-oak-folk.com
Dyed-in-the-wool folk pub, especially
noteworthy on Sundays.

Sandy Bell's
25 Forrest Rd., Edinburgh
Tel (0131) 225 2751
sandybells.com
Live folk music in traditional pub.

Whistle Binkies
4–5 South Bridge, Edinburgh
Tel (0131) 557 5114
whistlebinkies.com
Traditional pub with folk music.

Opera
Scottish Opera
39 Elmbank Crescent, Glasgow
Tel (0141) 248 4567
scottishopera.org.uk
Touring opera company.

Theater
Dundee Rep Theatre
Tay Sq., Dundee
Tel (01382) 223 530
dundeerep.co.uk
Home to the Scottish Dance Theatre
and Rep Ensemble.

Eden Court
Bishops Rd., Inverness
Tel (01463) 234 234
eden-court.co.uk
Plays, gigs, stand-up comedy, dance,
and art-house films.

Edinburgh Playhouse
18–22 Greenside Pl., Edinburgh
Tel (0844) 871 3014
atgtickets.com/venues/edinburgh-
playhouse
One of the UK's largest theaters
offers West End musicals to kids
shows.

Festival Theatre
13–29 Nicolson St., Edinburgh
Tel (0131) 529 6000
capitaltheatres.com
Big-budget dance, musical, and
theatrical productions.

His Majesty's Theatre
Rosemount Viaduct, Aberdeen
Tel (01224) 641 122
aberdeenperformingarts.com
Touring shows and musicals.

King's Theatre, Edinburgh
2 Leven St., Edinburgh
Tel (0131) 529 6000
capitaltheatres.com
Staging popular productions. Closed
for major repair at press time.

King's Theatre
297 Bath St., Glasgow
Tel (0844) 871 7648
atgtickets.com/venues/kings-the-
atre-glasgow
Theater, musicals, and comedy.

MacRobert Arts Centre
University of Stirling, Stirling
Tel (01786) 466 666
macrobertartscentre.org
Visiting theater, bands, and cinema.

Royal Lyceum Theatre
308 Grindlay St., Edinburgh
Tel (0131) 248 4848
lyceum.org.uk
Quality mainstream drama.

Theatre Royal
282 Hope St., Glasgow

Tel (0844) 871 7647
atgtickets.com/venues/
Theatre-Royal-Glasgow
Opera, ballet, and theater.

The Tolbooth
Jail Wynd, Stirling
Tel (01876) 274 000
stirlingevents.org/tolbooth-event
Atmospheric venue for theater, comedy, and music.

Traverse Theatre
10 Cambridge St., Edinburgh
Tel (0131) 228 1404
traverse.co.uk
Bringing the work of new Scottish writers to the stage.

Tron Theatre
63 Trongate, Glasgow
Tel (0141) 552 4267
tron.co.uk
Theater, comedy, and music, with its own theater company.

ACTIVITIES

Scotland's beautiful and varied nature lends itself to outdoor activities, from leisurely walks along forest trails and kayaking on dramatic lochs to mountaineering and skiing. A growing number of accolades have recognized Scotland as one of the best destinations in the world for climbing, diving, kayaking, mountain biking, and surfing. As a result more and more visitors, as well as Scots themselves, are taking part in adventure sports.

Fittingly for a country that yields itself so effortlessly to adventure activities, many of Scotland's facilities are also world class. Many adventure companies are also well-run operations with knowledgeable and highly trained staff. There is also a trend for adventure centers that run a mixed bag of adventure sports; some of these are residential.

Climbing & Hill Walking
Venues
Cairngorms
Cairngorms National Park Authority, 14 The Square, Grantown-on-Spey
Tel (01479) 873 535
cairngorms.co.uk
Brimming with mountains, moorland, forest, rivers, and lochs, Britain's largest national park is a haven for climbers and hill walkers, with plenty of opportunities for mountain biking.

Edinburgh International Climbing Arena,
Ratho, South Platt Hill, Newbridge
Tel (0131) 331 6333
edinburghleisure.co.uk
Hone your climbing skills at this world-class indoor center.

Glencoe
Glen Coe Visitor Centre, Glencoe
Tel (01855) 811 307
nts.org.uk/visit/places/glencoe
Eight Munros, 49 miles (79 km) of walking trails, and 20 major climbing sites make Glencoe one of Scotland's most popular climbing and hill-walking sites.

Isle of Skye
Skye is Scotland's most popular walking destination, with climbers and hill walkers drawn to the precipitous Cullin Mountain range that dominates the center. High-level walks can pose serious technical and physical challenges and are not for the inexperienced.

Loch Lomond & The Trossachs National Park
Loch Lomond & The Trossachs National Park Authority, Carrochan Rd., Balloch
Tel (01389) 722 600
westhighlandway.org
Loch Lomond, the hulking Ben Lomond, and the long-distance West Highland Way (west-highland-way.org) are just some of the attractions.

Nevis Range Mountain Experience
Torlundy, Fort William
Tel (01397) 705 825
nevisrange.co.uk
For many visitors and Scots the ascent of Britain's tallest mountain, Ben Nevis, is the ultimate goal of a climbing or hill-walking vacation in Scotland. There are other munros to hike, plus mountain biking and snow sports to enjoy.

Northwest Highlands

This region offers the chance to walk in and climb some of Scotland's most iconic mountains—including Stac Pollaidh, Suilven, and Ben Loyal—as well as the formidable peaks of Torridon, Dundonnell, and the Fannichs. Glen Shiel and Glen Affric also number among its attractions.

Pentland Hills Regional Park

Boghall Farm, Biggar Rd., Edinburgh, tel (0131) 529 2401
pentlandhills.org
With trails to suit all abilities from families to serious walkers.

Southern Scotland

Eschewed by those seeking vaulting Highland peaks, southern Scotland still has a lot to recommend it to walkers, with myriad trails dissecting the Lammermuir, Moorfoot, and Cheviot Hills. The south is also home to a number of long-distance walks including the Southern Upland Way (see pp. 126–127) and St. Cuthbert's Way.

Outfitters

Mountaineering Council of Scotland

The Granary, West Mill St., Perth
Tel (01738) 493 942
mountaineering.scot
Offering practical and safety advice about hill walking, climbing, and mountaineering in Scotland. Membership gives access to the club mountain huts.

North West Frontiers

Viewfield, Strathpeffer
Tel (01997) 421 474
nwfrontiers.com
Walking and hiking holiday specialists operating in the northwest Highlands, the Outer Hebrides, Orkney, and Shetland.

Torridon Outdoors

Torridon, tel (01445) 791 242
thetorridon.com/torridon-outdoors
Offering a multiactivity program in Torridon, including climbing, abseiling, guided walks, and mountain guiding.

Walking Scotland

visitscotland.com/things-to-do/outdoor-activities/walking
VisitScotland's official walking site links to outfitters and a huge database of downloadable routes.

Wilderness Scotland

Dalfaber Dr., Aviemore
(01479) 420 020
wildernessscotland.com
Specializes in walking and mountain-hiking trips throughout the Highlands and islands.

Diving

Scotland boasts some excellent diving destinations, including the Sound of Mull (see sidebar p. 233) and Orkney's Scapa Flow (see sidebar p. 314).

Halton Charters

3 Ness Rd., Stromness
Tel (01856) 851 532
clasina.co.uk
Wreck diving for accredited divers.

Lochaline Boat Charters

Auliston, Oban
Tel (07967) 419 025
lochaline-boats.co.uk
Offering guided dives with basking sharks and to wrecks around the Isle of Mull.

Puffin Dive Centre

Port Gallanach, Oban
Tel (01631) 566 088
puffin.org.uk
Offering diver training off the west coast.

Scottish Sub-Aqua Club
Caledonia House, 1 Redheughs Rigg,
South Gyle, Edinburgh
Tel (0131) 625 4404
scotsac.com
Offering accredited dive training.

Fishing

It is perhaps no surprise that, in a nation awash with lochs, blessed with rushing rivers and a coastline measuring 10,246 miles (16,490 km), angling is a popular pastime. In fact, clean and uncrowded waters make Scotland one of Europe's premier fishing spots. In the Tweed, Dee, and Tay Rivers, Scotland arguably boasts the best salmon fishing in the world. Scotland also has a large number of fisheries that permit angling. Many riverside hotels, particularly country house hotels, also have angling activities for guests.

Alba Game Fishing
Tel (07734) 810706
albagamefishing.com
This company specializes in bespoke fishing trips throughout Scotland, and provides fishing tackle, permits, and guides.

FishPal
fishpal.com
Everything you need to know about fishing in Scotland. The website covers the Dee, Tay, and Tweed Rivers, as well as fishing in lochs or in the sea. Anglers can book angling permits by selecting the relevant beat or fishery and the date through the online reservation system or through the booking office.

Scottish Anglers National Association
National Game Angling Centre,
The Pier, Loch Leven
Tel (01577) 861 116
sana.org.uk

Scotland's governing body for game angling with information about how, when, and where to do this type of fishing in Scotland.

Horse Riding & Pony Trekking

Swaths of dazzling scenery that incorporate vast sand beaches, gentle rolling hills, and vaulting mountains make Scotland a great destination for horse riding.

Highlands Unbridled
Murley Steading. Ballogie, Aboyne
Tel (01339) 887 676
highlandsunbridled.com
Riding lessons, day treks, and guided 3- to 17-day riding holidays throughout Scotland, with something for every ability.

Isle of Skye Trekking Centre
Croft 2, Suladale, Skye
Tel (01470) 582 419
theisleofskyetrekkingcentre.co.uk
Trek through some of Scotland's most enchanting scenery. Treks to suit all abilities.

North Sannox Pony Trekking
North Glen Sannox
Tel (07984) 256 664
northsannoxponytrekking.co.uk
Scenic treks for all abilities five years or older. Paddock rides available for three- to five-year-olds.

Riding Scotland
visitscotland.com/see-do/activities/horse-riding
VisitScotland's official horse-riding site with information on trekking and riding, links to riding and equestrian centers, and a map of routes and trails.

Ice Climbing

Thanks to its lofty mountains Scotland is the U.K.'s premier ice climbing destination. From late December to early April experienced mountaineers take to the ice in a test of their endurance, strength, nerve, and skill. It may not be for the novice climber, but it is possible to learn these skills in the relative safety of Kinlochleven's Ice Factor, home to the world's largest indoor ice wall.

Glenmore Lodge
Aviemore
Tel (01479) 861 256
glenmorelodge.org.uk
National outdoor training center offering a raft of skills courses.

Ice Factor
Leven Rd., Kinlochleven
Tel (01855) 831 100
ice-factor.co.uk
World-class indoor training facility for snow skills and ice climbing. Closed for repair at press time.

West Coast Mountain Guides
3 Kincardine Pl., Fort William
Tel (01397) 280 045
westcoast-mountainguides.co.uk
Guided ice-climbing courses and trips.

Golf
The home of golf has more than 550 golf courses. These range from public courses where golfers pay as they play to members-only courses. Guests staying at some of Scotland's more prestigious hotels can often bypass some of the membership regulations and secure a round of golf during their stay. See regional chapters in this guidebook for course recommendations.

Golfing Scotland
visitscotland.com/things-to-do/outdoor-activities/golf
Complete information about and links to golf courses plus advice about

planning a golfing trip, special offers, events, and competitions.

Scottish Golf
scottishgolf.org
The national governing body's website has handy "Find a Facility" and "Book a Tee Time" functions, plus links to forthcoming competitions.

Mountain Biking
Cairngorms (see p. 368)

Cycling Scotland
visitscotland.com/things-to-do/outdoor-activities/cycling
VisitScotland's official cycling website with links to mountain-bike centers, outfitters, events, and a database of routes.

Glentress
Glentress Forest, Peebles
Tel (01721) 721 736
forestryandland.gov.scot/visit/forest-parks/tweed-valley-forest-park/glentress
One of the best mountain-biking facilities with trails to suit all levels. Forestry and Land Scotland oversees other mountain bike centers throughout Scotland (forestryandland.gov.scot/visit/activities/mountain-biking).

Laggan Wolftrax
Strathmashie Forest, Laggan, Newtonmore
Tel (01528) 544 366
lagganforest.com
Home to some of Scotland's best purpose-built mountain-bike tracks from a beginners green run and a novice orange trail to a fast-paced red run and highly technical black run.

Nevis Range
Torlundy, Fort William
Tel (01397) 705 825
nevisrange.co.uk

The downhill trail here is the only World Cup venue in the U.K. and the only mountain course with gondola access. With a vertical drop of 1,722 feet (525 m) and a length of 1.65 miles (2.66 km), it is not for the faint-hearted, but mountain bike lessons and guided rides, including kids classes are offered.

The Torridon
Achnasheen, Wester Ross
Tel (01445) 791 242
thetorridon.com/torridon-outdoors
This luxury hotel's activity center offers bike hire and guided cycling trips and rugged mountain biking adventures.

Wilderness Scotland
Dalfaber Dr., Aviemore
Tel (01479) 420 020
wildernessscotland.com
This adventure company offers a choice of small-group mountain-and road-biking holidays.

Sailing
Stunning coastal scenery, clean waters, clean air, and good facilities make Scotland an excellent sailing destination, particularly on the west coast with its myriad offshore islands. Sailing schools provide lessons for novices, while the more experienced can organize a bareboat charter. Skippered cruises, for which guests don't need any experience, are also available.

Edinburgh Boat Charters
Shore Rd., S. Queensferry
Tel (0131) 554 9401
edinburghboatcharters.com
Half-, full-, and two-day excursion cruises out of Edinburgh and Oban.

Galloway Activity Centre
Loch Ken, Castle Douglas
Tel (01556) 502 011
lochken.co.uk

Offering a wide range of residential and nonresidential activities including sailing, powerboating, and windsurfing.

Loch Insh Outdoor Centre
Kincraig
Tel (01540) 651 272
lochinsh.com
Wide range of water sports—sailing, kayaking, windsurfing, and canoeing—plus land-based sports.

Loch Morlich Watersports
Glenmore Forest Park, Aviemore
Tel (01479) 861 221
lochmorlich.com
Sailing, waterskiing, canoeing, and windsurfing plus mountain-bike courses; equipment rental too.

Royal Yachting Association Scotland
Caledonia House, South Gyle, Edinburgh
Tel (0131) 317 7388
rya.org.uk/gbni/scotland
Scotland's national body for sailing has training centers that offer certified courses.

Sailing Scotland
visitscotland.com/things-to-do/outdoor-activities/sailing
VisitScotland's official sailing website with links to boatyards, marinas, sailing schools, and charter companies; a section on the country's canals and sailing events; and links for shipping forecast and tide information.

Shooting
Scotland has a long association with game hunting, particularly among the wealthy. While many country estates and country house hotels still organize stalking and shooting of game, (officially endorsed as a means of controlling the deer population) there has been a shift in recent years toward clay shooting.

Auchterhouse Country Sports
Burnhead Farm, Auchterhouse
Tel (01382) 320 476
auchterhousecountrysports.co.uk
One of the country's leading clay-shooting grounds regularly hosts national and international competitions. Lessons for all grades of shooter are also available, alongside quad biking, archery, falconry, and fishing.

Cluny Clays Activity Centre
Cluny Mains Farm, by Kirkcaldy
Tel (01592) 720 374
clunyactivities.co.uk
Clay pigeon shooting and air rifle shooting, plus archery and golf.

County Clays Dunkeld
Dunkeld House Hotel, Dunkeld
Tel (07845) 010 456
countyclays.co.uk
Air rifle and clay pigeon shooting, plus archery, off-road driving, quad biking, salmon fishing, game shooting, and falconry.

Rhidorroch Highland Estate
Ullapool
Tel (01854) 612 548
rhidorroch.com/Sporting.html
Mixed sporting estate offering deer stalking, clay pigeon shooting, and salmon fishing.

Skiing
Scotland has five ski centers, as well as a number of dry ski slopes where skiers can hone their skills.

Cairngorm Mountain
Aviemore
Tel (01479) 861 261
cairngormmountain.org
Runs to suit all grades of skier, 10 ski lifts, ski lessons, and equipment rental, as well as good après-ski.

Glencoe Mountain
Glencoe
Tel (01855) 851 226
glencoemountain.co.uk
Ski resort boasting 20 runs and 8 lifts. It is also home to the Fly Paper, the steepest black-graded run in Britain. Lift passes, equipment rental, and lessons available.

Glenshee Ski Centre
Glenshee
Tel (013397) 41320
ski-glenshee.co.uk
Facilities at the U.K.'s largest ski center include 36 runs, 21 lifts and tows, equipment rental, lift passes, and lessons.

Lecht
Strathdon
Tel (01795) 651 440
lecht.co.uk
This smaller resort located in the eastern Cairngorms offers 13 lifts, equipment rental, instruction, and passes.

Nevis Range
Torlundy, Fort William
Tel (01397) 705 825
nevisrange.co.uk
Skiing and snowboarding on Aonach Mor often possible until late spring. Facilities include a gondola to snow sports area, equipment rental, lift passes, and lessons.

Skiing Scotland
visitscotland.com/things-to-do/outdoor-activities/skiing-snowsports
VisitScotland's national skiing and snowboarding portal with information about travel, snow conditions, and links to ski centers.

Surfing & Windsurfing
Scotland is blessed with a number of great surfing spots. The clear standout is Thurso East, offering some of

the biggest breaks in Europe. The out-ermost island of the Inner Hebrides, Tiree, is also popular and hosts an annual international windsurfing competition, the Tiree Wave Classic in October.

Hebridean Surf Holidays
Barvas, Isle of Lewis
Tel (01851) 840 343
hebrideansurf.co.uk
Surfing holidays from novice to experienced. Lessons for beginners are given in secluded spots with manageable waves.

Wild Diamond
Burnside Cottage, Cornaig, Tiree
Tel (7712) 159 205
wilddiamond.co.uk
In addition to windsurf rentals and lessons, Wild Diamond offers surfboard rental and instruction in stand-up paddleboarding (and board rentals). Also instruction in sand-yachting and kitesurfing.

INDEX

ILLUSTRATIONS CREDITS